UNDERSTANDING & USING

Microsoft® Access 97

Bruce J. McLaren
Indiana State University

D1525753

JOIN US ON THE INTERNET
WWW: http://www.thomson.com
EMAIL: findit@kiosk.thomson.com   A service of I(T)P®

South-Western Educational Publishing

an International Thomson Publishing company   I(T)P®

Cincinnati • Albany, NY • Belmont, CA • Bonn • Boston • Detroit
Johannesburg • London • Madrid • Melbourne • Mexico City
New York • Paris • Singapore • Tokyo • Toronto • Washington

Managing Editor: Carol Volz
Developmental Editor: Cheryl Beck
Marketing Manager: Larry Qualls
Production Services: Labrecque Publishing

International Thomson Publishing

CONTENTS

Unit 3: Building a Select Query   A-66

Unit 4: Building a Form   A-94

Unit 5: Building a Report   A-120

Advanced Database Management with Access 97 . . . . .A-145

Unit 6: Relational Database Concepts and Advanced Queries   A-146

Unit 7: Working with Access Controls in Forms and Reports   A-172

Unit 8: Customizing a Form   A-198

Unit 9: Customizing a Report   A-220

Unit 10: Using Pictures, Images, and Graphs in Access   A-248

Unit 11: Introduction to Access Macros   A-276

Unit 12: Building an Application with Access   A-318

Unit 13: Connecting Access and Other Data Files   A-348

Index

Preface

Understanding & Using Microsoft Access 97 is about managing data with a personal computer. Even more, it will help you design forms and reports for retrieving and viewing the information necessary to run an organization. Because it is based on Microsoft Windows 95, Access is easy to use and a very powerful way to organize data. The built-in Wizard templates enable you to build attractive and useful database objects with no programming.

Why This Book?

It is our intention to offer a book that not only teaches how to use Microsoft Access, but also examines the design of databases in an understandable manner. Students are first drawn through the process of creating a database with just enough attention to detail to make them aware of optional features that can facilitate their work. Then more advanced concepts are presented in realistic scenarios with an emphasis on *why* rather than simply *how*.

This book serves a different role than the documentation packaged with Microsoft Access. The Microsoft documentation focuses on how to accomplish a specific task with a precise recipe and requires some prior knowledge on the part of the user to locate the proper section of the manual. By contrast, this book will lead you through Access tutorials in a step-wise fashion.

A realistic case study serves as a background for most of the database examples and exercises in this book. Hunter River Sporting Goods is a retail store that specializes in equipment for recreation. You will learn how a database management system like Access can be used to manage a small business, including such functions as ordering inventory, processing customer orders, and working with vendors. A second organization, Physician's Medical Clinic, is used in applications. A third organization and accompanying database appears in the Instructor's Manual.

Finally, *Understanding & Using Microsoft Access 97* serves as a member of THE UNDERSTANDING & USING SERIES published by South-Western Educational Publishing. It can be used alone, in combination with other books in the series, or to supplement any other book in a course where knowledge of Access is desired.

Content Highlights

Understanding & Using Microsoft Access 97 is divided into two main parts. The first part, comprising Units 1 through 5, offers a general overview of database management concepts and an introduction to Access for new users. It covers the use of Access for simple data files, using the built-in templates called Wizards. You will learn how to get started in Microsoft Access 97, build a data table, examine its contents through queries and forms, and print reports.

The second part of this book, comprising Units 6 through 13, builds on the concepts learned in the first part. Here you will learn how to prepare customized queries, forms, and reports. The relational database concept is introduced. A unit on Access controls forms the basis for making changes to Access objects that were prepared with the Wizards, or for creating new objects without the Wizards. The last section of the second part is aimed at those who want to know how to develop application systems using Access. Advanced concepts such as graphs and embedded pictures are covered in this part. It also covers use of Access programs called macros and modules that provide linked menus, forms, queries, and reports. The book includes the development of a medium-sized custom application using Access. This section also covers importing and exporting data files with Access.

How to Use This Book

You should complete the first five units of the first part to gain a basic understanding of Access database features. After that background, you can cover the material in the second part in the desired order. Units 7–9 contain important concepts about controls that can be used in building custom forms and reports. Although nearly all of the units are intended to be studied while sitting at the computer, you will benefit by first reading the unit, before trying the hands-on work. We strongly recommend that you work through *all* of the Guided Activities, Exercises, and Applications. As with other skills, with more practice your Access understanding will increase. Use this knowledge to solve problems from other courses, your job, or your personal life while you are learning Access. Each unit contains the following features:

CASE STUDY introduces you to a real world business setting where the unit's core objectives can be used. This makes the concepts and skills relevant to you.

LEARNING OBJECTIVES list the knowledge and skills covered in the unit. This gives you a framework to preview the unit and skim the topics that it covers. Objectives also give a means of self-evaluation.

THOROUGH DISCUSSION of the theory, techniques, guidelines, and practical considerations of the concept makes up the core of each unit. Each topic is discussed completely before diving into computer work, so that the book may be used to introduce topics and also can later serve as a useful reference. These discussions help you link the concepts to normal situations, to see where you can actually use the skills.

COMPUTER SCREENS are accurate copies of the screens you will see as you use Access. These screens place the various commands, buttons, and dialog boxes in the proper context.

GUIDED ACTIVITIES give step-by-step, hands-on illustrations of the database activities described in the text. Often the Guided Activities give you several ways to accomplish the same task, helping you develop flexibility and experience, rather than following a rigid, cookbook approach.

EXERCISES are additional assignments to give you hands-on practice of the knowledge and skills you gain in each unit. Some exercises have specific instructions, while others are less structured. Most exercises will use the computer.

APPLICATIONS are comprehensive, open-ended minicases that summarize the activities of the unit. Applications tend to be more challenging than exercises and test your ability to use Microsoft Access in a realistic fashion. These applications require you to apply your knowledge in a business situation.

Instructional Aids

A complete support package provides instructors and students everything they need to teach and to learn how to use Microsoft Access 97 in business applications. The textbook is augmented with these resources: a site on the World Wide Web, and an instructor's CD-ROM containing the electronic instructor's manual, the test bank, and the student data files.

WEB SITE a supporting home page on the World Wide Web is maintained for students and instructors, containing last-minute teaching tips, making updates available, and providing instant access to the data disks. The URL address for this page is http://www.indstate.edu/mclaren/access97.html and is case-sensitive.

WESTEST COMPUTERIZED TESTING In this updated version of South-Western's computerized testing, instructors can copy questions individually, sequentially, or randomly, and then arrange them automatically by type, randomly, or directly on-screen using the drag and drop feature. Users can also control the font and style, spacing, and margins. WESTEST also allows instructors to view exam summaries or test bank chapters, preview test pages, and import or export graphics.

ELECTRONIC INSTRUCTOR'S MANUAL contains general teaching suggestions, sample syllabi, test questions, and information about the student data files. Review Questions and answers to Exercises and Applications are also provided. A full database called University Bookstores is packaged with the Instructor's Manual and may be used for alternate applications or for testing purposes. An extra unit on Database Adminstration and a Glossary are included for additional instruction and reinforcement.

STUDENT DATA FILES that are used with Guided Activities, Exercises, and Applications are included on the accompanying floppy disk located on the inside back cover of the book. The files are stored in a compressed form and must be installed on your hard drive or on a local area network before they can be used. To install the Student Data files, insert the disk into the floppy drive. Select the Start Menu. Choose Run. Type `a:\setup.exe` and click OK. (Your floppy drive may be a different drive letter than a.) You can specify a directory where you want the files to be installed or use the default listed.

A Note of Thanks

- To Connie, my wife and colleague, for her steady encouragement and technical advice. Without her support this book would not exist.

- To our children, Anne and Cathy, who have unlimited patience with my writing habit, even on family camping trips.

- To Dean Don Bates and my colleagues in the School of Business at Indiana State University for their support.

- To Developmental Editor Cheryl Beck of South-Western Educational Publishing for initiating the project and incredible attention to detail.

- To Tory McLearn, Judith Abrahms, Terry O'Donnell, and others from Labrecque Publishing involved in the production of this book. Their professionalism and careful editing have made this an enjoyable task and a learning experience for me.

- To Emily Ketcham of Baylor University and the reviewers of the previous versions of the manuscript for their helpful comments and assistance in development of an accurate and appropriate textbook.

- To my students, who inspire me to write in a way that they can understand.

Bruce McLaren
Terre Haute, Indiana
October 1997
E-mail: *B-McLaren@indstate.edu*

Publisher's Note

This book is part of THE UNDERSTANDING & USING SERIES. This popular series provides the most comprehensive list of books dealing with microcomputer applications software. We have expanded the number of software topics and provided a flexible set of instructional materials for all courses. This unique series includes three different types of books.

1. *Understanding & Using Custom Editions* give instructors the power to create a spiral-bound microcomputer applications book especially for their course. Instructors can select the applications they want to teach and the amount of material they want to cover for each application—essentials or intermediate length.

   For more information about *Understanding & Using Custom Editions*, please contact your local ITP Representative, or call ITP Custom Solutions at (800) 245-6724.

2. General concepts books for teaching basic hardware and software philosophy and applications are available separately or in combination with hands-on applications. These books provide students with a general overview of computer fundamentals including history, social issues, and a synopsis of software and hardware applications.

3. A series of hands-on laboratory tutorials are software specific and cover a wide range of individual packages. These tutorials, written at an introductory level, combine tutorials with complete reference guides. A list of series titles can be found on the following pages.

   THE UNDERSTANDING & USING SERIES has been successful in providing you with a full range of applications books to suit your individual needs. We remain committed to excellence in offering the widest variety of current software packages. In addition, we are committed to producing microcomputing texts that provide you both the coverage you desire and also the level and format most appropriate for your students. The Managing Editor of the series is Carol Volz of South-Western Educational Publishing; the Developmental Editor is Cheryl Beck. We are always planning for the future in this series. Please send us your comments and suggestions:

Carol Volz
Managing Editor
South-Western Educational Publishing
5101 Madison Road
Cincinnati, OH 45227
Internet: carol_volz@swpco.com

Cheryl Beck
Developmental Editor
South-Western Educational Publishing
5101 Madison Road
Cincinnati, OH 45227
Internet: cbeck@swpco.com

We now offer these books in THE UNDERSTANDING & USING SERIES:

GENERAL CONCEPTS

Understanding Information Systems
Steven C. Ross

Understanding Computer Information Systems
Paul W. Ross, H. Paul Haiduk, H. Willis Means, and Robert B. Sloger

OPERATING SYSTEMS/ENVIRONMENTS

Understanding and Using Microsoft Windows 95
Steven C. Ross and Ronald W. Maestas

Understanding and Using Microsoft Windows 3.1
Steven C. Ross and Ronald W. Maestas

Understanding and Using MS-DOS 6.0
Jonathan P. Bacon

Understanding and Using MS-DOS/PC DOS 5.0
Jonathan P. Bacon

NETWORKS

Understanding Networks
E. Joseph Guay

Understanding and Using NetWare 3.x
Larry D. Smith

ONLINE SERVICES

Understanding and Using the Internet, 1997 Edition
Bruce J. McLaren

Understanding and Using Netscape Navigator
Jonathan P. Bacon and Robert Sindt

PROGRAMMING

Understanding and Using Microsoft Visual Basic 4.0
Jonathan C. Barron

West's Essentials of Microsoft Visual Basic
Jonathan C. Barron

Understanding and Using QBasic
Jonathan C. Barron

WORD PROCESSORS

Understanding and Using WordPerfect 6.1 for Windows
Jonathan P. Bacon

Understanding and Using Microsoft Word for Windows 95
Emily M. Ketcham

Understanding and Using Microsoft Word for Windows 6.0
Emily M. Ketcham

Understanding and Using WordPerfect 6.0
Jonathan P. Bacon and Robert G. Sindt

Understanding and Using WordPerfect 5.1
Jonathan P. Bacon and Cody T. Copeland

DESKTOP PUBLISHING

Understanding and Using PageMaker 5.0
John R. Nicholson

Understanding and Using PageMaker 4.0
John R. Nicholson

SPREADSHEETS

Understanding and Using Microsoft Excel 97
Constance McLaren

Understanding and Using Microsoft Excel for Windows 95
Steven C. Ross and Stephen V. Hutson

Understanding and Using Microsoft Excel 5
Steven C. Ross and Stephen V. Hutson

Understanding and Using Quattro Pro 6.0 for Windows
Lisa L. Friedrichsen

Understanding and Using Quattro Pro 5.0 for Windows
Larry D. Smith

Understanding and Using Lotus 1-2-3 for Windows Release 5
Dolores Pusins and Steven C. Ross

Understanding and Using Lotus 1-2-3 for Windows Release 4
Steven C. Ross and Dolores Pusins

DATABASE MANAGEMENT

Understanding and Using Microsoft Access 97
Bruce J. McLaren

Understanding and Using Microsoft Access for Windows 95
Bruce J. McLaren

Understanding and Using Microsoft Access 2.0
Bruce J. McLaren

Understanding and Using Paradox 4.5 for Windows
Larry D. Smith

Understanding and Using Paradox 3.5
Larry D. Smith

Understanding and Using dBASE IV Version 2.0
Steven C. Ross

Understanding and Using dBASE IV
Steven C. Ross

INTEGRATED SOFTWARE

Understanding and Using Microsoft Office 97
Emily M. Ketcham, Bruce J. McLaren, Constance McLaren, Karen Stites Young

Understanding and Using Microsoft Office for Windows 95
Emily M. Ketcham

Understanding and Using Microsoft Works for Windows 3.0
Gary Bitter

Understanding and Using Microsoft Works 3.0 for the PC
Gary Bitter

Understanding and Using ClarisWorks
Gary Bitter

PRESENTATION SOFTWARE

Understanding and Using Microsoft PowerPoint 97
Karen Stites Young

Understanding and Using Microsoft PowerPoint for Windows 95
Lisa L. Friedrichsen

A

Microsoft Access 97

■ This part gives you techniques for working with data. One of the main assets of any organization is the information it possesses, not only about its own products and processes, but also about its customers, suppliers, raw materials, employees, prospects, and so forth. This part presents an overview of Microsoft Access 97 that demonstrates the use of database objects such as tables, queries, forms, and reports.

Each type of data object (such as tables, queries, forms, and reports) is given its own introductory unit. Emphasis is placed on the use of Access Wizards to create attractive, functional data objects without needing to know database procedures in detail.

Hunter River Sporting Goods, Inc., was founded in 1947. Over the years, it grew from the seller of a single product line to a complete retailer of recreational and sports equipment. Hunter River carries a wide range of sporting goods and fitness, fishing, camping, and hunting products.

UNIT 1

Introduction to Database Management Concepts

In this unit, we discuss the basic terminology of database management and present some important factors to consider before you sit down at the computer to create a database system. The unit presents the basic database organization and describes the five main Access objects. Important Access tools and icons are introduced. Also included is a discussion of the documentation and Help systems that come with Access. The Guided Activities demonstrate how to start Access and open a database. The Exercises and Applications give you more opportunities to practice on your own in a less structured environment.

Learning Objectives

At the completion of this unit, you should be able to

1. define basic database management terms,

2. list important considerations before you begin to create a database system,

3. describe the basic database structures of Access,

4. explain what the basic Access toolbar buttons represent,

5. use the various Help systems packaged with Access,

6. design a simple database system on paper,

7. start Access and open an existing database,

8. use the Access Database window,

9. close databases and exit from Access.

Case Study

About four years ago, it became necessary for Hunter River Sporting Goods to modernize its record keeping. You have been hired as a consultant by Hunter River to manage their database systems. The company's database will need to contain information about products, vendors, customers, sales orders, employees, inventory, and more.

Database System Terminology

This section contains brief definitions of some terms that are illustrated in the next section.

Basic Database Terminology

A database management system (DBMS) is a package of computer programs and documentation that lets you establish and use a database. The Access package is a new personal computer DBMS designed for use with Microsoft Windows. A DBMS allows you to store data and retrieve it according to your own criteria.

A database is a collection of related data in tables, queries, reports, forms, macro programs, and so forth. A database contains data about a particular topic or for a particular purpose; it is not itself the programs that manage the data. The database is organized for easy user access. The Access database is stored in a single large file that contains all the database objects for a particular application.

A table is the part of the database that holds the data. A table is similar to a two-dimensional table in which the horizontal rows are records and the vertical columns are fields. In Access, the table is also known as the datasheet. In other DBMS packages, the table is known as a file.

A record is a group of related fields of information about one object or event in the database. A row of a table is analogous to a record.

The fields of a record contain the data items. Fields correspond to columns in tables. A field represents an attribute or measurement of some object or event. A field has certain characteristics such as data type and length. (Access contains text, number, currency, yes/no, counter, date/time, and graphic picture field types. We will discuss field types later in this unit, and in much more detail in Unit 2.)

An index contains a table of record numbers, called pointers, arranged in some order (for example, alphabetical, numerical, or chronological) to permit the rapid location of a particular record.

A key is an identifier for each record. It can be a single field, such as a catalog number, or a combination of several fields, such as last name and first name. All Access tables must have a primary key that uniquely identifies each record. Other keys for a table are known as secondary keys.

Additional Access Data Objects

A query is a set of conditions that provides for retrieval of certain records from a table. You can add more than one table to a query and relate tables by matching common fields. Unit 3 contains an introduction to Access queries.

A form represents a customized manner of inputting data into a database or presenting data on the screen. A form usually presents a single record at a time, or a single record from one table together with records from another table that match it. Unit 4 contains an introduction to Access forms.

A report provides the specifications for output of data in a tabular format. In Access, you can display a report on the screen or send it to the printer. A report usually has multiple records, organized in a particular order. Unit 5 contains an introduction to Access reports.

A graph is a way to present numeric data from multiple records in a graphic fashion. Access provides bar charts, line graphs, and other graph types that can be added to forms and reports.

A macro is a set of Access commands that cause an action. These commands are stored as a miniature program. A macro can be replayed when necessary without reentering its commands from the keyboard or with the mouse.

A module is a collection of Visual Basic for Applications (VBA) statements grouped together as a program. Modules are used to provide specialized processing calculations that cannot be accomplished with ordinary Access methods.

Database System Example

With the preceding definitions as a basis, let's consider an example of a database. Assume that you're the operator of a sporting goods store, Hunter River Sporting Goods, Inc. In your store, you stock recreational items from many suppliers for resale to retail customers.

Like many managers, you're concerned about your inventory. You want to minimize the amount of materials on hand because keeping inventory is costly. You also worry about obsolescence, particularly with clothing and other seasonal fashion items. Yet unless you have ample inventory on hand, a customer may be unable to make a purchase. Before you started using a computer, you kept your inventory on index cards that looked like Figure A1.1.

FIGURE A1.1
Inventory card

Stock Number: 20235

Description: Outdoor 285 Basketball

Unit Cost: 24.95

Quantity On Hand: 30

Date Of Last Order: 10/4/97

As a first step in database development, you transferred a portion of your inventory records from index cards to a sheet of paper, with a result that looked like Table A1.1. Many of the key database concepts can be illustrated by considering this example.

Each entry on the card, and each column in the table, is a *field*. Notice that the type of data is consistent as you read down the column: numbers, text, or date data. Fields are identified by *field names,* such as Stock Number, Description, Unit Cost, Quantity On Hand, and Date Of Last Order. (Some DBMS packages require us to use shorter names than these illustrations; Access permits field names of up to 64 characters long.) As you design a database, consider the types of information you want to keep, as a start toward field definition.

STOCK NUMBER	DESCRIPTION	UNIT COST	QUANTITY ON HAND	DATE OF LAST ORDER
20235	Outdoor 285 Basketball	$24.95	30	10/3/97
20237	Michael Jordan 285 Basketball	$15.95	12	10/3/97
20238	Larry Bird 33 Basketball	$19.95	5	8/1/97
20239	Girls League Basketball	$19.99	3	8/1/97
20241	NCAA Tourney Basketball	$24.95	10	10/3/97
20254	Joe Montana Football	$21.95	6	6/23/97
20255	Official NFL Football	$64.95	2	6/23/97
31204	Par72 Men's Stainless 8-Club Set, Right	$199.95	4	11/28/96
31205	Par72 Men's Stainless 8-Club Set, Left	$199.95	0	3/29/97
31211	John Boyd Driver	$129.95	5	3/29/97
31215	PowerHit 11-pc Golf Club Set	$229.95	10	11/28/96
31233	Professional Golf Balls 6-pack	$8.95	24	11/28/96
31234	Professional Golf Balls 15-pack	$17.95	13	3/29/97

The Stock Number field is a *key* field—a number or text string that is unique for each record. The DBMS allows us to locate a record rapidly, once we know its key number. As you become more familiar with the arrangement of your data, consider how you want to search for items (such as by stock number or perhaps by description). You'll use key fields to sort data in tables. Access requires that each table have a primary key.

Each card represents a separate *record*. Reading across the rows of the table, we also see what a record is: a group of related fields of information, treated as a unit. Read across the top row and note how the five fields are all related to each other: we have on hand 30 Outdoor 285 basketballs that sell for $24.95 each and were last ordered on October 3, 1997. We need one record for each unique unit, and we must make sure that the database system has sufficient capacity to hold records for all our products.

The computer stores this information in a *data table*. Without a computer, a data table might be simply a box of index cards or a manila folder in a file cabinet. At this point, we might want to start thinking of appropriate names for our data tables. Typically, we choose names that represent the kinds of objects that are stored in the table. Information about products, customers, vendors, and employees might be stored in tables named Products, Customers, and so on.

Collectively, these tables constitute the *database* of the business. Recall that the database is a collection of interrelated data. An Access database contains not just the data tables, but also the queries, forms, reports, and programs that manipulate the tables. As you will see in the next unit, Access stores all the database objects in a single database file.

Finally, the *database management system* is the method by which we manage all this data. Before computers, people used an amazing variety of colored index cards, and often inscrutable notes to themselves, to keep track of their information. A DBMS such as Access can enhance your ability to manage large amounts of data efficiently. The remainder of this book will explain how to do that.

Database System Design

When designing a database system, you must keep in mind the *purpose* of the database. You must decide *which facts* are needed by its users, and in *what format*. Sometimes the desired information is a list, such as a set of mailing labels or a sales report. Sometimes the desired information is a single item, such as the product with the most sales in the past month. For instance, if you wish to have a database that will provide you with a list of products that must be reordered from the vendor, you'll need both data that define reorder status (such as quantity on hand, current sales rate, last purchase date, and minimum order quantity) and data that enable you to contact the vendor (such as name, address, and telephone number). Also, you must consider whether you want to view the answers on the screen or get a printed report.

Design Components

Timing is important. *When* do we need the output, and when will we update the data? If you need daily lists, you must update the data daily. You might have a system that can collect data continuously, such as a computerized cash register, or, alternatively, your input might be based on periodic reports from others, such as monthly sales reports. A good rule of thumb is to update as often as possible, and at least as often as you expect to extract useful data.

Now is a good time to ask *where* the data comes from. Do you have or can you collect the necessary data using current organizational resources, or must you buy the data elsewhere? Suppose a salesperson wants to know the names of good customer prospects. This salesperson might have a record of previous purchases along with names and addresses, but might not know the customers' incomes or ages.

Now you're ready to consider *how* the computer provides the output, given the available data. Do we need to make calculations? Must we make decisions? Are there criteria for selection? Must we sort the output in a particular order? Should we summarize the data? Our salesperson might want mailing labels, sorted in zip-code order, of all persons who have made purchases in the past two years and whose household income is more than $20,000. He or she does not want to send more than one copy to a household, so duplicate addresses must be avoided.

Finally, you must decide *who* will design the system, who will build the tables and other database objects, and who will input the data. After you establish the database, who will be responsible for maintaining it: adding, deleting, or changing data, and making sure the programs continue to function as required? Who will be authorized to access the database? Who will maintain accounts for authorized users and see that unauthorized users cannot access the database? Who will be charged with backing up the data so that a safe copy is available in case of fire or a system failure causing loss of data?

Systems Analysis

Where would you find out the answers to these and other important design questions? A systems analyst is an individual who analyzes the organization and arrives at a design for a system that can solve the organization's problems. The analyst interviews workers and managers within the organization to learn about its operations. The analyst observes work being done within the organization and draws conclusions about improvements that could be made. The analyst will also want to talk with customers and suppliers to understand other views of the organization and its products.

The systems analysis procedure can be likened to peeling away layers. The layers represent levels of detail about the organization being modeled. As you learn more about the organization, you "peel back a layer" to build a better understanding of what information is needed for a particular department and how that information can best be delivered. Remember that first glances may not provide the most realistic understanding of the system being studied. In fact, because of familiarity with an existing system, the workers may make suggestions regarding the *old* system and may not see the benefits of taking a new approach. As the systems analyst, your role is to remain objective and draw conclusions only when the facts are well understood.

The process of designing a new system can be time-consuming, particularly when the organization is complex. It may be tempting to stop the investigation early and get to work on the computer, building database tables and the like. Most information system managers recommend that the analyst spend more time in the design stage before actually creating parts of the database. The extra time spent in planning will result in a database system that better reflects the needs of the organization and will need less reworking in the future.

However, it is also clear that organizations evolve over time. Customer needs change, products are modified, more locations are used, personnel come and go, suppliers have different interfacing needs, government regulations mount up. The end result is that a database with a good design can be modified to accommodate these changes. A poorly designed database will become increasingly difficult to change to fit new needs.

We will continue to address database design issues in the units that follow. For example, Unit 2, on building tables, contains information about how to choose a particular field type for a table. Other units on queries, forms, and reports will help you design those objects.

DBMS Capacity Considerations

Several aspects of database capacity are important to understand. First, the DBMS must allow enough fields to accommodate our needs (see Table A1.2 for a summary of Access capacity specifications). Second, the DBMS imposes a certain maximum number of characters per record. Third, the DBMS must be capable of maintaining the required number of records. Finally, the DBMS imposes a limit on the number of tables that can be in use at one time.

Your specific computer system might also impose capacity limitations. The hard disks of most PCs would permit storage of many thousands of records. Floppy disks have much less capacity, so organizations do not generally use them

TABLE A1.2
*Access capacity
specifications*

ITEM	CAPACITY
Maximum size of a database	1 gigabyte* (GB)
Number of objects in a database	32,768
Fields per table	255
Characters in object names	64
Characters per memo field	65,535
Characters per text field	255
Characters per record	2,000 (excluding memo fields)
Open tables	1,024
Maximum report size	22 inches wide; 22 inches high/section
Number of actions per macro	99

*Roughly, 1 billion bytes, or 1,000 megabytes

to store databases. Floppy disks do, however, provide a handy means of backing up and transferring data between computers. As a student, you can use a floppy disk while you learn Access.

The Hunter River Sample Database

For the remainder of this book, we will use Hunter River Sporting Goods, Inc., as the sample database for Guided Activities and Exercises. We introduced this fictional company earlier in this unit. Hunter River is a retail sporting goods company with a full line of sports, camping, hunting/fishing, fitness, and other merchandise. A different organization will be used for the Applications that appear at the end of most units.

The database for this company will contain information about products, customers, employees, departments, vendors, customer orders, purchase orders, and sales. We will use separate tables for each of these items. We will create other tables for reasons that are explained as you work your way through this book. The Hunter River database file is stored on the Student Data Disk that accompanies this book. Your instructor or lab assistant can provide more information about how to access the information from this database on your own computer and transfer needed files to your personal Student Data Disk. You can also download the data files from the author's Web site at **http://www.indstate.edu/mclaren/access97.html**.

Getting Started in Access

This section will describe the procedure for starting Access and using an Access database. It will also specify the hardware and software requirements for running Access under Windows 95 or Windows NT.

Software and Hardware Requirements for Access

Before you can use Access, it must be installed on your computer or local area network. In most schools, this will be done for you. In case you have your own copy of Access or wish to reinstall the software, this section will explain the software and hardware requirements. Access 97 must be installed under Microsoft Windows 95 or Windows NT, explained in the next section.

WINDOWS 95

Windows 95 introduces many new features, as well as a new user interface, for Windows users. Because Access 97 can work only with Windows 95 and NT, this textbook assumes you're using Windows 95. There is a version of this textbook for Access 95, also known as version 7.0. South-Western Educational Publishing has a previous version of this textbook for Access 2.0, which runs under Windows 3.1 or Windows for Workgroups 3.11. Access 2.0 also works under Windows 95.

SYSTEM REQUIREMENTS

Like many applications that run under Windows, Access uses a significant amount of system resources. If your system does not meet the following requirements, you will have difficulties when running Access under Windows 95 or NT.

Your system must have a 486 or higher microprocessor, 12+ MB RAM (16 MB recommended), 42 MB disk space available for full Access installation, and a mouse. A Windows-compatible printer is recommended.

Access can be run from a local area network server if insufficient local hard disk space is available. Instructions for installing Access on a network are provided in the Microsoft Access *Getting Results* manual.

Installing Microsoft Access

We will assume that Access has already been installed in your computer lab. Like other Windows applications, Access has a setup program that automates the installation process. If the setup program detects that your system does not have sufficient resources, a warning message is issued and the installation stops. The standard installation places three sample databases on the disk drive containing Access. These databases are used extensively in the Access documentation to describe various features and database techniques. If they are not present, consult your lab assistant or instructor.

 NOTE *We are using Microsoft Access 97 for the remainder of this textbook. Upgrades from previous versions are available.*

The Access (or Office Professional) setup program will add Access to the Start button menu under Programs. Your computer lab probably uses this convention and may have a separate program group for Access 97 or Office 97. Check with your lab assistant or instructor for any other special configuration information.

Each of the Microsoft Office applications is represented by an icon. The Access icon looks like a key and represents both the Access program and the Access databases. Other Office programs use similar icons. The MS Word word processor icon is a large *W*; the MS Excel spreadsheet uses an *X* as its icon. Your system may not contain all these icons.

Starting Microsoft Access

You can start Microsoft Access in at least three ways, depending on how your computer has been set up. Your instructor will have specific instructions for your computer lab.

- As with other Windows 95 applications, the preferred way to start Access is to click the Start button in the taskbar, then slide the mouse to the Programs entry. Select Microsoft Access by clicking its entry. Figure A1.2 shows the taskbar and the Windows 95 desktop. *Your desktop will probably not look like this one.*

- You can also start Access by choosing its icon. Locate the Access key icon on your desktop and choose it by double-clicking.

- If you open an Access database directly, Access itself will start and load the desired database. You can open a database file by double-clicking it in Explorer or selecting it from the Documents section of the Start button menu.

TIP

If you are not familiar with Windows terminology, go back to the Introduction and read the discussion of Windows.

If Microsoft Office is installed on your computer, the Office Shortcut bar may appear at the top or right edge of your desktop. To start Access from this toolbar, locate the Open Document button and click it once. When you see the set of databases, select one you want to open.

After a few seconds, a screen will appear with license and system configuration information. After that, you'll see the Access opening menu. The opening dialog box, shown in Figure A1.3, lets you create a new database or open an existing database. The opening dialog box of Figure A1.3 gives you two choices. You can create a new database, as indicated at the top of the box, or open an existing database, as indicated in the lower part of the box. A blank database has no tables or other objects. You must create the definitions for any objects added to the blank database. Databases created with the Database Wizard will have object definitions added automatically by Access. We cover the Database Wizard in Unit 2.

NOTE *If you click the Cancel button in the opening dialog box, no database will be opened or created, and you will see the blank Access screen. You will see the same screen when you close a database. Use this screen when you want to convert or repair a database, as described later in this unit.*

FIGURE A1.2
*Taskbar programs
on desktop*

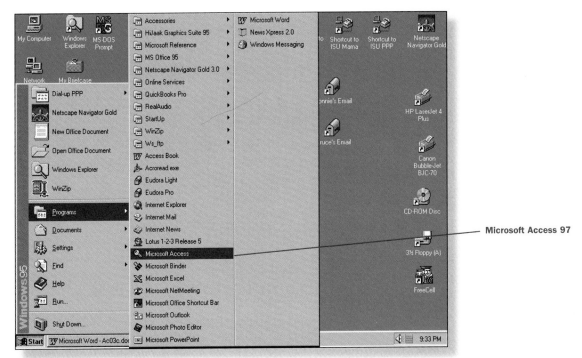

Microsoft Access 97

FIGURE A1.3
*Microsoft Access
opening dialog box*

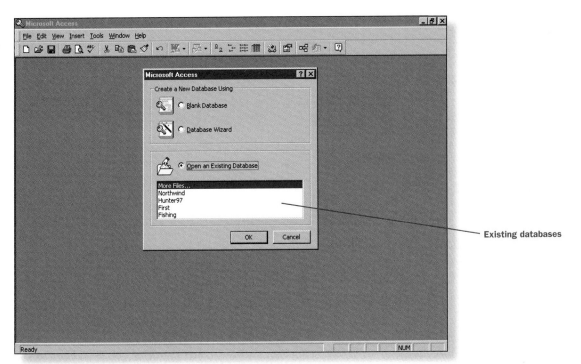

Existing databases

GUIDED ACTIVITY

1.1

Starting Microsoft Access and Opening a Database

In this Guided Activity, you will locate the Access icon and start the Access program. You will open the Northwind sample database packaged with Access. Three methods to open a database are discussed.

1. If you have not already started Windows 95, do so at this time.

2. Examine the desktop and locate the Access icon. Once you have located the Access icon, start Access by double-clicking the icon, then go to step 4.

3. If the Access icon is not present on your desktop, click the Start button in the taskbar. Slide the mouse up to the Programs line, then over and down to the Microsoft Access line. Click once on that line to start Access.

4. After a few seconds, the Startup window will appear. You may see the Northwind database listed in the lower portion of this box. If it is there, click once on its line to open this database, then click the OK button. Proceed to step 8.

5. If the Northwind database is not present in the file list (meaning that you have not opened it before), select More Files in the lower portion of the opening box, then click OK. You'll see the Open dialog box next. In the File Name box, type Northwind, then click the Find Now button. Access will search for *Northwind* and the file that contains the Northwind Traders database. When it appears in the large box in the center of the screen, click the Open button. Proceed to step 8.

You might have to use the Advanced button in the Open window to specify a new starting location for your file search.

6. If Access is already open, you can open Northwind directly. Use the mouse to select the File menu, then choose the Open Database command.

7. In the File Name list box, select Northwind. You may have to change to the Samples folder under C:\Program Files\Microsoft Office\Office\ to find the Northwind database. This is the large sample application that comes with Access. If this database is not listed, consult your instructor or lab assistant.

8. Access will display a welcome screen for the Northwind Traders database. Click the OK button to clear the message and open this database.

We will continue at this point in the next Guided Activity.

The Access Database Window

Access displays the Database window when you create a new database file or open an existing database file. The Database window contains all the database objects associated with that database, organized by type of object. From here, you can use one of these objects or create a new one of your own. Figure A1.4 shows the Northwind Database window.

FIGURE A1.4
Access Database window

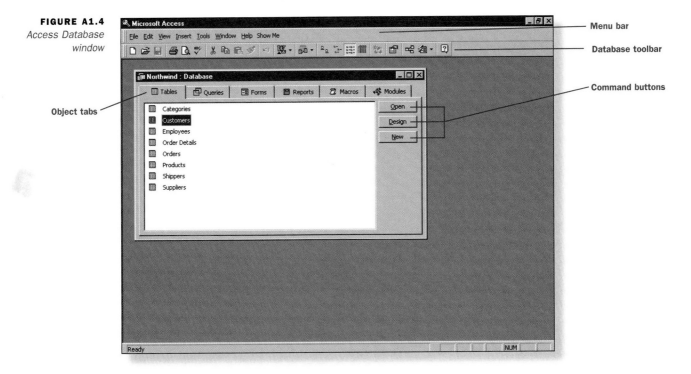

MDB Database File

Access stores all of the objects in the database in a single file with the MDB file extension (for "Microsoft database"). Unlike other database management packages, such as dBASE and Paradox, Access lets you copy a *single file* and transfer *all* the objects associated with that database. This also means that the DOS filename restriction of eight characters can be relaxed for objects stored within the database file. In Access, names of tables and other database objects can be up to 64 characters long, with embedded spaces. This makes it possible to accurately name your objects without ambiguity. Which is more meaningful, "1997 Sales Report by Region" or "SALES97R"? Of course, with Windows 95 you can use long descriptive names for files, too.

Object Tabs

The object tabs are shown across the top of the Database window. Notice that one of the tabs is selected; it forms the top of the large display in the center of the window. In this window, the Tables tab is selected. A list of objects in that category—in this case, the tables—appears in the middle of the box. If you were to click another object tab with the mouse, only the objects in the corresponding category would appear. Thus, you can examine all the objects in your database by cycling through the Tables, Queries, Forms, Reports, Macros, and Modules tabs. We will discuss each of the objects later in this unit.

Command Buttons

The Database window's command buttons appear at the right side of the window. The first two buttons work with the selected object, so be sure to select the correct object before using a command button. The Open button will open the existing object whose name is selected and display the object's contents, while the Design button is used to make a change in the design or structure of the highlighted object. The New button is used to create a new object of the type whose object button is selected.

The Access Display

The Access menu bar extends across the top of the screen, beneath the title bar, and lets you choose commands from the various menus. Many Windows 95 applications, including Access, *vary* the choices in the menu bar depending on which object is in use. For instance, if you had not opened a database in the opening dialog box, there would be different choices in the menu bar. Fortunately, Access presents choices that you are likely to need for each situation, but it does take some time to get used to different menu bars. The following sections will briefly explain the most important choices in each menu.

THE FILE MENU

The File menu is used to create a new database, open an existing database, change database properties, import and export data, print database objects, and exit from Access. As with most Windows applications, Access presents a dialog box in which you can specify the disk drive, folder, and file name when you open or save a database.

EDIT

The Edit menu is used with the Windows Clipboard and the Cut, Copy, and Paste commands. It is also used to undo changes that have just been made to the database object, and to rename a database object.

VIEW

The View menu allows you to choose the type of database object that appears in the Database window. The default choice is to view Tables, but you can select Queries, Forms, Reports, Macros, and Modules. You can also use View to choose the way objects will be shown in the Database window. The Toolbars command is used to select or customize toolbars used in Access 97.

INSERT

The Insert menu allows you to create a new database object (table, query, form, report, macro, or module) within the current database. You can select the type of object, as explained later in this unit. Most users will find it easier to use the Database window itself to add new objects to the database.

TOOLS

The Tools menu is used to manage the various utility programs that come with Access. You can check spelling through this menu, as well as analyze tables and set relationships between tables. Database security, such as establishing passwords and permissions for one or more users, is controlled through this menu. You can also create or change user groups. You also control Replication through the Tools menu. You can use the Options command from this menu to view and change system option settings. We will not work with the Tools choices in this unit. You can use the Help command to learn more about these settings.

WINDOW

Virtually all Windows 95 applications use the Window menu. This menu allows you to arrange windows on the screen, or to switch to a different active window. Most users will not need to use this command, because most Access windows are not maximized and always remain visible on the desktop. It is easier to switch to another visible window by clicking in some part of it with the mouse pointer.

HELP

The last menu choice in most Windows applications is the Help menu. With Help, you can search the online Access help system, even asking your own questions through the Office Assistant. Through Help, you can also find out the version of Access and get technical support information by choosing the About Microsoft Access command from the Help menu.

Access Database Objects

This section will describe the six main objects that make up an Access database. It gives a short example of each type of object, taken from the Northwind Traders sample database packaged with Access. This book contains separate units for most of these Access database objects.

Table

Recall that a database table is the basic structure that holds the data values for the database. It is called a table because its rows represent records and its columns are data fields. In Access you can have up to 32,768 tables per database. Most databases will have from 5 to 15 tables, depending on the complexity of the system modeled in the database. When you create a new table, you'll give the field name and data type for each column, along with the width of that column and any special rules for field values. When we examine the table's field definitions, Access displays it in Design view. We will build a new table in the next unit.

When we see the table and its field values, Access displays it in Datasheet view. This view resembles a spreadsheet, with fields across the top and records down the side. The icon for a table has the Datasheet view in its background. Figure A1.5 shows a table in Datasheet view.

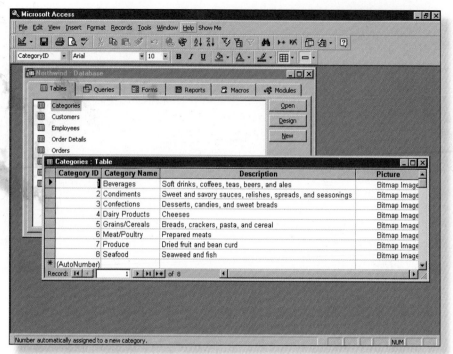

Query

In Access, you can use a query to display only the data that meet certain criteria. A query takes fields from one or more tables and allows you to enter criteria expressions to qualify records. In Access this facility is also referred to as query by example (QBE), because you provide an example of the kind of data that will qualify according to your criteria. You can also use the Query facility to link two tables so that records with matching field values appear together. For example, suppose you were working with an Order Details table that contained a product number that appeared in a recent order. You could match that table to a Products table that contained the product's name, and thus supply the name with the order. Figure A1.6 contains a query example in Design view that shows the link between two tables. Figure A1.7 shows the datasheet that appears when you run the query.

Form

A form is used to display records and allow the user to make changes to the field values in a record. Although the default Datasheet view can be used to examine data, the Form view allows customized designs that display field values, using such familiar Windows elements as list boxes and check boxes. You can also build forms that display the contents of more than one table at a time. Forms are designed primarily for screen output of one record at a time, although forms can also be sent to the printer. Figure A1.8 shows an Access form that shows product categories and a scrollable subform listing products from a given category.

FIGURE A1.6
Linked query in Design view

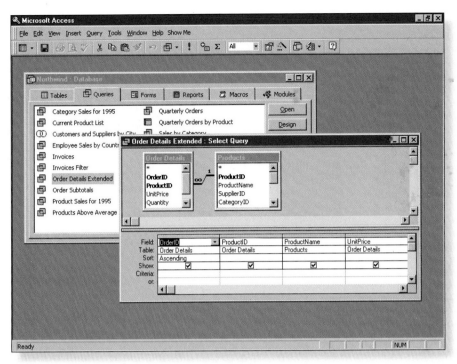

FIGURE A1.7
Datasheet view for the query from Figure A1.6

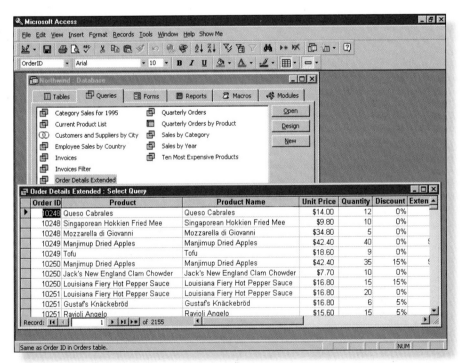

FIGURE A1.8
*Categories form
with Products
subform*

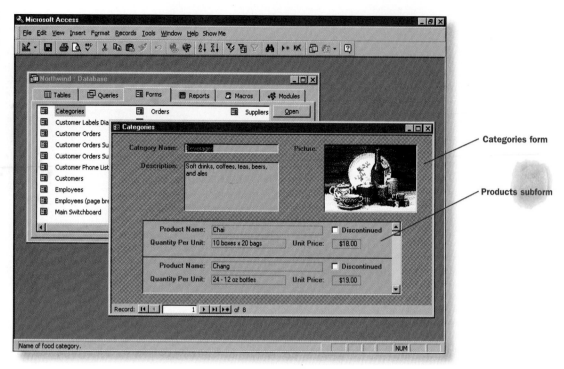

Report

A report is used primarily for printed output, although reports can also be viewed on the screen. You can design tabular reports that look like spreadsheets, or columnar reports with fields in different columns. Access has a facility for creating mailing label reports, and also allows you to design your own report formats. Figure A1.9 shows an example of an Access report. You cannot alter data in a report, nor would you want to.

FIGURE A1.9
*Print Preview of
alphabetical
products report*

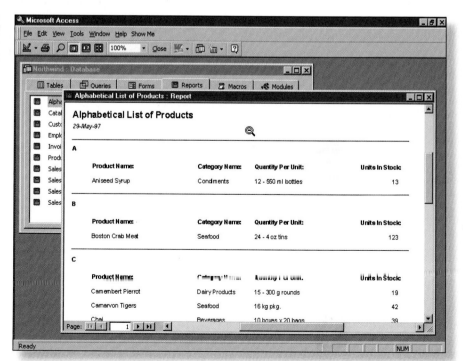

Macro

An Access macro is a list of actions that you use to automate repetitive tasks. Macros are stored by name, and can be attached to an on-screen toolbar button in such a manner that the macro executes when you click the button. Other macros can be called on to perform some action automatically when you open a particular database. Although some would consider this "programming," and are needlessly fearful of it, it is fairly easy for end users to create Access macros. Other applications, such as spreadsheets and word processors, use similar macros.

Module

Access contains a full programming language called Visual Basic for Applications, derived from the language used in Microsoft Visual Basic. Although most applications can be built without programming, this language is used for customized situations that cannot be handled otherwise. You can write custom modules in this language that perform automatic updates to your data.

Important Access Toolbar Buttons

Many Windows applications use tool buttons to represent frequently used commands. In Access, these tool button icons appear in toolbars, just beneath the menu bar. Access 97 has 22 toolbars for different situations, and many are used in other Office 97 applications. There are more than 50 toolbar buttons that are used in various circumstances. They do not all appear at the same time, but depend on the database object in use. The most important are described below. Individual toolbars for each Access object are also described in the appropriate unit of this book.

TIP

To display or hide a toolbar, right-click in the toolbar area, then select the desired toolbar from the list.

▦	Datasheet View	Display the table or query values in Datasheet view
◩	Design View	Display the Design view of the specified object (table, query, form, report) so that it can be modified
▣	Form View	Display the Form view of the data
▯	New	Create a new database file
☞	Open	Open an existing database file
🖫	Save	Save database object
🕮	Find | Replace Data	Find and/or replace specific data
✓	Spelling	Check spelling in text fields
▣	Print Preview	Display preview of printout on screen
🖨	Print	Print database object

	Build	Activate Access Builder
	Help	Activate Access screen tips help
	Undo	Cancel (erase) the last change made to the object
	Database Window	Display Database window
	Display Properties	Display properties box for indicated object
	Run	Run the current query or macro
	Primary Key	Denotes field that is the primary (unique) key field
	Office Assistant	Bring up Office Assistant help system
	Cut	Cut selected text to Clipboard
	Copy	Copy selected text to Clipboard
	Paste	Paste selected text from Clipboard
	Web Toolbar	Open Web toolbar

Access Documentation

Knowing what kind of documentation accompanies a package can often help you solve a problem more quickly, without having to go to other sources for help. The material from the manuals is available through online Help, discussed in the following section. *Getting Results with Microsoft® Access 97* is an introductory tutorial on Microsoft Office 97 and Access 97. It offers examples of many useful Access techniques. The *Getting Results* manual is also available in electronic form from the Office 97 CD-ROM. *Building Applications with Microsoft® Access 97* shows how to link Access objects into applications and serves as an introduction to the Access Visual Basic programming language. It is also available in print form from Microsoft.

Access Help Methods

This section will present the kinds of online Help available in Access.

ToolTips

Place the tip of the mouse pointer on a toolbar button and Access will display its name below the button. Use ToolTips to learn about new buttons.

Help Menu

The usual kind of Windows 95 help is available in the Access menu bar. You can display the contents of the help files, or search the index for specific help topics. Figure A1.10 shows the Help menu in Access 97.

FIGURE A1.10
*Access 97
Help menu*

OFFICE ASSISTANT

A new feature in Access 97 is the Office Assistant, a facility with which you can ask a question in plain English and Access will search through its help files for relevant information. An animated figure offers suggestions and delivers specific questions that you can choose from. The Assistant remembers what you have done and presents different choices based on what you're doing now. Figure A1.11 shows the default Clippit Office Assistant and a sample menu.

FIGURE A1.11
*Office Assistant
menu*

TIP

You can activate nine different animated figures for the Office Assistant. To select a new figure, click the Options button in the Office Assistant menu, then select the Gallery tab. You will need your Office 97 CD-ROM to change the figure, or you can download figures from the Microsoft Web site.

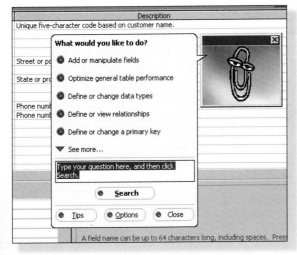

CONTENTS AND INDEX

This choice displays the standard Windows 95 Help system, with three tabs.

- Contents displays a broad table of contents for the Help system. Double-click a choice to see more detail. Select an index entry, then click Display to see the corresponding help screen.

- Index lets you search for a keyword, then links you to the help screens catalogued for that keyword. Click Display to see the help screen.

- Find searches through all help screens for instances of the keyword. This is the least efficient way to search for help.

MICROSOFT ON THE WEB

This choice, new with Access 97, links you to various Microsoft Web sites through your Web browser. You must have a live Web connection to use this command. You can view product information, see FAQs (frequently asked questions), reach online technical support, and so forth.

F1 Help Key

Press **F1** to activate the Office Assistant when no database object is open. You can press the **F1** function key in a dialog box and context-specific help about the highlighted object will appear. We suggest that you choose this method when you have a question about a particular entry or command.

Shift-F1 Help

If you press **Shift-F1** (or select What's This? from the Help menu), the pointer changes to an arrow question mark. You can then move the pointer to any object on the Access desktop and click the left mouse button to receive specific help about that object. What's This? help is particularly useful for information about toolbar buttons and menu bar commands. Press **Shift-F1** to turn off this feature.

Help Button

Some dialog boxes have their own Help button. Click this button to receive customized help for the particular box. Many Access dialog boxes have a ? button in the title bar. Click this button, then click an object within the box to get What's This? help for that choice.

GUIDED ACTIVITY

1.2   Using Access Help

This Guided Activity illustrates how to use the Help facility in Microsoft Access.

1. We assume that you have started Access and loaded the Northwind.mdb database, as shown in the previous Guided Activity. If you have not completed these tasks, go back to that activity now.

2. Select Help from the menu bar, then choose the Contents and Index command. Next, choose the Contents tab, as shown in Figure A1.12.

3. Select the second entry, "Introduction to Microsoft Access 97", then click Open. This choice will present a brief overview of Access database objects and terminology.

4. You'll see a list of several topics you can select. You can select any of these topics and Help will display information about that type of database object.

5. In this case, select the first topic, "Databases: What they are and how they work", and click Display. You'll see a box showing examples of databases.

FIGURE A1.12

Access Help Topics dialog box

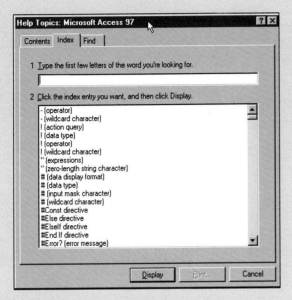

When you have finished reading that box, click the >> button to see the next box. The fifth screen is shown in Figure A1.13.

FIGURE A1.13

Fifth "What is a Database" help screen

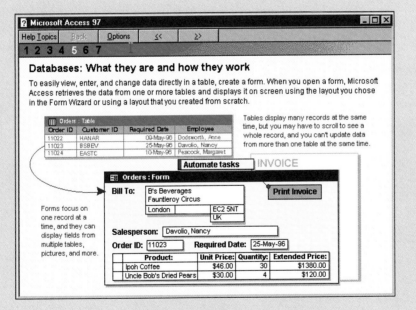

 NOTE *Move the mouse pointer to the Automate Tasks label. Click that label in the Help window and Access will display additional information about that option. Click again to close this box.*

6. After reading the seven illustrated Help boxes about databases, click the Help Topics button and you will return to Help Contents.

7. Click the "Creating a Database and Working in the Database Window" topic, just beneath the "Converting a Previous-Version Database to Microsoft Access 97" topic. Click Open to see the topics within this help line.

8. At this point, you could select the "Create a database" help topic and build a database object. We will pursue this course in the next unit when we build database tables.

9. Close the Help window by clicking the Close button in the upper right corner, then return to Access.

Closing a Database

To close the current database, use the File | Close command from the menu bar or click the window close button (marked with an X) in the upper-right corner of the Database window. Access will close all the windows associated with the current database. If you have unsaved changes for any database object, Access will prompt you to save them before closing that window.

 NOTE *Access databases are* automatically *saved when you close the database. There is no need to save the database itself. However, in future units you will learn how to create and save objects within the database.*

The Access desktop display becomes quite plain, as shown in Figure A1.14. The title bar shows just the name of the application, Microsoft Access. At this point, there are fewer commands in the menu bar. You will find that the choices in these menus have changed now that no database is open. The Tools menu is particularly important now, because it gives you access to the database utilities (convert, compact, and repair) as well as various security features.

FIGURE A1.14
Acess desktop with no database open

Leaving Access

Use the File | Exit command to leave Access. Nearly all Windows applications share a special feature: you can simply exit from the application and Windows will automatically close all files that are open. If you have made changes to any database object that is still open, you will be prompted to decide whether you want those changes to be made permanent. Take your time when closing objects, so that you do not inadvertently lose your work. After you reply, Access will close and you will return to the Windows 95 desktop.

GUIDED ACTIVITY

1.3 Leaving Access

In this Guided Activity, you will close the database and exit from Access.

1. Select File | Close from the menu bar. The Database window will close and you will see the plain Access desktop.

2. Select File | Exit from the menu bar. Access will close and you will return to the Windows 95 desktop.

3. If you're finished with Windows at this time, you can also shut down the computer by clicking the Start button in the taskbar, selecting Shut Down, and clicking Yes to Shut Down the Computer.

SUMMARY

One of the assets of any business is its information. Databases are collections of related information. Access contains in a single database file six types of objects that allow you to manipulate data: tables, queries, forms, reports, macros, and modules. Before creating tables and putting data into them, a systems analyst must determine what information is needed and in what format, when the data is needed, where the data comes from, and who will be allowed to look at (and to change) the information. Once the answers to these questions are determined, you can begin to plan the creation of the database using a database management system (DBMS) such as Access.

The Database window shows the objects that can be created in every database, plus the buttons that help you create a new object, open an existing object, or change the design or definition of an object. A table, also known as a datasheet, represents a spreadsheet with rows and columns; a table is used to hold data values. Queries are used to ask questions about the data. Forms display formatted records on the screen one at a time. Reports are also formatted, but are used mostly for printing. Macros are automated sequences of steps, which automate tasks by using Visual Basic programming.

EXERCISE

1.1   Academic Information Database

1. What tables would be appropriate for use by your school for keeping track of student academic information, including permanent information and classes taken?

2. Describe the fields within the tables.

EXERCISE

1.2   Video Store

1. Suppose you have just been hired by the manager of a local video rental store to help her design a database for the store. Describe the data tables that would be used with the database.

2. What kind of reports would this system need?

EXERCISE

1.3   911 Emergency System

1. The telephone company is putting together a 911 emergency information system for the local community. Describe the way this system will be used.

2. What tables would be used with this system?

3. What fields would be appropriate within these tables?

EXERCISE

1.4   Automobile Dealer Database

1. The local automobile dealer is interested in preparing a customer database. Describe the kinds of information that such a system would contain, and tell how it would be used.

2. What tables and fields would be needed?

EXERCISE

1.5 Computer Store

1. The Solutions With Computers store has hired you as an intern to assist its management in preparing a database. This company builds computers to order and also sells software, accessories, and service. What kinds of information would the company need to store in its database?

2. What tables and fields would be needed to support your system?

EXERCISE

1.6 Thrill Seekers Tours

1. The Thrill Seekers Tours travel agency has asked you to assist its personnel in preparing a database of its customers and tours.

2. Describe the kinds of information that such a system would contain, including the tables and fields needed.

3. List the forms and reports that Thrill Seekers Tours would need to conduct its business.

EXERCISE

1.7 Northwind Database Objects

1. Open Microsoft Access 97.

2. Open the Northwind.mdb database. By default, the Samples folder is located in the C:\Program Files\Microsoft Office\Office\ folder when you install Office 97. You may need to discuss the location of the sample databases with your instructor or lab assistant.

3. List the names of the tables stored in this database.

4. List the names of the forms and reports in this database.

Physicians' Medical Clinic: Designing the Database

In this Application, you will create on paper the preliminary design for a medical clinic database. In later Applications, you'll have the opportunity to use Microsoft Access and implement a portion of the database on the computer.

You have been hired by Dr. Thomas Greenway, chief administrator of the Physicians' Medical Clinic (PMC), to assist in the development of a working database system to handle patient visits, insurance, billing, and other pertinent transactions of a large medical office. There are nearly 50 physicians on the PMC staff, along with about 100 medical technicians, nurses, and business staffers. Although PMC operates a leased minicomputer-based information system, the administrator believes it is time to develop alternative database approaches that would make use of personal computers (PCs) and a local area network (LAN).

Goals for the PMC database would include storage of permanent patient information, information about patient visits to the clinic, costs of individual medical procedures and tests, insurance billings, employee information, supply inventory data, and information about supply vendors.

To help guide your thinking in the development of the PMC database, consider the following questions:

1. What tables would be useful for the PMC database? Remember that each kind of object in the database is usually represented by a separate table.

2. What kinds of reports would PMC want from the database? Arrange them in groups according to type of information. For example, you would have several reports dealing with individual patient visits to the clinic. Would these reports be printed *on demand*, or be based on a *fixed time interval,* such as daily or weekly? If the latter, how frequently should they be printed?

3. Describe the fields found in the permanent patient information table. That table contains information about the patient that doesn't change with each visit made to the clinic. What characteristics (field type, field size) should you consider for each field?

4. Next, describe the fields found in the supplies table. Give the name of the field, the type of data found in that field, and the approximate size of the field necessary to hold the largest value (or longest text phrase) that will appear in that field.

APPLICATION

APPLICATION

Hunter River Sporting Goods: Designing the Database

In this Application, you will create on paper the preliminary design for a retail sporting goods store database. In later Applications, you'll have the opportunity to use Microsoft Access and implement a portion of that database on the computer.

Assume that Hunter River is converting its information system from a manual one to a computerized database. You have been hired for an MIS internship to assist Hunter River management in making the conversion. Use the Hunter River background information that appears earlier in this unit. To help guide your thinking, consider the following questions:

1. What tables would be appropriate for Hunter River?

2. What kind of reports would Hunter River use in running the business? Consider such functions as point-of-sale transactions, inventory management, daily sales, employee payroll, customer lists, accounting reports, and so forth.

3. List the fields that might be found in the following tables: Customers, Employees, Products, Vendors, and Orders.

4. Suppose Hunter River wants to do business on the Internet. What activities would you suggest to management? What tables would be needed to support your recommendation? We will cover this in more detail in Unit 2.

UNIT 2

Building a Table

This unit will introduce you to building and working with database tables. This unit introduces the Database Wizard, which automatically creates tables with pertinent fields, forms, reports, and buttons for using the database. It will demonstrate how to open an existing table and access it in Datasheet view, as well as how to create a new table and populate it with data values. It will describe the various data types available in Access and show how to make changes to the design of a table in Design view. You will learn how to use the Table Wizard to create a new table. The unit concludes with a discussion about editing records and printing the contents of the table, including publishing a table on the Internet.

Learning Objectives

At the completion of this unit you should be able to

1. use the Database Wizard to create a complete database application,

2. create a new database in Design view,

3. explain the features of Datasheet view and Design view,

4. describe the functions of the various components of the Table window,

5. create a new table and define fields for the table,

6. list the nine data types used in Access 97,

7. make changes to the table definition,

8. add data and make changes to a table,

9. resize the columns and rows in a datasheet,

10. delete records,

11. print the contents of a datasheet,

12. use the Table Wizard to create a new table,

13. publish an Access table as an HTML document.

Case Study

Hunter River Sporting Goods has asked you to build database tables for such things as products, employees, vendors, and customers. An important criteria for the employees is entering information accurately into the database. In addition to building the tables, Sales Merchandise information needs to be published to the Internet as well as Employee information to the company's intranet.

Creating a New Database

As discussed in the previous unit, Microsoft Access uses a single comprehensive database file to hold all the database objects. To open an existing database, choose the File menu and select Open Database. Select the desired database, then click the Open button. Any database *already open* in Access will be closed automatically when you open or create a database.

There are two ways to create a new database: use the Database Wizard or start with a blank database. We'll start with the Database Wizard, then spend the rest of the chapter demonstrating the blank-database approach.

Access Database Wizard

The Database Wizard makes it very easy for novice database users to create a working database. You can choose among more than 20 templates from a wide variety of personal and business settings. Applications include

- Asset Tracking
- Book Collection
- Contact Management
- Event Management
- Household Inventory
- Inventory Control
- Membership

- Music Collection
- Recipes
- Resource Scheduling
- Service Call Management
- Students and Classes
- Time and Billing
- Workout

The Database Wizard creates a database for your application, complete with tables that contain appropriate fields with optional sample values. The Wizard also creates Access forms and reports for entering and displaying data values, all with little or no intervention by you. Your database is linked by a switchboard form with buttons for choosing various database functions (add data, view forms, print reports, exit) within that application.

GUIDED ACTIVITY

2.1 Using the Database Wizard

This Guided Activity demonstrates how to use the Database Wizard to create a membership database for the Fishing Club at Hunter River Sporting Goods.

1. If you have not already started the computer, do so now. Load Microsoft Access 97 and click Cancel when the opening Access dialog box appears.

2. Click the New Database button in the main Access toolbar (or use the File | New Database command) to start the Database Wizard.

3. Click the Databases tab. Select the Membership application, then click OK.

4. Specify Fishing as the database name and click the Create button.

5. When the Database Wizard window appears, click Next to approve each step as your application is built.

You could click the Finish button in step 5 to automatically accept all the default Wizard choices. We will go through each step in this Guided Activity.

6. Seven sample tables for the Fishing database, and the fields for each table, appear in the next Wizard window, as shown in Figure A2.1. You can add or remove fields in the database as appropriate for your particular situation. We will accept all of the Wizard's suggestions for this activity.

FIGURE A2.1
Database Wizard table and fields

Click here for sample data.

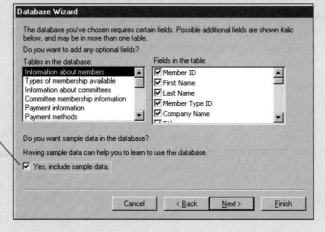

7. Click the check box to include sample data in the tables. Click Next to continue.

8. Click the Standard style used for screen displays, then click Next. (Forms are discussed in Unit 4.)

9. Click the Bold style for reports, then click Next. (Reports are discussed in Unit 5.)

10. Enter Fishing Club as the title for the database. Click Next to go on to the last step.

11. Finally, click Finish to complete the generation of your database. The Database Wizard will spend up to several minutes creating the database objects according to your specifications. The Database Wizard creates 8 tables, 1 query, 11 forms, 5 reports, and 1 module for this application.

12. The Main Switchboard menu is shown in Figure A2.2. Select other command buttons to see other options in this application.

13. When you are finished, close the Fishing Membership database window. We will continue with Access in the next Guided Activity.

You'll have another chance to work with the Database Wizard in an exercise at the end of this unit.

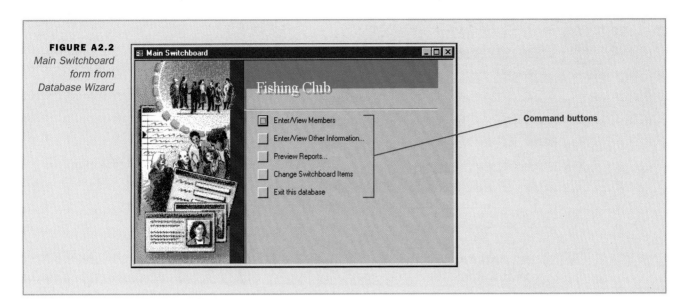

FIGURE A2.2
Main Switchboard form from Database Wizard

Command buttons

Create a Blank Database

To create a new blank database, click the New Database button or use the File | New Database command. Click the General tab, select Blank Database, and then click OK. You'll be asked to provide a name for your database. File names can be up to 255 characters, and can contain embedded spaces. Access automatically adds the MDB extension. The following Guided Activity demonstrates how to create a new database.

GUIDED ACTIVITY

2.2   Creating a New Blank Database

In this Guided Activity, you'll create a new database and store the MDB file on the drive of your choice. We will use this database for the remainder of this unit.

1. If you have not already started Access, do so at this time by choosing its icon. When the Microsoft Access opening screen appears, click the Cancel button. For now, we'll use the menu bar to create a new database.

2. Use the File | New Database command to create a new database. Click the General tab. You'll see the New window.

3. Double-click the Blank Database icon. You'll see the File New Database window, shown in Figure A2.3. Any database files you have previously placed in this folder will appear in the center of the window. (Your display will not look exactly like this one.)

 NOTE *By default, Access uses a folder called My Documents on the C: drive for your databases. Your computer lab may have a different default folder. Check with your instructor or lab assistant.*

4. Next, type `First` in the File Name box and press **Enter**. Access will create a file called First.mdb in the default folder and will display the First Database

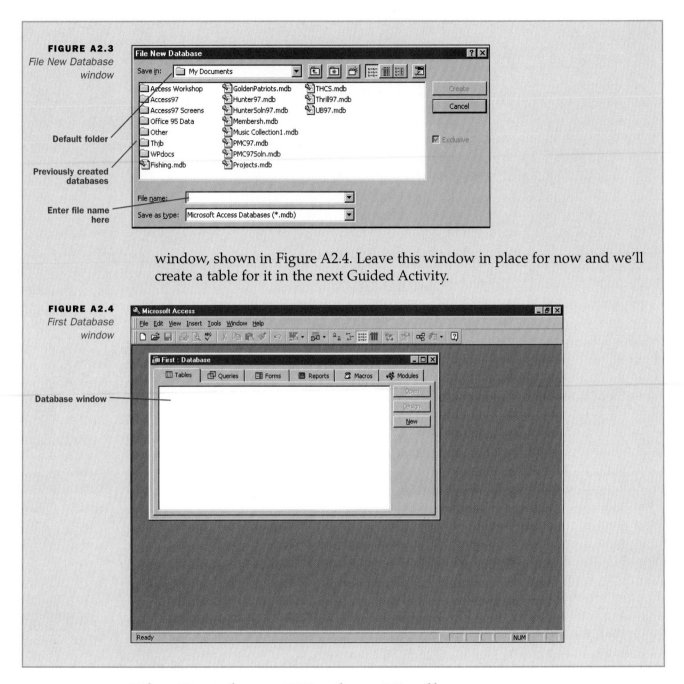

FIGURE A2.3
File New Database window

FIGURE A2.4
First Database window

window, shown in Figure A2.4. Leave this window in place for now and we'll create a table for it in the next Guided Activity.

The Database Window Toolbar

After you open a Database window, Access will display the toolbar shown in Figure A2.5. The first two buttons allow you to make a new database or open an existing database. The Save, Print, and Print Preview buttons appear next. You can spell

FIGURE A2.5
Database toolbar buttons

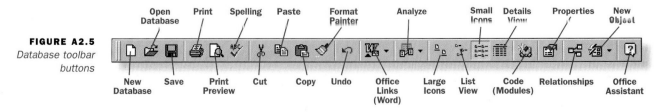

check your work with the Spelling button. The Cut, Copy, and Paste buttons let you work with the Windows Clipboard. The group of four buttons near the center of this toolbar lets you choose the way objects are displayed in the Database window. You can choose from Large or Small Icons, List view, and Details view. The Help button activates the Office Assistant. We will cover many of the other buttons in later units.

Working with the Table Window

You work directly with Access tables in Datasheet view, in which rows represent records and columns represent fields. This section also describes the process of creating a new table in Design view and the process of adding data to a table in Datasheet view.

Datasheet View

Datasheet view is similar to a spreadsheet. Access displays the records in rows down the screen and the fields in columns across the screen. You can scroll through the records one at a time or a screenful at a time. As with other Windows applications, Access lets you change the size of the rows and the columns to fit your data values. We will cover that procedure in a later section of this unit.

Design View

Before you can add data to a new table, you must first create the structure for the table in Access Design view. In this mode, you define each of the fields in the table. That is, you provide a name for the field, its field type, and an optional description of the field. There are numerous field properties for such things as field size, format, default values, validation rules, and index information. We will examine some of these properties in a Guided Activity.

Before you save the table definition, you must provide a primary key that uniquely identifies each record in the table. If you do not have a unique key in your field list, Access can create an autonumber field for this purpose.

Use the File | Save command to save the table definition. Access will ask you to enter a table name. Like other Access objects, table names can have up to 64 characters, including spaces and punctuation. The table name should be explicit; that is, it should describe the contents of the table without ambiguity. Within a single database, the table names must be unique. Tables and queries cannot share the same name. You may, however, use the same table name in *different* databases.

The Table Window Toolbar

Access provides shortcut buttons in the toolbar for Datasheet and Design views. They are located just below the File menu. Figure A2.6 shows the buttons in the

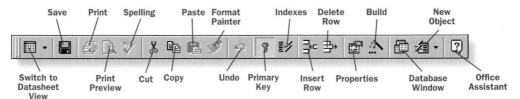

FIGURE A2.6
*Table toolbar
(Design view)*

Save   Print   Spelling   Paste   Format Painter   Indexes   Delete Row   Build   New Object

Switch to Datasheet View   Print Preview   Cut   Copy   Undo   Primary Key   Insert Row   Properties   Database Window   Office Assistant

Table window toolbar for Design view. The spreadsheet icon invokes Datasheet view; click this button and Access will show you table values. When you are in Datasheet view, the first button is a triangle with a ruler and pencil, signifying a switch to Design view. If you have a Table window open in either mode, you can immediately switch to the other view by clicking the corresponding button. If you have made changes to the design, Access will ask for your permission to save those changes before switching to Datasheet view. For information about other commands in the toolbar, use the Help system entry "Toolbars."

TIP

Although the subject is not covered here, this setting and others can be changed with the Tools|Options command.

The Status Bar

The lower portion of the desktop in Figure A2.4 contains the Access status bar. It will be displayed unless you have elected not to display it.

The left portion of the status bar shows messages such as field descriptions and menu explanations. It changes as you move the mouse cursor over various toolbar buttons. As in other Windows applications, the right portion of the status bar shows Caps, Num, and Scroll Lock status indicators.

Types of Data Fields

Your database can include a wide range of objects. Access employs 10 different data types to model your objects' attributes. Some data types represent numeric information; others represent text and dates. Each data type requires a different amount of storage space. These are described below, along with examples and an explanation of the uses for each data type.

TEXT FIELDS represent attributes or short descriptions of objects. You use text fields for such things as a name, address, state, color, size, manufacturer, course title, or telephone number. Remember that most database designers use text fields for number-like values that would not be used for arithmetic. Thus, zip codes, social security numbers, and box numbers should be text fields. You can specify the size of the field in characters; Access will not allow you to exceed that length, so select a field size that will hold your largest data items. It's possible to change the field size after you start using the database, however. The maximum length is 255 characters.

MEMO FIELDS are used for long textual descriptions or comments. Memo fields expand to fit the length of the entry in each record, up to a maximum of 64,000 characters per field. You can scroll a memo field in an Access form to display its contents a few lines at a time. By contrast, text fields are fixed-length fields and take up space whether you store anything in them or not; you may not want to use a text field where the contents of the field can be quite long or unpredictable in length.

NUMBER FIELDS are used to hold quantitative measurements about items in your database. The rule of thumb is to use a number field for an item when you might want to perform arithmetic operations on that field. Examples include number of shares, closing price, number of credit hours earned, grade point average, quantity on hand, and wholesale unit cost. Access provides a separate data type, called currency, for dollar and cents fields (described below). It is possible to create custom number field formats. The field size for numeric fields can be chosen to allow integers only, or to permit decimal places, as shown in Table A2.1. Generally, choose the shortest field size that will hold the largest number you'll store in the database.

TABLE A2.1
Number field sizes

FIELD SIZE	EXPLANATION	STORAGE SIZE
Byte	no decimals, range 0 to 255	1 byte
Integer	no decimals, range –32,768 to 32,767	2 bytes
Long Integer	no decimals, range –2.1B to 2.1B	4 bytes
Single	7 digits, range –3.4*10^38 to 3.4*10^38	4 bytes
Double	15 digits, range –1.8*10^308 to 1.8*10^308	8 bytes

DATE/TIME FIELDS contain date and time information about events. Examples include date of birth, course drop date, inventory transaction time, and date and time of admission to a hospital. Dates can be shown in four different formats; time can be shown in three formats. You can also create custom date and time formats. The Access Help screen contains instructions for creating custom formats. Remember that Access will not accept a nonexistent date for a date/time field. Examples of date and time formats are shown in Table A2.2.

TABLE A2.2
Date and time formats

FORMAT	EXAMPLE
General Date (default)	3/1/97 04:14 PM
Long Date	Saturday, March 1, 1997
Medium Date	01-Mar-97
Short Date	3/1/97
Long Time	4:16:33 PM
Medium Time	04:16 PM
Short Time	16:16 (24-hour time)

CURRENCY FIELDS are used to store numeric money amounts. By default, these fields show a dollar sign (or other currency indicator as set up in Windows) to the left of the value and show two decimal places, as in $99.95. Negative numbers are enclosed in parentheses. Numbers larger than 1,000 have a comma separator between the hundreds place and the thousands place, and so on (although this too can be modified in Windows). Currency fields can contain up to 15 digits to the left of the decimal point and up to 4 digits to the right of the decimal point. It is also possible to design a custom format for number fields that makes them appear with dollar signs, commas, and a fixed number of decimal places.

AUTONUMBER FIELDS are special numeric fields that increment (increase) by 1 in each successive record. They increase as you add new records, usually starting with 1. You could use an autonumber field for a check number, a purchase order number, or any other sequential value. An autonumber field is frequently used as the primary key for a table. Autonumber field values *cannot* be changed once they have been entered. You can also command Access to provide random number values for autonumber fields.

YES/NO FIELDS contain only the values yes (true) or no (false). They can be used to reflect a condition that is met or is not met by the data item. Examples include in-state student, graduate student, local alumnus, taxable item, and over 21. In each case the answer to a question can be stated as yes or no. Access 97 represents yes/no fields with a check box in a table.

OLE OBJECT FIELDS are a special Windows feature in which another *object* can be *linked* to the originating application and *embedded* in the Access database. The OLE (pronounced *oh-lay*) object can be a spreadsheet, unformatted text, a graph, a picture, or a sound. A linked OLE object remains tied to the originating application; if subsequent changes to the OLE object are made in that application, the changes are automatically made to the Access database that contains the OLE object.

HYPERLINK is a new data type with Access 97. Hyperlink fields are linked to other resources such as local files and Internet or intranet URL addresses. Hyperlink fields appear in color and are underlined, just like hyperlinks in a Web document's hyperlink address. When you click a hyperlink, your Web browser or Access will go to the specified location. For instance, you might use a hyperlink field to represent the Web address of a vendor's home page. Hyperlink fields can have up to three parts, each up to 2,048 characters, separated by # characters. The first part is an optional text description, the second is the address part, and the last is an optional subaddress within the main address. For example, consider the following hyperlink entry:

```
Internet Book#http://www.indstate.edu/internet_book#
```

Internet Book will appear in the field, but Access will link that entry to the actual URL. Hyperlinks that appear without the optional parts are acceptable. See online Help for more information about hyperlinks. Table A2.3 shows more possible hyperlink entries.

TABLE A2.3
Hyperlink examples

HYPERLINK	EXPLANATION
#http://www.microsoft.com	Microsoft's main Internet home page
#C:\My Documents\resume.doc	The resume.doc file in the C: drive's My Documents folder
#C:\Access\Hunter97.mdb#Form Vendors	The Vendors form in the Hunter97 database

LOOKUP WIZARD creates a field that lets you choose a value from a list of possible choices using a combo box or a list box. Choosing this option starts a Wizard to define the combo or list box for you. You can get the values from another table, from a query, or from a list of choices that you supply. Lookup fields are generally text fields.

Creating a New Table

In this section, we will design a table for sale merchandise at the Hunter River Sporting Goods store. In the Guided Activity that follows, you'll actually input the table specifications. The sale merchandise table contains information about regular products that the store wants to promote. Preliminary fields for this table should be those listed in Table A2.4.

TABLE A2.4
Fields for sales promotion

FIELD NAME	DESCRIPTION
StockNumber	A unique five-character code that identifies an item
Description	The item's description
Category	The store sales category for this item; choices are Camping, Clothing, Hunting, Sports, and Other
UnitCost	The most current cost per unit of the item
QuantityOnHand	The current quantity of the item in inventory
DateOfLastOrder	The date the product was last ordered from the vendor

TIP

Avoid using spaces in field names if you will frequently refer to the fields in Access expressions.

StockNumber, Description, and Category are all text data type fields. UnitCost is a currency data type field. QuantityOnHand is a number data type field. DateOfLastOrder is a date/time field.

You create a table in Design view using three steps:

1. Give the name, data type, and field size for each field in the table. You can add an optional field description that will appear in the bottom of the Table window whenever you select that field in a table or form.

2. Name the field(s) you will use as the table's primary key.

3. Save the table structure with the File | Save command.

GUIDED ACTIVITY

2.3   Creating a New Table in Design View

This Guided Activity will lead you through the process of creating the table definition for a new table. If you have not already completed Guided Activity 2.2, do so at this time.

1. Your computer should have Access running with the First Database window open. (Refer to Guided Activity 2.2.)

2. Click the Tables tab in the Database window to switch to Table mode, then click the New button to create a new table. Select the Design View line, then click the OK button. See Figure A2.7.

FIGURE A2.7
New Table window

3. Access will open a Table window in Design view, as shown in Figure A2.8. Note that there are blank rows for the field definitions at the top of the window.

FIGURE A2.8
Empty Table Design window

Field selector button

Bottom pane

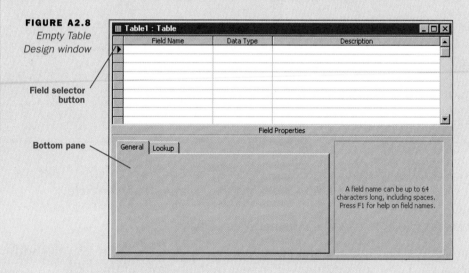

4. In the first row, type in the first field name, StockNumber. Press **Tab** to finish the entry.

5. Access will automatically move the pointer to the next column, Data Type, and highlight the default value, Text. That is the correct data type for this field. The lower pane of the Table window will show the highlighted default size of this field, 50 characters. Press the **F6** function key to switch the pointer to the bottom pane and key in 5, replacing the 50. Press **F6** again to return the pointer to the Data Type column. Accept this choice by pressing **Tab**.

NOTE   *You can change the default field size in the Tools | Options menu. Select the Tables/Queries tab.*

6. In the Description column, type A unique five-character code that uniquely identifies an item (primary key) and press **Tab** to move to the next row.

7. Repeat steps 4–6 with the second field, `Description`. It is also Text type, with a field size of 25 characters. Its description is `The item's description.`

8. The pointer should be on the third row of the Table window. Key in the third field's name, `Category`, and press **Tab**. For this Text field, type in `10` for the field size. The description for this field is `The store sales category for this item; choices are Camping, Sports, Clothing, Hunting, Other.` Press **Enter** to complete this field's definition.

9. For the fourth field, type `UnitCost` for the field name and press **Tab** to go on to the Data Type column.

10. This field will be Currency type. To display all the data types, click the arrow at the right of the Data Type drop-down list box.

11. From this list, choose the Currency type with the mouse and press **Tab** to complete the entry.

12. The description is `The most current cost per unit for this item.`

13. Next, enter the `QuantityOnHand` field name. Its data type is Number. Press **F6** to move the pointer to the lower pane.

14. Click the arrow on the right of the Field Size box to display numeric subtypes. Select Integer, press **F6** to move the cursor back to the top pane, and press **Tab** to move to the Description area. The description for this field is `The current quantity of the item in inventory.`

15. The final field is `DateOfLastOrder`. Its field type is Date/Time, and you should select Medium Date from the Format box in the lower pane. The description is `The date the product was last ordered from the vendor.`

16. Access requires that every table have a unique primary key. We will declare that the StockNumber field is the primary key. Use the mouse to position the pointer at the first field. Then click the Primary Key button that appears in the toolbar of the desktop. Access will place a smaller version of the key icon to the left of this field.

17. Figure A2.9 shows the table definition at this point. Go back and review the entries to be sure that each is correct. You can use the mouse to move the pointer to any item that is not correct.

18. You are ready to save the table. Click the Save button on the toolbar or give the File | Save command. When prompted, key in `Sales Merchandise` as the table name and click OK or press **Enter**. Access will save the table in the First database file.

19. Click the close box (marked with an X) in the upper right corner (or use the File | Close command) to close the Table window and redisplay the Database window. Figure A2.10 shows the First Database window with your newly saved table. We will work with the First database in the next Guided Activity.

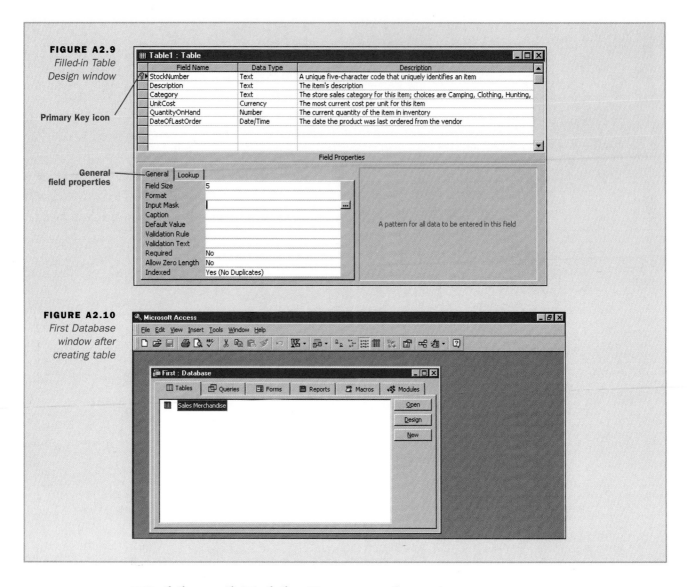

FIGURE A2.9
Filled-in Table Design window

Primary Key icon

General field properties

FIGURE A2.10
First Database window after creating table

Field and Table Properties

Access stores additional design information about database objects in property sheets. You can view properties of fields and tables in Table mode.

FIELD PROPERTIES

You have seen that the Table window's bottom pane in Design View contains property boxes for each of the fields. This pane will change slightly for different field types. The following list names the field properties and describes their meanings. For more information, you can refer to the *Getting Results* manual or see online Help.

FIELD SIZE   This is the length of the field in characters for text fields, the subtype of field (integer, single, double) for number fields, and the subtype for date/time fields.

FORMAT   This property enables you to customize the way the field will appear. You might use this property to format telephone numbers with parentheses around the area code or to insert hyphens into social security numbers.

DECIMAL PLACES   The number of decimal places to maintain for this number field.

INPUT MASK   A pattern for all data to be entered into this field. An input mask is useful for fields such as telephone numbers and social security numbers. Only the variable information is stored in the field, not the mask. The input mask definition can contain up to three sections separated by semicolons; for example, (999)000-0000!;0;" " could represent a telephone number input mask. Section meanings:

- First section—the input mask itself
- Second section—determines whether to store the literal display characters in the table
    - 0 = store literal characters with the value entered
    - 1 or leave blank = store only characters entered, not the mask literals
- Third section—character that is displayed for blanks in the input mask. You can use any character; type " " to display a space. If you leave this section blank, the underscore character is used.

You can find more examples of input masks by clicking the button with three dots to the right of the Input Mask property; this will start the Input Mask Wizard.

CAPTION   Access displays the full field name as the field's caption in the datasheet, forms, and reports. You can provide an alternate caption with this property. Some database analysts will choose a shorter name for the caption property.

DEFAULT VALUE   This property lets you establish a default value for the field that will always appear when a new record is added. Date/time fields could have the current system date as the default value. The user can override the value when the record is added or edited. Unless changed, the initial default value for text and date fields is blank, and for number and currency fields it is zero.

VALIDATION RULE   This property allows you to specify a condition for valid values. If the field does not meet the validation rule, Access displays the validation text and will prompt the user to enter a valid value.

VALIDATION TEXT   This is the message that you want to appear if the field does not meet the validation rule. The message should explain why the field does not meet the validation rule. If you give no validation text for a given rule, Access will display the message One or more values entered is prohibited by the validation rule set for <<this field>>.

REQUIRED   Lets you determine whether the user must make an entry in this field. Values are yes or no. If the field is required, the user will be prompted to enter a value before leaving the field. The primary key is required.

ALLOW ZERO LENGTH   Lets you determine whether to allow zero-length strings in this field. Values are yes or no.

INDEXED   This is a yes/no property that indicates whether Access is to create an index for this field. Indexes are used to speed up sorting and access to frequently used fields. If you have a large file, you should establish indexes in the appropriate fields.

NOTE *You can view the primary key and other indexes for a table by clicking the Index button or using the View | Indexes command from the menu bar.*

DISPLAY CONTROL   You can use the Display Control property from the Lookup tab in the Table window to specify the default method for displaying a Lookup field (list box or combo box).

TABLE PROPERTIES

The table properties are used to give a description of the table and other information about the table. To see the Table Properties window, use the View | Properties command or click the Properties button in the toolbar. You can move the Table Properties window by dragging its title bar if it blocks a vital part of the desktop, or you can close the window altogether.

CAUTION It is very important to complete the design of tables and fields, including properties, before going on to create forms and reports. If you establish properties for the fields in the Table window, Access will copy those properties into forms that you create. Any changes made to table and field properties *after* a form is created will not be copied to the form. Particularly important are the Format, Input Mask, Caption, Default, Validation Rule, and Validation Text properties. Also important is the field's Description property, which becomes the Status Bar Text property for a form control containing that field.

TIP

Make a backup copy of the database or the table before making a change to the design of the table where data loss might occur!

Changing the Table Design: Design View

After you save the table, you may find that you need to make changes to its design. You may need to add a field, change the size of a field, or remove a field. You can modify the field properties, provide a caption, or set up validation rules for the field. In most cases, Access will let you make the change without losing any data. If you change the data type or size for a field, however, data may be lost, particularly if the new field size is shorter than the original one.

ADDING A NEW FIELD

To add a new field at the end of the table, move the pointer to the next available row and begin typing the field definition. To add a field in the middle of a table, click the field selector button (previously shown in Figure A2.8) of the field that will *follow* the new field. Then issue the Insert | Rows command (or click the Insert Rows button in the toolbar) and Access will open a blank row for you to fill with the new field's definition, moving the other fields down to make room.

MOVING A FIELD TO A DIFFERENT LOCATION IN THE TABLE

Most applications have the fields in the sequence in which they are generally found in paper documents. To move a field to a different position in the record, first change to Design view. Select the field by clicking the field selector button immediately to the left of the field name. Access will highlight the entire row. Then click the field selector button (keep the mouse button depressed) and drag the field to a new location. Release the mouse button when you are satisfied with the new location. Access will rearrange the other fields to make room for this field.

DELETING A FIELD FROM THE TABLE

To delete a field definition from the table, click the field selector button to highlight the field row(s) to be deleted. Then press the **Del** key (or click the Delete Rows button in the toolbar) and the field will be permanently removed from the table. All data in that field will be permanently lost.

 NOTE *You will be given a second chance to confirm the design change(s) when you close the Design view window or save the table. If you do not save the design changes, Access will reverse all the changes made since the table was last saved.*

GUIDED ACTIVITY

2.4   Changing the Table Design

In this Guided Activity, you will make changes to the Sale Merchandise table design that was created in the preceding Guided Activity. We will add two new fields and provide a validation rule for the Category field.

1. Make sure you have the First.mdb Database window open on your desktop, then click the Tables tab to switch to Table mode.

2. Click the icon for the Sales Merchandise table to select it.

3. Click the Design View button to work with the table in Design view.

4. We will add a new field to the end of the table. Move the pointer to the row following DateOfLastOrder.

5. The new field's name is `NowOnOrder`. It is a yes/no field and the description is `Is product now on order?`

6. We also need to insert a field into the table before the Category field. Move the pointer and click the field selector button to the left of the Category row. The whole row will now be selected. Use the Insert I Row command and Access will create a blank row, as shown in Figure A2.11.

 NOTE *You can drag the vertical border between the column headings in the Table window to adjust the column widths. In Figure A2.11, the Field Name and Data Type columns have been narrowed to show more of the Description column.*

7. The new field will be `Vendor`. It is a 15-character Text field whose description is `Name of the product vendor.`

FIGURE A2.11
*Table design with
blank inserted row*

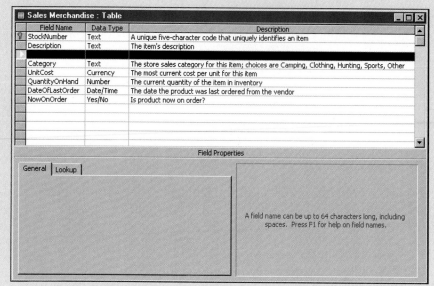

8. Next, we need to add a validation rule to the Category field. Click anywhere in the Category row and press **F6** to move to the bottom pane.

9. Click the Validation Rule line and enter this expression: `In("Camping","Sports","Clothing","Hunting","Other")`. As you type the expression, it will scroll across the small box. This *In* function in this validation rule will prevent you from entering any other category names not in the list. You can add more departments to the list at a later time by modifying this validation rule.

10. When you have finished typing the validation rule expression, use the **Left arrow** and **Right arrow** keys to check it. If you want to see the entire expression at once, click the Build button at the end of the Validation Rule property line or on the toolbar, shown in Figure A2.12. You can make changes to the expression in this window. When you're finished with this Expression Builder window, click OK to close it.

 When you enter the validation rule expression, it is usually not necessary to type the quotes around the Category names; Access will add those automatically when you finish the entry. You do have to type quotes when one of your words in the expression is an Access key word. For example, if you use a validation rule for state and choose IN to represent Indiana, Access would interpret that word as the Access In function. Put quotes around "IN" and it will be accepted as a regular text string.

11. Use the File | Save As/Export command to save this table in the current database with a new name. When prompted, type `Final Sales Merchandise` as the name. If you had chosen the File | Save command, Access would replace the original table with the revised table; with File | Save As/Export, you now have two tables under different names.

 12. Click the Datasheet View button in the Access toolbar (or use the View | Datasheet View command) to display the table in Datasheet view, as shown in

FIGURE A2.12
Expression Builder box for Category validation rule

Build button

Datasheet View

Validation rule

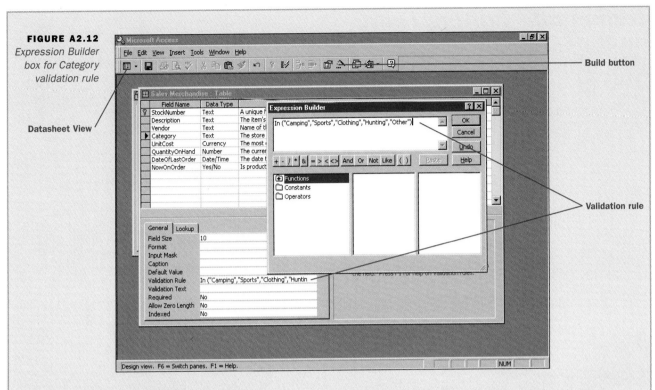

Figure A2.13. We will use this view in the following section and in the next Guided Activity.

 NOTE *Figure A2.13 also shows the Formatting toolbar. Use the View | Toolbars command to select this toolbar.*

FIGURE A2.13
Table window in Datasheet view

Document control buttons

Formatting toolbar

Record button

Column

Add New Record

Last Record

Next Record

Current Record Number

Previous Record

First Record

Record navigation area

Status bar

Record

Number of records

Field scroll bar

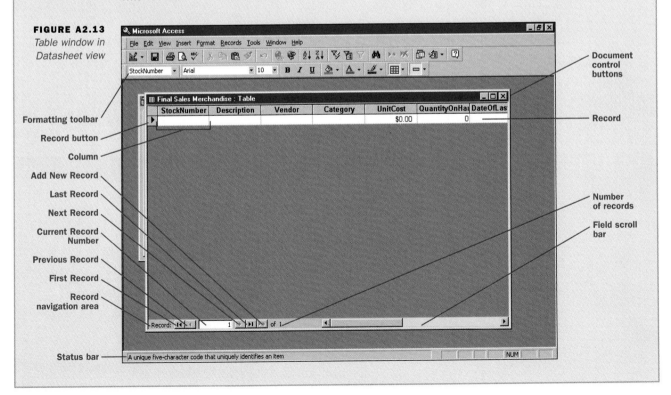

Adding and Editing Data

Now that you have created the table, it's time to add data to it. This section discusses the procedure for adding data and making changes to data in the table. The user customarily uses the Datasheet view or a form for this purpose. You'll learn about forms in the next unit.

The Table Window in Datasheet View

Access provides the Table window to display rows and columns in Datasheet view. Figure A2.13 shows the Table window. The components of this window and their purposes are explained below.

TITLE BAR   shows the name of the table.

DOCUMENT CONTROL BUTTONS   control the presentation of the document window. The three buttons are Minimize, Maximize, and Close, from left to right.

COLUMN   represents a field, with the field name at the top of the column.

RECORD BUTTON   The right-pointing triangle shows the location of the current record. This button changes shape as you work with a table. For instance, when it appears as a pencil, you have made changes that have not yet been saved in the database.

NAVIGATION BUTTONS   move the record pointer. Individual buttons are explained in Figure A2.13.

RECORD SCROLL BAR   If there are more records than one screen can hold, Access will display a vertical record scroll bar at the right edge of the window. (This scroll bar is not seen in Figure A2.13.)

FIELD SCROLL BAR   The table contains a horizontal field scroll bar if the table is wider than the screen can display at one time.

GUIDED ACTIVITY

2.5   Adding Data to the Table

In this Guided Activity, you will add several records to the table created in the previous Guided Activity.

1. If it is not already open, load Access and open the First.mdb database and select the Tables tab in that window.

2. If it is not already highlighted, move the pointer to the Final Sales Merchandise table.

3. Click the Open command button. Access will open the Table window for this table. You should see columns headed with the field names for this table, similar to those in Figure A2.13.

4. With the pointer positioned on the first row in the first column, type in the first StockNumber, 13021. If you make any mistakes, rekey the correct value.

5. Press **Tab** to move to the next column. Type in the Description, Cold 30 Cooler. If you notice an error in an earlier column, you can use the mouse to reposition the pointer, or press **Shift-Tab** to move to a previous column.

6. Press **Tab** and type in the Vendor name, Icicle.

7. Press **Tab** and type in the Category name Camp. You are deliberately misspelling this name. Press **Tab**.

8. Your validation rule will catch the incorrect category value. After reading the message, click OK, then enter the correct category spelling, Camping. Press **Tab** and type in the wholesale UnitCost, 59.95.

9. Press **Tab** and type in the QuantityOnHand, 12.

10. Press **Tab** and type in the DateOfLastOrder, 5/3/97.

11. Press **Tab** and move to the NowOnOrder field. This is the final field of the first record. Access displays this yes/no field as a check box. Note that Access scrolled the columns over to display this field; the first column no longer appears on the display. Larger displays may be able to display the entire record without scrolling. Press **Tab** because the product is not on order at this time.

NOTE *As a shortcut to repeat the value from the previous record, press **Ctrl-'**. Access will insert the value from the corresponding field of the previous record into the desired field of the current record. In the next step, you can use this shortcut for the Vendor and Category fields.*

12. Key in the remaining record values as shown below. Remember that Yes for the NowOnOrder field is indicated by clicking the check box.

```
13034   Cold 36 Cooler          Icicle   Camping  129.95  7   5/3/97   No
13037   Ice Cold Lunch Tote     Icicle   Camping   14.95  3   5/3/97   No
13066   40-Qt. Cooler Kit       Slaw     Camping   29.95  0   4/14/97  Yes
20238   Larry Bird 33 Basketball Johnson Sports    19.95  5   8/1/97   No
20239   Girls League Basketball Johnson  Sports    19.99  3   8/1/97   No
20241   NCAA Tourney Basketball Johnson  Sports    24.95  10  10/3/97  No
```

13. Figure A2.14 shows the Datasheet view for this table after the data are entered. Note that your date entries appear in DD-Mon-YY medium date format, as you specified when you entered the table definition. We will use this table in the next Guided Activity.

14. Your table will be saved automatically when you close the window. If you have to quit Access now, you can return to this point.

FIGURE A2.14
Table window with added data

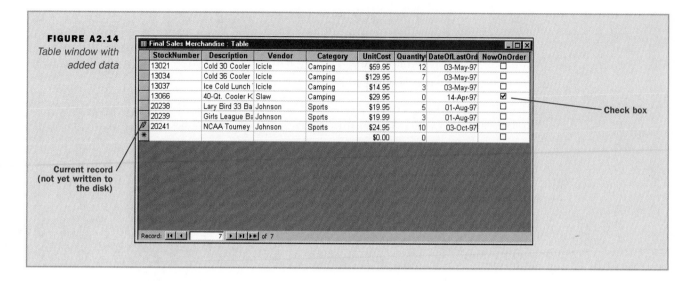

Check box

Current record
(not yet written to
the disk)

Moving the Record Pointer

Notice the value of the current record number at the bottom of the Table window. It should agree with the location of the current record button in the left margin of the table. You can manipulate the record pointer in several ways.

USE Tab AND Shift-Tab KEYS

The **Tab** key will move the pointer rightward, to the next field in the current record, or down and left to the first field of the next record if you are in the last field when you press **Tab**. The **Shift-Tab** key combination has the opposite effect: it moves you leftward, to the previous field.

USE THE MOUSE POINTER

You can simply move the mouse pointer to any field in the desired record and click the left button. The record pointer will automatically move to the field in that record.

USE THE ARROW KEYS

You can use the **Up arrow** and **Down arrow** keys to move the pointer to the previous or next record. You can also use the **Left arrow** and **Right arrow** keys to move to the previous or next field. The default setup is for the **Right arrow** key to duplicate the effect of the **Tab** key.

NOTE *You can change the meaning of the Right and Left arrow keys so that they move from character to character in the same field instead of moving to adjacent fields. This and other custom settings can be accomplished with the Keyboard tab in the Tools | Options command.*

USE THE NEXT/PREVIOUS RECORD BUTTONS

The Next and Previous Record buttons are located on either side of the current record indicator in the table. Click either button to move one record at a time in either direction.

USE THE FIRST/LAST RECORD BUTTONS

The First and Last Record buttons are located next to the Previous and Next buttons at the bottom of the Table window. Clicking these buttons will take you to the table's first and last records, respectively.

USE THE SCROLL BARS

Like other Windows objects, Access uses scroll bars in Datasheet view. The horizontal scroll bar at the bottom of the table appears when there are fields that do not appear in the Table window. The vertical scroll bar at the right side of the table appears when there are records that do not appear in the window.

GUIDED ACTIVITY

2.6 Moving the Record Pointer

In this Guided Activity, you will practice moving the record pointer.

1. Open Access, and open the First.mdb database. Make sure the Final Sales Merchandise Table window is open in Datasheet view on your desktop.

2. Position the record pointer at the first record by clicking its record selector button with the mouse.

3. Press the **Down arrow** key twice to position the record pointer at record. 3

4. Use the mouse to click the Last Record button. Note the value that appears in the current record number.

5. Use the mouse pointer to click the Minimize button in the upper right corner of the Table window.

6. Click the minimized table in the lower part of the desktop. Select Restore from the Control menu, or click the Restore button in the upper right corner of that window.

7. Click the First Record button in the record navigation area in the lower part of the window. Leave the table open on your desktop; we will work with this table in the next Guided Activity.

Deleting Records

You can delete records in Datasheet view using the keyboard or the mouse. In either case, first select the record(s) to be deleted by clicking the row selector button(s). Access will highlight the selected records. Press the **Del** key on the keyboard or select Delete Record from the Edit menu. You can also click the Delete Record button on the toolbar, or even right-click that record and choose Delete Record. Access will prompt you to confirm this *permanent* deletion. Click Yes to complete the delete operation, or No to cancel the delete command.

GUIDED ACTIVITY

2.7 Deleting a Record in Datasheet View

In this Guided Activity, you will add one record to a table, then delete it using the keyboard.

1. Open Access, and open the First.mdb database. Make sure the Final Sales Merchandise Table window is open in Datasheet view.

2. Click the Add Record button at the bottom of the window to add a new record. Access will display a new blank record at the end of the table.

3. Type the following entry in this row. The exact values don't matter (other than a valid Category) because you will immediately delete this record.

    ```
    11111  Sample Product    Smithton    Sports    9.50    0   5-29-97  No
    ```

4. Examine the Table window to be sure Access has added this record.

5. Click the record selector button of the record you just entered. Press the **Del** key or use the Edit | Delete Record command.

6. When prompted to confirm the deletion, as shown in Figure A2.15, click Yes. Access will permanently remove the selected record.

FIGURE A2.15
Confirm deletion dialog box

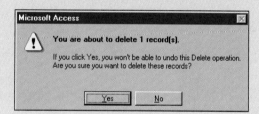

7. Just to check whether this was an irreversible action, try clicking the Undo button. What happens? Leave the table open for now.

Changing the Table's Appearance

You may want to make changes to the way the table appears in Datasheet view. It is easy to do so by dragging the table's row and column borders with the mouse. For example, in the last table (shown in Figure A2.14), some fields were wider than others.

GUIDED ACTIVITY

2.8   Changing the Table in Datasheet View

This Guided Activity will show you how to make changes to the physical appearance of the table's rows and columns in Datasheet view.

1. We will begin with the Final Sales Merchandise table in Datasheet view. Notice that each column is the same width in Datasheet view, regardless of its contents.

2. Practice slowly moving the mouse pointer over the border between the UnitCost and QuantityOnHand columns in the field name area of the Table window. The pointer should change to a double-headed arrow pointing left and right. If your cursor does not change its shape, make sure you're moving it in the area just above the first record.

3. Hold down the left mouse button and slowly drag the pointer to the left. Notice that the UnitCost field gets smaller and the fields to its right move over into the space left by it. Adjust the column's width until you're satisfied that the header (field name) fits, but make it no wider than that. Release the mouse button when you're finished.

4. Next, move the pointer to the border between the QuantityOnHand and the DateOfLastOrder fields. You may have to use the field scroll bar to move to this area.

5. Following the same procedure as in step 3, drag the border to the left until only the word Quantity shows in the field name area, then release the mouse button.

6. Notice that the Description field seems to be chopped off. We can make this column wider, or adjust the row height and have the Description appear on two lines. We'll do the latter.

7. Move the pointer to the record button area between records 1 and 2. Notice that the pointer changes into a two-headed arrow pointing up and down. If your cursor does not change shape, make sure it is just to the left of the first column.

8. While holding down the left mouse button, drag the border down until there are approximately two lines for each record. Notice that longer descriptions will now spread over both lines. Release the mouse button when you're finished.

9. Use the File | Save command to save the changes to your worksheet; accept the changes to the layout. Access will remember layout changes made to a table or other database object. Figure A2.16 shows the Table window after these appearance changes. Remember that nothing has changed in your data themselves, just the way they appear in this view.

FIGURE A2.16
*Resized table in
Datasheet view*

StockNumber	Description	Vendor	Category	UnitCost	Quantity	DateOfLastOrd	NowOnOrder
13021	Cold 30 Cooler	Icicle	Camping	$59.95	12	03-May-97	☐
13034	Cold 36 Cooler	Icicle	Camping	$129.95	7	03-May-97	☐
13037	Ice Cold Lunch Tote	Icicle	Camping	$14.95	3	03-May-97	☐
13066	40-Qt. Cooler Kit	Slaw	Camping	$29.95	0	14-Apr-97	☑
20238	Lary Bird 33 Basketball	Johnson	Sports	$19.95	5	01-Aug-97	☐
20239	Girls League Basketball	Johnson	Sports	$19.99	3	01-Aug-97	☐
20241	NCAA Tourney Basketball	Johnson	Sports	$24.95	10	03-Oct-97	☐
*				$0.00	0		☐

Final Sales Merchandise : Table

Record: 1 of 7

Editing Data in the Table

You may want to add more data to a table, or make changes to the contents of records already in the database. Access makes it easy to do so in Datasheet view. Simply use the mouse pointer to select the record and field you wish to change. Then type in the correction.

The last status box in the lower right portion of the Access desktop shows the insert status. Access starts in Insert mode; that is, if you position the cursor in a word and begin typing, characters to the right of the pointer are moved over to allow space for the new characters. If you press the **Ins** key, Access will display OVR in the insert status box, indicating that you are in Overtype mode. Any new characters typed in at the current insertion point will *replace* characters already present.

Changes to the table's field values are made permanent when you move the record pointer to a new record. If Access displays a pencil icon in the record selection button, it means that the record has changed but has not yet been saved to the database, as shown in Figure A2.14. You can issue the File | Save command at any time to save all the changes made to the table's layout.

NOTE *The File | Save command will only prompt the user to save changes to the layout if changes have been made to the appearance of a table's datasheet.*

GUIDED ACTIVITY

2.9 Editing Data in the Table

In this Guided Activity, you will make some changes to the field values in the table and work with the validation rule for the Category field.

1. Make sure that the Final Sales Merchandise table is open on your desktop.

2. Move the pointer to the Category field of the first record.

3. Replace the `Camping` category name with `Coolers` and press **Enter**. What happens? Remember that you established a validation rule for category names.

4. Change the `Coolers` value back to `Camping`.

You can do this quickly by using the Edit | Undo Typing command or by clicking the Undo button on the toolbar.

5. Move the pointer to the record with Stock Number 20239. Change the Unit Cost from `19.99` to `18.99`.

6. Move the pointer to the date field of the same record. Change the date to `8/32/97` and press **Tab**. What happens? Remember that Access automatically checks for invalid dates (it even recognizes a leap year) and prompts you when it finds one that is invalid. If you can't fill in a valid date in a date/time field, it is best to leave it blank.

7. Click OK to clear the message box. Change the date back to `8/1/97` by clicking the Undo button or giving the Edit | Undo Typing command.

8. If a small pencil icon appears in the record button, Access has *not* yet committed your changes to the database. Your changes to the table are made permanent when you move the pointer to another record or close the table. We will work with this table in the next Guided Activity.

Sorting Records in Datasheet View

Access allows simple ascending or descending sorts on a single field while in Datasheet view. First click the field you want to sort by, then click the Ascending Sort button or the Descending Sort button on the toolbar. Access instantly sorts all rows in the table. To return to the natural order record sequence (by the primary key), click in the primary key column and click the Ascending Sort button. More sophisticated sorts are performed with Access select queries, covered in Unit 3 of this book.

Printing the Data from a Table

A simple print capability is built into Datasheet view. You can print all the records in the table, or print certain records by clicking their record selection buttons. You can change print orientation (portrait or landscape) and print margins with the File | Page Setup command.

Activate print preview by clicking the Print Preview button on the toolbar. This button will format the datasheet and show a report preview on the screen. You have the option of scrolling through the print preview or zooming in on a portion of the report for careful scrutiny. You can send the output to the printer or cancel the print request and return to the datasheet.

Our sporting goods sales report will resemble a spreadsheet with a box around each field. Although this datasheet print facility is easy to invoke, it lacks basic formatting capabilities that are found in the Report mode of the database, which will be discussed in more detail in Unit 5.

GUIDED ACTIVITY

2.10   Printing the Datasheet

This Guided Activity will demonstrate how to print the table in Datasheet view.

1. Open the Final Sales Merchandise Table window if it is not already open.

2. Use the mouse pointer to select the Print Preview toolbar button, or use the File | Print Preview command from the menu.

3. After a few seconds, you'll see the first page of the datasheet in the preview window. While in the datasheet preview, the pointer resembles a magnifying glass. You can move it to any part of the page and click the left mouse button to zoom in on that portion of the output and inspect it in detail. Figure A2.17 shows the initial Print Preview window; Figure A2.18 shows a zoomed-in portion of that report.

FIGURE A2.17
Print Preview window

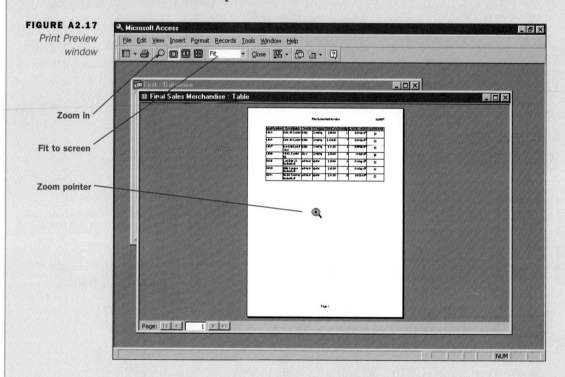

4. Notice that the status line at the bottom of the preview window contains a page number reference. If you had a larger table, you could scroll back and forth through multiple pages of the print preview output, using the page navigation buttons in the status area.

5. If you have a printer attached to your computer that is set up for Windows output, click the Print button to send the output to the printer.

6. Click the Close button to return to Datasheet view.

7. Close the table and return to the Database window.

FIGURE A2.18
Print Preview in
100% size

Zoom out

One page

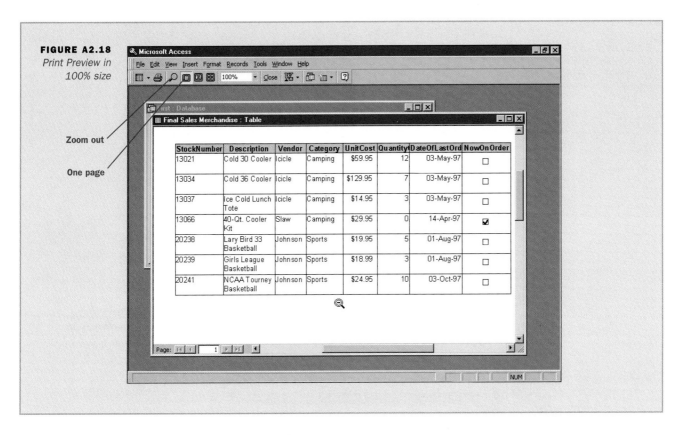

Using the Table Wizard

Earlier in this unit, I mentioned that Access provides an easy-to-use capability for designing new tables. The Table Wizard provides dozens of sample tables, each with its own appropriate fields. You must choose between Business and Personal categories, then select your table. Choose individual (or all) fields by clicking the > or >> button. Access will quickly create the table and all the appropriate fields and properties. Figure A2.19 shows the opening Table Wizard window.

GUIDED ACTIVITY

2.11 Using Table Wizard to Create a Table

This Guided Activity will demonstrate how to use the Table Wizard to create a new table.

1. If you are not already there, return to the First Database window. Make sure you're in Table mode.

2. Click the New button, select Table Wizard, and click OK. You should see a dialog box similar to the one shown in Figure A2.19, with the Business category selected.

3. Click the down arrow in the Sample Tables list box until you locate the Projects table. Click the Projects table once to bring up the sample fields for that table.

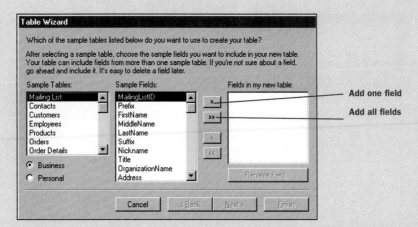

4. Click the >> button to select all the fields for this table, then click Next to go on to the next step.

5. In Figure A2.20, Access has displayed `Projects` as the name for this new table. Accept this suggestion and click Next to let Access choose a primary key for you.

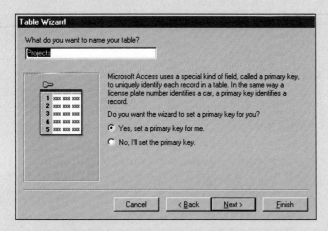

6. Click Next in the following screen: the Projects table is not related to any existing table.

7. You can choose to modify the table design or open the table in Datasheet view. Select Modify The Table Design and click Finish. Figure A2.21 shows the new table in Design view.

8. For now, close the table without making any changes. Access has already saved the table.

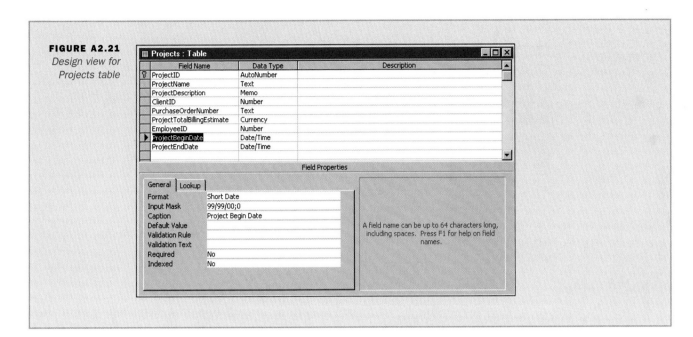

FIGURE A2.21
Design view for Projects table

Publishing a Table on the World Wide Web

Access 97 introduces the built-in ability to publish database objects on the World Wide Web. Thus, you can view the contents (not the design) of tables, queries, forms, and reports on the Internet or on your intranet using a Web browser. Web documents are coded with Hypertext Markup Language (HTML) formatting commands. Access 97 is able to create those HTML documents directly—you don't need to know anything about HTML. Use the File | Save As HTML command to start the Publish to the Web Wizard. The next Guided Activity will take you through the Wizard's steps.

GUIDED ACTIVITY

2.12   Publishing a Table on the Web

This Guided Activity will take you through the Publish to the Web Wizard. It is not necessary to have an Internet connection to complete this activity, but you should have a Web browser on your computer.

1. If you are not already there, return to the First.mdb database.

2. Use the File | Save As HTML command to start the Publish to the Web Wizard. The opening window is shown in Figure A2.22. Click Next to begin.

3. Next, you must select the object(s) that you wish to publish to the Web as shown in Figure A2.23. The object tabs appear at the top of this window, just as they do in the Database window. For this Guided Activity, select the Final Sales Merchandise table and click Next.

FIGURE A2.22
Opening Web
Wizard window

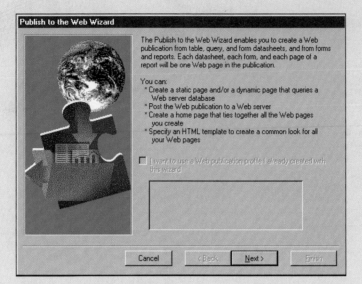

FIGURE A2.23
Web Wizard
selection window

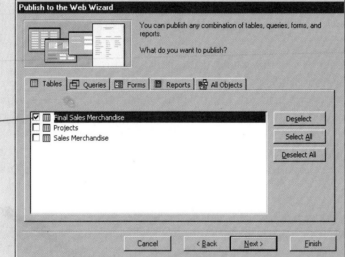

**Click here to
select**

4. The next step asks you to specify a default HTML template. We'll skip this step, so just click Next.

5. Figure A2.24 shows the three kinds of HTML documents that can be saved. We'll pick the first one—Static HTML. A static HTML document stores the values that are in that database object at the time you create the HTML file. The other two dynamic HTML options let the user query the contents of the database when he or she links to the HTML document. Click Next.

6. The next window asks you where the HTML document is to be saved. The top portion asks for a local folder, defaulting to C:\My Documents\. (Change this field to the folder where you customarily save documents.) The optional bottom portion asks for the Web server where the document will be published. At this point, we'll skip the Web server part. Click Next to continue.

FIGURE A2.24
Web Wizard HTML document window

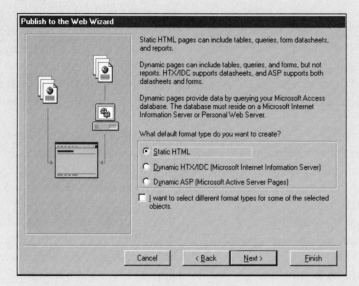

7. The next window asks for the URL of a home page. Click Next to skip this step.

8. Click Finish to complete the Publishing to the Web Wizard process. Access will create a file called Final Sales Merchandise_1.html and save it in the location you specified in step 6.

9. Figure A2.25 shows what your document looks like in Internet Explorer. If you have a browser, open it and give the File | Open command, then specify the location and file name for the HTML document.

FIGURE A2.25
HTML document in Internet Explorer browser

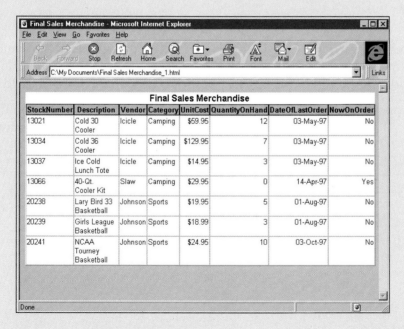

10. You can close your browser. You can close Access unless you are going to work on the Exercises or Applications.

SUMMARY

Before you can create tables to hold information, you must first create the database. Access provides the Database Wizard for creating more than 20 kinds of standardized databases. You can also start with a Blank Database and create the tables yourself. You can view tables in two ways: Design view, which is used to define the fields and their properties, and Datasheet view, which resembles a spreadsheet.

The columns of a table are called fields. The data in each field can be any of nine data types: text, memo, number, date/time, currency, autonumber, yes/no, OLE objects, and hyperlink. In Design view, you can specify several other properties as well as data type: field size, format, decimal places, input mask, and validation rule, among others.

Use Design view to modify the structure of a table; for instance, to add new fields or rename fields. Use Datasheet view to add and edit data values. You can delete records while in Datasheet view. You can also sort the records in Datasheet view, and you can print them. Access 97 supports Web publishing by saving Access objects as HTML files. Access comes with a Publish to the Web Wizard to simplify this process.

EXERCISE

2.1   Create Employees Table

1. Open the First.mdb database.

2. Create a new table called Employees in the First.mdb database. Fields are shown below, along with data type and size. The primary key is the EmployeeNumber field. You should make up an appropriate description for each field.

3. Suppose you learned that the EmployeeNumber field is actually the person's social security number. What input mask would be appropriate for this field? *Hint:* Use the Build button to start the Input Mask Wizard.

FIELD NAME	DATA TYPE	FIELD SIZE
EmployeeNumber	Text	11
FirstName	Text	10
LastName	Text	15
Department	Text	10
DateOfHire	Date/Time	
CurrentSalary	Currency	0 decimal places

EXERCISE

2.2 Add Data to Employees

1. Open the First.mdb database.

2. Add the following data to the Employees table in the First.mdb database. You should insert your own name as the last record in the table, with suitable information.

3. How would you handle Barbara Smith's middle initial?

4. Print the datasheet after you save it to the database.

```
123-44-5678  Mark Cameron       Accounting   6/19/93   25,400
666-77-1111  Kelsey Palmer      Sales        1/29/93   21,200
001-42-0009  Elizabeth Crow     Sales        2/1/90    40,000
555-66-7890  William Prince     Shipping     11/30/92  16,955
987-65-4321  Barbara K. Smith   Sales        8/19/78   35,400
124-76-0000  John Roberts       Accounting   3/4/92    22,600
234-45-8237  Jean Sullivan      Sales        12/01/91  16,200
567-89-0123  Emily Hilton       Management   8/3/95    33,500
```

EXERCISE

2.3 Modify Employees Table Design

1. Open the First.mdb database.

2. Add a new field to your Employees table definition. Called PartTime, it is a yes/no field that indicates whether an employee is considered part-time only. Palmer and Sullivan are considered part-time employees.

3. Print the revised datasheet.

EXERCISE

2.4 Create Table with Table Wizard

1. Open the First.mdb database, then create a new table using the Table Wizard.

2. From the Personal sample tables, select the Exercise Log table and copy all the fields over to a new table with the same name. Let Access choose a primary key for you.

3. List the field names in this new table and the data type for each field. (Hint: Choose the Design View button to see the data type.)

EXERCISE

2.5 Music Collection Database Wizard

1. Use the Access Database Wizard to create a database for your music collection. Make sure you request that sample data values be created.

2. List the names of the tables, queries, forms, and reports that the Database Wizard creates for this application.

3. Print a copy of the datasheet for the first table listed in the Database window.

EXERCISE

2.6 Hunter River Sample Database

Open the Hunter97.mdb database on the Student Data Disk. We will be using this database for the remaining activities and exercises in this book. The Hunter97 database duplicates the work you did with the First.mdb database in this unit and adds many new objects for the Hunter River store.

1. List the tables in this database.

2. Open the Employees table and print a copy of its contents in landscape orientation. *Hint:* Use the File | Page Setup command to change Orientation.

3. Open the Customers table and write out its structure.

EXERCISE

2.7 Publish a Web Table

We'll continue with the Hunter97.mdb database file for this Exercise.

1. Start the Publish to the Web Wizard from the Database window.

2. Select the Employees table and publish it to your local hard disk or network account. What is the name of this file?

3. Start your browser and load this file. Print a copy of the file from your browser.

4. Print a copy of the *text version* of the HTML file. You can do this with Windows Notepad, located in Accessories. *Hint:* Notepad will only list TXT files by default. Be sure to search all files when you open this HTML file.

APPLICATION

Physicians' Medical Clinic: Building a Table

You have been hired to assist with the development of a patient database for the clinic. Some database design planning has already been done, and your next task is to create a table for permanent patient information. Tables for information about specific patient visits, doctors, standard procedures, insurance companies, and other database objects will be created later.

Use the file named PMC97.mdb to assist you in creating a new table called New Patients. You decided information needs to be entered as fields. The first field, PatientNumber, will be the primary key. Other fields include FirstName, LastName, AddressLine1, AddressLine2, City, State, ZipCode, DateOfBirth, EmployerName, InsuredName, InsuranceCompany, and InsurancePolicy.

Use your own information or imaginary data to add two records to the table. The first record should be your own record as head of household. Make the second record that of a dependent of yours who will use your own health insurance policy. You will need to figure out how to print the contents of the New Patients table and submit it to the hospital administrator.

Hunter River: Building a Table for the Web

Management at Hunter River Sporting Goods wants to create a Web site for the company's product line. You have been asked to help them get started with this process. You will need to conduct research on what kinds of information prospective customers want to find on the Web as well as research for Web sites of similar companies to see what the competition is doing. Use the Publish to the Web Wizard and create an HTML document. Use your Web browser to show the company officers your Web page as well as present them with a printout. Collect any other information that the company officers may want to include on the Web page.

UNIT 3

Building a Select Query

In this unit you will use Access queries to display data from one or more tables that meet specific conditions known as criteria. You will create a simple select query, then use the query to sort records and provide totals for groups of records within the database. The unit contains a detailed list of Access expressions and functions that can be used in queries as well as in other Access objects.

Access queries provide an easy way to select data that meet certain criteria that you set up. You specify the conditions in the form of an example; hence the name QBE (query by example). You choose the fields that are retained by the query, by dragging the field names from the data tables to the query. Once the query is prepared, you can use the resulting data as the basis for a form, report, graph, or another query.

You can use a query to link two or more tables that share common data values. For example, suppose you wanted to link a Department table with the Employees table, showing only the employees who are members of that department. Or you might want to link the products from a particular vendor with information from the Vendor table that is not stored in the Products table. One of the strongest features of Access is its ability to create queries that link two or more tables.

Learning Objectives

At the completion of this unit, you should be able to

1. define the types of queries available in Access,

2. list the important functions that can be used in queries,

3. create a simple select query,

4. build a criteria expression for selecting records,

5. sort records and prepare group totals for the datasheet,

6. print a query result,

7. save a query as a static HTML document,

8. explain why dynamic HTML documents are needed for Access queries.

Case Study

You are the database administrator at Hunter River. They want to query groups of products that are overstocked, and prepare lists of products that were ordered in certain months. They also want to determine what employees meet certain conditions.

Types of Queries

SELECT QUERY

The select query is the most common. It provides for selection of records that meet the criteria you specify. After you run the query, the records that meet the criteria are displayed in a datasheet. The records that match the criteria are dynamic; that is, the datasheet changes if the underlying table values change. The datasheet is not a regular data table, although its current contents can be saved as one if desired.

ACTION QUERIES

When you want to make changes to your data, use an action query. You can make changes to a selected set of records with one query command. There are four kinds of action queries:

- An update query can make changes to field values in an existing table.

- An append query can append records that match the criteria to another table.

- A make-table query creates a new table with records from the query's datasheet.

- A delete query is used to delete records that match the criteria.

ADVANCED QUERIES

Parameter queries allow you to create a query, save it, and then rerun it whenever you wish with *new* criteria values. For example, suppose you build a conventional query that specifies a particular department of the store. Each time you run this query, it will select records that match that department. If you make that value a parameter, Access will allow you to input a new value for the query's department criterion without modifying the original query.

Crosstab queries are used to categorize data into groups. Access shows the record count or field sums for the records in each group in a two-dimensional format. We will not cover crosstab queries in this unit.

SQL queries are created using SQL expressions rather than the usual Access query grid. SQL stands for structured query language, the English-like statements used to manipulate some relational databases.

The Query Window

Figure A3.1 shows the Query window for a select query. At the top of the window are the tables used in the query. At the bottom is the design grid. Its columns represent the fields you have added to the query. Each column provides for the field name, sorting instructions, a show box for that field, and rows for the criteria expressions.

The query Design view toolbar is shown in Figure A3.2. Many of the buttons are similar to those on other Access toolbars. The overlapping tables let you specify the tables used for the query, and the exclamation mark (!) button is used to run the query. The summation (Σ) button is used to add calculations and totals to the query. We will discuss these buttons in more detail as we build queries in this unit.

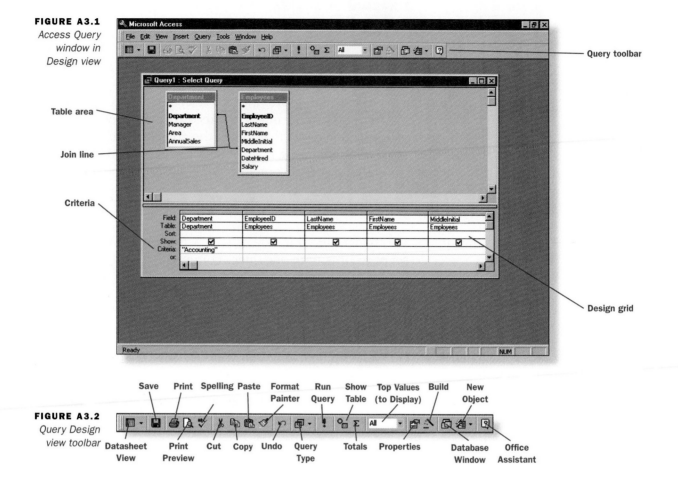

FIGURE A3.1
Access Query window in Design view

Table area

Join line

Criteria

Query toolbar

Design grid

FIGURE A3.2
Query Design view toolbar

Save   Print   Spelling   Paste   Format   Run   Show   Top Values   Build   New
                                   Painter   Query   Table   (to Display)   Object

Datasheet   Print   Cut   Copy   Undo   Query   Totals   Properties   Database   Office
View   Preview   Type   Window   Assistant

Building a Select Query

In this section, we will demonstrate how to create a simple select query using the manual method. There are six steps in building a simple select query in Access. Each step is discussed below.

1. Open the Database window, select Query mode, and choose New.

2. Choose the New Query (manual) method to build the query.

3. Add one or more tables or queries from the Show Table window.

4. Drag the fields to be added to the query from the tables to the design grid.

5. Specify field criteria in the design grid for inclusion in the Query datasheet.

6. View the results of the query in a datasheet.

Creating a New Query

The first step is easily accomplished. When the Database window is open, click the Queries tab and then click the New button. Alternatively, you can use the Insert |
Query command from the menu bar.

Choosing the Method for Building the Query

You can build a query manually in Design view, or choose the Select Query Wizard and have Access build the query for you. For now, we'll focus on building the query by hand so that you will understand its components. After choosing Design View, you'll see the blank query in its Design view.

Adding Tables to the Query

Access shows you a list of tables and queries from the current database in the Show Table window. Select the tables and/or queries that you want to add to this query. These tables and queries form the data source for your query. Only the fields from these selected tables and queries will be available in the query. Of course, you can add more tables at any time by modifying the design of the query. Figure A3.1 shows two tables in the query, linked by the common Department field. When you are finished adding tables, click the Close button.

Adding Fields to the Query Design Grid

There are several rows in the design grid.

- Field contains the name of a field or calculated expression.

- Table gives the name of the table where the field is found.

- Total is used for totals queries for calculating sum, average, maximum, and so forth.

- Sort is used to indicate ascending, descending, or no sort for a particular field.

- Show contains a box; if it is checked, that field will be included in the query's output.

- Criteria holds the criteria expression for that field.

- Or provides for additional criteria rows.

You can add *all* the fields from a table to a query at one time by double-clicking the table's title bar to highlight all the fields, then dragging them to the design grid. You can add *individual* fields to a query by dragging them from the table box to the design grid. Most users will select specific fields rather than the entire table. Because fields will appear in the datasheet in the order in which they are listed in the design grid, you should consider order when you're dragging fields to the grid. Access also lets you rearrange the field order after the query has been created, as we will discuss later.

You may want to add an expression involving several fields in the Field row of the design grid. For instance, you could place an expression consisting of the city, state, and zip code for an address. Or you could place both first and last names in the same query field box. For more details on this procedure, see the section "Concatenation Operators," later in this unit.

If you do not want a field's value to appear in the datasheet, click that field's show box to erase the check mark that Access places there. By default, all the fields in a query will be displayed. All five fields in the query shown in Figure A3.1 will appear in the datasheet.

Creating Simple Criteria Expressions

Next, you can add an optional criteria expression to the query. The query will display only those records that match the criteria provided. A simple query uses a criteria expression for one field. For example, you might place a particular vendor's name in the Vendor field in the Criteria row. Only records from that vendor would appear in the datasheet. If no criteria are supplied, *all* records will match the criteria and will appear in the datasheet. As shown in the criteria expression of Figure A3.1, only records from the Accounting department will appear in that datasheet.

The most common simple query uses a constant value as the criterion, such as the vendor name or department name discussed above. You can also enter a more elaborate expression to indicate a condition. If the field name contains a space or other punctuation, you must enclose it in brackets; brackets are optional for other field names. Examples of criteria expressions are shown in Table A3.1.

We will cover Access expressions in more detail in a later section of this unit.

Running the Query to View the Results

After creating the query and its criteria, click the Run Query (!) toolbar button or the Datasheet toolbar button. Access will process your query and display the results in a table called a datasheet. The Query window in Datasheet view looks just like Datasheet view for the Table window. Only the records that match your query are displayed in the datasheet, as shown in Figure A3.3.

FIGURE A3.3
*Query
Datasheet view*

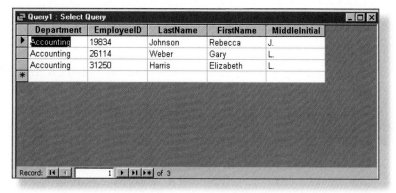

Saving the Query Design

As with other Access objects, you can use the File | Save command to save the query design. You will be asked to supply a name for the query. If you want to save the query under a *different* name, use the File | Save As/Export command. A query cannot have the same name as a table in the database. After saving the query, you can close the Query window and return to the Database window, or go to Datasheet view to view the datasheet that the query has produced.

TABLE A3.1
Typical criteria expressions

EXPRESSION	MEANING
"John"	This field's value must be the text value John.
="John"	Same as the previous expression.
<=50	The field must be less than or equal to 50.
Quantity>10	The Quantity field must be greater than 10.
Between 10 and 50	The field must be at least 10 and no more than 50.
[Order Date]< #1-Jan-98#	The Order Date must be earlier than January 1, 1998.
Between #1-Oct-97# and #3-31-97#	The date must be between these dates.
(Open+Close)/2>=30	The average of opening and closing prices must be at least 30.
[Name] is Null	The Name field is <>null, meaning that it is empty and has no value.
"Sports" or "Other"	Allows the use of either the Sports department or the Other department.
In("Sports","Other")	Either Sports or Other (same as previous expression)
S*	The field must start with the letter S.

GUIDED ACTIVITY

3.1 Creating a Select Query

In this Guided Activity, you will use the Products table of the Hunter97.mdb database to prepare a simple select query.

1. Start Windows and Access as usual. Open the Hunter97.mdb database.

2. In the Database window, click the Queries tab to switch to Query mode. Then click the New button, select Design View, and click OK to open the Select Query window.

3. Access displays the query's Show Table dialog box, shown in Figure A3.4. Scroll down, then click the Products table line. Click Add to add this table to the query.

4. We will use just a single table for this Guided Activity, so click Close to complete the add table portion of the query design.

5. Next, you must select the fields for the design grid. For this simple query, we will choose three fields. With the mouse, drag the Description field to the first column of the design grid. That is, move the pointer to that field in the Products table, then hold down the left mouse button and drag the field to the first column of the grid, and finally release the left button.

FIGURE A3.4
*Query Show Table
window*

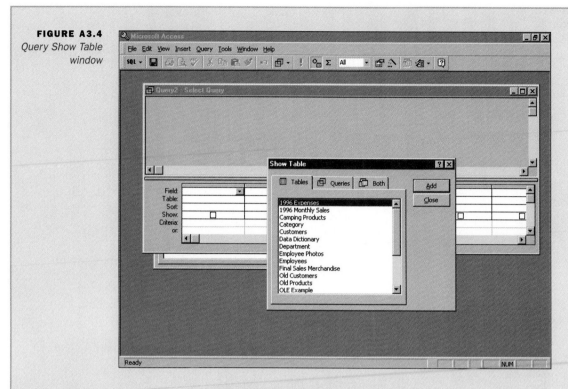

6. Repeat the process, placing the Category field and the QuantityOnHand field in columns 2 and 3. Your screen should look like Figure A3.5.

FIGURE A3.5
*Query window
after step 6*

Datasheet View

Products table

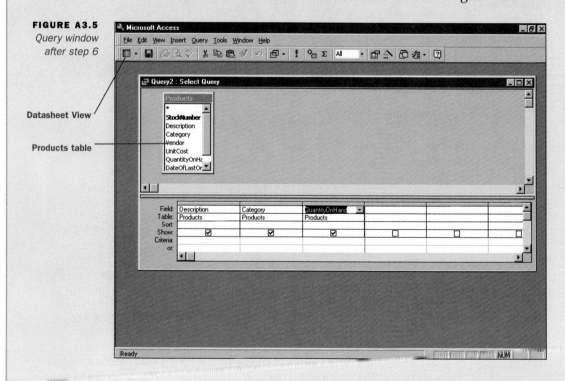

7. If you click the Datasheet button in the toolbar, Access displays the records in the datasheet that match the query. Notice that all records qualify because no criteria condition was specified.

8. Click the Design View button in the toolbar to return to the query design. This time, specify `Camping` in the Criteria row in the Category column of the design grid. Notice that Access automatically places quotes around the `Camping` text value when you press the **Enter** key.

9. Again, click the Datasheet button to see the new datasheet, shown in Figure A3.6.

FIGURE A3.6
Query datasheet after step 9 (Camping records)

Description	Category	QuantityO
Cold 30 Cooler	Camping	12
Cold 36 Cooler	Camping	7
Ice Cold Lunch Tote	Camping	3
40-Qt. Cooler Kit	Camping	0
48-qt Cooler	Camping	10
Outdoor grill -30K btu	Camping	10
Super Sport Stove	Camping	6
Double Burner Stove	Camping	0
2-Room Cabin Tent	Camping	3
12x10 Deluxe Family Dom	Camping	5
12x9 Tent with Awning	Camping	0
10x8 Cabin Tent	Camping	12
6x6 Square Dome Tent	Camping	15
Twin Tube Lantern	Camping	25
Powerhouse Lantern	Camping	15
South Rim Lantern	Camping	18

Record: 1 of 18

10. Use the File | Save command to save the query from step 9. Give it the name `Camping Overstock`. We will modify this query in the next Guided Activity, when we demonstrate how to create a more complex query.

NOTE   *If the Camping Overstock query already exists in your database, you may replace it with this query.*

Access Expressions and Built-In Functions

Earlier in this unit, we saw sample expressions that are available in Microsoft Access. In this section, we will elaborate on expressions and functions that are available for Access queries, table properties, forms, and reports. Much of the material here is included for future reference, when you use Access for real database systems.

Parts of the Expression

Access provides a general format for expressions. Suppose we have an expression:

```
[DateOfLastOrder]<Date()-30
```

This expression asks the question: Is the DateOfLastOrder field more than 30 days earlier than the current date? Each part of the expression is explained below.

- [DateOfLastOrder] is an identifier, which describes a data field or other data source. If you refer to an identifier that contains spaces or punctuation, you must enclose it with brackets.

- The < sign is an operator, meaning *less than* in this case.

- Date( ) is a function, referring to the current system date within the computer you are using.

- The minus sign (−) is another operator in this example.

- The 30 is a literal, which can represent a number, a string of text characters, or a date. A Yes/No literal is known as a constant.

Rules for Access Expressions

Access expressions follow algebraic rules similar to those you have used before, in your math classes. This section contains a summary of the rules for expressions.

ARITHMETIC OPERATORS

Access uses the usual +, −, *, and / arithmetic operators to represent addition, subtraction, multiplication, and division. Exponentiation is denoted by the ^ character. The \ operator is used for integer division; 7\4 would divide one integer by another and return an integer answer, in this case 1. The Mod operator returns the remainder of a division operation; 7 Mod 4 would return 3.

COMPARISON OPERATORS

Access uses combinations of <, =, and >—comparison operators—to compare pairs of values. < means less than, <= means less than or equal to, and so on. <> is used to denote not equal. The result of a comparison operation is True or False.

Another group of operators can be useful when comparing two items. It is simpler to use Like, In, and Between than to build compound conditions. Examples are shown in Table A3.2.

TABLE A3.2
Like, In, and Between operators

EXPRESSION	MEANING
Like "Camp*"	Finds a field that begins with "Camp". * is the wildcard character that means any number of characters can follow.
Like "3????"	Finds a field of five characters that begins with a 3. ? is the wildcard character that means any other character in that position.
Like "X[A-C]##"	Finds a field starting with the letter X, and then any letter between A and C, followed by two digits. # is the wildcard character that means any digit.
Like "*/*/'97"	Finds a date field in 1997.
In("IN","IL","OH")	Finds a field that matches "IN", "IL", or "OH".
Between 2 and 4	Finds a field whose value is at least 2 and no more than 4.

LOGICAL OPERATORS

You may use logical operators to make conjunctions between pairs of logical (Yes/No or True/False) expressions in a way similar to the use of the compound criteria described earlier in this unit. And and Or are the most commonly used. The And operator implies that both expressions must be true for the overall expression to be true. The Or operator implies that either expression may be true for the overall expression to be true. For example, `X=6 And Y=4` is true *only* if both parts of the expression are true. Likewise, `X=6 Or Y=4` is true if either part, or both parts, of the expression are true. Access uses the not condition operator to reverse the meaning of a condition. For instance, `Not "IN"` implies that the field cannot have the value of `IN`. You can search for "Expressions" in online Help to see more examples of these and other logical operators.

CONCATENATION OPERATORS

Access uses the concatenation operator to join two text strings. Suppose you keep last name and first name in separate fields. You can join (concatenate) them with the expression: `First+Last` or `First&Last`. The + and & operators both perform the same task in Access. Access trims trailing blanks from the two text strings, and does not place a space after the First field. Thus, the words in the concatenated fields will appear run together. To solve this, use `First&" "&Last` to insert a space between the concatenated strings.

You could place the `First&" "&Last` expression in the Field row of the query to place both first and last name fields in the query. Remember that field names with embedded spaces must be enclosed in brackets when used in expressions.

IDENTIFIERS

You may need to specify more than a field name in an Access expression. You can use a form or report name, table name, field name, and other identifiers as part of the expression. Separate each with an exclamation point. For example, the expression `Forms![Product Entry]![QuantityOnHand]` refers to the QuantityOnHand field from the Product Entry form. `[Products]![Category]` refers to the Category field from the Products table. In the latter example, brackets are not needed because neither identifier contains spaces or other punctuation. You can specify just the field name if you're referring to a field from the current active data object.

Access Functions

A function returns a value to the expression in which it is used. Access 97 provides more than 160 functions, many of which are used in Visual Basic for Applications. We will discuss a few of the more common functions in this section. For an alphabetical list, search Access Help for "Functions, Reference Topics."

MATH FUNCTIONS

Access provides 13 mathematical and trigonometric functions. Common math functions are shown in Table A3.3. Trigonometric functions (Atn, Cos, Sin, Tan) use radians as the parameter and return angle answers in radians.

TABLE A3.3
Math functions

FUNCTION	MEANING
Abs( )	Absolute value. Example: Abs(−4.3)=4.3
Exp( )	Exponential of value. Example: Exp(2)=7.38906
Int( )	Integer part of value. Example: Int(9/2)=4
Log( )	Natural log of value. Example: Log(4)=1.386294
Rnd( )	Random number between 0 and 1. Example: Rnd( )=0.77474
Sqr( )	Square root of value. Example: Sqr(16)=4

DATE AND TIME FUNCTIONS

Access can provide the current system date and time, and can also extract the individual components from any date or time number. There are nearly 20 date and time functions. Common functions are shown in Table A3.4.

FINANCIAL FUNCTIONS

Functions that pertain to the time value of money are built into Access. Functions for depreciation and payments are included. Table A3.5 shows some of the most common financial functions. You can look up the specific syntax of these functions by searching online Help for the particular function name; examples of some of the more popular functions are shown.

TEXT MANIPULATION FUNCTIONS

These functions work with text field–type data, also known as strings. The most common text manipulation functions are shown in Table A3.6.[1]

MISCELLANEOUS FUNCTIONS

Access provides miscellaneous functions for other purposes, as shown in Table A3.7.

---

[1] Access 97 does not contain a useful function called Proper( ). This function capitalizes the first letter of each word in a text string, sometimes known as "proper case." Proper("TEXT BOOK") would return "Text Book". This function is found in the UtilityFunctions module in the Hunter97.mdb file, and can be exported to your own databases.

TABLE A3.4
Date and time functions

FUNCTION	MEANING
Date( )	Current system date and time as a date field subtype 7. Example: 3/25/95
DateDiff( )	Difference between two dates. You can specify whether that difference should be expressed in seconds, minutes, hours, days, weeks, months, quarters, or years. Example: DateDiff("d",Now( ), #12/25/98#) will return the number of days between now and December 25, 1998.
DateSerial( )	Allows you to enter date by giving separate values for year, month, day. Example: DateSerial(95,3,25)
DateValue( )	Allows you to enter date as string and converts to date type. Example: DateValue("3/25/95")
Day( )	Integer day of the month for a specified date value, between 1 and 31. Other functions are Month( ) and Year( ), which also return integer answers. Example: Day(#7/16/95#) returns 16.
Hour( )	Integer hour of a specified time. Other functions are Minute( ) and Second( ), which return integers between 0 and 59.
Now( )	Current system date and time. Example: 3/25/95 10:30:06
Time( )	Time portion of system clock as date field subtype 7.
TimeValue( )	Allows you to enter time as a string and converts to date field type. Example: TimeValue("10:30:06 AM")
Weekday( )	Day of the week for a specified date value. Answer is between 1 and 7, beginning with Sunday. Example: Weekday(#12/25/95#) returns 2, meaning that Christmas in 1995 was on Monday.

TABLE A3.5
Financial functions

FUNCTION	MEANING
DDB( )	Double-declining balance depreciation. Example: Ddb(10000,2000,4,3) returns 500, the depreciation for year 3 for an asset that costs $10,000 with a salvage value of $2,000 and a life of 4 years.
FV( )	Future value of an investment based on a series on constant payments. Example: FV(.015,36,–100)=4727.60.
IPmt( )	Interest portion for a particular payment on an installment loan or annuity.
IRR( )	Internal rate of return for an investment with periodic cash flow amounts. MIRR( ) will calculate the modified rate of return.
Nper( )	Number of payments necessary to pay off a loan. Example: Nper(.12/12,–200,5000)=28.9 months.

NPV( )	Net present value of an annuity.
Pmt( )	Amount of the periodic payment for an installment loan or annuity. Example: Pmt(.08/12,3*12,–5000,0,0)=156.68 or the monthly payment for $5,000 loan for 3 years at 8% annual interest.
PPmt( )	Principal portion for a particular payment on an installment loan or annuity. Example: PPmt(.08/12,5,36,–5000,0,0)=126.67 or the amount of principal paid in the fifth of 36 payments on a $5,000 loan at 8% APR.
PV( )	Present value of an annuity paid in equal installments.
Rate( )	Interest rate of a loan or annuity based on equal installments.
Sln( )	Straight-line depreciation of an asset for a single period. Example: Sln(10000,2000,4)=2000 or the annual depreciation for an asset that costs $10,000 with a salvage value of $2,000 and a life of 4 years.
Syd( )	Sum-of-years' digits depreciation of an asset for a specified period. Example: Syd(10000,2000,4,3)=1600 or the depreciation for year 3 for an asset that costs $10,000 with a salvage value of $2,000 and a life of 4 years.

TABLE A3.6
Text manipulation functions

FUNCTION	MEANING
Asc( )	ASCII numeric code for a particular character string. Asc("M") returns 77.
Chr( )	Character for a particular ASCII code. Chr(77) returns "M".
Format( )	Formats an expression according to format code. Format(Date( ),"dd-mmm-yy") returns 3-Mar-94.
InStr( )	Position of one string within another. InStr("ABCD","C") returns 3.
LCase( )	Lowercase version of a string. UCase( ) returns uppercase version.
Left( )	Leftmost characters of a string. Left("ABCDEF",3) returns "ABC".
Right( )	Returns rightmost characters of a string. Right("ABCD",2) returns "CD".
Len( )	Length of characters in a string, as an integer. Len("ABCDE") returns 5.
LTrim( )	Trims leading spaces from a string. RTrim( ) trims trailing spaces from a string.
Mid( )	Returns a portion of a string. Mid("ABCDEFGH",3,2) returns "CD".
Str( )	Converts number data value to a string. Val( ) converts a string to a numeric value.
Trim( )	Trims leading and trailing spaces from a string. Trim("ABC") returns "ABC".

TABLE A3.7
Miscellaneous functions

FUNCTION	MEANING
Choose( )	Returns a value from a lookup list based on the sequence in the list. Choose(Key,"ounce","pound","ton") would return one of the three strings based on the value of Key (1, 2, or 3).
IIF( )	Returns one value if the expression is true, another if the expression is false. IIF(Hours>40,Rate*1.5,Rate) will return Rate*1.5 if Hours is greater than 40, and Rate otherwise.
IsEmpty( )	True if the indicated field is a noninitialized value, false otherwise. Access can distinguish between the Null value and a noninitialized value.
IsNull( )	True if field is null, false otherwise.

Creating Compound Criteria Expressions

A compound condition query uses criteria expressions for two or more fields in the same query. If you provide criteria expressions for more than one field, Access will process the query in the following manner:

■ If the expressions are in the same row of the grid, *all* conditions must be true in order for the record to qualify for the datasheet. This is known as an And condition. Remember that you can create a compound condition in which no records will appear in the datasheet.

■ If the expressions are in different rows of the grid and *any* condition is true, the record will qualify for the query's datasheet. This is known as an Or condition. We will prepare a compound criteria query in the next Guided Activity.

GUIDED ACTIVITY

3.2 Creating a Compound Query with a Calculated Field

In this Guided Activity, you will create a more complex query with multiple criteria expressions. We will start with the query from step 10 of the preceding Guided Activity.

1. Make sure that Access is loaded and that Hunter97.mdb is open. Go back to Design view for the Camping Overstock query.

2. Leave Camping in the Category column and add >=10 to the criteria row of the QuantityOnHand column. Make sure both criteria expressions are in the *same* row of the design grid, as shown in Figure A3.7.

3. Now go to Datasheet view to see the records in the current datasheet. You should see 10 products that *both* are Camping *and* have balances that are at least 10 units.

FIGURE A3.7
*Query Design view
with compound
criteria*

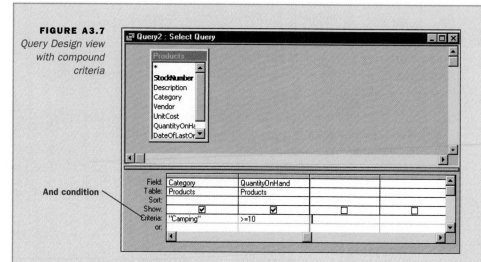

And condition

4. Go back to Design view. This time, place the expression `Other` in the Criteria row directly beneath `Camping`. You are now specifying that Camping products whose balances are at least 10 units *or* Other products will meet the criteria in your query.

5. Go to Datasheet view to see the new datasheet. You should see 18 records.

6. Go back to Design view and delete all the criteria conditions. You can easily do this by moving the pointer slowly at the beginning of the Criteria row in the design grid. When the pointer changes to a right-pointing arrow, click once to highlight the entire grid row. Then press the **Del** key to erase the criteria expressions. Repeat with the next Criteria row in the grid.

7. Go to the QuantityOnHand field cell, then enter the expression `[QuantityOnHand]*[UnitCost]` and press **Enter**. Access creates a new calculated field called Expr1. You should highlight Expr1 in Design view and change the name to something more meaningful.

8. Type `>=250` in the Criteria row. This condition specifies that the cost of the current inventory must be at least $250. Click the Run Query button (!) to view the new datasheet. How many records now qualify?

9. Now go back to Design view again. Let's add another field to the query. Instead of dragging the DateOfLastOrder field from the Products table to the design grid, click in the Field row of the first blank column in the design grid. Access will display a pull-down list box; click the down arrow to display the list. Click the DateOfLastOrder field once to place it in that row.

10. On the *same* row as the criteria expression from step 8, place the criteria expression `<1/1/97` in the column you just added and press **Enter**.

NOTE   *When you press* **Enter**, *Access will convert your date string to* `<#1/1/97#`.

11. Run the query and examine the resulting datasheet, shown in Figure A3.8. Access should display nine products that were last ordered before January 1, 1997, and whose current inventory value is at least $250. Close the query, but do not save it.

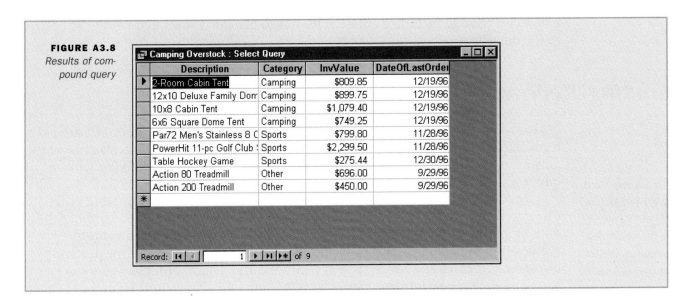

FIGURE A3.8
Results of compound query

Making Changes to the Query Design

You may find that the query is not quite correct. You can rearrange fields, insert new fields, and delete fields in a manner similar to the one you learned with Access tables in Design view.

Rearranging the Fields

You can easily rearrange the fields in a query by highlighting the field's column and dragging it with the mouse. Click in the field selector area at the top of the column to select the column. Then drag the column to the desired location in the design grid. If Access leaves the field in the wrong position, you can easily repeat the process to correct the error.

Inserting a New Field

From the field list in the table section of the Query window, select the field you want to insert. Then drag the field to the desired location and release the left mouse button. Access will insert the field into the design grid and move other fields to the right to make room.

Deleting a Field

Click in the field selector area of the field's column that you want to delete. When the column is highlighted, press the **Del** key. Or choose the Edit | Delete command from the menu bar.

Hiding a Field

Ordinarily, when you add a field to the query design grid, its show box is checked. When you run the query, that field will appear in the datasheet. If you *uncheck* the show box, that field's values will not appear in the datasheet. Use this approach when you want to include a criterion for a field but don't want that field to appear in the datasheet.

Sorting Records in a Query

TIP

Access also has a quick sort feature for sorting records in Datasheet view for tables, queries, and forms. Look for the Sort Ascending button (A–Z) or the Sort Descending button (Z–A) in the Datasheet or Form toolbar.

It's easy to give sorting directions in the design grid for an Access query. Each field has a Sort row in the design grid. The default is no sorting, so the datasheet records appear in natural order, the order in which they appear in the underlying table or query.

You can choose an ascending sort, in which values appear in increasing order. The descending sort places items in decreasing order. For number and currency data types, these types of sorts are obvious. For text items, you can substitute alphabetical order for ascending sorts and reverse alphabetical order for descending sorts. For dates and times, Access will use chronological order for ascending sorts and the reverse for descending sorts. Memo, OLE Object, and Hyperlink fields cannot be sorted.

To choose a sort type, click once in the Sort row in a field's design grid. Click the down arrow and choose Ascending or Descending. To remove the sort command, choose the (not sorted) line in the Sort row of the design grid.

If you specify sorts for more than one column, Access uses the *leftmost* sort column in the design grid as the primary sort key and uses remaining sort columns to break ties in higher-level sort keys. If your query's primary sort key is not leftmost among sort columns, drag the fields in Design view to the proper order. The next Guided Activity will demonstrate this procedure.

GUIDED ACTIVITY

3.3   Sorting Records in a Query

In this Guided Activity, you will add sort commands to a query.

1. Use the Camping Overstock query created in Guided Activity 3.1. Select Design view for this query.

2. Highlight the Category column and make sure the Camping restriction has been removed.

3. Click once in the Sort row of the Category field. Pull down the sort menu and choose Ascending.

4. Run the query and view the records in the datasheet. Notice that the product records now appear in alphabetical order by Category.

5. Next, go back to Design view and click once in the Sort row in the Description field. Set up an Ascending sort for this field.

6. Run the query and view the records in the datasheet. Was this a useful sort? Remember that Access uses the leftmost sort field as the primary sort key.

7. We need to move the Description field so that it appears *after* the Category field. Switch back to Design view. Move the pointer to the field selector border just above the Category field column. The cursor will change to a down arrow. Click once to highlight the Category column.

8. With the pointer in the field selector area, drag the Category field to the Description field and release the mouse button. Access will switch the two fields' positions in the query. Figure A3.9 shows the new column order. Note the shape of the mouse pointer in the field selector area of the Description column.

FIGURE A3.9
Query window in Design view

Field selector area ⎯

Rearranged columns ⎯

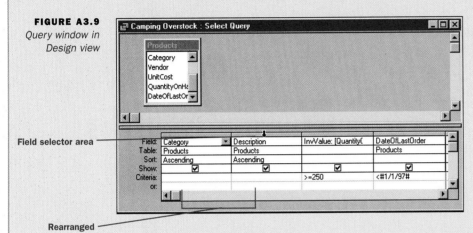

9. Run the query and examine the record sequence. With Category first, you should see an alphabetical listing of products within each category.

10. Use the File I Save As/Export command to save this query as Sorted Products by Category. Close the query.

Totals for Groups of Records

Microsoft Access queries can also group records that share a common value and can provide totals as well as perform other calculations on fields in those groups. Calculations are performed only on records in the datasheet from the query, so you can provide specific criteria if desired.

Types of Total Calculations

You can perform the following types of total calculations on number, autonumber, currency, and date/time fields in a query. The operation is specified by typing its name into the Total row in the design grid for a particular field. You can also select the operation from the pull-down list in the Total row.

Calculation	Meaning
Sum	Total of all values in the field
Avg	Arithmetic mean average of all values in the field
Min	Minimum value of the field
Max	Maximum value of the field

StDev	Standard deviation of all values in the field
Var	Variance of all values in the field
Where	Specify a particular value for a field *not* used to group data

The following types of calculations can be performed on number, autonumber, currency, date/time, yes/no, text, memo, hyperlink, and OLE object fields:

Calculation	Meaning
Count	Number of non-null values in the field
First	Field value from the first record
Last	Field value from the last record

Calculations on All Records

You can find summary information for all records in the table or datasheet. The basic procedure has four steps:

1. Create a new query and drag all the fields to be totaled to the design grid.

2. Click the Totals button on the toolbar (a Σ, or summation sign). You can also choose View | Totals from the menu bar. You will see a new Total row appear in the design grid with the words Group By under each field.

3. In the Total row under the field(s) you want to total, replace Group By with Sum or the appropriate calculation name.

4. Run the query to view the datasheet that results from the query. Access will display names in the columns that reflect the type of calculation done on each field. You'll see the results of the group totals calculation in a single row of the datasheet.

Calculations on Groups of Records

In this case, Access calculates values for groups of records, rather than for all records. This procedure is similar to the All Records procedure. The difference is that you must also drag the Group By fields to the design grid. For example, you might want to find the average salary of employees in each department. In this case, the Department field is the Group By field, and the Salary field would be the Sum entry on the Total line. You might also want to know the oldest DateOfLastOrder in the Products table for each product category. You cannot group by memo fields or by OLE object fields. You'll work with groups of records in a Guided Activity later in this unit.

Calculations for One Group

In this application, you create the query as before, but you also add a criteria expression that defines the group for which you want totals. When you run the query, only those records that match the criteria will be selected for totals.

In addition, you can establish criteria for the total field. For instance, you might want to know the average number of units in stock, but only for those products that have nonzero QuantityOnHand values. In that case, you would specify >0 as the criterion in the QuantityOnHand field, as well as entering Avg in the Total row for that field.

Calculations for Subgroups

You may want to break groups down into subgroups for purposes of totaling them. This procedure is analogous to sorting on more than one field. Access will take the first Group By field it encounters from the left side of the design grid and make it the primary group. It will then subdivide that group by the next Group By field it finds, proceeding from left to right.

Suppose you wanted to count the number of products from each vendor within each product category. The leftmost Group By field would be Category, and the next Group By field would be Vendor. We will demonstrate this feature in the next Guided Activity.

GUIDED ACTIVITY

3.4   Creating a Query with Total Calculations

In this Guided Activity, you will build a simple totals query, then modify it for several situations.

1. Open the Hunter97.mdb database and click the Queries tab. Click the New button, select Design View, and click OK.

2. In the Show Table window, select the Products table, and click Add. Close the Show Table window.

3. Drag the QuantityOnHand field to the design grid.

4. Click the Totals button (the summation sign) on the toolbar. You will see the Total row appear in the design grid.

5. Replace the Group By expression with `Sum` in the Total row.

6. Run the query and examine the datasheet. You will see a single row labeled `SumOfQuantityOnHand` with the value `439`. Why is there just *one* row in the resulting datasheet?

7. Click the Design View button to return to the Query window.

8. Drag the Category field to the design grid, then run the query to view the datasheet, shown in Figure A3.10. The first column was widened to show the full name of that column. Why do you see four records in the datasheet at this time?

FIGURE A3.10

Results of totals query after step 8

Column widened to show name

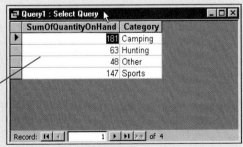

9. Return to Design view and place the criteria expression `Camping` in the Criteria row of the Category field.

10. Rerun the query. You should now see only the total for the Camping products.

11. Return to Design view and remove the Camping criteria expression from the Category field.

12. Drag the Vendor field to the design grid, then place the expression `Count` in the Total row under the QuantityOnHand field. `Group By` appears in the Total row under the Vendor field.

13. Run the query. You should see 14 records in this datasheet, one for each combination of Vendor and Category.

14. Use the File | Save As/Export command to save this query under the name Product Count by Vendor. In the next section, you'll learn how to print the contents of the datasheet for this query.

Printing the Query

As with Access tables in Datasheet mode, you can print the datasheet resulting from the query. Open the Database window and switch to the Query mode. Highlight the query you would like to print, and click the Print Preview button, or use the File | Print Preview command from the menu bar. Access will prepare the print job, and then display the first page of the output on the screen. You can use the magnifying glass pointer to zoom in on a portion of the output. If you want to send the output to the printer, click the Print button. Click Close if you wish to cancel the Print Preview command.

You can also send the output directly to the printer, without previewing, if you choose the Print button on the toolbar.

GUIDED ACTIVITY

3.5   Printing the Query's Datasheet

In this Guided Activity, you will print the datasheet resulting from the query of the preceding Guided Activity.

1. Open the Hunter97.mdb Database window and click the Queries tab.

2. Click the Product Count by Vendor query in the Database window and click Open.

3. Click the Print Preview button on the toolbar, or give the File | Print Preview command from the menu bar.

4. After a few seconds, Access will show you the first page of your print output on the display screen. Use the magnifying pointer to zoom in on a portion of the output.

5. If a printer is attached to your computer, click the Print button to send the output to the printer. Otherwise, click Close to cancel the Print Preview command. The print preview output is shown in Figure A3.11. If you are not continuing with the Exercises, you can close the database and exit from Access.

FIGURE A3.11
Sample query print preview

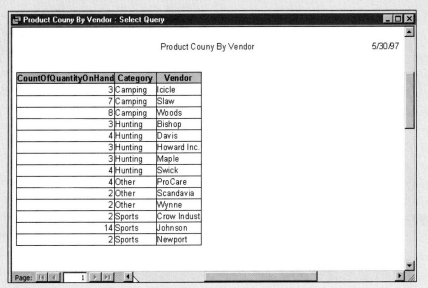

Product Couny By Vendor   5/30/97

CountOfQuantityOnHand	Category	Vendor
3	Camping	Icicle
7	Camping	Slaw
8	Camping	Woods
3	Hunting	Bishop
4	Hunting	Davis
3	Hunting	Howard Inc.
3	Hunting	Maple
4	Hunting	Swick
4	Other	ProCare
2	Other	Scandavia
2	Other	Wynne
2	Sports	Crow Indust
14	Sports	Johnson
2	Sports	Newport

Publishing a Query to the Web

Just as Access 97 can publish a table as an HTML document, it can also create an HTML file for a query's datasheet. The File I Save As HTML command will launch the Publish to the Web Wizard to help you with the steps. However, if you create a static HTML document, only a snapshot of the data that matches the query at the time you created the HTML document will be saved. Use static HTML when the data doesn't change very often. When the data changes, recreate the static HTML document.

If the database changes frequently and you expect to get current data from a query when accessing it via the Web, you'll need to choose one of the dynamic HTML document protocols available through the Wizard. These protocols set up a link between the Access database and the Web server, building the HTML documents on demand. Access 97 includes these dynamic HTML protocols for use with Microsoft's Internet Information Server, a Windows NT server application:

- IDC/HTX files that run an SQL query to fill an HTML template with current data

- ASP or ActiveX Server Page documents for accessing ODBC databases

Although the details for building and running dynamic HTML documents are beyond the scope of this book, you can find more information about dynamic HTML documents in online Help. Search under Dynamic HTML Format.

SUMMARY

In order to get specific information out of your database, you use queries. The Design view for a query allows you to specify what table(s) will be queried, which fields will be included in the answer, and what criteria must be met for records to be retrieved. When you run a select query, Access selects only the specified fields or records that meet the defined criteria, and displays the results in Datasheet view. Queries may have one criterion, or several criteria using And or Or conditions. Queries allow you to sort on one or more database fields. Clicking the Totals button adds a new row to a query that calculates the sum, average, count, and other functions for a field.

Exercises

Use the Hunter River database contained in the Hunter97.mdb file on the Student Data Disk for these Exercises. *Be sure to identify any printed output with your name and both the Exercise and part numbers.*

EXERCISE

3.1

Select Queries I

Create a select query that includes the following fields from the Employees table in the sequence given: LastName, Department, Salary. So that your instructor will know how you solved the exercise, write the appropriate query expression for each column on the printed output for each part. Modify the same query to solve each part below, but save it only after the last part.

1. Print the query for *all records*.

2. Print the query for the Accounting department *only*.

3. Print the query for Accounting *or* Sales department employees.

4. Print the query for all employees who earn at least $15,000 annual salary.

5. Save the query under the name Exercise 3-1.

EXERCISE

3.2

Select Queries II

Prepare another select query for the Employees table. This query should contain *all* fields from the table, in the default order of the table definition. Modify the query to solve each part below. Write the criteria expressions on the printed output for each part so that your instructor can see how you got your answer.

1. Print the query for employees whose last names begin with letters between A and M.

2. Print the query for employees who were hired during 1993.

3. Print the query for employees who were hired during 1993 *and* who are in the Sales department.

4. Print the query for employees who were hired *after* January 1, 1992 *and* who are *not* in the Sales department.

5. Print the query for employees whose *monthly* salary is from $1,000 to $1,500. Show only the last name and annual salary fields. Save the query as Exercise 3-2.

EXERCISE

3.3

Select Queries III

Write the query criteria expressions directly on the output, using fields from the Employees table that would match the following conditions. Run each query to test your expressions, and print the results for each part. Save the final query as Exercise 3-3.

1. Employees hired during the month of March in any year

2. Employees hired during the first quarter (January–March) of any year.

3. Employees who have worked for the Hunter River store for at least 48 months; use the current date when you solve this problem. (*Hint*: Use the DateDiff( ) function.)

4. Employees whose salary is above the average salary for all employees in the table. (*Hint*: Use the Davg( ) function.)

EXERCISE

3.4

Sorting within Queries

Prepare a query that will accomplish the tasks in the following parts. Modify the query for each part and print each part individually. Include LastName, FirstName, Department, Salary, and DateHired fields from the Employees table in the query.

1. Alphabetical listing of all employees

2. Alphabetical listing of employees broken down by department; departments should appear in alphabetical order

3. Same as part 2, except that first and last names should appear within one field (*Hint*: Use the concatenation operator in the Field row of the design grid.)

4. Listing of employees by salary, in descending order

5. Listing of employees by salary, broken down by department, in ascending order. Save this query as Exercise 3-4.

EXERCISE

3.5

Products Total Queries I

Prepare a totals query that will accomplish the tasks in each of the following parts. Use appropriate fields from the Employees table. Print each part individually.

1. Calculate the sum of all salaries.

2. Calculate the average salary for each department.

3. Add the Salary field twice to the design grid and show both the minimum and maximum salary values for all records.

4. Count the number of employees in each department.

5. Calculate the average salary for those employees hired in 1993. (*Hint:* Use the Where calculation in the Total row to select only 1993 hires.) Save this query as Exercise 3-5.

EXERCISE

3.6

Products Total Queries II

Prepare a query that will accomplish the tasks in each of the following parts. Include fields from the Products table. Print each part individually.

1. Show the products that were last ordered in the month of November.

2. Show the products that were not ordered during 1997.

3. Show the products whose current inventory value (unit cost multiplied by quantity on hand) is between $20 and $100, inclusive.

4. Show the products that were not ordered during 1997 and that are currently out of stock. Save this query as Exercise 3-6.

EXERCISE

3.7

Using Functions in Queries

For this query, select any table as the data source but do not drag any fields to the design grid. Use the design grid Field row to key in the appropriate Access function to answer each of the following questions. Let each question be in a different column. Write down the function expression and provide the answer. For example, enter `Pmt(.08/12,3*12,-5000,0,0)` in the Field cell, then run the query to find out that the payment should be $156.68. Save the query as Exercise 3-7.

1. Find the monthly payment for borrowing $7,000 for 4 years at 9% per year. Remember to enter the *monthly* interest rate and number of months for the loan.

2. Find the depreciation for year 6 of a 10-year asset whose initial cost was $75,000 and whose salvage value is $15,000. Assume the double-declining balance method.

3. Find the day of the week for your own birth.

4. Find the number of days since your own birth using the DateDiff function.

EXERCISE

3.8   Another Way to Publish an HTML File

This exercise will demonstrate a quick way to save an Access object on the Internet without going through the Web Wizard.

1. Open Hunter97.mdb, then select Query mode. Open the Inventory Value query already saved in the database.

2. Use the File I Save As/Export command (*not* File I Save As HTML).

3. Select To An External File Or Database and click OK.

4. In the Save Query As dialog box, change the Save As Type to HTML Documents. Accept the default name and click Export.

5. Print a copy of the HTML file from your browser. How does this output differ from the Web Wizard approach?

Physicians' Medical Clinic: Using a Select Query

Dr. Greenway and the hospital board are very concerned about the effects the proposed national health program may have on PMC. They have asked you to prepare some select queries to examine patient statistics. Using the PMC97.mdb database, create a select query, display and print the datasheet, modify the query, and repeat the process as specified below. Indicate clearly which printed output goes with which part of the application.

You have been asked to provide a list of patients from the Patients table in patient number order. The following fields are requested: PatientNumber, FirstName and LastName as one field with a space between, EmployerName, and DateOfBirth. Print this list. Modify the previous query of this application to select only those patients *from the State University employer*. Print this list.

Prepare a query to select patients from any employer who are *younger than age 21*. Use the current date to determine actual age. Print this list in *descending age order* (oldest first). Prepare and print another list showing names, home address fields, and employer names for those patients who have *no insurance company* listed. This list should appear in alphabetical order.

Finally, prepare a list of patients who are insured by the *US Insurance Company* or by *Municipal Insurance*. Print this list in order of insurance company and within each company by patient number. Include the patient number, last and first names, and insurance company name.

Hunter River—Creating a Query for the Web

You are continuing you work on the Web site for Hunter River. The corporate officers want you to create a query called All Products that includes StockNumber, Description, Category, UnitCost, Vendor, and QuantityOnHand. Use the UnitCost field to create an expression for sales price that is marked up by 35%; that is, divide UnitCost by 1–.35. Call this expression SalesPrice.

Publish this query to the Web and print a copy from your Web browser.

Their next request is query only Camping items, and they want this saved as Web Camping Products. They would like the query published to the Web and printed out from the Web browser. The company officers also want to create a service for the customers over the Internet by giving them the ability to use the Web page to request products in a particular sales category.

UNIT 4

Building a Form

In this unit you will learn the basics of forms, including the types of forms available with the Access Form Wizard. You will create a simple form using the Form Wizard, then use that form to view data and add data to a table. This chapter demonstrates how to use filters to limit the records that appear. You will learn also to develop and print main/subforms.

Learning Objectives

At the completion of this unit, you should be able to

1. list the various types of forms used in Access,

2. discuss the advantages of using a form to display data,

3. create a form using the Access Form Wizard,

4. use the form to display data from a table,

5. add data to a table using a form,

6. print the data with the form,

7. use a filter to show certain records with a form,

8. use Access wildcard expressions.

Case Study

Hunter River needs a form to add new customers and employees. You have been asked to develop and print a more complicated main/subform to assign the employees of Hunter River to departments.

Form Basics

Access forms provide a visually attractive way of presenting data on the screen, usually one record at a time. You can arrange the record's data fields in any location on the desktop and format the fields as desired. Fields can be arranged in a specific order within the form to make data input easier and more accurate. Generally, it is easier to use forms to enter and edit data than to use the underlying tables in Datasheet view.

Form Controls

Forms are made up of the standard Windows graphical objects for displaying data in a custom manner. These graphical objects, known as controls, include such items as labels, text boxes, lines, rectangles, check boxes, drop-down lists (combo boxes), buttons, option groups, picture objects, charts, and so on. Samples of these controls are shown in the Northwind Orders form of Figure A4.1. Note that the Bill To drop-down list has been pulled down to illustrate this feature. The Print Invoice button at the bottom will cause an Access event procedure or macro to run, printing the invoice. Some of the same controls are also used in Access reports.

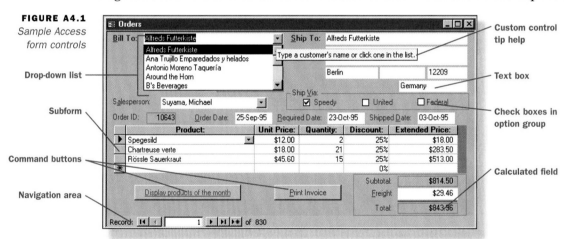

FIGURE A4.1
Sample Access form controls

You can build many forms automatically by using the Form Wizard. This unit primarily discusses forms created with the Form Wizard. You do not need to work with the controls on a form created with the Form Wizard unless you want to make changes to the form. For more customized forms, you may need to learn more about controls.

The Form View Toolbar

The Form view toolbar is shown in Figure A4.2. It uses many of the same buttons as the table Datasheet and Query views. As with other views, the first button can be used to choose from Form, Datasheet, and Design views. There is a different toolbar for Form Design view.

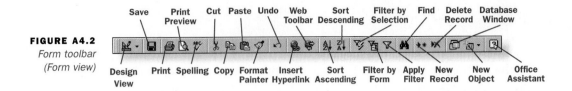

FIGURE A4.2
Form toolbar
(Form view)

Designing a Form

This section will discuss the types of forms and the various styles available through Access Forms.

Types of Forms

As with tables and queries, you create a new form by clicking the Forms tab, then clicking the New button. Figure A4.3 shows the New Form window. Choose the form type from the top of this window, then specify the table or query where the form's data are found.

FIGURE A4.3
Access New Form
window

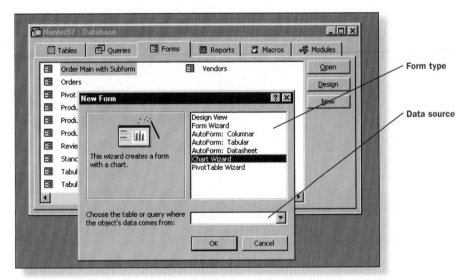

DESIGN VIEW

Design view represents the manual method for building a form. In Design view, you start with a blank form and drag the various fields and controls to the form. This method lets you create a custom form to match a given situation, but it is the most difficult to use.

FORM WIZARD

Access provides an easy-to-use tool called the Form Wizard for creating forms. The Form Wizard leads you through an interview process, asking questions about the appropriate information for the form and the kind of form you would like to build. You tell Access which fields are to be used on the form, and in what order. You can specify the background style for your form and can provide a form title. Form Wizard provides four types of forms, described next.

COLUMNAR FORM   A columnar form displays the field values from a record down the screen in one column, one field per line. Preceding the field is a label, which defaults to the field name or to the caption you provided as a field property for that field when you defined the table. It is also possible to "snake" extra fields into two columns, newspaper-style. That is, the fields can go down the first column, then continue at the top of the second column. Figure A4.4 shows a columnar form for Product Entry with Standard style.

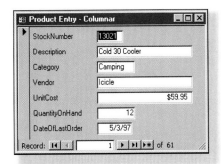

FIGURE A4.4
Columnar Form Wizard form

TABULAR FORM   The tabular form presents fields in row and column format, similar to Datasheet view. You can display multiple records with a tabular form, as shown in Flax style in Figure A4.5. Fields proceed across the form, from left to right. This kind of form is useful when there are fewer fields to display. Long fields can be displayed over two or more lines. Unfortunately, as you see in the figure, the font choice for this form means that the field names are not displayed fully.

FIGURE A4.5
Tabular Form Wizard form

StockNu	Description	Cate	Vendor	UnitCost	yOnHand	LastOrder
13021	Cold 30 Cooler	Campi	Icicle	$59.95	12	5/3/97
13034	Cold 36 Cooler	Campi	Icicle	$79.95	7	5/3/97
13037	Ice Cold Lunch To	Campi	Icicle	$14.95	3	5/3/97
13066	40-Qt. Cooler Kit	Campi	Slaw	$29.95	0	4/14/97
13068	48-qt Cooler	Campi	Slaw	$57.69	10	4/14/97
17221	Outdoor grill -30K	Campi	Woods	$199.99	10	5/15/97
17226	Super Sport Stove	Campi	Woods	$119.99	6	5/15/97
17239	Double Burner Sto	Campi	Woods	$79.99	0	5/15/97
17344	2-Room Cabin Ter	Campi	Woods	$269.95	3	12/19/96
17345	12x10 Deluxe Fan	Campi	Woods	$179.95	5	12/19/96
17346	12x9 Tent with A	Campi	Woods	$139.95	0	12/19/96
17348	10x8 Cabin Tent	Campi	Woods	$89.95	12	12/19/96
17350	6x6 Square Dome	Campi	Woods	$49.95	15	12/19/96
17542	Twin Tube Lanter	Campi	Slaw	$29.99	25	4/14/97

Record: 1 of 61

DATASHEET FORM   The datasheet form displays data in row and column order, in Datasheet view. However, when you switch to Form view, this form displays a single record at a time, across the screen. Figure A4.6 shows the datasheet form in Datasheet view.

JUSTIFIED FORM   The justified form is new with Access 97, displaying data in tabular form but in several rows per record, depending on how many fields you have in the record. The width of each field is proportional to the relative size of the

FIGURE A4.6
*Datasheet Form
Wizard form*

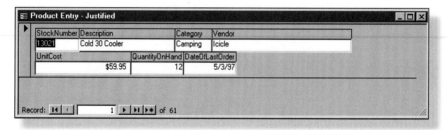

field in the table's design. This form is particularly useful when the data source has many fields. Figure A4.7 shows an example of a justified form.

FIGURE A4.7
*Justified Form
Wizard form*

AUTOFORMS

Access 97 includes three types of AutoForms that closely resemble three Form Wizard forms: Columnar, Tabular, and Datasheet. AutoForms are useful in that you need specify only the table or query containing data for the form, and Access builds that form for you automatically. It will use all fields in the order in which they appear in the underlying table or query, and will use the table's or query's name as the form title. The final result for an AutoForm is similar to the Form Wizard form using the Standard style.

CHART WIZARD

A Chart Wizard form depicts numerical data in a graph. Figure A4.8 shows a chart form. If you customize graph forms, it may be appropriate to combine this type of form with one of the others in a comprehensive screen.

PIVOT TABLE WIZARD

The Pivot Table Wizard creates a Microsoft Excel Pivot Table form. A pivot table is similar to a crosstab report; it displays summarized data with row and column subtotals, along with grand totals. For instance, suppose you want to count the number of products from each vendor within each sales category in the Products

FIGURE A4.8

Chart Wizard form
(bar chart)

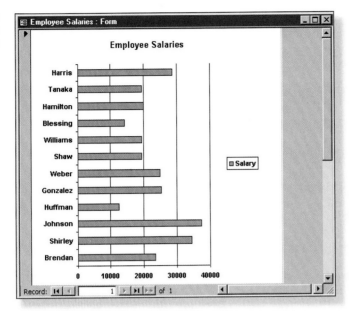

table. Click the Edit Pivot Table button to load Excel. Use a pivot table form for this purpose, as shown in Figure A4.9. Notice that the menu bar and toolbars belong to Excel, the OLE server in this instance. Closing the form will close Excel and return you to Access. We'll leave the creation of this pivot table form for an Exercise at the end of this unit.

FIGURE A4.9

Pivot table form
shown in Excel OLE
window

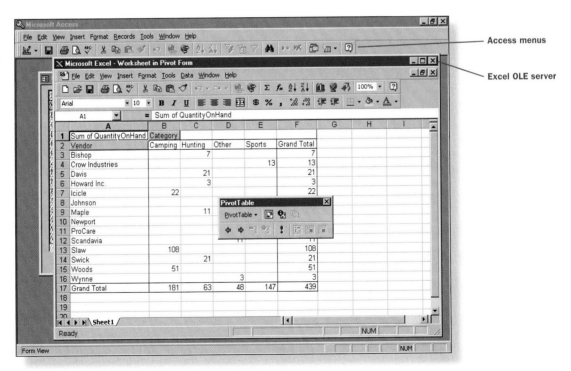

MAIN/SUBFORM

You may want to link two tables that contain matching field values. For instance, you might have a customers table and an orders table; these tables can be linked by matching their customer number fields. A main/subform is used to display matching records from the two tables together. In this example, the top portion (main) of the form in Figure A4.1 contains information about the customer order. The bottom portion (subform) shows all the products within that order. It is necessary to declare a one-to-many relationship between the two tables before a subform can be created and properly linked.

You can add a subform to an existing form, create it in a Form Wizard, or even add more than one subform to a main form. We will create a main/subform design in a later Guided Activity.

GUIDED ACTIVITY

4.1   Creating a Form with AutoForm

In this Guided Activity, you will use the AutoForm to create a columnar form.

1. Start Windows and load Access.

2. Use the File | Open Database command to open the Hunter97.mdb database. This database can be found on the Student Data Disk.

3. Click the Forms tab in the Database window.

4. Click the New button to open the New Form window, previously shown in Figure A4.3.

5. Select AutoForm: Columnar.

6. Click the down arrow in the table or query box at the bottom of the New Form window, then choose the Employees table. Click OK.

 NOTE *Press **E** to jump directly to tables beginning with the letter E. This feature is available in most Access drop-down lists.*

7. After a few seconds, Access will display the Employees form in Form view. Notice that the fields are displayed down the left side of the Form window, one per line. The title of the form defaults to Employees, the name of the table containing the data.

8. Click the close button in the Employees Form window. When prompted, save the form under the name `Employees AutoForm`. We will return to the Forms page of the Database window in the next activity.

Using the Form Wizard

This section will cover the use of the Access Form Wizard to create a form. The subsequent Guided Activities will help you to easily build your own forms.

Steps in Building a Form with Form Wizard

The Form Wizard helps you create the form by presenting a series of questions. As you fill in the answers to these questions, the form is created automatically. You do not have to remember long steps on your own when using the Form Wizard to build a form.

Although the form created in this process is complete, you might want to make some changes to its design. You can use Form Design view to make corrections manually. However, because the Form Wizard is so easy to use, we recommend that you create a new form with the Form Wizard, at least until you have more experience with Access. This unit does not cover making manual changes in Form Design view.

Before starting the Form Wizard, you should open the Database window for your database, then select the Forms tab in the Database window. To create a form, click the New button and choose Form Wizard. Then answer the questions presented by the Form Wizard.

When using the Form Wizard, you must provide the following information:

- Which table or query the form will use for its data source (the table or query from which the form gets its data values)

- Type of form layout to build (Columnar, Tabular, Datasheet, or Justified)

- Order of fields to place in the form

- Which style to use (Clouds, Colorful1, Colorful2, Dusk, Evergreen, Flax, International, Pattern, Standard, or Stone)

- Title (form name) to appear in the title bar at the top of the form

After you have specified this information, Access will give you a chance to open your form or to make changes to its design. You can also use Access Help to make changes to the form's design. After examining the form, you must give the form a name and save it in the database.

Form Wizard Layout

You can choose from the four layout options: Columnar, Tabular, Datasheet, and Justified. Keep in mind that the columnar layout provides the most room for longer fields on a form, but only a single record appears at one time. The tabular and datasheet layouts show multiple records but do not do a good job when there are many or long fields to display. Justified is particularly good when you have a large number of fields. In a main/subform design, the main form is predominantly a columnar design, while the subform is a datasheet design.

Form Wizard Field List

You must decide which fields to place in the form, and their sequence, called tab order. Many people will add data to the form from a paper document, so field sequence should match the order of fields in the paper document. When you have finished with a field, the **Tab** key will take you to the next field on the form. **Shift-Tab** will take you to the preceding field. You can override the tab order with the View | Tab Order command. Search Access Help for "Tab Order in Forms" for more information.

You may decide to add all the record's fields to the form or to select a subset of fields. For example, you might use a supervisor version of a form with all fields available, but use a separate form for lower-level employees that does not include certain sensitive fields, such as salary or date of birth.

Form Wizard Styles

After you specify the type of form, Form Wizard asks you what style you want to use. These styles do not affect the data or the form itself, only the way fields appear on the screen. In each case, the field name appears as a label next to the field text box. You can click each style line in this box to see a preview of the style in the left portion of the box.

GUIDED ACTIVITY

4.2   Creating a Form with the Form Wizard

In this Guided Activity, you will use the Form Wizard to create a single-column (columnar) form.

1. Start Windows and load Access.

2. Use the File | Open Database command to open the Hunter97.mdb database if it is not already open.

3. Click the Forms tab in the Database window.

4. Click the New button to open the New Form window.

5. Choose Form Wizard and click OK. We will choose the table or query later.

6. Click the selector button to the right of the Tables/Queries combo box in the Form Wizard window. Access will display an alphabetical list of all the tables and queries associated with the current database. Click once in the Products table but *do not* press **Enter**.

7. The Products table will become the data source for this new form, shown in Figure A4.10. Access will display a list of Products fields on the left and the selected fields on the right. You can add fields one at a time, in the desired order, or click the >> button to add all the fields from the Products table in the order in which they were placed in the table definition.

8. For this example, click the >> button to add all the fields to the form, then click Next to go to the next step.

NOTE *If you accidentally added the wrong field to the form, highlight the field, then click the < button.*

9. Access will display a window with the layouts you can build with the Form Wizard. Select Columnar, then click Next.

10. The Form Wizard window now shows the form styles, with a picture of the currently selected style at the left side of the window. Choose Standard, then click Next.

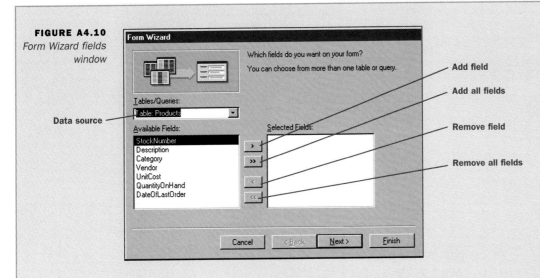

FIGURE A4.10
Form Wizard fields window

Data source

Add field
Add all fields
Remove field
Remove all fields

11. In the form title box, key in `Product Entry`. This title appears at the top of the form whenever it is used.

12. Click the Finish button to open the form with data in it, similar to the one shown in Figure A4.4 earlier in this unit. Notice that Product Entry appears in the title bar of the Form window.

NOTE *If the Product Entry form already exists in your copy of Hunter97.mdb, you may replace it with this form.*

13. You may use the navigation buttons at the bottom of the Form window to scroll through the records in the Products table.

14. When you are finished examining the data from the Products table, click the form's Close button to close the form (or use the File | Close command).

The usual style is Standard, with a plain gray background. This was the style illustrated in Figures A4.3–A4.5. The remaining styles add background graphics and color to enhance the look of the form. Forms with these styles are similar, except in appearance.

Form Design View

Although we will not explain how to make changes to form design in this unit, you may be interested in seeing what Access uses to represent the form design. While the Product Entry form is active, you can click the Design View button to see the form in Design view, shown in Figure A4.11.

There are two toolbars in Design view—the Form Design toolbar on top, and the Formatting toolbar just below it. You can customize the contents and location of the toolbars, even changing their shape—right-click the toolbar area and select Customize.

NOTE *As mentioned in Unit 2, Access will use the Caption property of a field for its caption in forms and reports. If the Caption property is empty, Access uses the field's name as a caption.*

FIGURE A4.11
Design view for Product Entry form

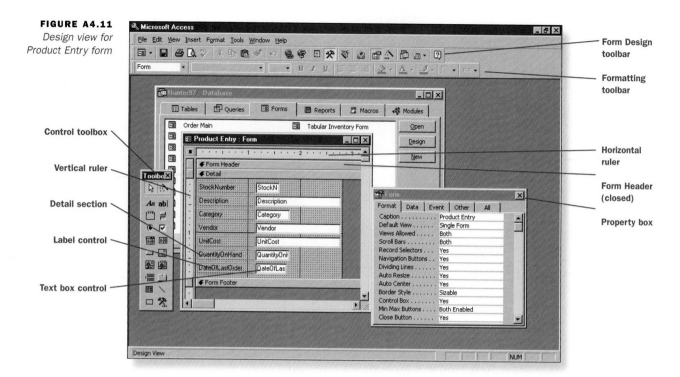

The title of the form appears in the title bar of the form. You could also place the title in the header section, using a larger font. The fields appear in the form detail section, one per line. Like the header section, the footer section is also empty. Surrounding the form are the horizontal and vertical rulers, used to indicate placement of the boxes on the form.

The boxes within the detail section are called controls, mentioned earlier. Adjacent to each text box is a label, in this case the field name. You will also see the Control toolbox in the lower left portion of the screen. The buttons in this toolbox are used to place different kinds of controls in the form design. An experienced Access user is able to manipulate controls individually and can customize the form. For example, you could click a text box control to display its size/move handles, then drag a handle to resize the control to better fit the data.

In the next Guided Activity, we introduce a more complicated form, again created with the Access Form Wizard.

GUIDED ACTIVITY

4.3 Creating a Main/Subform

In this Guided Activity, you will use the Form Wizard to create a more complex form that shows the Hunter River departments at the top and the employees in each department at the bottom. The activity is based on the one-to-many relationship between Department and Employees that already exists in the Hunter97.mdb database.

1. Load Access and open the Hunter97.mdb Database window.

2. Click the Forms tab and click New.

3. In the New Form window, select Form Wizard. Click OK to start the Form Wizard.

4. Select the Department table in the Tables/Queries box, then click >> to add all of the Department fields to the main form.

5. Next, choose the Employees table, then click >> to add all the Employees fields to the subform. Click Next to go to the next step.

It is critical that you have the relationship between the Department and Employees tables set up properly. For this activity, we have created the relationship for you in the Hunter97 database. If the one-to-many relationship is not set up properly, the Form Wizard will place all the fields in the main form. If the relationship is set up properly, you will get additional instructions on setting up the subform relationship, described next.

6. If the proper relationship between the Department and Employees tables exists, Access will ask how you wish to view the data in the form. Select the default choice, By Department, and make sure that the Form With Subform(s) button is selected. Click Next.

7. When you are asked for the subform layout, choose Datasheet. Click Next to go on to the next step.

8. For now, choose the Standard style and click Next.

9. In the Form Title box, enter `Employees by Department`. Keep the default value for the Subform Title, `Employees Subform`. Then click the Finish button. Access will create two forms—the main form and the Employees subform.

NOTE *If the Employees by Department subform already exists in your copy of Hunter97.mdb, you may replace it with* this *form.*

10. Next, you will see the finished main/subform, shown in Figure A4.12. The fields from the Department table appear as a single-column main form, while the fields from the Employee table appear in the tabular subform at the bottom of the Form window. Each part of the form has its own record selector area.

FIGURE A4.12
Employees by Department main/subform

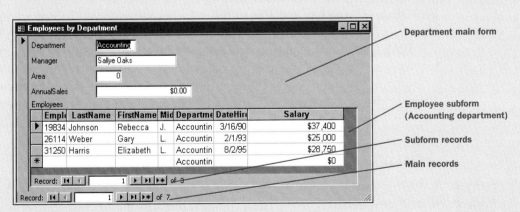

11. Click the Department Next Record button, and the subform will change to reflect employees in that department.

12. We will work with this form shortly, in Guided Activity 4.5. Click the Close button to save this form as Employees by Department.

13. Leave the Hunter97 Database window open.

Viewing and Editing Data with a Form

TIP

Some applications may require that users only view data. If a control is read-only, you will not be able to make changes to its value in the form. To make a control read-only, change its Locked property from No to Yes.

In this section, you will view and edit data from the Hunter97.mdb database using several Access forms. A form generally displays a single record at a time, and you can use the navigation buttons to move data from the table through the Form window. Any changes made to data in the form are automatically made to the underlying table, even if you have used a query as the form's data source.

Viewing Field Values

Ordinarily the form consists of a set of field labels, each with an attached text box that contains field values. The form opens with the pointer in the first field of the first record. You can move from field to field in the form by pressing the **Tab** key, or by clicking the field you wish to see. If there are more fields than will fit in the window, you may need to use the vertical and horizontal scroll bars to see them.

When you open the form, Access sizes the window just large enough to display all the fields unless there are more fields than can fit on the screen. You can resize the Form window by dragging the corners or sides of the window. You can also use the minimize and maximize buttons to change the window size.

Moving the Record Pointer in the Form

With the single-column form, you will see the fields from a single record at a time. You can scroll through the records by using the navigation buttons at the bottom of the Form window. They work just like the navigation buttons in the datasheet's Table window—the inner arrow buttons move one record backward or forward, and the outer arrow buttons move to the first and last records, respectively. You can also use the **Page Up** and **Page Down** keys to scroll from record to record, or the Edit | Go To command from the menu bar to go to a specific record.

With a tabular form, you will see several records at one time, displayed across the screen. You can move the record pointer by clicking the record selector button or by using the navigation buttons in the status bar, the **Page Up** and **Page Down** keys, or the Edit menu.

Record: |◄ ◄   1   ► ►| ►* of 7

Adding Data with a Form

Working with the form is very similar to working with the datasheet. If you want to add new records to the underlying table, use the Records | Data Entry command (or click the New Record button in the toolbar) to display a blank form. Another method is to move to the last record with the navigation buttons. Then click the Next Record button (or press **Page Down**) and Access will display a new blank record on the form. You can key in new values on the form and they will be stored in the underlying table.

Editing Data with a Form

To edit data with the form, position the record selector on the desired record, then click the field that you want to change. Make changes to the values as necessary, then go to the next record to be changed. Access will display a pencil icon in the record selector area in the left portion of the Form window while you are making changes to the record, indicating that the changes have not yet been committed to the database. When you move to a different record, the new values are automatically saved in the table, just as in Datasheet mode. You can undo changes to the current record with the Undo button in the toolbar.

Deleting Records with a Form

To delete the current record, click in the record selector area. Then press the **Del** key, click the Delete Record button, or use the Edit I Delete command from the menu bar. Access will ask you to confirm that you want to delete the highlighted record(s). *Remember that deletions are irrevocable*—once you have deleted the record and confirmed it, the data are gone. You will have to key them in again if the deletion was made in error.

GUIDED ACTIVITY

4.4 Working with Data Using a Form

In this Guided Activity, you will use a form to make changes to the Hunter97.mdb database.

1. If it is not already open, start Access and open the Hunter97.mdb Database window.

2. Click the Forms tab, then open the Product Entry form, previously shown in Figure A4.4.

3. Notice the size that Access chose for the Form window. Use the mouse to increase the box size, dragging the lower right corner to the right.

4. Use the mouse to resize the window to its original size. Alternatively, you can close and reopen the form to restore its original size.

5. Use the navigation buttons to directly move the record pointer to record 8. Increase the quantity on hand by one unit. Notice that Access displays the pencil icon in the record selector area in the upper left corner.

6. Click the Last Record button, then examine the contents of this record. Access is able to move the record pointer there very quickly.

7. Next, click the New Record button or use the Records I Data Entry command to display a blank form. The navigation area should say Record 1, even though there are many more records in the table.

NOTE *You can also click the New Record button to add a new record.*

8. Add the following record to the end of the table. Semicolons separate fields:

   ```
   63050; 5" Combination Knife; Hunting; Swick; $14.70; 9;
   1/15/97
   ```

9. When you have entered all the fields, press **Enter**. The pencil icon will change to a right triangle in the record selection area, indicating that your record has been written to the disk drive. Close the form by clicking the Form window Close button.

10. Open the form again and click the Last Record button. You should see the record that you just added to the Products table.

11. Click the record selector area of the form, then press the **Del** key to delete the record you just added. Confirm the change when Access prompts you.

12. Close the form. Any changes are automatically saved in the Products table.

The next Guided Activity will explore the use of the main/subform that you created earlier in this unit.

GUIDED ACTIVITY

4.5 Working with Data in a Main/Subform

In this Guided Activity, you will work with data using a main/subform created in an earlier activity.

1. Load Access, and open the Hunter97.mdb database. Open the Employees by Department form, previously shown in Figure A4.12.

2. The main form uses the Department table as its data source. Because this table is indexed by its primary key, department name, the departments will appear in alphabetical order. The Accounting department is listed first, along with its three employees. The Employees table is indexed by its primary key, employee number, and its records appear in that order.

3. Click the Next Record button in the Employees navigation area in the *middle* of the Form window to move to the next employee of the Accounting department. Remember that the main form has its own navigation buttons at the bottom of the form.

4. Click the Next Record button twice in the navigation area at the *bottom* of the Form window. You should see the next department (Marketing) and its employees appear in the form. If you had accidentally pressed the Employees navigation button, you would see the second employee of the Accounting department.

5. Let's add a new employee in Marketing at this time. Move the cursor to a blank row in the Employees subform datasheet and fill in fields in the subform. The new employee data is shown below. When you're finished, scroll through the departments and view the employee data.

   ```
   23111; Oak; Joseph; M.; Marketing; 9/10/95; 42,500;
   ```

   Figure A4.13 shows the form with this new entry in the Marketing department.

FIGURE A4.13
Employees by Department form with new record

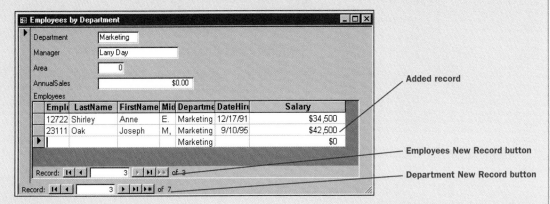

6. Manipulate the navigation buttons to find the fourth employee in the Sales department.

7. Form windows can be moved like any other window. Use the pointer to drag the window's title bar to a new location so that you can view other objects on the desktop. When you're finished, close the Employees by Department form.

Applying Filters

Although forms can be based on either tables or queries, sometimes you still need to restrict the data so that it meets certain criteria. This is done by applying a filter, which is similar to a query, to the form. Filters may be applied in four ways: Filter By Selection, Filter By Form, Advanced Filter/Sort, and Filter For Input. Filters restrict records so that only those that meet your criteria will be displayed in a table, query, or form.

Filter Wildcard Expressions

You can use wildcard characters in filter expressions. Similar to those presented for queries, the wildcard characters let you specify just a portion of the filter criteria. The asterisk (*) stands for any number of characters in the asterisk position and following it; with this asterisk, unlike the DOS asterisk wildcard, you *can* specify characters that follow it. The question mark (?) stands for any single character in its position. A number sign (#) stands for a single digit in its position. Square brackets [ ] allow you to specify several matching characters for a single position. The exclamation point (!) is used to define characters that you *do not* want to match. For example, if you specify [!X], Access will find all characters in that position except the letter X.

Examples of wildcard expressions are shown in Table A4.1.

EXPRESSION	MATCHING VALUES
MIS*	MIS 320, MIS 276, MIS major
MIS 3??	MIS 320, MIS 399, MIS 3FH (but not MIS 276)
*76	276, 376, 476, 1776
*ville	Charlottesville, Evansville (but not Hovilles)
MIS 3##	MIS 320 (but not MIS 3FH)
MIS [34]##	MIS 376, MIS 430, MIS 476 (but not MIS 276)
MIS [3-5]##	MIS 376, MIS 580 (but not MIS 276)
M[IG][ST]	MIS, MGT, MIT, MGS (but not MIG)
M[!G][!T]*	MIS 475, MIS Major (but not MGT)

Filter By Selection

To use the fastest, easiest option, highlight a portion of an entry in a field in a form, table, or query datasheet, then click the Filter By Selection button. The result is that only records with that value in the same field appear in the form or datasheet. This is essentially the same thing as a simple select query with a text string matching criteria. To remove the query and see all the records, click the Apply Filter button. Figure A4.14 shows the filtered datasheet for the Products form. Notice that "(Filtered)" appears in the navigation area to indicate that a filter is in place.

FIGURE A4.14
*Filtered Products
datasheet for
Camping products*

Stock Numbe	Description:	Category:	Vendor:	Unit Cost:	Quantit	Date of Last Ord
13021	Cold 30 Cooler	Camping	Icicle	$59.95	12	5/3/97
13034	Cold 36 Cooler	Camping	Icicle	$79.95	7	5/3/97
13037	Ice Cold Lunch Tote	Camping	Icicle	$14.95	3	5/3/97
13066	40-Qt. Cooler Kit	Camping	Slaw	$29.95	0	4/14/97
13068	48-qt Cooler	Camping	Slaw	$57.69	10	4/14/97
17221	Outdoor grill -30K btu	Camping	Woods	$199.99	10	5/15/97
17226	Super Sport Stove	Camping	Woods	$119.99	6	5/15/97
17239	Double Burner Stove	Camping	Woods	$79.99	0	5/15/97
17344	2-Room Cabin Tent	Camping	Woods	$269.95	3	12/19/96
17345	12x10 Deluxe Family	Camping	Woods	$179.95	5	12/19/96
17346	12x9 Tent with Awnin	Camping	Woods	$139.95	0	12/19/96
17348	10x8 Cabin Tent	Camping	Woods	$89.95	12	12/19/96

Record: 1 of 18 (Filtered)

Note filtered records

Filter By Form

Again place the cursor in the field you want to query. If you click the Filter By Form button, a window appears with a copy of the form or datasheet with blank fields, as seen in Figure A4.15. Fill in the criteria on the Look For tab (and the Or tab, if it is necessary to provide alternate criteria), then click the Apply Filter button. The result

FIGURE A4.15
Filter by Form window

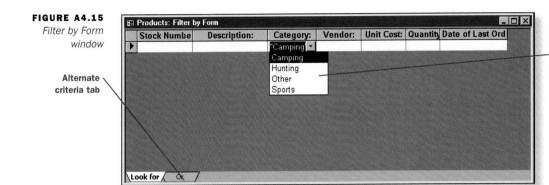

Select choice

Alternate criteria tab

is that only the records satisfying the criteria are displayed in the form. To remove the filter, click the Apply Filter (now called Remove Filter) button again.

NOTE *If you right-click the Filter By Form selection, the shortcut menu offers an Apply Filter choice.*

Sorting with a Filter

  With Filter By Form and Filter By Selection, you can sort on a single field at one time by using the Sort Ascending and Sort Descending buttons in the toolbar. After the filter is applied, click in the field you want to sort on. Then click the appropriate Sort button.

Saving a Filter as a Query

Ordinarily the filter is discarded when you close the form or datasheet. It is possible to save the filter as a query so that you can reuse it later. Use the File | Save As Query command or choose Save As Query from the shortcut menu. When prompted, give the filter a name. Then open the filter query as you would any other query. It is not possible to convert a query to a filter, however.

GUIDED ACTIVITY

4.6   Applying Filters to a Form

1. Load Access. Open the Product Entry form in the Hunter97.mdb database.

2. Click the down arrow next to the View button to change to Datasheet view.

3. Scroll down to the record whose StockNumber is 20235. Double-click to highlight *just* the word Basketball in the Description field.

4. Click the Filter By Selection button. Access will display records that contain the word *basketball* in the Description field. This filter restricts the form to five records, as shown in Figure A4.16.

5. Remove the filter by clicking the Remove Filter button.

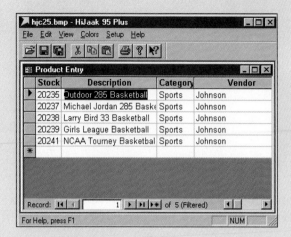

6. Click the down arrow next to the View button to switch to Form view.

7. Click the Filter By Form button to see the blank form. Press **Del** to remove the Like "Basketball" criteria.

8. Click in the blank Category field. Click the arrow that appears, then select Sports from the drop-down list.

9. Click in the QuantityOnHand field, then type >0 in that field, as shown in Figure A4.17.

10. Click the Apply Filter button. This results in 17 filtered records that are from the Sports category and that have some units in stock.

11. Click the Remove Filter button to show all the records in the form.

12. Click the Close button to close the form.

Other Filters

Access 97 offers two other filter types, Advanced Filter/Sort and Filter For Input. Advanced Filter/Sort virtually duplicates the Access select query environment for more complicated filter situations. Start with Filter By Form, then use the Filter | Advanced Filter/Sort command. Add fields and criteria to the filter design grid, then apply the filter. We will not demonstrate this feature here.

Filter For Input is new to Access 97. Open a table, query, or form in Datasheet view, or a form in Form view. To specify the exact field value you want the filtered records to contain, right-click the field, and then in the Filter For box on the shortcut menu, type the value. Press **Enter** to apply the filter. To remove the filter, right-click the field and choose Remove Filter.

Printing the Form

Although forms are primarily designed for displaying data values on the screen, Access provides a way to print them. Unfortunately, Access may not keep all fields from one form together on a single printed page. Thus, the printed form output may leave something to be desired. Access reports are usually a better way to print information.

It is possible to modify the form properties to force Access to print each form on a separate page. The default is to place forms together, one after another, until the printed page is full and the output overflows to the next page.

As we did with printing the table in Datasheet view, you can use the Print Preview button to see how the printed output will look. To do this, open the Database window and switch to Forms. Click once on the form you wish to print, then click the Print Preview button. Access will show you a reduced view of the printed form. You can place the magnifying-glass pointer on any part of the reduced page and click once to zoom in on that portion. You can click the Print button to print the form as is, or click the Close button to return to the Database window.

GUIDED ACTIVITY

4.7   Printing a Form

In this Guided Activity, we will print a form on the printer. If your computer is not able to print, you can still preview the output and see how the printed page would appear.

1. Start Access and open the Hunter97.mdb Database window. Click the Forms tab to display the forms in this database.

2. Select the Product Entry form by clicking it once. You need not open the form to print it.

3. Click the Print Preview button and Access will create a print preview on the screen. You should see four or five forms repeating on one page.

4. You can use the magnifying-glass pointer to zoom in on a portion of the page. Move the pointer to the desired location and click the left mouse button to zoom in on the desired part of the report.

5. If a printer is attached to your computer and configured to print under Windows, click the Print button to print the output. Otherwise, click Close in the preceding screen to return to the Database window.

6. This is the final Guided Activity for this unit. If you are finished working with Access, exit by double-clicking the Control menu box or use the File | Exit command.

Publishing a Form on the Internet

You can publish a form on the Internet in the same way as you did with tables and queries. First create the form, then use the File | Save As HTML command. The Publish to the Web Wizard will start up and guide you through the process. If you prefer to take a shortcut, use the File | Save As/Export command and select HTML as the data type. You will not see the Wizard's prompts for the latter method. Access forms provide a visually attractive means of presenting data on the screen,

SUMMARY

usually one record at a time. Several types of forms are easily created using the Form Wizard. Columnar forms, tabular forms, justified forms, and main/subforms are the most commonly used types, but charts and pivot tables are also easy to create. You can view any form in three ways: Design view, Form view, and Datasheet view. Fields can be arranged in a specific order to make data input easier and more accurate. Generally, it is easier to use forms to enter and edit data than to use the underlying table datasheets. You can also use Access filters to restrict records viewed in a form (or in a table or query datasheet) according to certain criteria.

Exercises

Use the Hunter River database contained in the Hunter97.mdb file on the Student Data Disk for these Exercises.

EXERCISE

4.1   Customer AutoForm

1. Use the AutoForm Columnar Wizard to create a form for the Customer table.
2. Print a copy of the data in the form.
3. Save the form with the name Exercise 4-1.

EXERCISE

4.2

Products Tabular Form

1. Create a tabular form for the Products table. Use the Clouds style.
2. Place only the following fields in the form in the order given, not the order in the table definition.

   `StockNumber; Vendor; UnitCost; QuantityOnHand`
3. Save the form with the name Exercise 4-2.
4. Print just the first page of this form.

EXERCISE

4.3

Expenses Columnar Form

1. Use the 1996 Expenses table to prepare a single-column standard form.
2. Use all fields in the default order.
3. Print a copy of the data in the form.
4. Save the form with the name Exercise 4-3.

EXERCISE

4.4

Vendor Products Main/Subform

1. Use the Vendors and Products tables to prepare a main/subform for Hunter River management. Which table should be used for the main portion of this form?
2. Which vendors do not have any products in the current Products file?
3. Can you tell whether there are any products that do not have a matching vendor in the Vendors file?
4. Save the form with the name Exercise 4-4.
5. Print a copy of the form for the Woods vendor only.

4.5   Employees Columnar Form

1. Use the Form Wizard to create a columnar form with all fields for the Employees table using the Standard style.

2. Save the form with the name Employee Information.

3. Print a copy of the form with data from the Employees table.

4.6   Orders Justified Form

1. Use the Form Wizard to create a justified form using the Orders table.

2. Save the form with the name Exercise 4-6.

3. Print a copy of the form with data from the Orders table.

4.7   Product/Vendor Pivot Table

In this Exercise, you will create the pivot table form shown earlier in Figure A4.9.

1. Select the Forms tab and click the New button.

2. Select Pivot Table Wizard and specify Products as the data source.

3. Add Category, Vendor, and QuantityOnHand fields for the pivot table.

4. When Excel opens and displays an image of the pivot table, drag Category to the COLUMN area, drag Vendor to ROW, and drag QuantityOnHand to DATA.

5. Click Finish, then save your pivot table as Exercise 4-7.

6. Print a copy of the pivot table.

4.8   Employee Photos Form

1. Select the Forms tab and click the New button.

2. Select Form Wizard, then specify `Employee Photos` as the data source. This table includes a small photograph of the employee as an OLE object field.

3. Add all the fields to the form.

4. Select the Columnar layout.

5. Select the Standard style.

6. Finish the form and save it as Employee Photo Form.

7. Print a copy of record 1 only. *(Hint: Use the File | Print command instead of clicking the Print button; use the Selected Record(s) option.)*

EXERCISE

4.9 Using Filter By Form (I)

In this Exercise you will use a filter (not a query) to display only records that meet certain criteria. For the purposes of this Exercise, answer the indicated questions and write down the record numbers that match the filter criteria. Use the Customers form.

1. Find the first occurrence of a customer from Martinsville.

2. Find all the customers whose zip codes begin with 478.

3. Find the *third* customer from Illinois.

4. Find the *last* customer from Indiana. What is the simple way to do this with just one Find command?

5. Find the customer whose first name is Kelsey.

EXERCISE

4.10 Using Filter By Form (II)

In this Exercise, you will use a filter (not a query) to display only records that meet certain criteria. For the purposes of this Exercise, answer the indicated questions and write down the record numbers that match the filter criteria. Use the Employee Entry form.

1. How many employees work in the Sales department?

2. How many employees work in Sales and have been hired since January 1, 1995?

3. Which employees earn at least $25,000 per year?

4. Which employees earn no more than $20,000 per year *or* work in the Sales department?

Physicians' Medical Clinic: Building a Form to View Data

Because of the large number of lengthy fields in the Patients table, Dr. Greenway of the Physicians' Medical Clinic has requested that you create a form to facilitate data entry. All fields in this table must be included in the form, but you have some latitude in the sequence and placement of fields on the form. Remember that the sequence should follow the order in which data are obtained from the patient. Use the PMC97.mdb database. Design your form on paper first, then use the Form Wizard to create the form. Save a copy of the blank form, then print a copy of the blank form. You will enter the following information for one patient. Do not type the hyphens in the Patient Number field. After you finish entering the data below, print the form for this patient.

```
555-12-9876   Henry, Kelsey J.   1552 Fifth Avenue      Paris, IL 61944

02/01/1950    State University   US Insurance Company   B-35524-9867
```

You have been told that it takes too long to enter all the information for new patients, and you have to streamline the data entry process. You know that most patients are from a single city and state, that probably 75 percent of new patients are employed by four major employers, and that three health insurance companies cover 80 to 90 percent of patients. Modify the design of the form to make use of this information.

Hunter River: Designing a Custom Form to Enter and View Customer Orders

Design a form to enter and view customer orders for Hunter River Sporting Goods. Your form should make use of data from at least four tables: Customers, Orders, Order Items, and Products. To help your thinking, locate an invoice or statement from some store or service. Analyze the overall layout of the invoice:

- Large type or the company's logo appears at the top.

- Information about the customer typically appears beneath the large type or the logo, along with information about the order such as order number, order date, and so forth.

- Information about line items appears in the middle of the invoice, including data fields from the Order Items and Products tables.

- The bottom of the invoice contains calculated amounts such as subtotal, sales tax, amount due, and so forth.

Sketch the layout for an on-screen form for a point-of-sale (POS) computerized cash register that will handle a customer order. Show the location of each field and its proportional length on the form layout. Indicate which fields are calculated values.

UNIT 5

Building a Report

This unit will illustrate the use of Access reports to display printed data from one or more Hunter River tables. In this unit, you will learn the report basics, including the types of reports available with the Report Wizard. You will create a simple report using the Report Wizard, then view that report in Print Preview. You will learn how to make manual changes to the report design. The unit includes a section on mailing labels, and concludes with a section on publishing Access reports in Microsoft Word.

Learning Objectives

At the completion of this unit, you should be able to

1. list the types of reports available in Access 97,

2. create a report with the Report Wizard,

3. create a grouped report with the Report Wizard,

4. make minor modifications to the report design,

5. build a sorted report,

6. create a mailing labels report,

7. publish an Access report in Microsoft Word.

Case Study

At Hunter River Sporting Goods, you have been asked to build reports to display printed data from one or more tables. The types of reports needed are mailing labels, employee service reports, group reports about products, and a vendor list. You may be required to publish these reports to the Internet.

Report Basics

Access reports provide a visually attractive means of presenting data in printed form, usually for all records in a table or query's datasheet. You can arrange the sequence of the data fields used and format the fields as desired. You can combine fields and create calculated fields. Totals and subtotals are available in Access reports.

Reports Versus Forms

Reports and forms are very similar. Both show records from one or more tables, but reports provide more control over the way printed data will appear. Reports also give you more flexibility for handling summarized data than do forms. While forms require you to create a main form with a related subform (each with its own table or query) to show detailed data, reports can group data within a single table or query.

Like forms, reports allow you to combine graphical information and Access controls. Most of the techniques used to build forms can also be used with reports, including AutoReport and the Report Wizard. However, reports are designed expressly for printing. They can be viewed on the screen only in Print Preview fashion. You cannot use a report to input or edit data as you can with a form.

The Report Design View Toolbars

Figure A5.1 shows the Report Design toolbar and Formatting toolbar. They share some buttons with Datasheet view and Form view. The top toolbar deals with the report as a whole, while the lower toolbar lets you make changes to the format of a selected object within the report. The Report Design view is covered later in this unit.

FIGURE A5.1
Report Design view and Formatting toolbars

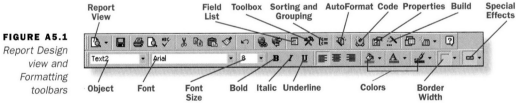

Creating a Report

In this section, we will discuss the types of reports and styles available through the Access Report Wizard.

Types of Reports

As with forms, Access organizes the development of reports to make it easy for novice users. Figure A5.2 shows the New Report Wizard dialog box.

FIGURE A5.2
*New Report
window*

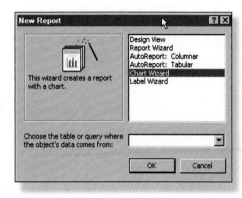

DESIGN VIEW

Design view represents the manual method for building a report. Here you start with a blank report and drag the various fields and controls to the report. This method lets you create a custom report to match a given situation, but is the most difficult to use. Occasionally, you will build the report with another method, then switch to Design view to modify the report as needed.

REPORT WIZARD

Access provides an easy-to-use tool called Report Wizard for creating reports. The Report Wizard leads you through an interview process, asking questions about what kind of report you wish to build and eliciting the appropriate information for the report. The Report Wizard options for grouping similar records, preparing subtotals, and sorting are described later in this unit.

AUTOREPORT COLUMNAR REPORT

The AutoReport columnar report automatically creates a single-column report with each field on a separate line and the field name to the left of the field value, running down the page in one long column. Columnar reports are used with many fields or with long fields. You can modify the report settings in Design view to display just one record per printed page.

AUTOREPORT TABULAR REPORT

The AutoReport tabular report displays data in columns, from left to right, similar to a tabular form. Each record appears in a new row. Labels appear at the top of each column. Tabular reports are useful when you have few fields or shorter fields. Figure A5.3 shows an AutoReport tabular report.

CHART WIZARD REPORT

The Chart Wizard report displays numeric information as a graph. The Form and Report Chart Wizards are very similar, invoking Microsoft Graph to create the chart using data that you specify.

FIGURE A5.3
AutoReport tabular report

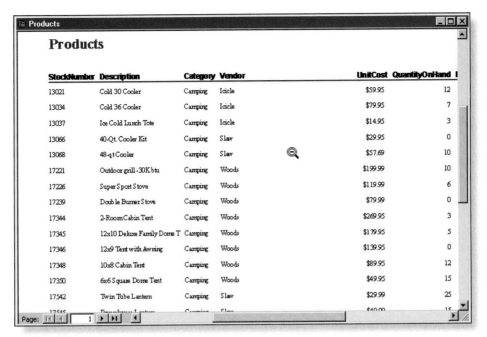

LABEL WIZARD REPORT

The Label Wizard report prepares mailing labels. Field values appear like entries on a mailing label, usually one per row, although there can be one or more labels across the page in a grid, depending on the size of the label and the paper used. Access does not print field labels with this report type. Mailing labels are particularly useful when printing labels for envelopes, but are also useful for displaying short blocks of related data on regular paper when the other two types are not appropriate.

GUIDED ACTIVITY

5.1 Creating a Report with AutoReport

In this Guided Activity, you will use AutoReport to create a tabular report.

1. Start Windows and load Access.

2. Use the File | Open Database command to open the Hunter97.mdb database. This database can be found on the Student Data Disk.

3. Click the Reports tab in the Database window to display the reports stored in the database.

4. Click the New button to open the New Report window, previously shown in Figure A5.2.

5. Select AutoReport: Tabular.

6. Click the down arrow in the table or query box at the bottom of the New Report window and choose the Products table.

7. Click OK to activate AutoReport.

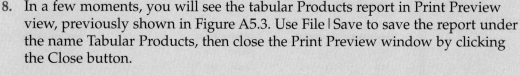

8. In a few moments, you will see the tabular Products report in Print Preview view, previously shown in Figure A5.3. Use File | Save to save the report under the name Tabular Products, then close the Print Preview window by clicking the Close button.

NOTE *If the Tabular Products report already exists in your copy of Hunter97.mdb, you may replace it with this report.*

Using the Report Wizard

As with the Form Wizard, you can use the Report Wizard to create a variety of report formats. This section will cover the use of the Report Wizard to create reports. The subsequent Guided Activities will help you to easily build your own semi-custom reports.

Steps in Building a Report with the Report Wizard

The Report Wizard helps you create the report by presenting a series of questions. As you fill in the answers to these questions, the report design is created automatically. You do not have to remember long steps on your own when using the Report Wizard to build a report.

Although the report created in the process is complete, you may want to make some changes to its design. You can use Report Design view to make corrections manually, or use the Report Wizard and build a new report with the desired features. This unit covers making only minor manual changes in Report Design view.

Before starting the Report Wizard, you should open the Database window for your database, then select the Reports tab in the Database window. To create a report, click the New button. Then answer the questions presented by the Report Wizard.

When using the Report Wizard, you must provide the following information:

■ Which table or query the report will use for its data source; this binds the report to its data source (you can use a query to limit reports to certain records)

■ Order of fields to place in the report

■ Fields to group by (optional)

■ Fields to sort on (optional)

■ Summary calculations such as Sum, Avg, Min, Max (optional)

■ Report layout (Stepped, Block, Outline 1, Outline 2, Align Left 1, Align Left 2), print orientation (Portrait or Landscape), and whether to adjust field widths to fit the report on one page

■ Which style to use (Bold, Casual, Compact, Corporate, Formal, Soft Gray)

■ Title to appear at the top of the report

■ Whether to preview the report or modify its design

Report Fields

As with Access forms, the first step is to specify the fields for the report. You can select them one at a time with the > button, or choose all fields with the >> button. Most Access reports are tabular, with the fields appearing across the page similar to a datasheet. Take care in choosing your fields so that they all fit across the page.

Grouping Levels

The group report resembles the datasheet or tabular form. Field name or caption labels appear as column headings, spread across the page. Field values appear beneath the headings, one row per record, with groups of data that share a common value such as product category, employee department, and so forth. You can choose more than one level of grouping. It is not necessary to specify a group field.

Sort Order

You can specify up to four fields to sort your report by, in ascending or descending order. For instance, you can sort mailing labels by zip code to take advantage of lower postage rates. Sales reports might be sorted by salesperson, date, and territory. A product report could be sorted by category and stock number. It is not necessary to specify a sort field.

Summary Options

The summary options are used to calculate summaries for groups of records. You can choose among sum, average, minimum, and maximum calculations, and can display the calculated values in the group footer section of the report. You can display only the calculated values in the report, or show them with the detail record values. Use the Summary Options button in the Sort Order window to select the summary options.

Report Layout

As with Access forms, you can choose from several layouts using the Report Wizard. The layouts include Stepped (the default), Block, Outline 1, Outline 2, Align Left 1, and Align Left 2. You can also choose between Portrait (upright) and Landscape (sideways) page orientation. Access has the ability to adjust field widths so that all fit on a single page—a very useful feature. As you select a layout, the Form Wizard shows you how your report will look with that layout.

Report Styles

After you specify the report layout, the Report Wizard asks you what style you want to use. These styles do not affect the data or the fields in the reports, only the way they appear on paper. As you create the report with the Report Wizard, Access will show you a preview of the report in the style you have chosen. In most cases, you can "back up" by clicking the Back button and change your selection to a different style.

The default style is Compact, in which the title and field labels appear in bold text. Other styles include Bold, Casual, Corporate, Formal, and Soft Gray. Access may use different fonts in different styles. The best way to choose among report styles is to print a page in each style and select the one that best fits your application.

Previewing and Printing the Report

After you have specified this information, Access will give you a chance to preview your report or to make changes to its design. The procedure is essentially the same as with other Access data objects: after selecting the report to preview, click the Print Preview button in the toolbar. Access will generate an image of the report for the screen and allow you to zoom in on any portion for close scrutiny—for example, a subtotal. The navigation buttons at the bottom of the preview window can be used to select other pages of the report. You may want to check the last page to see end-of-report grand totals. You can then send the report to the printer or cancel the preview command and return to the Report window.

If you have saved a report in the database, you can still preview the report before printing it. In the Database window, highlight the report's name, then click the Preview button in the Database window.

Saving the Report

Finally, you must give the report a name and save it in the database. The File | Save command is ordinarily used to save the report design. If you close the Report window without saving the report design, Access will prompt you to save the report or cancel the Close command.

GUIDED ACTIVITY

5.2   Creating a Report with Report Wizard

In this Guided Activity, you will use the Report Wizard to create a group report and preview it on the screen.

1. If Windows is not already open, start it and load Access.

2. Use the File | Open Database command to open the Hunter97.mdb database.

3. Click the Reports tab in the Database window to switch to Report mode. Click the New button to open the New Report window, previously shown in Figure A5.2.

4. Select Report Wizard in the New Report window. Click OK to start the Report Wizard.

5. Click the selector button to the right of the Tables/Queries box at the top of the next Report Wizard dialog box. Access displays an alphabetical list of all the tables and queries associated with the current database. Click once in the Products table.

6. Access will display the available fields at the left and the selected fields at the right. You can add fields one at a time, or click the >> button to add all the fields from the Products table in the order in which they were placed in the table definition. See Figure A5.4.

FIGURE A5.4
*Field selection
window*

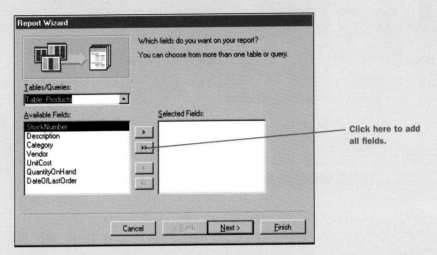

7. For this example, click the >> button to add all fields to the report. Click Next to go to the next step.

8. Next, Access asks you to specify a field to group the report by. Highlight the Category field and click the > button. The Report Wizard shows you that it will group data by this field, shown in Figure A5.5. Click Next to go to the next step.

FIGURE A5.5
*Grouping level
window*

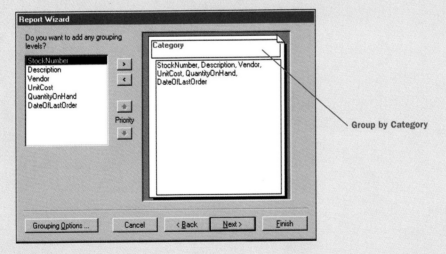

9. Access asks you to specify fields to sort on, as shown in Figure A5.6. In the first sort box, select UnitCost as the primary sort field. Click the sort order button at the right of the sort box; it will change to a descending sort.

10. Click the Summary Options button in the lower part of the window. Figure A5.7 shows the Summary Options dialog box, where you can choose among sum, average, minimum, and maximum. Click the Avg check box for the

FIGURE A5.6
Sort order window

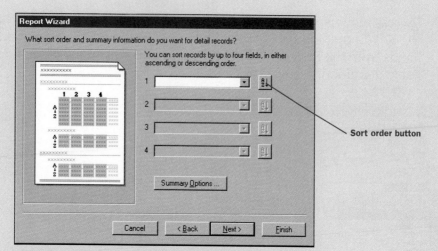

FIGURE A5.6
Sort order window

Sort order button

FIGURE A5.7
*Summary Options
window*

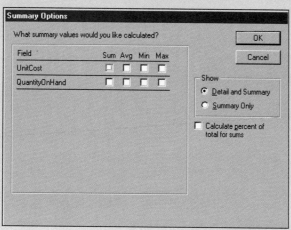

UnitCost field. Click OK to return to the sorting window, then click Next to go on to the next step.

11. Next, you need to specify the layout for your report. Keep the default Stepped layout. The Report Wizard dialog box will next show you a picture of the currently selected layout in the left portion of the window, as you see in Figure A5.8. Choose the Landscape print orientation. Click Next.

12. Now you can specify the style for your report. For now, let us keep the default Bold style. Click Next to go to the last step.

13. In the report title box, type Products by Category. The title appears at the top of the first page of the report. Access will also save the report design under this name in the Hunter97 database.

14. Click the Finish button to see a preview of the printed version on the screen, shown at 70% of actual size in Figure A5.9. The system date when the report is printed and the page number appear in the lower part of the report.

NOTE   *If the Products by Category report already exists in your copy of Hunter97.mdb, you may replace it with this report.*

FIGURE A5.8
*Layout/Orientation
window*

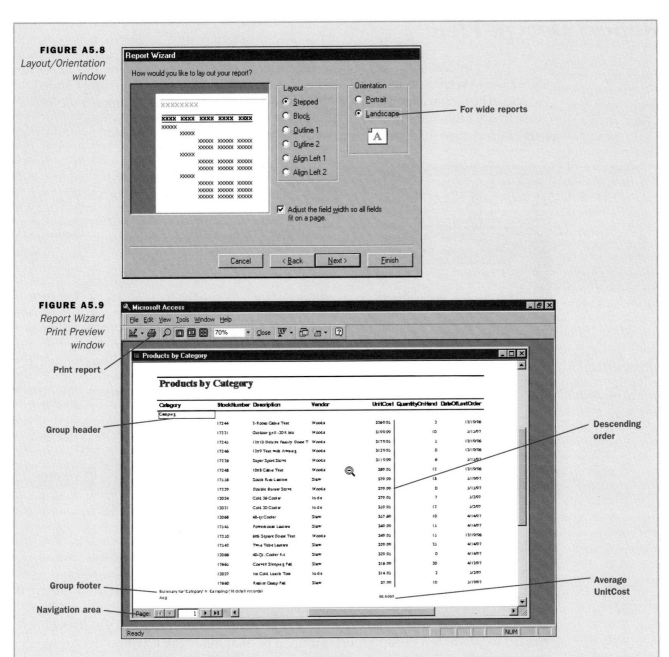

FIGURE A5.9
*Report Wizard
Print Preview
window*

Print report

Group header

Group footer

Navigation area

**Descending
order**

**Average
UnitCost**

15. You can use the magnifying glass pointer to zoom in or out on a section of the report. Use the navigation buttons at the bottom of the window to scroll to various pages of the report.

NOTE *If your computer has a printer attached, click the Print button to send the output to the printer.*

16. Use the File | Close command to close the Report window and return to the Database window.

Report Design View

You may be interested in seeing how Access represents the report design. Figure A5.10 shows the Design view for the Products by Category report of the preceding Guided Activity. The Control toolbox covers up a small portion of the last few report sections. You can drag the title bar of the toolbox to a new location so that it does not hide a part of the design that you want to work with, or turn it off temporarily.

FIGURE A5.10
Report Design view window

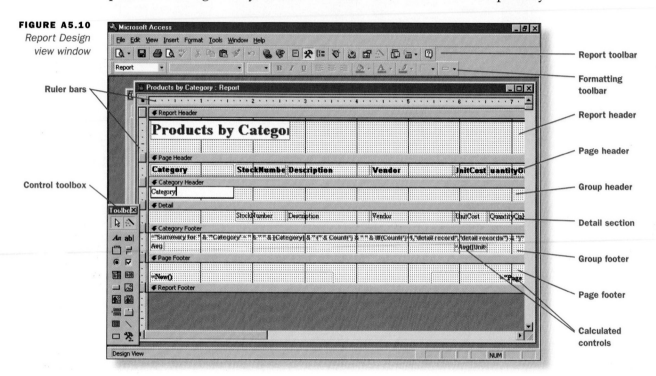

Report Sections

Like many other database management products, Access uses a report section structure to hold parts of the design. The Products by Category report, described below, has seven sections. All but the Category header and footer sections are standard in all reports. The Category header is present because we asked the Report Wizard to produce a group report, grouped by that field. The Category footer holds the average UnitCost summary that we requested in the Report Wizard.

Report sections help you organize the information that goes into the report. Fields and other controls are placed in the sections as needed. A control's section will determine where and how often that control is printed in the report. Report sections are very similar to form sections, discussed in Unit 4. A discussion of each section follows.

REPORT HEADER SECTION

The report header section contains information that is printed only on the first page of the report. The Report Wizard places the report title in the report header section, along with horizontal rule lines that separate the title from the rest of the report. You might want to place a logo or other graphic in the report header section as well.

TIP

If you want the report title to print on all pages of the report, move it from the report header section to the page header section.

PAGE HEADER SECTION

The page header section appears at the top of every page of the report except the first page, where it appears just beneath the report header. Place column headings in this section for tabular reports. The Report Wizard was able to squeeze the field names into the page header section because we chose landscape orientation. If you are creating a custom report, place long field-name column headings on two or more lines.

GROUP (CATEGORY) HEADER SECTION

The group header section appears at the beginning of a new group of records. The field *name* used for grouping (in this case, Category) is displayed in a text box in Design view. Access substitutes the value of the group by field in the actual report output. Access normally leaves a blank line before a new group begins, but you can override that to start a new group on a new page. You will see this demonstrated in Guided Activity 5.4.

DETAIL SECTION

The detail section contains the values for fields you have chosen for the report, one record per line in the detail section. Tabular reports display fields side by side, so a long field will take up considerable room in the detail section. In such a case, you might choose to display less than the full field or to spread the field over two or more lines.

GROUP FOOTER SECTION

The group footer section appears at the end of a group of records. You can add group totals in this section, or display a count of the number of records in the group. Unless you specify summary options in the Report Wizard, the group footer section will not appear.

PAGE FOOTER SECTION

The page footer section appears at the bottom of each page in the report. The Report Wizard places the system date and page number fields in it. You can also use it for additional information not contained in the report title. Not all users will need a page footer.

REPORT FOOTER SECTION

The report footer section appears at the end of the report, on the last page. You can use it for report totals and record counts. The report footer section will appear before the page footer on the last page of the report. Because we did not specify totals or subtotals in the preceding Guided Activity, the Report Wizard did not create a report footer section.

Making Changes in Report Design View

As we suggested with Access Form Wizard forms in Unit 4, it may be necessary even for casual users to make some slight modifications to the report design provided by the Report Wizard.

To make changes to the report's design, highlight the report name and click the Design View button in Report mode of the Database window. You can move, resize, or delete controls in the design by clicking their corresponding Design view. The following Guided Activity will show how to make a few changes to the design without going into detailed Report Design view instructions.

GUIDED ACTIVITY

5.3   Changing the Report Design Manually

In this Guided Activity, you will make three small changes to the Products by Category report design created by the Report Wizard in the preceding Guided Activity.

1. In the Hunter97 Database window, switch to Report mode.

2. Highlight the Products by Category report name. Click the Design View button to open Report Design view. You should see the same screen previously shown in Figure A5.10.

3. With the mouse, click once in the label box containing the title of the report in the report header section. Wait a second, then click once more. The insertion point cursor should be blinking in the label box. If a report property box appears instead, click one more time in the label box to open the label box for editing.

4. Use the arrow keys (or the mouse) to move the pointer to the letter b in by. Change this letter to a capital B and press **Enter**.

5. Next, click once in the box in the page header containing DateOfLastOrder.

 NOTE   *The upper left handle at the edge of this box will let you move the control. The other seven handles let you resize the control.*

6. Highlight, then delete the DateOf portion of this label control by pressing the **Del** key.

7. Repeat the process to delete the Quantity portion of the QuantityOnHand label in the same section.

8. To view your efforts, click the Print Preview button. (Or use the File | Print Preview command in the menu bar.) Click the Two Pages button in the Print Preview toolbar to see two side-by-side pages of the report, as shown in Figure A5.11.

9. You should see that the report title has been modified and that the two column heading labels were shortened.

FIGURE A5.11
*Two-page preview
for modified report*

Two-page display

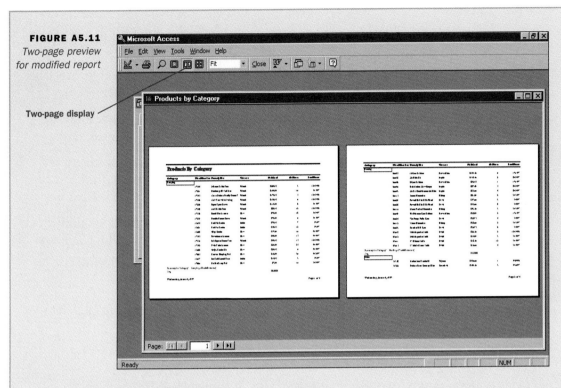

10. Use the File | Save As/Export command to save the changes made to the report design. When prompted, use Modified Products by Category as the name. Close the Report window.

 NOTE *If the Modified Products by Category report already exists in your copy of Hunter97.mdb, you may replace it with this report.*

The following activity will give you a chance to build a more complicated sorted groups/totals report with the Report Wizard.

GUIDED ACTIVITY

5.4

Building a Sorted Group Report with Totals

In this Guided Activity, you will use the Report Wizard to create a report with two group levels and subtotals.

1. Open the Hunter97 Database window and click the Reports tab.

2. Click the New button to create a new report.

3. Select the Report Wizard and click OK.

4. In the Tables/Queries combo box of the initial Report Wizard dialog box, select the query called Inventory Value. Only records that match this query will appear in the report.

5. Add these fields in the order specified: Category, Vendor, Description, and Expr1. The Expr1 field is an expression, calculated in the query as [UnitCost]*[QuantityOnHand] for each product in the Products table. We will not use the DateOfLastOrder field. Click Next to go to the next screen.

6. In the next Report Wizard dialog box, click > to specify these fields to group by, in the order given: Category, Vendor. Click Next to go to the next step.

7. Now sort by the Expr1 field, so that items will appear by order of inventory value within each group and subgroup. Either type Expr1 in the first sort box or click the down arrow in that box and select Expr1. Do *not* click Next yet.

8. Click the Summary Options button to display the Summary Options dialog box. Click the Sum check box to display the sum of the Expr1 field. Click OK to return to the sorting window.

9. Click Next to go to the next step.

10. Use the Outline 1 layout for this report and Portrait orientation, then click Next.

11. Use the Corporate style. Click Next to go on to the next step.

12. The report title should be Inventory Value Group Report.

NOTE *If the Inventory Value Group Report already exists in your copy of Hunter97.mdb, you may replace it with* this *report.*

13. Click the Finish button to view your report, shown in Figure A5.12. Notice that the left side of the Expr1 field has been chopped off. The Expr1 label is not very informative.

FIGURE A5.12
Print Preview

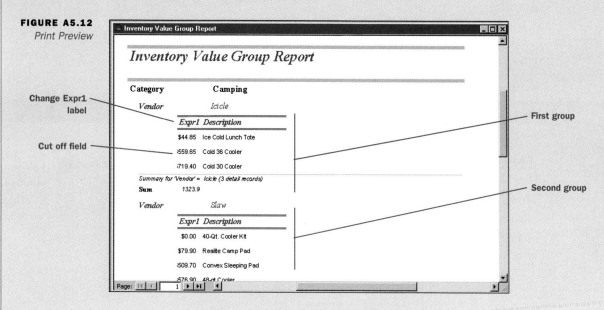

14. Click the Close button to close the Print Preview window and return to Design view for this report. You will see the design that the Report Wizard created for your report. In the next few steps, you will make corrections to the controls discussed in step 13.

15. In Design view, click twice *slowly* in the box containing Expr1 in the Vendor header section. (Make sure that you don't click the similar box in the detail section.)

16. Use the **Del** key to delete the letters `Expr1`. Then type `Inventory Value`. The box will expand to contain your new column heading label. Press **Enter** when you are finished.

 NOTE   *If you are not satisfied with the label `Expr1` as the column heading for inventory value, you can also go back to the query, change the column name there, and save the query. Then repeat this activity.*

17. Click the cut-off Expr1 text box control in the detail section. Drag its left move handle to the left so that the control starts at about .75 inches on the horizontal ruler.

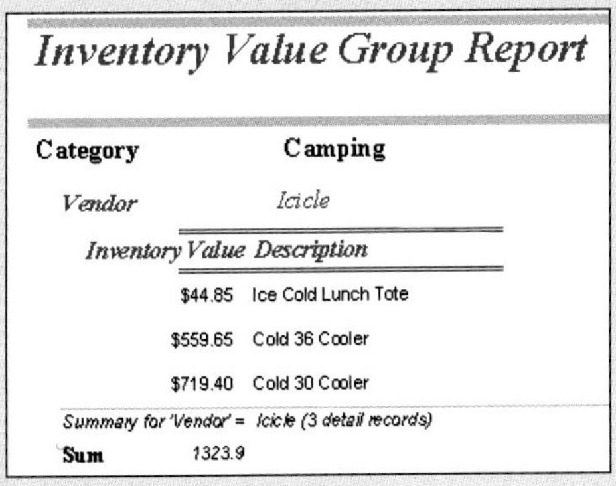

FIGURE A5.13
Corrected report in Print Preview

Inventory Value Group Report

Category   **Camping**

Vendor   *Icicle*

Inventory Value Description

$44.85   Ice Cold Lunch Tote

$559.65   Cold 36 Cooler

$719.40   Cold 30 Cooler

Summary for 'Vendor' = Icicle (3 detail records)
Sum   1323.9

18. Click the Print Preview button in the toolbar. Access shows you the modified report. If a printer is attached to your computer, print the report. Figure A5.13 shows a portion of the Print Preview window for this report.

19. Click the Save button. Close the Report Design window and return to the Database window.

Creating Mailing Labels

The Label Wizard requires a little more effort than the regular Report Wizard. Although the basic approach is the same, you must provide the dimensions of the labels to be used, and also specify which fields are to be placed on each line of the label design.

Using the Label Wizard

Figure A5.14 shows the mailing label format screen in the Label Wizard sequence. At the top is a picture of the general format of a label report. The left of the window shows the field list, with >> and << buttons to add those fields to the report design or remove them from it. At the right is a prototype label box that shows the label appearance as you add fields and punctuation to it. You can type in a text phrase and add that to the label format.

As you build the label format, the Label Wizard will create a report design similar to those of previous reports. In fact, after you preview the mailing labels and close the Print Preview window, Access will display the report design. Only three report sections appear in a mailing labels report design, and two of those are closed. The page header and page footer sections appear with no space allotted for them. Only the detail section contains field values.

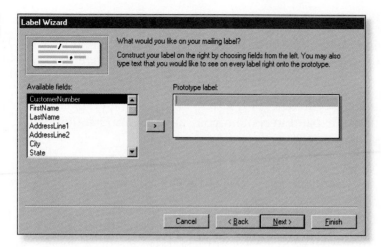

Making Changes to the Design

You can make changes to the report design as needed. For instance, some laser and inkjet printers are unable to print on the top ½ inch of the page. Access may "chop off" the top portion of the labels if printed with such printers. To remedy this problem in Design view, drag the border of the page header section down about ½ inch, creating a blank header for the top of each page. The laser printer will skip down about ½ inch before printing the first row of labels. Of course, you must properly align the blank labels in the printer to ensure that they line up with the printed text. Dot-matrix printers are usually able to print to the edge of the page and do not suffer from the "chopped-off" effect. (See more about margins in the next section.)

Adjusting the Printer Setup

With the Page Setup window, you can set the page margins for a particular report. Highlight the report name in the Database window, then give the File | Page Setup command from the menu bar. The first Page Setup window is shown in Figure A5.15. You can change left, right, top, and bottom margins in this window.

FIGURE A5.16
*Page Setup
Orientation*

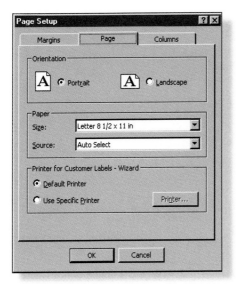

FIGURE A5.17
*Page Setup
Columns*

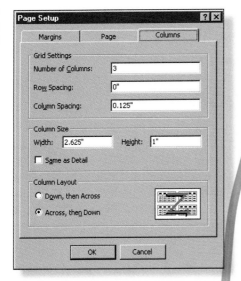

To see additional report choices for mailing labels, click the Page tab, shown in Figure A5.16. You can choose the printer for your report and tell the printer whether you want the report orientation to be portrait or landscape. Landscape (horizontal) orientation will print the page sideways, or 11" × 8 ½"; the default is portrait (vertical), or 8 ½" × 11". Not all printers are capable of printing in landscape mode.

Click the Columns tab shown in Figure A5.17 to see more choices for mailing labels. Access will display information about the number of columns in the mailing labels grid along with the column and row spacing for the grid. You can also choose whether to use the standard horizontal layout or a vertical layout, in which the labels are printed down the page rather than across the page. Any changes made here are stored in the report design.

Printing the Labels

When you print the mailing labels report, Access will substitute the values from each record into the report, filling in the labels from left to right if you have selected a label design with multiple labels per row. Trailing blanks in text fields are automatically trimmed when they are inserted in the report. If the *entire* row of a label is blank, Access will skip that row and move lower rows up in its place. For example, you may need to keep two lines for street addresses; the first line might be used as an office or suite number, and the second line for a building name or a street address. If a record does not need the second line, Access will simply omit it from the label report. The following Guided Activity will demonstrate this feature.

TEST FIRST!

GUIDED ACTIVITY

5.5   Creating a Mailing Labels Report

This Guided Activity will demonstrate how to create a mailing labels report using the Label Wizard.

1. Load Access, and open the Hunter97.mdb database. Click the Reports tab.

2. Click the New button to create a new report.

3. Select the Label Wizard report type, then select the Customers table in the Tables/Queries combo box. Click OK to go to the next screen.

4. In the first Label Wizard screen, you should specify the dimensions of your labels. Access provides the Avery brand label stock codes for more than 60 different sizes of labels. First select the Sheet Feed label type button, then scroll through the list until you find the correct size. In this case, we will use the Avery 5160 1" × 2 ⅝" × 3 across. This means there are three labels across (called "3-up"); each label is 1" high and 2 ⅝" wide. With standard fonts, you can print approximately 5 or 6 lines on each label, with about 25 to 30 characters on each line. With smaller, proportionally spaced fonts, you can squeeze more information onto each label. Now click Next.

NOTE *The Customize button can be used to create a custom label specification.*

5. The next screen lets you choose the font name, size, weight, and text color. Click Next to accept the default values (Arial, 8 point, Light, black color) for these font settings.

6. Access will display the label formatting screen and ask you to select fields for the label. Select the FirstName field, then click the > button to place that field on the first row of the label. Notice that Access shows you this field in the prototype label box at the right of the window.

7. Any text you type is placed directly in the label design. Press the **Spacebar** to place one space after the FirstName field. Then add the LastName field to the first row of the label. If you make a mistake, use the **Backspace** key to remove the last item placed in the label format.

8. Press **Enter** to go to the second line of the label.

9. Select the AddressLine1 field and place it on the second line of the label. Press **Enter** to go to the third line of the label.

10. Select the AddressLine2 field for the third line of the label. Press **Enter** to go to the fourth line.

11. On the fourth line, place the following fields and punctuation. Remember to click the > button after you select each field.

```
City<comma><Space>State<Space><Space>PostalCode<Space>
Country<Enter>
```

12. Figure A5.18 shows the completed label format. Review the label appearance box and make any corrections necessary. When you are finished, click the Next button to go to the next step.

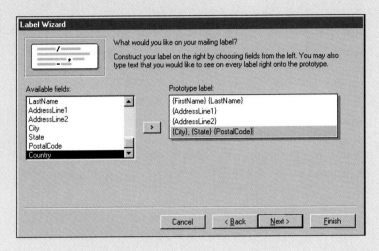

13. Access will ask for fields to sort the output on. Select the PostalCode (zip code) field and click the > button to sort on it. Click Next to go to the next screen.

14. Next, enter the title for the mailing labels report as 3-Up Customer Labels.

NOTE *If the 3-Up Customer Labels report already exists in your copy of Hunter97.mdb, you may replace it with this report.*

15. Click the Finish button to view the labels that Access prepares. If a printer is attached to your computer, print the labels. Figure A5.19 shows the labels from

16. Close the Print Preview window. Access will display Design view for your labels. Close this window and return to the Hunter97 Database window. If you are not ready to work the Exercises in this unit, close the Hunter97 database.

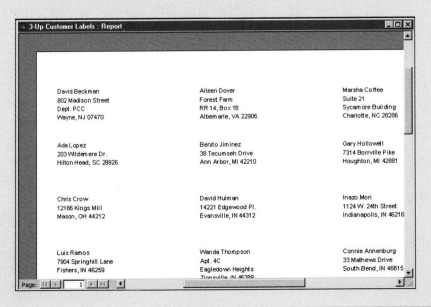

Publishing a Report with Word

You can publish an Access 97 report with Microsoft Word using the Tools | Office Links | Publish It With MS Word command, or click the same button in the toolbar. Simply highlight the report, then click the Word button. Access will automatically create a word processing file with the same name as the report, but with an RTF (rich text format) extension—and open Microsoft Word. Then you can add new formats, change fonts, adjust margins, and create other special effects that Access itself is unable to provide. When you are finished, you can save the Word document or print it.

Access also supports the Merge It With MS Word command, which is appropriate when you want to merge print Access data (from a table or query) in Word. Select the data source, then click the appropriate Office Links button. The Mail Merge Wizard will begin, and will lead you through the process of creating a source document that calls for values of Access data fields.

SUMMARY

Unlike forms, reports are used primarily for the printed page, not on the screen. Like forms, they are easily created using AutoReport and the Report Wizard. Several types of reports may be created with the wizard. While a columnar report shows many fields in a vertical list, a tabular report arranges fields horizontally, across the page. Reports can also be used to create charts and mailing labels using data values from the database.

In creating reports, you are given options not only to choose the type of report to create but also to specify which fields are placed where, whether fields are grouped into categories or sorted, and whether any summary calculations should be made. You can also add a title to the report.

Print Preview is used to see the results of the report on-screen before printing. Design view shows many of the same tools and controls that you saw in Design view for forms. The standard sections of a report and their functions are listed below:

- Report header shows titles and text to be printed once at the beginning of the report.

- Page header prints information at the top of every page.

- Group header prints the category for each grouped section.

- Detail section contains the specific fields of data from each record.

- Group footer is used to print subtotals and counts of values for each grouped section.

- Page footer prints at the bottom of every page.

- Report footer contains grand totals or any text displayed once at the end of the report.

Exercises

Use the Hunter River database contained within the Hunter97.mdb file on the Student Data Disk for these Exercises.

EXERCISE

5.1   Vendors AutoReport

1. Use the AutoReport feature to create a tabular report for Vendors.
2. Print the report and save a copy as Exercise 5-1.

EXERCISE

5.2   Salary Group Report

1. Use the Report Wizard to prepare a group report showing employee salaries by department.
2. Within each department, sort alphabetically.
3. Save the report design as Exercise 5-2.
4. Print a copy of your report.

EXERCISE

5.3   Customers Group Report

1. Create a group report for the Customers table based on the State field.
2. Include all fields except Customer Number and Country.
3. Print the report and save a copy as Exercise 5-3.

EXERCISE

5.4   Customers Sorted Mailing Labels

1. Create a set of mailing labels for the Customers table, but limit the labels to Indiana and Illinois only. (*Hint*: Use a query.)

2. Labels should appear in Postal Code (zip code) order.

3. Print the report and save a copy as Exercise 5-4.

5.5   Employees Tabular Report

1. Use the Employees table to prepare a tabular report.

2. Include all the fields in the report, but do not present groups or totals.

3. Use a suitable title for your report.

4. Print the report.

5. Save the report design as Exercise 5-5.

5.6   Vendor Mailing Labels

1. Use the Report Wizard to create a Vendors mailing label report.

2. Assume three-across labels (Avery 5160 is a good choice for sheet-feed printers).

3. Use the first six fields in the table in the customary mailing label format, with City, State, and Zip code together on the fourth line.

4. Save the report as Exercise 5-6.

5. Print a copy of your report.

5.7   Product Catalog Published in Word

In this Exercise, you will create an Access report, then publish it in Microsoft Word.

1. Create a product report in mailing label format showing the following items:

```
Stock Number    Category    (three spaces between fields)
Description
UnitCost    Vendor
```

2. The format should be three-across labels, and should be sorted by the Category field.

3. Save the report as Product Catalog.

4. Print a copy from Access.

5. Use the Access Publish It With MS Word command to prepare this report in Word. Access will create a file called Product Catalog.rtf, then open that file in Microsoft Word.

6. Add a header to the catalog document in Word. The left portion should be Hunter River Sporting Goods. The middle portion should be Product Catalog. The right portion should be Page followed by the page number button (#).

7. Add a footer to the catalog document in Word. It should contain the current date, centered.

8. Print a copy of your product catalog document in Word.

9. Save the changes to the Product Catalog.rtf file.

EXERCISE

5.8   Employee Service Web Document

1. Create a report showing years of service of employees. You may choose which other fields are to be included.

2. Save the report as Exercise 5-8.

3. Publish this report as an HTML document.

4. Print a copy of the report with your Web browser. How is this output different from the normal Access report printout?

EXERCISE

5.9   Inventory Value Group Report (Design View Changes)

1. Open the Inventory Value Group Report that was created in Guided Activity 5.4.

2. Switch to Design view.

3. Change the Sum text box control's Format property to Currency. (Hint: click the Properties button while the Sum control is highlighted.) Widen the control by dragging its left side.

4. Repeat step 3 for the Grand Total Sum text box control.

5. Save the report as Exercise 5-9.

6. Print a copy of the report with your changes.

Physicians' Medical Clinic: Creating a Report

In this application, you will create a report to show information in various ways. You will open the PMC97 database, create a report with the Report Wizard, print the report, make changes and print the new report, and then repeat the process. Read the directions carefully. Clearly identify which output goes with which part of the application.

Dr. Greenway has asked that you create a group report that shows all the patients within each insurance company, sorted alphabetically. Include the patient name fields, zip code, patient number, date of birth, insurance company, and policy number. Print the report, then save its design.

After presenting the report to the administrator, you learn that he is really only interested in the patients from the US Insurance Company. Create an appropriate query and repeat the report from step 1. Of course, you will not have to use the group report type, but you should show the insurance company name in the report title.

The insurance office has asked that you create a set of mailing labels for all patients who have a positive balance forward. These should be 2-across labels and should show the name and address fields, and they must include the patient number. Sort the labels in ascending zip code order.

Hunter River: Publishing an Access Report on the Internet

You have been asked to publish a Products group report as a HTML document that can be viewed over the Internet. Use the Hunter 97 database and create the products group report including only those items whose current inventory value (quantity*unit cost) exceeds $200. Please include the name and address of the vendor for each item in the report. The officers of Hunter River want the information sorted from highest to lowest inventory value. Make sure that you save the report and publish it on the company Web site for the officers to view. Also obtain a printout of your HTML document.

A

Advanced Database Management with Access 97

PART TWO continues the development of database objects using Microsoft Access. While Part One focused on creation of tables, queries, forms, and reports with the wizards, Part Two examines customized database objects. Unit 6 allows you to create customized queries and introduces the concept of relational databases. Because similar Access controls are used in forms and reports, Unit 7 discusses working with these controls. Units 8 and 9 deal with how to create and edit custom forms and reports. Unit 10 shows how to embed pictures and graphic images in Access forms and reports and how to create charts using Microsoft Graph. Unit 11 shows how to create macros in Microsoft Access. Unit 12 deals with creating applications with Access and with the responsibilities of the database administrator. You learn how to import and export data in Unit 13. The final two units deal with creating applications with Access and with the responsibilities of the database administrator.

UNIT 6

Relational Database Concepts and Advanced Queries

This unit will extend the knowledge you have gained from previous units to allow you to create customized queries. It will formally introduce the relational database concept and show how tables can be joined together with a query. The Hunter River full relational database design will be presented. The unit covers action queries in which changes to tables are made through the Query view. A section on parameter queries illustrates preparation of queries whose criteria can be changed when the query is run. The chapter concludes with a brief discussion of SQL, the industry-standard Structured Query Language.

Learning Objectives

At the completion of this unit, you should be able to

1. explain the overall concept of a relational database,

2. list the kinds of action queries Access supports,

3. describe the purpose of a parameter query,

4. discuss the use of a crosstab query,

5. join tables with a query,

6. create an update query to make changes to a group of records,

7. use a delete query,

8. create a parameter query,

9. use the built-in Access SQL support.

Case Study

As database administrator at Hunter River, you have been asked to prepare queries that make changes to prices in the database for sale merchandise. Hunter management also needs to know if Access is capable of handling SQL queries.

Relational Database Concepts

In this book, until now, we have dealt primarily with individual tables. Real-world applications frequently involve multiple tables that must be joined to retrieve appropriate information. In fact, the Hunter97.mdb database is a good example of a relational database, in which data are stored in numerous two-dimensional tables that can be linked by matching common data values in several tables. For instance, we store permanent information about departments in a Department table, rather than storing that information in the Employees table; by joining the Department table to the Employees table, we gain access to that store of information when dealing with an employee in a given department.

Joining Separate Tables

Although there is a large body of formal mathematical literature concerning relational databases, they can be described more simply in common-sense terms. We want to establish a separate table for each entity in the system. That is, we want to store information about a single type of data object in a table for data objects of that type. If certain information is shared across most or all of the members of the data object group, we should place that information in a different table. Hence, we store information about individual employees in the Employees table; this could include employee number, name, address, date of birth, salary, and department name. Information about departments, such as department manager, department address, and department telephone number, could go into the Department table and not be *duplicated* for each member of that department. Both tables must contain a common value, department name, so that information about a given employee's department can be linked to that employee. Figure A6.1 shows the link between Products and Vendors.

FIGURE A6.1

Link between Products and Vendors tables

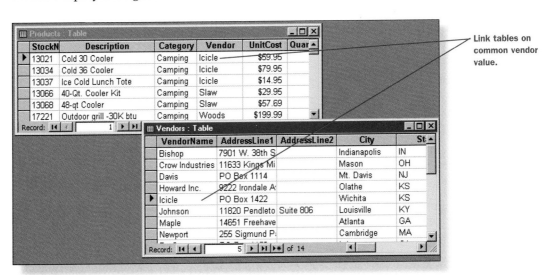

Link tables on common vendor value.

So far, we can describe the following tables in the Hunter97.mdb database: Products, Employees, Department, Customers, and Vendors. Products can be linked with the Vendors table by matching vendor name. Employees can be linked with Department by matching department name. We can introduce a table called Orders that will contain information about customer orders. It can be joined to the

Customers table by matching customer number. You might be tempted to use the customer name field for matching these two tables, but proper names are notoriously poor for providing *unique* identifiers. (Is there someone else at your university with your name?) We will develop the Hunter River relational model in more depth later in this unit.

Deciding What Fields Go into What Tables: Normalization

Database students usually have some difficulty at this point in the database design. Most database designers use a procedure called normalization, which begins with all fields in one huge table. Through the normalization process, fields are methodically moved into successively smaller tables until certain conditions have been met. Each stage of the process results in a normal form: first normal form, second normal form, third normal form, and so on. We will discuss the goals of the normalization process before giving some examples of the normalization result.

REPEATING GROUPS

We often encounter repeating groups of fields in a database. For instance, one customer may place several orders over a period of time. We could store all information about customers, including their orders, in a single table. But how can we define fields that describe an unknown number of orders? It becomes impossible to work with these data unless the order information is moved to a separate table. Thus, the Customers table would contain permanent information about the customer, which doesn't change from order to order (until, say, the customer moves). The Orders table would contain information about each order, such as order date, order number, customer number (but not customer name, which is contained in the Customers table), total amount of the order, and so on. If one customer placed five orders, there would be five records in the Orders table, one per order for that customer. As part of the normalization process, we move repeating groups of fields to their own separate table.

ANOMALIES AND REDUNDANCY

A normalized database is easier to work with than one that is not normalized. Certain anomalies, or irregularities, can occur when records are added to, modified in, or deleted from nonnormalized databases. Suppose *all* the data about departments were stored only in the Employees table. If Hunter River were to change a department manager's name, *every* employee record belonging to that department would have to be modified. If we place departmental data in a separate Department table, however, we need only change the manager's name in one place. Having the department manager's name in every employee record is redundant and should be avoided. Examine your tables for redundant information that can be placed in a separate table.

CALCULATED FIELDS

It is generally accepted that calculated fields are *not* stored separately in a table. Rather, when needed, these fields should be calculated from the underlying values that are stored in the record at hand. For instance, the calculation for grade point average (GPA) is given as total points divided by total credit hours. It is necessary to store the latter two items. When the GPA is desired, perform the operation. By eliminating redundant calculated fields, you will save storage space in the database.

There are instances, however, when storing a calculated field is desirable. In the GPA example, schools frequently group or sort by GPA. In such a case, the GPA would have to be calculated and stored, at least temporarily. Use your judgment when deciding whether to eliminate calculated fields from tables.

PARTIAL DEPENDENCY

Each field in a table should depend on the whole primary key, not just on a portion of that key. Suppose you had a table in which a concatenation (combining) of two fields was the primary key. To do this in Access, **Ctrl**-click the field selector buttons of the adjacent primary key fields, then click the Primary Key button on the toolbar. Access will place the key icon in front of both fields and treat their concatenation as the primary key.

For example, you might have an Order Items table that contains the individual products in one customer order. A customer purchases a basketball, a basketball rim with backboard, and a basketball goal pole. Although these items make up a single order, the order would have three repeating groups, and thus the line items in the order should be placed in a separate table. The primary key for the Order Items table would be the concatenation of order number and product number.

If the table is properly normalized, all the nonkey fields should depend on the *entire* concatenated key and not just on one of the key fields. If you placed the unit price field in the Order Items table, it would depend on the product number but *not* on the order number. Thus, there is a partial dependency in the Order Items table design. To resolve this problem, remove the unit price from the Order Items table and place it in the Products table, where the price depends only on the primary key, the product number. Can you think of an instance in which the unit price *would* depend on both the product number and the order number? In other words, when would you have a price for this particular order that is different from the standard price given in the Products table?

Putting It All Together

My database design advice for beginning students is to develop tables that meet the three normalization criteria. First, remove repeating groups and place them in their own table; look for redundant or duplicated information and place it in a master table, where information can be looked up when needed. Second, eliminate calculated fields that can easily be recalculated. Finally, examine each table to make sure that the entire primary key uniquely identifies each field in that table. If not, consider moving the field to another table in which it depends only on the full key. Other normalization rules can be found in database management textbooks. For a more thorough treatment, read more about this issue in such books. The three normalization criteria are as follows:

NORMAL FORM	DESCRIPTION
First Normal Form	Use a flat file structure without repeating groups. All Access tables are automatically in first normal form.
Second Normal Form	Data are in first normal form and there are no partial dependencies: no nonkey field depends on only part of the key.
Third Normal Form	Data are in second normal form and contain no transitive dependencies: no field depends on any other field that is not a key field.

Normalizing a database results in more tables, with fewer fields in each one. Most applications require that you join two or more tables to make use of their information at one time. As you pursue normalization, remember that it will take a short time for the computer to join the tables. Some database designers are willing to accept a slightly less normalized design in order to eliminate some of the links necessary when joining tables. However, with today's faster hardware, most database designers prefer the modeling advantages of normalized data structures.

Access Table Analyzer

You can use a relatively new Access feature to analyze the structures of your tables. It is called the Table Analyzer Wizard; you start it with the Tools | Analyze | Table command. It looks for duplicated information and attempts to split your original table into new tables in which each piece of information appears only once. You can adjust, accept, or reject the Wizard's suggestions. Because the Hunter97.mdb database is already normalized, we will not demonstrate the table analyzer at this time. Try it on one of your own nonnormalized databases.

The Hunter River Relational Model

This section will describe the tables used in the Hunter River relational database model. We can describe the base tables with their table names and field names, with the primary key coming first. For the purposes of this book, the primary key fields are shown in italics. It is not necessary that common fields used to link tables have the same name; rather, they must have the same value for the match to occur. By convention, we frequently use the same name in the table design, although it is not strictly necessary. For instance, we can use both *Stock Number* and *Product Number* to refer to the same field in different tables. Because Access permits the use of long, descriptive data names, we can accurately describe our fields. Some database packages restrict data names to 10 characters or fewer, making it more difficult to understand the precise definition of a field.

The base tables are as follows:

CUSTOMERS   (*CustomerNumber*, FirstName, LastName, AddressLine1, AddressLine2, City, State, PostalCode, Country)

ORDERS   (*OrderNumber*, CustomerNumber, OrderDate, TotalOrderAmount, EmployeeID, TaxableSale, MethodOfPayment)

ORDER ITEMS   (*OrderNumber, ProductNumber,* OrderQuantity)

PRODUCTS   (*StockNumber*, Description, Category, Vendor, UnitCost, QuantityOnHand, DateOfLastOrder)

EMPLOYEES   (*EmployeeID*, LastName, FirstName, MiddleInitial, Department, DateHired, Salary)

DEPARTMENT   (*Department*, Manager, Area, AnnualSales)

VENDORS   (*VendorName*, AddressLine1, AddressLine2, City, State, ZipCode, ContactPerson, TelephoneNumber)

Suppose we wanted to prepare an invoice for a customer order. At the top of the invoice would be the order number, order date, and customer information (name, address, and so on). In the middle of the invoice would be the items purchased for this order, one line per item. Each line would contain the item number, its description, the number of units purchased, the cost per unit, and the extended cost obtained by multiplying the number of units by the unit cost. At the bottom of the invoice would be a subtotal for the items ordered, plus the sales tax information.

How would we obtain this information? First, decide which table is the most important. Because we are preparing an invoice for a specific order, the Orders table is most important. Notice that the Orders table can be joined to the Customers table by the CustomerNumber field in each table. Next, we want only those Order Items that match this order number. Notice that the OrderNumber field is present in both the Orders and Order Items tables. Finally, for each line item we will need to look up the description and unit cost from the Products table, matching ProductNumber in the Order Items table with StockNumber in the Products table. These relationships are summarized graphically in the Relationships window, shown in Figure A6.2. We will describe the Tools | Relationships command later in this unit.

FIGURE A6.2
Relationships window for Hunter River relational design

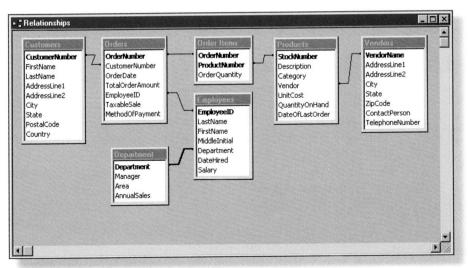

The PMC Relational Model

Recall the Physicians' Medical Clinic (I) application. You were asked to design a database that met the needs of patient medical data, billing, and insurance. This section will sketch out a possible relational model that meets these needs. Not all the details are given; some are left as an exercise for you. This model is similar to the Hunter River model.

The main tables are Patients, Visits, Payments, Procedures, Insurers, and Doctors. The Patients table corresponds to the Customers table from the Hunter River example. The Visits table corresponds to the Order Items table; we can assume that a patient visit represents a single line item such as a checkup, X ray, or the like. The Procedures table corresponds to the Products table and represents the list of possible procedures, their descriptions, and their costs. When a patient comes to the clinic, the doctor fills out a form and checks off the procedure after it is completed. If you want to allow more than one line item per visit, break the Visits table into two tables, Visits and Visit Items. The Payments table includes payments and insurer reimbursements.

How will we relate the tables? Patients are linked to the Visits table by matching the patient number. The Visits table contains a procedure number that allows a lookup in the Procedures table. To prepare an insurance billing, the patient's insurance company from the Patients table can be used to look up the matching name in the Insurers table. The PMC Relationships window is shown in Figure A6.3.

FIGURE A6.3
Relationships window for PMC database

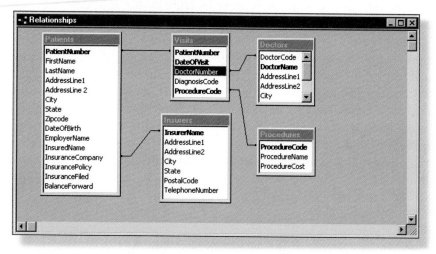

Joining Multiple Tables with a Query

In previous units, we have seen how a simple select query can select records from one or more tables. The tables appear in the top portion of the Query window. We can use the drag method to join the two matching fields; Access will draw a line between these fields, representing the fact that the tables are now joined. As you move the pointer in one datasheet, Access will attempt to move the pointer in the other table so that the linked fields maintain the *same*, common values. The best way to illustrate this is with an example, shown in the following Guided Activity.

GUIDED ACTIVITY

6.1 Using a Query to Join Two Tables

In this Guided Activity, we will create a query that joins the Employees and Department tables.

1. Begin Windows 95 and load Access as usual. Open the Hunter97.mdb database.

2. Click the Queries tab and click the New button. Then select Design View and click OK to manually create a new query. The Query Wizard can be used for some of the advanced queries, discussed later in this unit.

3. Add the Employees table and the Department table in the Show Table dialog box. Click Close to signify that you are finished adding tables.

4. Because they have the same name, Access will automatically draw a line between the two Department fields, as shown in Figure A6.4. This link is called a join line. If the fields to be joined have different names, you could drag a field from one table onto the other table, then release the left mouse button, to create the join line.

FIGURE A6.4
Joined tables in Query window

Join line

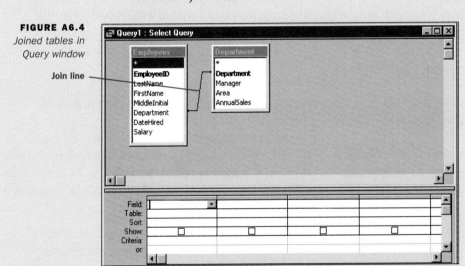

 NOTE *The join line is also drawn automatically if there is a relationship between two tables.*

5. Select the following Employees table fields for the design grid: Department, FirstName, LastName, and Salary. Drag each to the design grid.

6. Drag the Manager field from the Department table to the design grid.

7. Run the query by clicking the exclamation point (Run) button on the toolbar (or click the Datasheet button on the toolbar). The resulting datasheet is shown in Figure A6.5. Notice that Access has pulled the correct manager for each employee's department, as a result of the join you created above.

8. Save this query as Employees with Managers, then close the Query window.

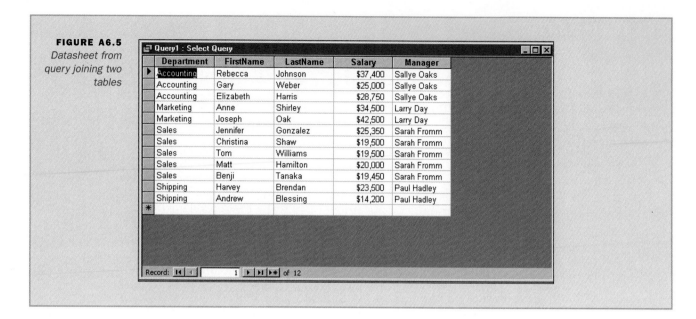

FIGURE A6.5
Datasheet from query joining two tables

Types of Joins with a Query

Three kinds of joins are possible with Access queries: inner joins, outer joins, and self-joins. You can control whether records that *don't* match are included in the query, as explained below.

INNER JOINS

Unless otherwise instructed, Access will match up all combinations of matching records in the two tables. Called an inner join, this join creates as many rows in the resulting datasheet as there are matching combinations in the two joined tables. In the preceding example, there are 13 employees and 7 departments. There are 12 rows in the datasheet: all employees but one have a matching department, so 12 employee records were selected. One of the employee records had a department (Maintenanc) that does not exist, so that employee does *not* appear in the inner join.

NOTE

The match must be exact—if there were a Maintenance department in the Department table, that would not *match "Maintenanc." We will discuss the concept of referential integrity shortly.*

OUTER JOINS

Not all the departments appear in the inner join: only four of the departments are now represented by employees. The three departments without listed employees—Management, Purchasing, and Other—are not shown. To include these departments without matching employees, you can create an outer join. To create this type of join, double-click the join line between the two tables to bring up the Join Properties dialog box, shown in Figure A6.6. Choice 1, the default, produced the inner join we created in the preceding example.

There are two possible outer joins with this query. Clicking on choice 2 will display all departments whether or not there are employees that match; departments without employees will be displayed with just a Manager listed. Choice 3 will

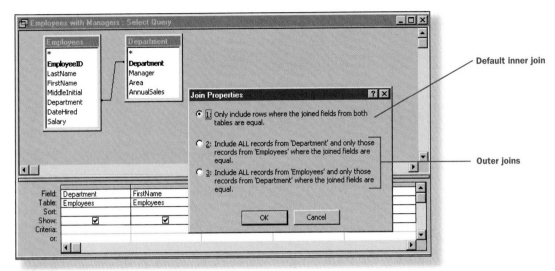

Default inner join

Outer joins

display all employees whether or not there are departments that match. Figure A6.7 shows the query datasheet for choice 2. Notice the missing employee information for three departments. If you had pulled the Department field from the Department table, the department's name would appear in Figure A6.7. When you select an outer join, Access places an arrow on the join line that points *away from* the table where all records are used.

Employees with Managers : Select Query

Department	FirstName	LastName	Salary	Manager
Accounting	Rebecca	Johnson	$37,400	Sallye Oaks
Accounting	Gary	Weber	$25,000	Sallye Oaks
Accounting	Elizabeth	Harris	$28,750	Sallye Oaks
				Joe Derek
Marketing	Anne	Shirley	$34,500	Larry Day
Marketing	Joseph	Oak	$42,500	Larry Day
				John Lucas
Sales	Jennifer	Gonzalez	$25,350	Sarah Fromm
Sales	Christina	Shaw	$19,500	Sarah Fromm
Sales	Tom	Williams	$19,500	Sarah Fromm
Sales	Matt	Hamilton	$20,000	Sarah Fromm
Sales	Benji	Tanaka	$19,450	Sarah Fromm
Shipping	Harvey	Brendan	$23,500	Paul Hadley
Shipping	Andrew	Blessing	$14,200	Paul Hadley

Record: 1 of 15

Departments with
no employees

SELF-JOINS

This type of join relates values within the same table. For example, you might have a table showing both employees and managers. In this scenario, you could have a ReportsTo field in the Employees table that gives the EmployeeID of the manager. You can use a self-join to determine which employee reports to which manager. To have access to the name of that manager, add a second copy of the Employees table to the query, then link the ReportsTo field in the first Employees table to the EmployeeID field in the second Employees table. You can drag the appropriate fields to the design grid and view the resulting datasheet.

NOTE   *Another way to create this self-join is to link the LastName field with a portion of the Manager field. Unfortunately, matching names is not very precise—large organizations might have more than one person with the same name.*

Defining Table Relationships

Access provides another way to define join relationships between tables and queries. Using the Relationships dialog box, you can create a permanent link between two tables. This relationship is automatically transferred to subsequent queries, forms, and reports using the tables, so that you can view data from both tables at the same time. Create table relationships before you build queries using the tables.

For instance, if two tables are joined in a relationship, Access will automatically draw a join line between them if they are added to a query. If the tables are used in a main/subform or main/subreport, Access will display the proper matching records in the subform or subreport.

The Relationships Dialog Box

To view the relationships in a database, choose the Relationships command from the Tools menu. You have seen the Hunter River Relationships window in Figure A6.2. Double-click a join line between two tables. The Relationships dialog box for the Employees-Department join is shown in Figure A6.8. You should identify the primary table and a related table. The primary table is the master or lookup table, such as the Department table from the preceding Guided Activity. The related table contains one or more records that match some or all of the records in the primary table, such as the Employees table from the preceding example.

FIGURE A6.8
Relationships dialog box for Employees-Department join

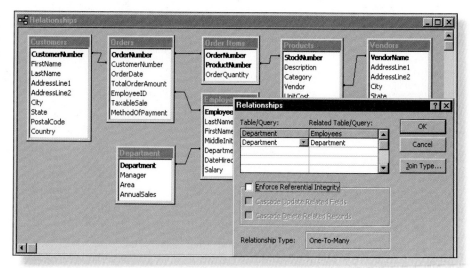

The key field in the primary table is compared with the specified field in the related table to join the two tables. In this example, both tables contain a field called Department. It is not necessary that the tables be joined on fields with the same names. An exercise appeared earlier in this book that asked you to produce a main/subreport listing the Vendors and the Products supplied by each vendor. In the Vendors table (primary table), the key field was Vendor Name. In the Products table (related table), the matching field was Vendor. A relationship between these two tables already exists in the Hunter97.mdb database.

The Join Type button refers to inner join (default), outer join, or self-join, as discussed in the previous section. By default, only records that have matching values in the linked fields will appear in the join.

REFERENTIAL INTEGRITY

Referential integrity refers to the requirement that any record placed in the related table *must* have a matching record in the primary table. If you choose to enforce referential integrity with the check box in the Relationships dialog box, any changes to either table must not violate referential integrity. For example, Access would prevent you from deleting the parent record from the primary table if it had a matching record in the related table. Similarly, Access would not allow you to add a record to the related table if a matching parent record did not already exist in the primary table.

CAUTION In this case, because we already have some Employees records without matching records in the Department table, Access will not let us require referential integrity in this relationship. To resolve this problem, edit the tables to eliminate the inconsistency, then return to the Relationships dialog box and click the Enforce Referential Integrity check box.

The relationship can be one-to-one or one-to-many. In one-to-many relationships, a record from the primary table can match more than one record in the related table. The one-to-one relationship type states that only one record from the related table can match a record from the primary table. In this case, there can be more than one employee in a particular department, so the one-to-many type is appropriate.

CASCADE UPDATE AND CASCADE DELETE

These two characteristics may be chosen *only* if you activate referential integrity. Notice that they are dimmed in Figure A6.8.

Cascade Update will cause the matching linked field value to change when you change the primary linked field value. For example, if you change the name of the Accounting department to ACCT and have Cascade Update checked, Access will automatically update every matching Department field in the Employees table to ACCT.

Cascade Delete instructs Access to delete any matching records in the related table (Employees in our example) if you delete the matching record in the primary table (Department here). Use this option with extreme caution—an inadvertent deletion of a department record could cause every employee for that department to be permanently deleted.

CREATING THE RELATIONSHIPS IN A DATABASE

Although the Hunter97.mdb and PMC97.mdb databases already have relationships established, it is easy to create relationships for a new database. Here are the steps:

1. Open the database.

2. Use the Tools | Relationships command to open the Relationships window.

3. Use the Relationships | Show Table command to display a list of tables and queries.

4. Add tables to the Relationships window just as you did with queries, then close this window.

5. Drag matching fields between appropriate tables just as you did with queries.

6. Double-click a join line and establish the relationship properties:

    ■ Specify primary table and related table.

    ■ Join type (choose inner or outer).

    ■ Referential integrity (optional).

    ■ Cascade Update (optional).

    ■ Cascade Delete (optional).

7. Close the Relationships window and save your changes.

Building Action Queries

In an earlier unit, we created simple select queries that determined which records qualified for the datasheet. The query itself did not make any changes to the underlying tables. In this section, we will demonstrate how to create queries that perform some type of action based on the criteria in the query.

Types of Action Queries

When you run an action query, changes are made to the underlying tables. To help remind you that these queries can be dangerous, Access places a small exclamation point next to the query name on the Queries tab of the Database window. In addition, another icon appears to identify the type of update query.

The four types of action queries are briefly described below. Following that discussion are examples of each type of action query.

UPDATE QUERIES

An update query can be used to change every record in the underlying table(s) that meets the criteria of the query. Similar to the Edit | Replace command, an update query is more flexible, allowing you to specify expressions with most field types, not just with text fields. There are some restrictions on update queries with multiple tables; search online Help for more details about multiple-table update queries.

An update query appears in the Database window with a pencil icon in front of the exclamation point.

DELETE QUERIES

The delete query will cause a group of records that meet the criteria to be permanently deleted from the database. This is much faster than manually deleting each record. The *Getting Results* manual suggests that you can delete records from only a single table at a time unless the Cascade Delete option is set in the Relationships dialog box. A delete query appears in the Database window with a script *X* icon before the query's name.

 Use delete queries with care! Once deleted, data is gone forever.

MAKE-TABLE QUERIES

The make-table query saves in a new table those records that match your criteria. These records also remain in the original table. You can select a subset of the fields for the new table; this will have the effect of making any forms or reports using the new table run faster. The make-table query will save records as of a certain point in time; subsequent changes to the original tables will *not* be reflected in the new table unless you run the make-table query again to extract the appropriate records. A make-table query appears in the Database window as a table icon with a yellow starburst in the corner.

APPEND QUERIES

You can use an append query to add certain records from one table to the end of another existing table. Only records that meet the criteria will be appended to the other table. The appended records also remain in their initial table. This is a good method for copying some or all records from one table to another table. An append query appears in the Database window as a plus icon.

Creating an Update Query

In this section, we will demonstrate how to create an update query to make changes to an existing table. There are four steps in creating an update query. First, create a select query as usual with the proper selection criteria expressions; run the query to view the datasheet in Datasheet view to be certain the correct records have been selected. Second, switch back to query Design view and choose the Query | Update command from the menu bar; the name of the window will change to Update Query, and Access will insert an Update To row in the design grid. Third, insert the new expression in the proper column of the design grid. Finally, run the query to make the changes. Remember that these changes will be permanent if you click the OK button after Access performs the update. *The Undo button will not be able to reverse the changes.* If you do not want to commit the changes to the database, click the Cancel button instead. The following Guided Activity will illustrate the preparation of an update query.

GUIDED ACTIVITY

6.2   Creating an Update Action Query

This Guided Activity will illustrate how to create an update action query to mark down prices for a clearance sale.

1. Close any open windows and return to the Hunter97.mdb Database window. Select the Queries tab.

2. Click the New button to create a new query design, then select Design View and click OK.

3. In the Show Table dialog box, add the Final Sales Merchandise Table and close the Show Table box.

4. Drag the following fields to the design grid: StockNumber, UnitCost, QuantityOnHand, and NowOnOrder.

5. In the QuantityOnHand column, enter the criteria expression >0. In the NowOnOrder column enter the criteria expression No in the same criteria row. You are creating a condition for marking down prices of closeout units that are in stock and not now on order.

6. Click the Run Query button on the toolbar to execute the select query. Notice which products qualify, and write down the unit costs for the first and last products. Six records should qualify.

7. Return to Design view. Now we will convert this select query into an update query. Select the Update command from the Query menu, or select Update from the Query Type button on the toolbar. Access will insert an Update To row in the design grid.

8. Beneath the UnitCost column, enter [UnitCost]*0.85 in the Update To row, as shown in Figure A6.9. If you forget the brackets around the field name, Access will incorrectly convert your update expression to text.

9. Run the query by clicking the Run button on the toolbar (or use the Query | Run command on the menu bar).

10. Before you make the changes permanent, Access will ask you to confirm the update. Click Yes to commit the changes.

11. Close the Update Query window. You do not have to save the query design.

12. Select the Tables tab and open the Final Sales Merchandise table. You should see the changes to the unit cost fields.

13. To reverse the effects of the price change, repeat steps 2–7 to prepare the same select query. This time, use the Update To expression [Unit Cost]/0.85, then run the query. You do not have to save the query design.

FIGURE A6.9
Update Query design

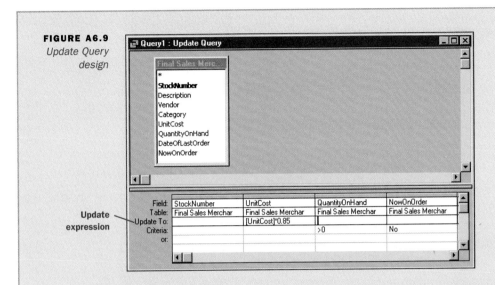

Update expression

14. Open the Final Sales Merchandise table to confirm that the original change was nullified in step 13.

Creating a Delete Query

The process of creating a delete action query is similar to creating an update query. First, create a select query with the correct criteria for those records to be deleted. Then choose the Delete command from the Query menu and Access will convert the Query window into a Delete Query window. When you run the query, Access will delete all records that meet the criteria. As with the update query, you are given a chance to cancel the command before its changes become permanent.

Creating a Make-Table Query

With a make-table action query, all records that meet the criteria are copied to a new table. First, create a select query with appropriate fields; only the fields that are included will be copied to the new table. Second, establish criteria expressions if necessary. Third, run the select query to confirm the settings in the design grid. To convert the select query to a make-table query, give the Query | Make Table command. You will see a Query Properties box, in which you specify the name of the table in the current database. There is a check box to specify that the table belongs in a different database. The following Guided Activity will show how to create a make-table action query that joins two tables.

GUIDED ACTIVITY

6.3 Creating a Make-Table Query

This Guided Activity will show you how to copy records from joined tables to a new table, using a make-table action query.

1. Close any open windows and return to the Hunter97.mdb Database window.

2. Open a new query in Design view.

3. Add the Employees and Department tables to the query and close the Show Table dialog box. Access will automatically place a join line between the Department fields of these two tables.

4. Drag the following fields to the design grid: FirstName, MiddleInitial, Last-Name, Department (all from Employees), and Manager (from Department).

5. Select the Make Table command from the Query menu. Your desktop should look like Figure A6.10.

FIGURE A6.10
Make Table Query window

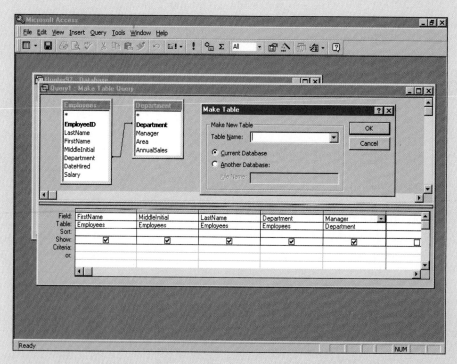

6. In the Table Name box, specify `Employees/Managers` and press **Enter**.

7. Run the query to create the new table. Access will ask you to confirm the creation of the new table with 12 records. Click Yes.

8. Close the Make Table Query window. Do not save the query design. Switch to Table mode to see the Employees/Managers table.

CAUTION

You cannot use the same name for a table and a query. Thus, if you were to save the query of this activity, you would need to choose a different name from that of the table you created.

Creating an Append Query

Not surprisingly, the append action query works in much the same manner as the other action queries. The first step is to create a select query with the appropriate fields and criteria. Only the fields that are included in the query will be copied to the other table. Next, select the Append command from the Query menu. Access will display the Append box, in which you can specify the name of the existing table to which you wish to append records. To complete the procedure, run the query. The extracted records are placed at the end of (are appended to) the existing table. If you were to accidentally execute the same append query twice, the records would be added *twice* to the existing table.

You can display the Query Properties box by clicking the Properties button on the toolbar, or by using the View | Properties command. The Unique Values property in the Query Properties box can restrict the append query to unique field values only; if it is Yes, Access will examine the primary key value and append only records whose primary key does *not* already exist in the table.

Using a Parameter Query

There may be occasions when you want to reuse a previous query several times, making changes in the criteria each time. You can speed up the process by saving the query as a parameter query. When you run a parameter query, Access displays a dialog box and asks you to enter the criteria as a parameter (characteristic element). The query then runs normally. This way, you can specify the criteria whenever you run the query without having to formally change its design in a Query window.

Parameter queries can be useful when you are printing reports for a specific time period. For instance, use a parameter query as the basis for a monthly report, and specify the month in the parameter box. Access will print the report, including the records for just that month. If you specify more than one criterion in brackets, Access will prompt you for each one, in order. These will be considered "And" criteria—all must be true in order for the record to qualify.

To create a parameter query, first prepare a select query as usual. In the Criteria cell you want to use as a parameter, enter the parameter prompt, enclosed by *square brackets*. This may be entered as an imperative statement, such as `[Enter the Department name:]`, or just the name of the field for which you are entering the criteria. You may have more than one parameter in a single query. Save the query normally.

When you run the query (or open a form or report that uses the query as its data source), Access displays the parameter box with your prompt(s) and asks you to fill in the entry. Your responses are transferred into the query, and the resulting datasheet reflects the same criteria that would have been input directly into the Query Design window.

The following Guided Activity will illustrate the Access parameter query.

GUIDED ACTIVITY

6.4   Creating a Parameter Query

In this Guided Activity, you will create a parameter query for the Products table.

1. Close any open windows and return to the Hunter97.mdb Database window.

2. Switch to Query mode and click the New button.

3. Choose Design View and click OK.

4. Choose the Products table for the query and click Add. Then click Close.

5. Drag the Description, StockNumber and Category fields to the design grid.

6. In the Criteria cell in the Category column, type [Enter category name].

7. Click the Run Query button. You will see the Enter Parameter Value dialog box and the design grid behind it, shown in Figure A6.11. When you key in a value, it will be substituted as the Category criteria.

FIGURE A6.11
Parameter query design grid and parameter box

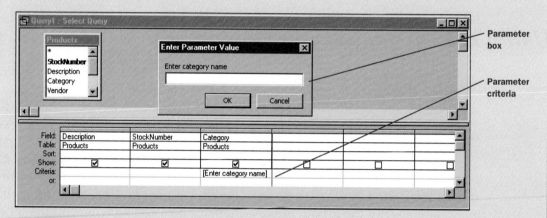

8. Type Camping in the box and click OK. The results of the query are shown in Figure A6.12. The 18 Camping products appear.

FIGURE A6.12
Result of Camping parameter query

9. Switch back to Design view, then run the query again. This time, leave the criteria expression empty in the parameter box. How many records qualify? Experiment with other product categories.

10. You can close the Query window without saving the query.

Creating a Crosstab Query

The final query introduced in this unit is useful when you are tabulating results *across* groups of records. The crosstab query will present summaries of these groups in a two-dimensional, crosstab format. In one dimension appears one variable (field value) and in the other dimension appears the other variable, both in groups. The crosstab format is easier to read than the long list that results from a select query. The pivot table form (previously discussed in Unit 4) is virtually the same thing as a crosstab query.

The method for creating a crosstab query is similar to that used for the previous queries. First, create a new query and add tables to the Query window. Drag appropriate fields to the design grid. Choose Crosstab from the Query menu. Access will add two new rows to the design grid: Total and Crosstab. The Crosstab cell is used to specify which fields will become the horizontal and vertical headings in the crosstab matrix, and which field is to be summarized. The Total cell for the summarized field specifies the type of summary calculations (Sum, Avg, Min, Max, Count, StDev, Var, First, Last, Expression, and Where). Then run the query to view the crosstab datasheet.

You will create a crosstab query as an exercise in this unit.

SQL—Structured Query Language

Structured Query Language is a common language used with many relational database management systems to retrieve information, using near-English queries that are more comprehensible than those in most computer languages. SQL queries are procedural in nature—that is, you must explain what to do, using an SQL command verb and listing each field involved plus any selection criteria within the query statement itself. Complicated queries can result in an extremely long SQL statement.

Most Access users will not find it necessary to know or use SQL statements. Access translates your select or action query into SQL before submitting it to the database engine for processing. The database engine breaks the SQL query down before applying it to the database. Because Access must work with data from sources other than itself, its ability to translate queries into standard SQL statements makes it compatible with a great many database systems, such as Oracle and SQL Server.

Viewing the SQL Box in an Access Query

In the event that you are curious enough to view the SQL statement that is equivalent to your own Access query, choose the SQL command from the View menu in query Design view or select SQL from the Query View button on the toolbar. Access will display the SQL statement in a box. Figure A6.13 shows the SQL statement corresponding to a select query. Can you work out the purposes of the various parts of the SQL statement that correspond to the Access query? The answer is left to you as an exercise.

FIGURE A6.13

SQL view for a select query

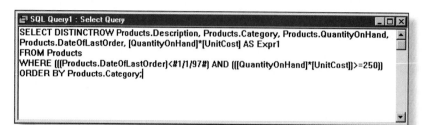

```
SELECT DISTINCTROW Products.Description, Products.Category, Products.QuantityOnHand,
Products.DateOfLastOrder, [QuantityOnHand]*[UnitCost] AS Expr1
FROM Products
WHERE (((Products.DateOfLastOrder)<#1/1/97#) AND (([QuantityOnHand]*[UnitCost])>=250))
ORDER BY Products.Category;
```

Making Changes to the Query with the SQL Box

If you know how to use SQL, you can make changes to queries by modifying the SQL statements in the SQL box. Make changes directly to the statements in the box. If you want to add a new line, press **Enter**. When you exit from the SQL dialog box, Access will make changes to the query to reflect the SQL statement.

You can use SQL statements in some Access properties and in Visual Basic modules. See the Access *Building Applications* manual for more details about modules.

Creating a New Query in SQL

You can create a query completely in SQL. Switch to Query mode, click New, and select Design View. Close the Tables window, then select View I SQL View from the menu bar. You will see a plain SQL window with SELECT; as the statement. The basic format of the SQL Select statement is

```
SELECT <field list> FROM <table name> WHERE <condition>
ORDER BY <sort fields>
```

The WHERE and ORDER BY parts are optional; use WHERE to give a criterion for including the record, and use ORDER BY to sort by one or more fields. You can add ASC or DESC after the sort field name to specify ascending or descending sorts. Fill in the rest of the SQL statement as needed. Search online Help for "SQL statements" to learn more about Access SQL queries.

SUMMARY

One of the strengths of Access is that it is a full relational database system. It joins tables by matching fields with common values. The process of creating these smaller related tables is called normalization. Normalization involves segregating repeating groups into their own tables, eliminating redundancies and calculated fields, and watching out for fields that do not access the entire primary key. The Access Table Analyzer Wizard can give you suggestions on how to split tables to remove repeating information.

Access creates relationships between tables in two ways. In the Query window, you can create a temporary connection between two tables by dragging a field from one table to the matching field in another table. You can also manage the relationship between tables by selecting Tools | Relationships in the Database window. Joins between two tables can be inner joins, in which only matching records from both tables appear, outer joins, which do not require a matching field from the other table, and self joins, in which records match other records in the same table.

Action queries, like select queries, are created by selecting tables and establishing criteria. They are different in that when an action query runs, it causes a change to the database. Because of these database changes, action queries are marked with an exclamation point to tell you to be cautious when running them.

- Update queries change selected field values, similarly to the Word Replace command.

- Delete queries delete records that match the criteria.

- Make-table queries create a new table from the query's datasheet.

- Append queries will add records that match the criteria to another table.

Another type of query lets you change the criteria each time you run it. A parameter query employs a user prompt (enclosed in brackets) in the Criteria row. When you run the query, Access prompts you to enter the criteria. When you type in a value, it is substituted for the criteria expression. Crosstab queries are useful for viewing a summary of results across records, in a two-dimensional table. Queries offer another view, SQL view, which displays the SQL—Structured Query Language—statements behind the query. SQL is the standard language used by information systems professionals to retrieve data from mainframe relational databases.

Exercises

Use the Hunter River database contained within the Hunter97.mdb file on the Student Data Disk for these exercises, except Exercise 6.1.

EXERCISE

6.1 University Student Information System Relational Design

1. Design a relational database for a university student information system. Your database should store information about students, classes they have taken, grades received, courses available within the university, and instructors who teach those classes.

2. Be sure to consider how the tables will be joined to produce desired forms and reports.

3. Write out the tables and fields in parenthesis notation: Table Name(<u>Field1</u>, Field2, …). The underlined field is the primary key.

4. Use dotted underline for *foreign keys*, the fields that are primary keys in the lookup table.

EXERCISE

6.2   Orders and Order Items Query

1. Prepare a query that links the Orders and Order Items tables.

2. Print the resulting datasheet for the orders.

3. Prepare a group report using your query so that all the order lines that are related to a particular order appear together as one group.

4. To document your query design from step 1, open the query in Design view and press the **PrtSc** key. This will copy the screen to the Windows Clipboard. Immediately return to the Start button on the taskbar and open a word processor such as Word or WordPad. To copy the contents of the Clipboard into the word processor, choose the Paste command from the Edit menu. Then print the document on your printer.

5. Save the query as Exercise 6-2.

 NOTE   *You might want to try the Tools | Analyze | Documentor command for more detailed documentation about your query.*

EXERCISE

6.3   Make-Table Query for Plan I Employees

1. Create a make-table action query for the Employees table. Only employees who were hired prior to January 1, 1995, should be included in the new table.

2. Use all fields.

3. The new table should be called Plan I Employees.

4. Print a copy of the datasheet for this new table.

5. Save this query as Exercise 6-3.

EXERCISE

6.4   Bonus Update Query

1. Open the Plan I Employees table in Design view from the preceding exercise. Create a new currency field called Bonus.

2. Prepare an update query in which each employee whose salary is below $20,000 receives an 8% bonus; employees at $20,000 or above are to receive a 6% bonus. Remember to enclose the field name in square brackets if you use it

in an Update To expression. *(Hint:* This will require two different update queries.)

3. Print a copy of the resulting datasheet.

4. Save the query as Exercise 6-4.

EXERCISE

6.5   Customers Parameter Query

1. Create a parameter query for the Customers table, using the State field as the parameter.

2. Save the query under the name Customer State Parameter Query.

3. Execute the parameter query and substitute IN for the state.

4. Print the resulting datasheet.

EXERCISE

6.6   Monthly Product Orders Crosstab Query

1. Use the Crosstab Query Wizard and the Products table to create a crosstab query that has Vendor as the row header and DateOfLastOrder as the column header.

2. Count the number of orders placed each month.

3. Print a copy of your query's datasheet.

4. Save the query as Exercise 6-6.

EXERCISE

6.7   Interpreting a Query's SQL Statements

1. Switch to Query mode in the Database window.

2. Select SQL Query 1. Switch to SQL view with the View menu.

3. Copy the SQL query on paper and write down the meanings of the following parts:

   a. SELECT DISTINCTROW Products.Description, Products.Category, Products.QuantityOnHand

b. WHERE (((Products.DateOfLastOrder)<#1/1/97#) AND
(([QuantityOnHand]*[UnitCost])>=250))

c. ORDER BY Products.Category;

EXERCISE

6.8   Creating an SQL Query

1. Switch to Query mode.

2. Create a new query in Design view. Add the Employees table to the query.

3. Use the View | SQL View command to switch to SQL view.

4. Using SQL statements only, create a query that will show last name, department, salary, and date hired for employees hired before January 1, 1995. The query should be sorted chronologically by date hired.

5. Print a copy of the query's SQL statements.

6. Print a copy of the datasheet for this query.

7. Save the query as Exercise 6-8.

Physicians' Medical Clinic: Building an Action Query

As the database administrator for Physicians' Medical Clinic, you have been asked to create a query that joins the appropriate tables from the PMC97.mdb database. You know that this query will need information about patients, visits, payments, procedures, and insurers as described in Unit 6. Assume that there is no more than one procedure per patient visit, but that a patient will probably have several visits over the billing period, one calendar month. Sketch out the format for the patient billing statement, but do not create a report format at this time.

Create an action query from the join query you just created. Copy into this temporary table all the records that fall in the months of March and April. Use an appropriate name for the new table to reflect its contents. Make sure that you have all the fields necessary to create the patient billing statement. Print a copy of the datasheet corresponding to this new table.

Finally, you will need to prepare a tentative group report for the clinic using the Report Wizard. There may be a limitation with the Report Wizard, so you may need to modify the report design. Print a copy of the report for the March/April patient visits.

Hunter River: Building Action and Parameter Queries

For this application, you will append records from the Products table with an append action query that is based on a parameter query. Create a new table called Special Items. It should have the same fields as the Products table but should have no records. (*Hint:* Copy the Products table using the Windows Clipboard, rename the copy of Products, then delete all records in the copy.) Add two more fields to Special Items: ContactPerson and TelephoneNumber, both taken from the Vendors table.

Create a query that joins the Products and Vendors tables. In the Category column of your query, use the following criteria expression: [Enter Product Category]

Run the select query and select Sports as the category. Finally, convert your query to an append action query, using Special Items as the name of the recipient table. Run the query for Sports and Camping categories. How would you *remove* the Camping records from Special Items?

APPLICATION

UNIT 7

Working with Access Controls in Forms and Reports

This unit acts as a building block for the ultimate preparation of customized Access forms and reports. The unit describes the types of controls available for Access data objects. You will learn how to add, move, and resize controls that are used in forms and reports. There are sections on use of the Access Toolbox to place new controls in a form or report. The unit also contains a discussion about control properties.

Learning Objectives

At the completion of this unit you should be able to

1. move a control,

2. resize a control,

3. add a control with the Access Toolbox,

4. create a calculated control,

5. display and change control properties,

6. select the appropriate control for a custom form or report.

Case Study

Hunter management wants you to develop a custom entry form that goes beyond the simple objects available with Form Wizard. They have asked you to learn more about Access controls and Form Design view.

Control Basics

Controls are graphical objects used to display text, lines, boxes, data values, or graphic images on a form or report. When you used the wizards to create forms and reports in the first part of this book, Access generated the controls for you and placed them on the design surface for you in predefined ways. In those units we suggested that you would probably find it easier to re-create the data object with the wizards than to make the changes manually by adding, moving, and resizing controls.

In this unit we discuss how to work directly with those controls to create custom forms and reports. Some users will still prefer to let the wizards build the form or report and then make manual changes to the design. Other users would rather start with a blank screen and add the controls necessary for the final design. In this unit we discuss controls themselves. In future units you will learn details on how to use these controls with forms and reports.

Classes of Controls

There are three general classes of controls in Access. Bound controls and calculated controls depend on field values in tables or queries, whereas unbound controls are not connected with fields. Each is described below.

BOUND CONTROLS

Bound controls are those that show data from tables or query datasheets. We say that the controls are *bound* or connected to a field from the table or query. Each record in the table or datasheet will have a different field value for that control. Bound controls include text, number, date/time, yes/no, memo, counter, and OLE object data types.

UNBOUND CONTROLS

Unbound controls show text, lines, rectangles, images, or OLE pictures and are not bound to a field of a table or datasheet. Unbound controls can include messages or anything that remains unchanged from record to record in the table or datasheet. Unbound controls are used to format and highlight forms and reports, as well as to provide messages and prompts that are not based on particular field values.

CALCULATED CONTROLS

Similar to bound controls, calculated controls get their data values from an expression of one or more fields. As you navigate through the table or query, the value of the calculated control will change as the expression is recalculated. In an earlier unit we created an inventory value expression that multiplied Unit Cost by Quantity on Hand. In a form or report this would be considered a calculated control.

Types of Toolbox Controls

The Toolbox is a collection of icons that is automatically displayed when you open a form or report in Design view. Shown in Figure A7.1, the Toolbox is a normal window that can be moved by dragging its title bar or closed by clicking the close button.

FIGURE A7.1
Access control Toolbox in vertical shape

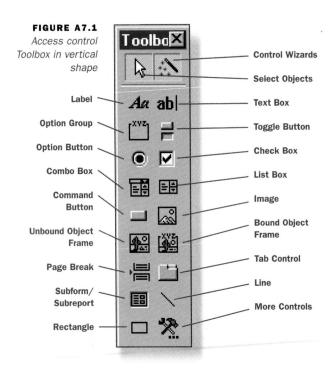

This section will discuss the types of controls that are accessible through the Toolbox. Instructions on use of the Toolbox appear in the following section.

The Select Objects (Pointer) tool is used to select commands from a menu and to select, move, size, and edit objects in the Design window. This is the default tool when the Toolbox is opened.

CONTROL WIZARDS

The Control Wizards tool is used to turn Control Wizards on or off. If this button is selected, the Control Wizards will assist you when you add an option group, combo box, or list box control. You can also use the View | Control Wizards command to toggle the Control Wizards. The default setting is to have the Control Wizards active, as shown in Figure A7.1.

LABEL

The Label tool is used to place a descriptive text phrase on the screen. Examples include report title, column headings, explanatory messages, and hyperlinks. The label is not to be confused with the text box, which is described next. A label is an unbound control.

You can insert a label containing a hyperlink in Access 97.

TEXT BOX

A text box is used to enter or display data of all types, including text, numbers, and pictures. A text box control is usually associated with a field, whereas a label is an unbound control. When you add a text, number, date, memo, currency, autonumber, or hyperlink field by dragging it from the field list box, it is stored in a text box. A text box can have scroll bars if there is a lot of information to display.

OPTION GROUP

An option group control is used to create a group of buttons or boxes in an option group. Only one button in an option group can be selected at a time. In Access 7.0, the Control Wizards can help you create an option group.

TOGGLE BUTTON

A toggle button is used to select a response from a group of values. It may be used by itself to select a Yes/No value. The toggle button, option button, and check box all do the same thing and differ only in their appearance.

OPTION BUTTON

Similar to a toggle button, the option button can be used in an option group to select one response from a set of values. Option buttons are sometimes referred to as *radio buttons* because they resemble a round knob on a radio. The option button may be used by itself to select a Yes/No value. When selected, the option button appears as a small filled-in circle and means "Yes."

CHECK BOX

Similar to toggle and option buttons, the check box can be used in an option group to select a response from a set of values. When used by itself, it may be used to select a Yes/No value. It is a rectangular box and, when selected, appears with a small check mark in the box, meaning "Yes."

COMBO BOX

A combo box lets you select a value from a list by choosing it with the pointer or lets you fill in the value in the box. Many Windows dialog boxes use a combo box for user responses, such as when you save a file and specify the file name. In Access 7.0, the Control Wizards can help you create a combo box.

LIST BOX

With a List Box you can choose a value from a list. Although a list box is similar to a combo box, you cannot enter a value by keying it into a list box. In Access 7.0, the Control Wizards can help you create a list box.

COMMAND BUTTON

The Command Button tool can be used to insert a command button in a form. You associate the command button with an Access macro. The command button executes a set of commands when selected.

IMAGE

The Image tool is used to place a static image in the form or report. The image is *not* an OLE object, and therefore cannot be edited from within Access after being placed in a form or report. An example of a static image is a logo or other artwork. Use bound or unbound object controls for images that must be edited after they are placed in the form or report.

UNBOUND OBJECT FRAME

The Unbound Object Frame tool is used to hold an unbound OLE object in the form or report. An unbound OLE object is a picture or graphic image that is *not* bound to a field within the database.

BOUND OBJECT FRAME

The Bound Object Frame tool is used to hold an OLE object that is bound to a field in a table. The OLE object is usually stored within the database.

PAGE BREAK

The Page Break tool is used to place a page break in the form or report, causing the printer to begin a new page. This tool is used with the screen and with a printed page.

TAB CONTROL

The Tab Control tool is used to place a tab control in the form, with two or more pages for displaying information. You can copy or add other controls to the tab control. Right-click the tab control in Design view to modify the number of pages, page names, page order, and other tab properties.

SUBFORM/SUBREPORT

The Subform/Subreport tool is used to place a subform within a main form or a subreport within a main report.

LINE

The Line tool is used to add a straight line to the form or report. The line is an unbound object. Lines are used to separate portions of the form or report and can make the output appear more like a printed document. You can use buttons on the Formatting toolbar to change the width and color of the line.

RECTANGLE

The Rectangle tool is used to place a rectangle in the form or report. Rectangles can highlight items from one group and can produce a shadow effect when placed beneath another control. The color of the rectangle can be changed with the property sheet (discussed later) or the buttons on the Formatting toolbar.

MORE CONTROLS

The More Controls button will open a dialog box with specialized ActiveX controls available in Access 97. The calendar control is an example of an ActiveX control. The specific controls available on your machine will depend on what applications you have installed.

Adding a Control from the Field List

Before we learn how to insert the custom controls with the Toolbox, we should discuss the method to insert field text boxes directly into the form or report from the field list. Open the form or report in Design view, and then click the Field List button on the toolbar. (Or use the View | Field List command from the menu bar.)

Using the mouse, drag a field from the field list to its desired location in the design grid. Access will create *two controls* for each field—a label containing the field name (or alternate caption, if you have defined one) and a text box bound to the field value. Access will copy the field properties you created when you designed the table to the control property sheet. Thus field properties such as format, validation information, and default value are consistent wherever you use that field.

 If you change a field property after the control using that field has been created, that property will *not* be transferred to the control as well. Access will check validation rules for that field wherever it appears, however, even if you add one after the control tied to that field was created.

GUIDED ACTIVITY

7.1 Adding a Control from the Field List

In this Guided Activity you will create a control in a form by dragging it from the field list.

1. Start Windows 95 and load Access. Open the Hunter97.mdb database file.

2. Click the Forms tab and click the New button to open a new form.

3. Choose the Customers table in the New Form dialog box. Choose Design View, and then click OK to open Form Design view.

4. If the grid dots are not already present, use the View | Grid command to display the placement grid. These dots do not appear in the final form or report. Notice that Access also places black gridlines at 1-inch intervals to help you place controls in the form.

5. If the field list is not already present, click the Field List button on the toolbar or issue the View | Field List command from the menu bar. Access will display a box containing the field names from the Customers table. Move the field list box to the side, out of the way, by dragging its title bar.

6. Drag the LastName field from the field list to the design grid so that the text box is approximately 0.5 inch down and 1.5 inches across, according to the rulers in the Form Design window. The crosshairs pointer indicates the location for the text box control, *not* its label. Release the mouse button. If you placed the boxes in the wrong location, press the **Del** key to delete these two controls and repeat this step.

7. Access will create two controls as shown in Figure A7.2. The left control is a label that contains the field's name (or caption, if you have entered one in the Caption property); the right control is a text box that is bound to the LastName field. Access always places the upper left corner of the text box control at the location you indicate with the pointer.

FIGURE A7.2
Add a control from the field list

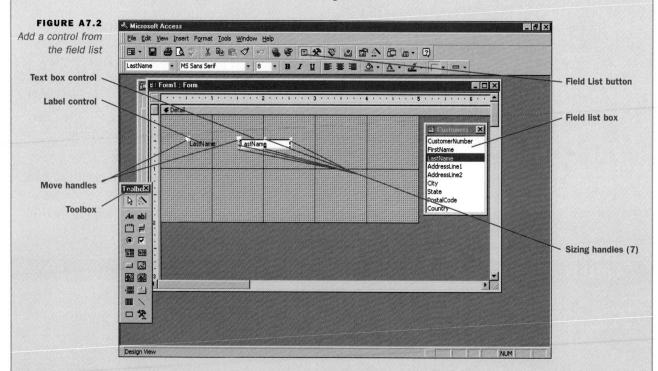

8. The text box on the right was added with the sunken effect, giving it a 3-D look. We will show you later how to change special effects associated with controls. Leave the form open for now; you will modify it in the next activity.

We will discuss the purpose of the handles that appear at the edges of these controls in the next section. Leave the form design on the screen at this time and we will add more to it in a later activity.

Moving and Resizing Access Controls

After placing a control in the Design window, you may want to move it or change its size. The control handles that appear at the edges of the control box are used for these purposes. In Figure A7.2 you can see that the LastName text box on the right has eight handles around its edges. Use these handles to move and resize this box. Note that when you move or resize the text box control, its accompanying label does *not* change. Each box can be adjusted separately or both can be adjusted together.

Moving a Control

The upper left corner handle is larger than the others. This is the move handle. You can move the control by dragging its move handle. Slowly move the pointer on this handle until it changes to a small hand shape with one index finger. Then hold down the left mouse button and drag the control to its new location. When you release the left mouse button, Access will redraw the control with its upper left corner at that location.

If you position the mouse pointer over the text box control until the pointer turns into a hand with all fingers outstretched, you can move *both* controls (if they are both selected) at the same time. If you want to move both boxes, it is sometimes easier to delete both boxes and create them again in the desired location.

Resizing a Control

The other seven handles on the text box control are sizing handles. The top and bottom sizing handles are used to expand the box size up or down, while the left and right handles can be used to expand the box sideways. The three corner handles are used to change the size in two directions at once, just like dragging the corner border of a window. Notice that the label control does not have any sizing handles. It can be expanded in the horizontal direction when you edit the text in the label box. This is covered later.

The Grid System for Aligning Controls

Access uses a grid system in the Form and Report Design windows. The grid appears as a series of evenly spaced dots, usually 24 dots per inch if you are using the U.S. measurement system. (For metric users, Access uses 5 dots per centimeter.) Use the View | Grid command to turn the grid on or off. Access uses the grid system to help you align controls horizontally and vertically. Horizontal and vertical gridlines appear at 1-inch increments in Access.

If the Snap To Grid command on the Format menu is checked, Access will snap all four corners of the control to the nearest grid coordinates. That is, when you add, resize, or move the control, it will be aligned horizontally and vertically with the grid dots. You can't place the control's location between the dots when this command is on. You can toggle the grid alignment off by using the Format | Snap To Grid command again. You can temporarily defeat the snap to grid feature by holding down the **Ctrl** key while you complete the control move or resize operation.

Access defaults to Snap To Grid, but your computer site may have changed this setting. Use the Format menu to see the current setting. You can also change the spacing of the dots with the form or report property sheet by changing the GridX and GridY properties. Search Help for "Grid (forms and reports) fineness (granularity)." You can turn off the grid with the View I Grid command, but the Snap To Grid setting remains active even when the grid is not visible.

The Format I Align command is helpful in aligning a group of selected controls. You can specify that one or all of the edges of the selected controls align to a control or a certain point on the design grid. Thus, you can align a column of controls, or a row of controls, so that they match. This is particularly useful after you have made a series of changes to the controls and they are out of alignment. We will demonstrate this in a future activity.

GUIDED ACTIVITY

7.2   Moving and Resizing a Control

In this Guided Activity you will practice moving and resizing an Access control.

1. We will begin with the custom form started in the previous activity. If you have not already completed the activity, do so at this time. Refer back to Figure A7.2.

2. First we will move the LastName text box control to the right. Be sure it is selected so that its handles appear. If the handles are not present, click once on the control to select it.

3. Position the mouse pointer on the move handle at the upper left corner of the control on the right so that the pointer turns into the hand icon with a single pointing finger.

4. While pressing the left mouse button, drag the control to the right until the pointer is at the 2-inch mark on the ruler. Notice that Access displays a shadow of the box on the ruler bar while you are dragging it. Release the mouse button to move the box.

5. Repeat step 4, but this time try to move the box to a point *between* the grid dots. When you release the mouse button, the box will snap to the nearest grid dot.

6. Next, you will resize the box. Position the mouse pointer on the lower left sizing handle until the pointer turns into a diagonal arrow with two heads.

7. While pressing the left mouse button, slowly drag the left border to the left to increase the size of the box. When the left edge of the box reaches the 1.5-inch mark, release the mouse button. Access will resize the box to your specification.

The next activity will illustrate how to align two controls on the same form.

GUIDED ACTIVITY

7.3 Aligning a Group of Controls

In this Guided Activity you will add another control and align it with the previous control already in the form from Guided Activity 7.2.

1. We will begin with the form from the previous activity. If you have not already completed that activity, do so at this time.

2. Examine the form from the previous activity. The LastName text box control should start at the 1.5-inch mark.

3. Use the pointer to drag the FirstName field from the field list box to the form. Place its upper left corner 0.25 inch down and 2 inches across on the grid.

4. Select the FirstName label and drag the move handle of the FirstName label so that it aligns with the LastName label just beneath it.

5. Click the Select Objects tool in the Toolbox if it is not already selected. Then move the pointer to a point about 0.125 inch down and 1.5 inches across. While holding down the left mouse button, drag the pointer to draw a rectangle to enclose a portion of both of the text boxes. This is one way to select more than one field in the Form or Report Design window. (The other way is to hold down the **Shift** key, click on each item to be selected, and then release the **Shift** key.)

6. Choose the Align command from the Format menu. From the submenu, choose Left with the pointer. Access will align the two fields at their left edges. The Design window should look like Figure A7.3.

FIGURE A7.3
Aligned controls

Form Selection button

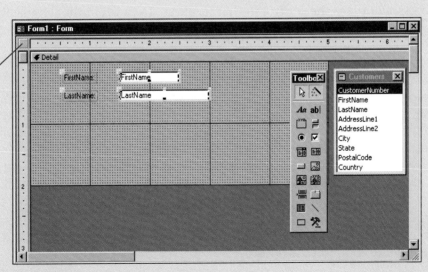

NOTE   *If you inadvertently move the wrong controls, or place them in the wrong position, use the Edit | Undo command (or click the Undo button) to reverse the effects of your last command.*

7. Close the Form Design window without saving the form.

TIP

If more than one control is selected, you can choose other Format|Size command options, including sizing all controls to the tallest, shortest, widest, and narrowest in the group.

We will address more custom form design issues in the next unit of this book.

Size to Fit Option

Ordinarily, you will specify the size of the control when you add it to the design. If you choose the Size | To Fit command from the Format menu, Access will automatically adjust the size of the control to fit the item it contains. For instance, if you change the font size in a label, command button, or toggle button, the control's height and width can be adjusted to fit its contents. The Format | Size | To Fit command will adjust only the height of a text box, list box, or combo box if the font size of text within is changed. You must resize the box to change the width of the box.

Using the Toolbox to Add a Control

When you add a control to a form or report by dragging from the field list box, Access will create only label and text box controls. In this section you will learn how to use the Toolbox to insert other types of controls in a form or report.

General Procedure to Add a Control

First switch to Design view for the form or report you're working on. If the Toolbox is not already present, use the View | Toolbox command (or click the Toolbox button on the toolbar) to make it appear. Click the desired control tool in the Toolbox, and then move the pointer to the upper left corner of the desired location for the control. Access will change the pointer shape to reflect the tool you selected. Use the mouse to drag the control box to the desired size and release the left mouse button. Access will place the control in that location. Then fill in the details about the control, and make changes to the control's property sheet if necessary.

Viewing the Property Sheet

There are three ways to display the property sheet for a control, form, or report. The easiest way is to double-click on the object, and the property sheet will appear. To use the other ways, you must first select the object by clicking it once in the Design window. You can select the form or report itself by clicking the Form Selection or Report Selection button in the upper left corner of the form or report, as shown in Figure A7.3. Then click the Properties button on the toolbar or use the View | Properties command from the menu bar. Once a property sheet window appears, Access will display the appropriate property sheet when you select a different object. You can close the property sheet window or move it out of the way to make more room on the desktop.

Fill in the Property Sheet

The details about the control depend on the type of control you insert. Label controls contain text phrases. A text box is tied to a specific field or calculated value. Toggle buttons, option buttons, and check boxes are also tied to a particular Yes/No field. Combo and list boxes are tied to a field and must be given a set of values to choose from. Image and object frame controls are associated with a graphic image or an OLE object. Line and rectangle controls are drawn directly in the Design window, using the mouse pointer.

Although there are properties for nearly all of the options for each control, you may find it easier to use the toolbar and other tools to fill in some of the properties. For instance, we saw in the first part of this book that you can use the Formatting toolbar to choose colors and line widths for controls. You can select a font, font size, and other features such as bold or italic from the toolbar. These settings are automatically transferred to the appropriate property. We will cover properties later in this unit.

GUIDED ACTIVITY

7.4   Adding a Line Control with the Toolbox

In this Guided Activity you will add a line control to a blank form with the Toolbox.

1. We will begin with a new form, so close the previous Form Design window and return to the Hunter97.mdb Database window.

2. Click on the New button in Form view in the Database window. Specify the Products table in the New Form box, choose Design View, and then click OK.

3. Drag the bottom edge of the Form Design window down to about 3 inches to make more room in the form. You may want to drag the Toolbox over to the right side of the desktop so that the entire form design surface is visible.

4. We need to place a title in the upper portion of the form. Click the Label button in the Toolbox. On the Formatting toolbar click the Font Size drop-down list and choose 14 points. This will produce a large font for the top of the form.

5. Then position the pointer at about 0.25 inch down and 0.5 inch across the ruler lines. Press the left mouse button and drag the box to the 0.5,4.0-inch coordinates, and then release the mouse button. Access will create a label control and leave the pointer blinking inside.

6. You can key in the desired heading for the form. Notice that the pointer is taller than normal, indicating your use of the 14-point font. Key Sample Custom Form Heading Label and press **Enter**.

7. Next, click the Line button in the Toolbox. Move the pointer to the grid location just 2 dots beneath the lower left corner of the heading label. Press the left mouse button and drag the line to the right until it just lines up with the right edge of the label box. Keep the line horizontal so that it aligns with the grid dots. Release the mouse button.

8. Access will draw the line in the indicated location, using the default thin line width. Click the arrow next to the Line/Border Width button on the Formatting toolbar. Click the Width button marked 2 (2 points) to make the line heavier. Figure A7.4 shows the form design at this stage.

9. Leave the form design on the screen, as it will be used in the next Guided Activity.

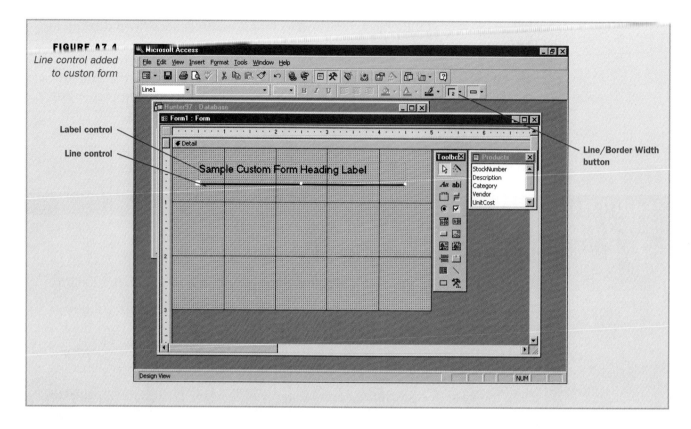

FIGURE A7.4
Line control added to custom form

Label control

Line control

Line/Border Width button

Adding a List Box Control

We could use a similar procedure to add a list box that shows several values for the field. Select the List Box tool in the Toolbox, and then drag the desired field from the field list to the form design. Access will create two controls—a label attached to the list box and the list box itself. However, to use the list box to display data, you must fill in details in the control's property sheet.

With the list box control selected, click the Properties button on the toolbar to display the property sheet for the control. You must specify the number of columns (usually one) for the list box and indicate where Access can find the row values to be displayed in the box.

There are three Row Source Types for the list box control: Table/Query, Value List, and Field List. The Table/Query type assumes that the data comes from a table or a query named in the Row Source line, and is the default setting. The Value List type assumes that the data comes from a list of values typed into the Row Source line. The Field List type assumes that the data is a list of field names from the table or query named in the Row Source setting.

Access contains a List Box Wizard that will make creating the list box much simpler. The following Guided Activity will illustrate how to add a list box control to the form, using the Value List row source for the Category field of the Products table.

GUIDED ACTIVITY

7.5 Adding a List Box Control with the Toolbox

In this Guided Activity we will add a list box control to the form started in the previous activity. The list box will make it easier to enter or view the product category.

1. This activity will add on to the form design begun in the previous activity. If you have not completed that activity, do so at this time.

2. Be sure that the Control Wizards button is selected in the Toolbox. Click the List Box tool in the Toolbox.

3. Drag the Category field from the field list box to the Form Design window, placing it at the 1,1-inch coordinates.

4. After a few seconds, the first List Box Wizard window will appear, as shown in Figure A7.5. You can have Access get the list of values from a table or query or from a fixed list. Because we are going to use values from a table, click Next to go to the next step.

FIGURE A7.5
List Box Wizard

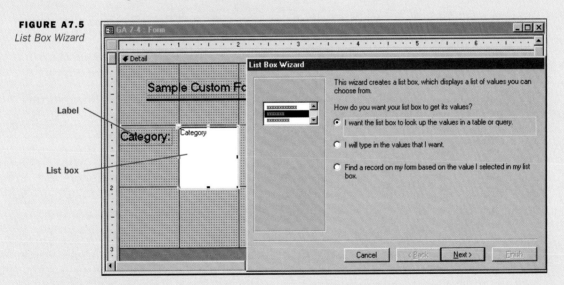

5. Access will ask which table or query contains the values for the list box. Choose the table Category and click Next. Click the > button to select the Category field. Click Next to continue.

6. Access will display the values from the Category table and ask how wide you want the column to be. Accept the default and click Next.

7. At the next screen, click Next to signify that you will store the value in the Category field of the Products table. Then click Finish to use the default label and return to Design view.

8. To view the results of your form, click the Form View button on the toolbar, or issue the View | Form View command from the menu bar. Figure A7.6 shows the form with the list box for the first record.

FIGURE A7.6
Form view of list
box control

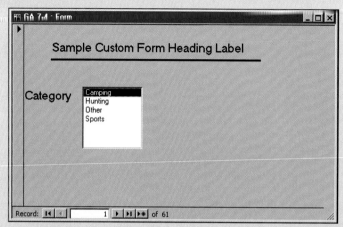

9. You can use the record navigation buttons at the bottom of the window to move to different records. The list box will show the value of the Category field for each record. Don't make any changes on the form at this time—the new values would be saved in the Products table!

10. The label for the Category field is too large—it used the same size as the form heading label you selected. Click the Design View button on the toolbar to return to Design view. (Or use the View | Form Design View command from the menu bar.)

11. Click once on the Category label (*not* the list box) to select it. Notice that the label box now has handles at all corners, and the list box control has only a move handle.

12. With the label control selected, click once on the Font Size drop-down list on the toolbar and choose 10 points. Access will immediately change the label to this font size in the Design window. Although we will not illustrate it here, you can select a different font from the Font box adjacent to the Font Size box on the toolbar.

13. The list box is also a little larger than necessary. Click once on the list box control to select it, and then drag the bottom middle handle up to about the 1.7-inch mark. Go to Form view to see how the list box appears.

14. Close the Form window without saving the form.

Properties of Controls

Although each type of control has different properties, the controls are similar. To view the property sheet for a control, select the control and click the Properties button on the toolbar (or issue the View | Properties command from the menu bar). You can also double-click a control to open its property sheet. To view the default properties for a type of control, click its button in the Toolbox with the property sheet open.

Properties for Label Controls

Figure A7.7 shows the full property sheet for the label control. Ordinarily, you cannot see all of the choices at the same time. Access tabs are a way to view a subset of the properties; in this case, all properties are displayed. The property sheet is a box like other Windows objects and can be moved or resized as desired. For this figure, it was resized to show more properties.

FIGURE A7.7
Label control property sheet

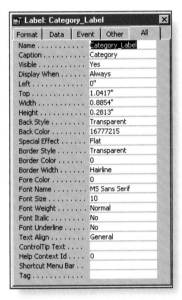

The Name gives the name of the control. It must be unique for this form or report. If you drag a field from the field list box, Access will use the field name as the control name. If you create an unbound control, Access will assign a unique name. In this case, Category_Label represents an unbound label.

The Caption property reflects the label contained within the control itself. If you change the Caption property, the form will also change. Likewise, if you change the name on the form design, the property sheet will reflect that change.

The Hyperlink Address property contains the string expression for the path to a Web document or file. If you type a hyperlink URL caption in a label field, Access will convert it to a hyperlink and store it in the Hyperlink Address property. (This property doesn't appear unless it contains a hyperlink.)

The Visible property describes whether the label appears. The default is Yes, but you may want to control this property based on a condition within the data itself. For example, if a customer payment is past due, you might display a warning message on the form. You can make changes to Access properties in macros.

The Display When property can be used to always display the field or to display it only on the screen form or on the printed form.

The next few properties reflect the location and size of the control. In this case, the left edge of the label is at the 0-inch mark and its top is near the 1-inch mark. If you move or resize the control, your changes are stored in the property sheet.

The following few properties are used less frequently. Back Style allows you to create a transparent control that permits other controls in the same location to appear, such as in an option group where the option group control contains other buttons or boxes. The Special Effect property indicates whether the item is to be normal or flat or to be raised or have a sunken appearance. The colors are shown as Access codes; to make changes to colors or special effects, use the Formatting toolbar.

The font properties can be adjusted more easily with the buttons on the Formatting toolbar. You can choose the font name and size; select from bold, italic, and underline; and choose text alignment (general, left, right, center). General alignment means that character values are left-aligned while number and date values are right-aligned.

The ControlTip Text property lets you attach a short description to a control that appears when you move the mouse pointer to the control. Many Access buttons contain ToolTips; ControlTips work in the same manner.

The Shortcut Menu Bar property lets you specify a series of choices to be available when you right-click the control on a form.

Properties for Text Box Controls

With a text box control on the form, Figure A7.8 shows its resized property sheet. Many of the properties are the same as the label control properties, but there are some new properties described below. Not all of these appear in the Property window; to see them, use the scroll bar.

FIGURE A7.8
Text box property sheet

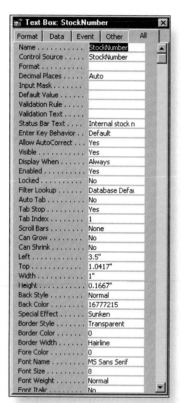

Several of the properties for this control are taken directly from the table design for the StockNumber field. Name, Format, Decimal Places, Input Mask, Default Value, Status Bar Text, and the Validation Rule properties follow what has been defined for the field to which this control is bound. Status Bar Text defaults to the field Description in the table definition. (The Caption property is used for the label control that accompanies this text box.)

The Before Update and After Update properties describe Access macros or Visual Basic user functions that are to execute before and after, respectively, the data in the text box control updates the field value in the underlying table. Typical applications for these macros or user functions are validation procedures that are too complicated for a single validation expression.

The On Enter and On Exit properties describe a macro or user function that is to execute when that control receives the focus (when it becomes the active control). The On Enter procedure executes when the control first gets the focus; the On Exit procedure executes when the control is about to lose the focus.

The Locked property makes a field read-only. That is, the field using that control will display data, but you may not change the data. This is useful in applications where the user has the authority to read the value but not to erase or change the data in the field. In this example, the control is not read-only.

The Scroll Bars property allows you to define whether horizontal, vertical, or either type of scroll bar appears with the control, which is useful with larger fields. The default is no scroll bars.

The Can Grow and Can Shrink properties describe how Access will handle data values that are too big or too small for the current control box size. The default is No for both properties, meaning that values that are too large to fit are truncated (shortened). Items that are smaller than the box result in a box with blank space.

The Help Context ID property allows you to identify a particular custom help topic for this control. When the user presses the **F1** key, Access will check the Help Context ID property for the control that has the focus. If available, your own custom help message will appear. See Access Help for assistance on this property.

TIP

For a complete list of all control events and their associated properties, search the "Events and Event Properties" reference in online Help.

Properties for Other Controls

Earlier in this unit we described the property sheet for list boxes. In fact, most of the Access form controls share similar property sheets. If you have questions about a particular property, highlight that line and press the **F1** key to display Help screens. Access Help contains examples of most of the properties. Coverage of bound and unbound OLE object controls appears in Unit 10 of this book.

Adding Controls to a Report Design

Forms and reports share many features, including use of controls in the Design window. Of course, forms permit you to add or edit data, while reports only permit you to *display* data values. Although most of the controls covered earlier in this unit apply equally to forms and reports, the most common for reports are label, text box, and line controls.

Recall from Unit 5 that Access report designs are broken into sections. The Page Header section contains the report title, page number, date, and column headings. The Detail section contains actual data values for records. The Page Footer section may contain explanatory information such as footnotes. Other sections may be used in reports to accommodate grouped data, title/cover page, and report summaries. We will focus on report controls for these three report sections in this unit. Unit 9 will cover custom reports in more detail.

When you drag a field from the field list box, position the pointer where you want the text box to be located. Access will place an attached label in front of the text box. In most reports you will delete the attached label and use column headings in the Page Header section to identify the text box values. Click the control you want to delete once, and then press the **Del** key.

You can drag the section borders to adjust the space. If there is any room above or below the controls in the Detail section, Access will duplicate that blank space above and below the data values in the report. Most users will want to eliminate that blank space. The following Guided Activity will show how to create a simple custom report by placing controls directly in the design.

GUIDED ACTIVITY

7.6 Adding Controls to a Report

This Guided Activity will demonstrate how to create a report by adding controls directly to the report design.

1. Close any open windows and return to the Hunter97.mdb Database window.

2. Switch to Report mode and click New to create a new report.

3. Choose the Products table for the data source and select Design View. Click OK to open the Report Design window.

4. If the Toolbox is not visible, use the View I Toolbox command. If the field list box is not present, use the View I Field List command.

5. You will have to drag the bottom border of the Page Header section down to allow the title and other headings to fit. Make this section approximately 0.75 inch tall.

6. Click the Label button in the Toolbox. Then move the pointer to the Page Header section and create a label box at 0.25 inch and stretching across to 3 inches. In this box, type `Hunter River Product List` and press **Enter**.

7. With the label control selected, change the font size to 14 points for the report title.

8. Next, issue the Format command and select Size | To Fit. Access will resize the box to hold the title.

9. Add another label control to the Page Header section for `Product Number` under the previous label control. While this control is still selected, click the Bold button on the toolbar. Issue the Size | To Fit command from the Format menu to resize the control.

10. Repeat step 9 with another Label control for `Product Description`, just to the right of the Product Number label. While this control is selected, click the Bold button on the toolbar. Then issue the Size | To Fit command from the Format menu.

11. Click the Text Box button in the Toolbox, and then drag the StockNumber field from the field list to the Detail section. Select the attached label by clicking on it once, and then press **Del** to remove its label from the Detail section. Place the text box right below the Detail section border so that it aligns with the Product Number heading, and then release the mouse button. (Do *not* remove the Product Number label you placed in the Page Header section.)

12. Repeat step 11 with the Description field. Remove its attached label from the Detail section and make it align with its column heading.

13. Finally, drag the Page Footer section border up to reduce the size of the Detail section. Your screen should look like Figure A7.9.

FIGURE A7.9
Report design with controls

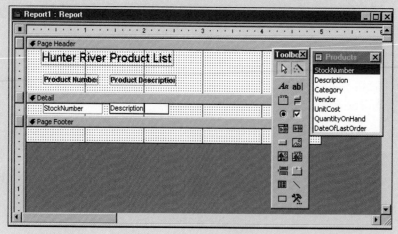

14. To preview your report, click the Print Preview button on the toolbar or choose the Print Preview command from the File menu. See Figure A7.10.

FIGURE A7.10
Print preview for custom report

15. Click the Save button or use the File | Save command to save this report as Hunter River Product List.

SUMMARY

This unit introduces Access controls, used when creating custom forms and reports. Controls are added to the design grid in Design view. You can drag a field from the field list box or create a new control from the Access Toolbox. The grid system allows you to align controls easily.

The Access Toolbox supports more than 16 different control types. The most common controls are labels, text boxes, rectangles, lines, command buttons, check boxes, and images. The Control Wizards will help you add option groups, combo boxes, and list box controls.

You can move a control on the design grid by dragging its move handle to the desired location. Access will change the pointer to a hand with outstretched fingers when you are moving a group of controls or a single index finger when moving a single control. The control's property sheet gives the characteristics for that control.

Exercises

Use the Hunter River database contained within the Hunter97.mdb file on the Student Data Disk for all of these exercises.

EXERCISE

7.1

Customers Form

1. Create a form with the following control specifications using the Customers table.

2. Place a 14-point label containing CUSTOMER ENTRY FORM at the top of the form. Be sure to return the default label font size to 8 or 10 points after you create this label box.

3. Place *two* horizontal lines beneath the label. Use the default line width.

4. Drag the FirstName field to the form.

5. Drag the LastName field to the form, beside the FirstName text box.

6. Change the label control for the FirstName field to Cust Name: and resize the label control as needed to fit.

7. Delete the LastName label box.

8. Move the LastName text box to place it closer to the FirstName text box.

9. Print a copy of one page of your completed form. Save the form as Exercise 7-1.

EXERCISE

7.2

Modified Customers Form

Continue with the form you created in Exercise 7.1, adding the following elements.

1. Drag the AddressLine1 field to the form, allowing one row of grid dots between the name and the Address field.

2. Drag the AddressLine2 field to the form, placing it directly beneath the previous Address field box. Delete the label for this field.

3. Drag the City field to the form, placing it directly beneath the previous Address field box. Delete the label for this field.

4. Drag the State field to the form, placing it to the right of the City text box. Delete the label for this field.

5. Drag the PostalCode field to the form, placing it to the right of the State text box. Delete the label for this field.

6. Reposition the State and PostalCode text boxes so that there is a single grid dot between fields.

7. Change the AddressLine1 label box to read Address: and move the box so that its right edge aligns with the CustName label box.

8. Print a copy of one page of the completed form. Save the modified form as Exercise 7-2.

EXERCISE

7.3

Customers Custom Report

In this exercise you will create a custom report using the Customers table. Follow the directions below.

1. In the Page Header section, place a title Customer List. With the box still selected, change the font size to 14 points. Use the Format | Size | To Fit command.

2. Drag the CustomerNumber field to the Detail section. Delete the attached label.

3. On the same row of the Detail section, create a text box. Delete its attached label box. Within the text box, enter the expression =[FirstName]&" "&[LastName] and press the **Enter** key. This tells Access to concatenate (combine) the customer's first and last names with one space between. Don't forget the equal sign, which tells Access to create this calculated field.

4. Add suitable column headings to the Page Header section. They should appear in bold.

5. Adjust the space in the sections to match the example in Guided Activity 7.6, and then print a copy of one page of your report.

6. Save the report as Exercise 7-3.

EXERCISE

7.4

Employee Form with List Box

Create a custom form using the Employees table.

1. Prepare a suitable form title, and then add the EmployeeID, FirstName and LastName, and Department fields.

2. The Department field should be in a list box that uses the Department table as its data source. Adjust the size of the list box to fit the information.

3. Print one page of the form, and save it as Exercise 7-4.

EXERCISE

7.5

Modifying a Form Wizard Form

1. Make sure the Hunter97.mdb database is open, and switch to Form mode.

2. Open the Products form already in the database, and view it in Form view.

3. Switch to Design view and rearrange the controls by dragging them into two columns.

4. Print a copy of the form, and save it as Exercise 7-5.

EXERCISE

7.6

Custom Products Form with List Box

1. Start with the form you developed in Exercise 7.5, and modify it so that the Vendors control is a list box, not a text box. Make the list box very short so it has a vertical scroll bar.

2. Print one page of the form, and save it as Exercise 7-6.

EXERCISE

7.7

Formatting Controls in the Products Form

1. Open in Design view the Products form from Exercise 7.5.

2. Change the background color of the form from gray to light blue. *Hint: click in the background of each section, then use the Fill/Back Color button on the Formatting toolbar.*

3. Make all the label controls appear in dark or royal blue. *Hint: Shift-click each of the controls to select them at one time, then use the Font/Fore Color button on the toolbar.*

4. Make all the text boxes appear in shadowed special effect. *Hint: draw a box in the Detail section that incorporates a piece of each of the text boxes to select them all at one time.*

5. Print one page of the form, then save it as Exercise 7-7.

EXERCISE

7.8   Hunter Menu Form

1. Design a main menu form for Hunter River on paper. Sketch out the location for command button controls for the following four menu choices: View Forms, Preview Reports, View Database, Quit. Include a label control for the name of the organization and put text boxes for the current date and time near the bottom of the menu.

2. Use Access to create the form with your design. The background for the form should be dark (hunter) green, and the label text should be deep yellow.

3. Include the command button controls with appropriate labels, but don't assign any macros or event procedures at this time. *Hint: make sure the Control Wizards button is off, then click the Command Button tool in the Toolbox to create the button. Access will leave a plain button without a macro assignment; change the label text appropriately. We will cover command buttons in a later unit.*

4. Print a copy of the form. Save it as Exercise 7-8.

Physician's Medical Clinic:
Building a Custom Physician Form

The chief administrator in the clinic wants you to design and build a custom form for entering doctor information for Physician's Medical Clinic. The form should be easy to use and provide controls for all physician information. Print a copy of the form for one doctor.

UNIT 8

Customizing a Form

This unit covers preparation of customized Access forms. It builds on the discussion of controls found in the previous unit and the forms introduction in the first part of this book. You will learn how to modify an existing form design as well as how to format text and controls. Advanced form features are covered, including the design and construction of complex forms that take advantage of the graphical user interface elements available in Access.

Learning Objectives

At the completion of this unit you should be able to

1. modify an existing form,

2. create a custom form using the blank form method,

3. create a list box control,

4. create an option group control,

5. set the font, font size, style, and alignment of text in a control,

6. link a main form and subform,

7. create a calculated subtotal.

Case Study

Hunter River needs a custom employee data entry form, as well as forms for products with vendors. You have been asked to create a customized order form that shows detail line items and calculates the total cost of the order.

Designing the Custom Form

We touched on the design of forms in the first part of this book. With the Form Wizard you can prepare a single-column form, a tabular form, a graph form, or a main/subform. While these form types provide some flexibility, you may need to prepare a combination of these types for use in a particular application. Our study of controls from the previous unit indicated that check boxes, toggle buttons, list boxes, and a variety of other helpful controls can make it easier for you to understand and work with the database. This section will show you how to create a custom form that incorporates these controls.

Steps in Creating the Custom Form

There are five steps in creating a custom form, described next. Starting with understanding the information needs, this process emphasizes how the user will work with the form.

UNDERSTAND THE PURPOSE OF THE FORM

The first and most important step is to understand the purpose for the form. Is it to enter data? Will the data be transferred from paper records? Is the form simply to show records? Will the form be used for making changes to (editing) the data? Who will be using the form? How many records will be examined? How much data should be presented on the form? What fields should appear on the form?

The answers to these and other questions will make it easier to design a form that meets the needs of the organization. Remember that these needs are often not stated precisely by the users. In fact, you will often be called on to prepare a prototype data object, whether it be a form or a report, and then you will let the users react to the model and make notes on their observations. Because it is so easy to make changes to Access data objects, you can quickly cycle through several iterations (versions) to be certain that the form meets the organization's needs.

CREATE THE DESIGN ON PAPER

You should sketch out a few rough ideas on paper, before you sit down at the computer. Although some people can create excellent forms directly on the screen, we generally recommend that you develop ideas first on paper. From the previous step you will know what information is to be displayed on the form. This step provides feedback on how to display and work with that data. For instance, if there are a great many fields, it may be necessary to use scrolling text boxes to reach them all, to provide a tabbed control, or even to associate multiple screens with a single form.

Look for examples of good form design in other forms used by your organization. Some paper forms have been carefully crafted and can serve as a guide for your computer forms. Consider the tab order sequence of data on the form. Do you want to give users choices in list or combo boxes, or provide buttons or check boxes? Do you want to provide validation rules for certain fields so that incorrect values can be eliminated at the source of data entry? We will talk more about form designs when we introduce form sections.

BUILD THE FORM DESIGN

You can either start with a Form Wizard design, then make changes, or create the form yourself by placing controls in the blank Design window. Because it is so easy to place fields on the screen, you will probably choose the latter. Our first activity will show how to make changes to an existing form design. Later activities will start with a blank form.

Main/subform designs combine two forms. First build the main form portion and save it. Then build the subform portion. Finally, add the subform to the main form and save the combined form as one unit.

TEST THE DESIGN

This important step involves presenting the form to users and asking for their feed-back. Expect them to "take it for a test drive" as they try to use the form with real-istic data. This step usually results in valuable feedback about changes that should be made. Also expect users to tell you things that they neglected to mention earlier in the process. Experience shows that once a user can do hands-on work with the real object, good progress is made toward the development of the best design for that object.

MODIFY THE DESIGN

After receiving feedback from the users, rebuild the form with corrections and enhancements. Retest the design with the same users to be certain that the revised form meets their needs. It is not unusual to go through several cycles at this stage.

Form Sections

Like reports, Access forms also have sections. Among these form sections, the Detail section contains the text boxes and command buttons that the user manipu-lates while working with the form. So far, most of our custom form examples have used the Detail section for all of the form elements.

The Form Header appears one time per form, at the beginning. The form header contains titles, instructions for the user, and other preliminary information about the form. It may also contain command buttons that accomplish certain tasks such as opening a second form. The Page Header appears at the top of each printed page. Likewise, there are Form Footer and Page Footer sections. Page headers and footers do *not* appear in Form view, but will appear when the form is printed. The page header and footer are used for column headings, date and time, page number, and other information that is pertinent for printed output.

Form headers and footers are added as a pair, using the Form Header/Footer command from the View menu. Likewise, page headers and footers are added as a pair using the Page Header/Footer command from the View menu. Once active in the Design window, you can drag the lower portion of the section borders up or down to shrink or enlarge the size of the section. Figure A8.1 shows a form design that uses sections.

The Form Header contains the form title in a label box. The Detail section con-tains the seven fields in the single-column format. The Form Footer is empty. From the form property sheet window, the Default View property is Single Form, mean-

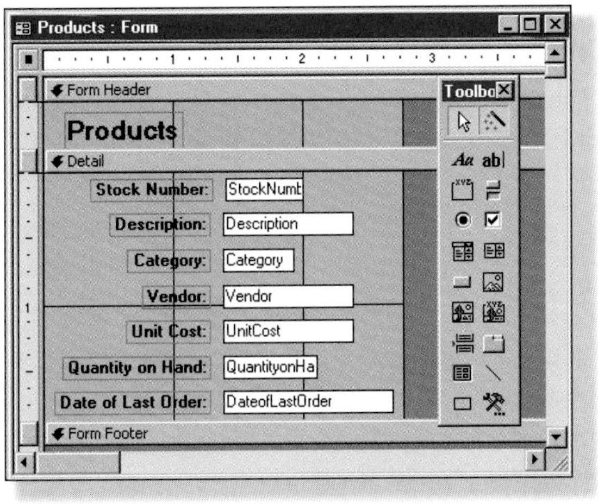

FIGURE A8.1
Form design showing form sections

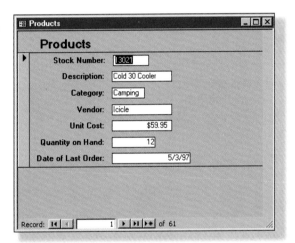

ing that the form for only one record will appear on screen at a time. Figure A8.2 shows Form view for this form.

FIGURE A8.2
Single Form view

Use of Controls in Form Designs

As we discussed in the previous unit, Access uses controls to represent labels, data values, OLE objects, lines, and other features that appear on forms. The Form Wizard uses labels, text boxes, and lines when Access creates forms automatically. You might want to add other kinds of controls to your forms. While the previous unit covered types of controls, in this unit we will discuss how to apply those controls to enhance your forms.

TEXT BOXES VERSUS YES/NO CONTROLS

Suppose we are looking at the Category field in the Products table. Its value, Camping, is displayed in the text box of Figure A8.2. When adding new records or changing the category for a particular product, the user must key in the entire name of the department. It must be spelled correctly to match other tables.

Because there are only a few product categories, it might be simpler to design a form with an option group containing a check box (or perhaps option buttons or toggle buttons) for each category. The user can then simply click the box representing the category for that product, saving time and increasing accuracy. Access will make sure that only one check box in the option group is turned on at a time (making it, in effect, a Yes/No control). The major limitation of an option group is that the Option Value returned by clicking one of the check boxes must be numeric. You might have to redesign the table in order to make use of such values. For instance, Camping could be 1, Hunting 2, and so forth.

TEXT BOX VERSUS A LIST BOX CONTROL

The list box control provides a drop-down list of values from which the user can choose. This control would also be suitable for the product Category. The user must move the pointer to the proper choice, and then click. For anything more than a few choices, the list box is more efficient than an option group of separate check boxes. With four current product categories, the list box would be a useful substitute for an option group of four boxes or buttons. We will later demonstrate how to replace a text box with a list box control.

TEXT BOX VERSUS A COMBO BOX CONTROL

Although similar to the Category field in the previous discussion, the Vendor field is less predictable. Thus, we might have a new vendor that is not already in the list. A combo box control provides a list of items to choose from, but also allows the user to key in a new value not in that list. Thus, a combo box control would be necessary for the Vendor field unless there were a way to guarantee that the vendor was already in existence before the user adds a product to the database. We will later demonstrate how to add a combo box to the form.

Creating a Custom Form

After the design is complete, it is time to build the form. If you start with a Form Wizard form design, you can go to Form Design view and manipulate existing controls to match the design. Certain kinds of custom forms are easier to build this way: if the Form Wizard can come close to your design, save yourself some effort and adopt this method. For other forms, it would be more trouble to make changes to the Form Wizard version than to start from scratch. We will demonstrate both methods in this unit, starting with modifying a Form Wizard design.

GUIDED ACTIVITY

8.1 Modifying a Form Design with a List Box and a Combo Box

In this Guided Activity you will modify a form design created by the Form Wizard, adding a label control, a list box control, and a combo box control.

1. Start Windows and load Access. Open the Hunter97.mdb Database window. Click the Forms tab and highlight the Product Entry form.

2. Click the Design button. If they are not already present, use the View menu to add the Toolbox, property sheet, and field list box. Drag the right side of the Form window border right to about the 5-inch mark.

3. Drag the border of the Form Header section down to about the 0.5-inch mark to make room for a form heading in this section.

4. Click the Label button in the Toolbox, and then create a label in the Form Header section, similar to the header shown in Figure A8.1. Use Product Entry Form as the text for this label, and select 14-point size.

5. Select the Category text box in the Detail section by clicking within its box. Press the **Del** key to delete this control and its attached label control.

6. Next, we will manually add a list box control for the Category. Click once on the List Box button in the Toolbox. Make sure that the Control Wizards button is *not* selected. Then drag the Category field from the field list box to the Detail section, placing it to the right of the other fields, about 4 inches over.

    Access will create two controls: the list box itself and an attached label control.

7. You should reduce the size of the list box by dragging the sizing handle. Make it about 0.75-inch tall.

8. In Guided Activity 7.5 in the last unit we created a list box with the Control Wizards. Here we must manually modify the list box property sheet to contain the values for the departments. Click once on the list box to select it, if it is not already selected.

9. In the property sheet, make the following changes. The Row Source Type should be Value List. On the Row Source line, type Camping;Hunting;Sports;Other and press **Enter**.

10. To preview the results, click once on the Form View button on the toolbar. The Camping choice is highlighted, signifying that the first record is from that Category. Your screen should resemble Figure A8.3.

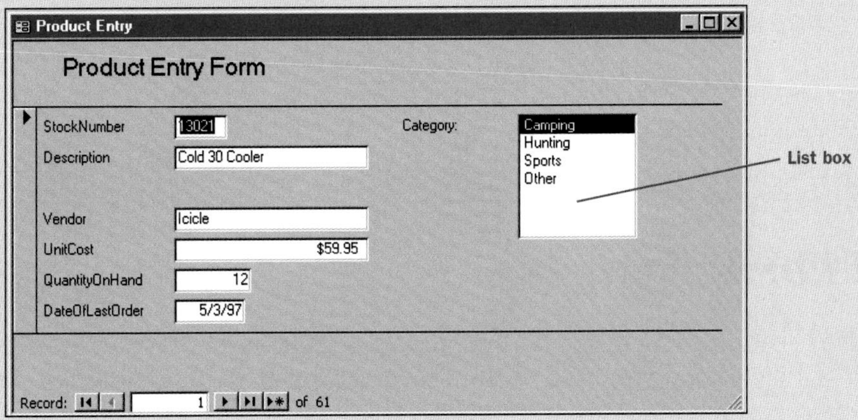

FIGURE A8.3
Form view with list box control

11. Next, we will replace the Vendor field with a combo box with help from the Control Wizards. Return to Form Design view. Select the Vendor text box and press the **Del** key to remove it and its attached label.

12. Click the Combo Box button in the Toolbox. It is to the left of the List Box button, and directly below the "bull's-eye" (Option Button) icon. Make sure the Control Wizards button is selected in the Toolbox.

13. Drag the Vendor field from the field list box to the Detail section, placing it beneath the Description field where the Category field used to be. Align the combo box with the other fields.

14. The Combo Box Wizard screen will appear after a few seconds. Click Next to have the combo box look up values from a table. At the next screen select the Vendors table and click Next.

15. At the next step click the > button to select the VendorName field. Click Next to go on.

16. Click Next to accept the default column width. Click Next again to store the value in the Vendor field of the Products table. Finally, click Finish to add the combo box to your form.

17. Click the Form View button on the toolbar to view your form. It should look like Figure A8.4. The combo box is expanded to display choices.

FIGURE A8.4
Form view with combo box control

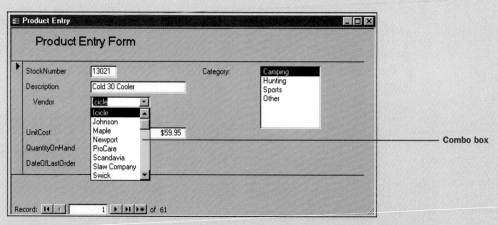

18. Close the Form window without saving the revised design.

Advanced Form Features

This section will present several advanced features possible with Access forms. We also discuss how to build custom forms from scratch, starting with a blank form.

Creating an Option Group

As mentioned previously, an option group is a control that contains several Yes/No choices or options, represented by check boxes, option buttons, or toggle buttons. Only one choice can be selected (Yes) at a time; all the other choices are (No). The option group control returns the numeric value associated with the selected Yes/No control, storing that value in the field it is bound to.

The option group Control Wizards procedure is similar to that used for other form controls. Build the form as normal, adding other controls as needed. When you are ready for the option group, click on the Option Group button in the Toolbox. With the Control Wizards button selected, drag the field from the field list that is to be bound to the option group. Place that field in the Form Design window, most likely in the Detail section. Access will create two controls—a label with the name of the field bound to the option group, and the option group itself, represented by a large rectangle.

First type in the labels for each value in the option group. The Option Group Wizard presents a grid that resembles the datasheet. Then choose whether to have a default value for the option group, and specify the values used for the various options. They are usually 1, 2, 3, and so forth. Specify which field in the form's data source (underlying table or query) will receive the value from the option group; typically, it will be the field you dragged to the form for the option group.

Next, select the style and Yes/No control type that will represent the choices in the form. After choosing the label text for the option group, you are finished with the Option Group Wizard and you can see the design. The following example will show how to create an option group in a custom form.

GUIDED ACTIVITY

8.2   Adding an Option Group to a Form Design

In this Guided Activity you will use the Option Group Wizard to add an option group to a form design.

 NOTE   *The Access Advanced Wizards must be installed to complete this activity. By default this option is not selected when you install Office 97.*

1. Close all open windows and return to the Hunter97.mdb Database window.

2. Switch to Form mode and select the Order Entry form in Design view. It should resemble the design shown in Figure A8.5.

3. If necessary, move the field list box and property sheet out of the way. Use the View | Toolbox command to make sure that the Toolbox is displayed.

 4. Make sure the Control Wizards button is selected, then click the Option Group button in the Toolbox. It is the rectangle directly beneath the Aa (Label) tool. Then drag the MethodOfPayment field from the field list box, placing it at the 1,3-inch coordinates (down 1", over 3") in the Detail section.

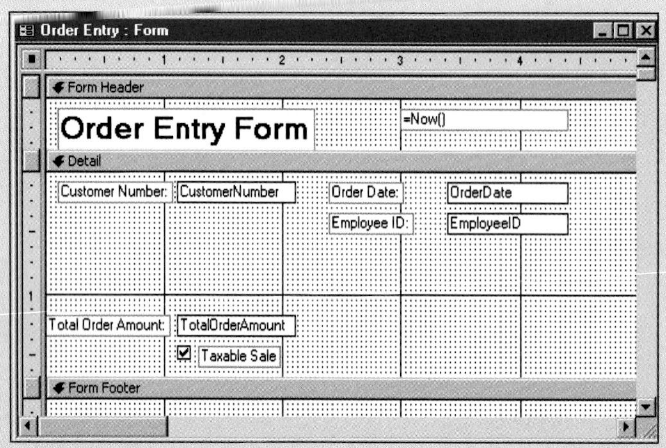

FIGURE A8.5
Order Entry preliminary form design

5. The Option Group Wizard will ask you to type in the label names for each option item. The values are `Cash`, `Purchase Order`, and `Credit`. Type each on a separate line, and then click Next.

6. You will be asked if you want one option to be the default value. Select no default method of payment, and then click Next to go to the next step.

7. The Option Group Wizard chooses the values of 1, 2, and 3 for the three option choices. Click Next to accept these values.

8. Click Next once more to signify that you want Access to store the option value in the MethodOfPayment field.

9. Make sure that the Option Buttons choice is selected. We will use the Etched style for the option group. Click Next to go on.

10. For the option group's label, enter `Method of Payment` and click Finish to place the option group in the form. Figure A8.6 shows the form's Design view.

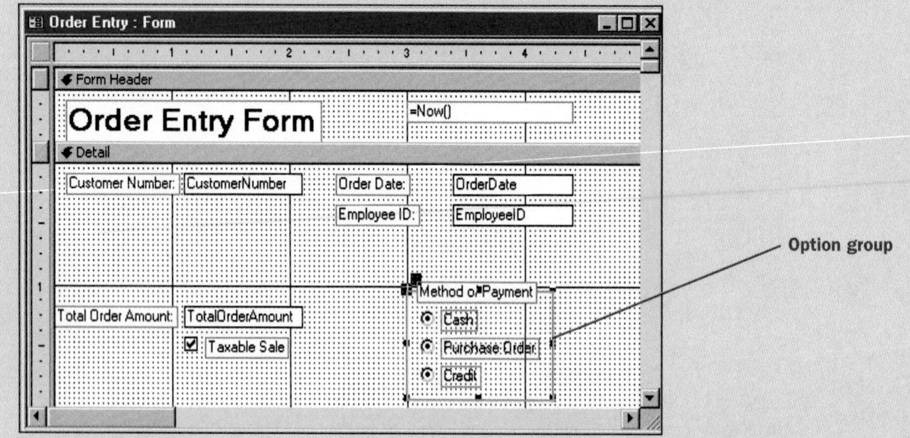

FIGURE A8.6
Order Entry form design with option group

11. Finally, we will view the form. Click the Form View button on the toolbar (or give the View | Form command). Figure A8.7 shows the form for a record in the Orders table.

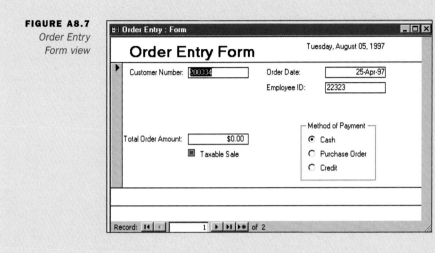

FIGURE A8.7
Order Entry
Form view

12. Save the changes under the same form name. Close the Form window.

Improving the Form's Usefulness

It is possible (and desirable) to make the form easier to use by improving its layout and visual image. Rearranging fields, enclosing similar fields with rectangles or lines, adding sunken or raised 3-D special effects, and using color are all techniques that will help the user. Refer to the previous unit or search Help for suggestions in these areas. Some other suggestions follow.

FORMATTING TEXT: FONT, SIZE, STYLE, AND ALIGNMENT

As mentioned earlier in this book, Access shares many desirable Windows features, including choice of font and font size. The font refers to the particular typeface used such as Arial, Courier, and Times Roman. Your choice of fonts depends on which fonts were installed on your system. Beginning with Windows 3.1, built-in TrueType fonts are scalable; that is, Windows can automatically enlarge or shrink the font to the desired size. TrueType fonts can be displayed on the screen and printed on nearly any printer. Typical font size for a form title is 14 or 18 points. Text box labels may be 8 or 10 points. The Font and Font Size buttons appear on the Formatting toolbar whenever a text control is selected.

The text style refers to normal, bold, and italic. To change the style of text in a control, select that control, and then click the appropriate style button on the toolbar. You can format a portion of the text in a control by highlighting just the portion that you want to change. As mentioned in the previous unit, you can change a single control or change the default values for all new controls of a specific type.

Text alignment refers to where a value appears within its column. The default text alignment is General, in which numbers and dates are aligned at the right side of the control box, and other values are aligned with the left side of the control box. You can also select Align Left, Center, or Align Right. Select the text control, and then click the appropriate buttons on the Formatting toolbar.

INSERTING A PAGE BREAK

When there are numerous fields, you may need to break the form into several screens. The page break control is used for this purpose. You can move back and forth between the screens of the form as necessary. Create the form as usual, filling the form's Detail section with controls. Then click the Page Break button in the Toolbox. Move the pointer to the location in the form design where you want to put the page break, and click the left mouse button. Access will insert the page break and mark it next to the left ruler with a short dotted line.

CHANGING THE TAB ORDER IN A FORM

TIP

It is possible to change the behavior of the arrow keys, in the Options dialog box. Use the Tools|Options command to display the Options dialog box. Select Keyboard, and then change the arrow key behavior to move a character at a time instead of a field at a time.

Access will sequence the fields' controls in the order you add them to the form. If you have made mistakes or rearranged controls, the tab order may not be correct. Recall that the tab order is the order in which a user will go through the controls in a form. You can press the **Tab** or **Enter** key to go forward through the fields in the form. Press **Shift+Tab** to go in the reverse order. The **Right arrow** and **Left arrow** keys will usually work in the same manner, sending you to the next or previous field.

The standard tab order is top-to-bottom, or left-to-right. To change the tab order, open the form in Design view. Choose the Tab Order command from the View menu. Figure A8.8 shows the Tab Order dialog box for the previous form. Select the form section you wish to change (Form Header, Detail, or Form Footer). To select the standard order, click the Auto Order button. If you want a custom tab order, click the field selector button to the left of the field name to select the field. Then drag that field to the proper sequence and release the mouse button. Access will insert the selected field and rearrange the other fields. Click OK to save the new tab order.

FIGURE A8.8
Tab Order dialog box

USING A COMMAND BUTTON TO OPEN ANOTHER FORM

From the previous unit you likely will remember that a command button is used in a form to cause some action to occur. The command button is attached to an Access macro or a user procedure. You can use the command button to open another form on demand; that is, you can choose to see another form based on characteristics of the data. You can add a command button manually, or use the Command Button Wizard.

If the Control Wizards button is not selected, simply add the command button control like any other control. Then modify the property sheet to indicate what action the button is to take, as shown in Figure A8.9. For example, the On Click property can give the name of the macro that runs when the button is clicked. That macro can cause the requested form to be displayed. Macros are covered in Unit 11 of this book.

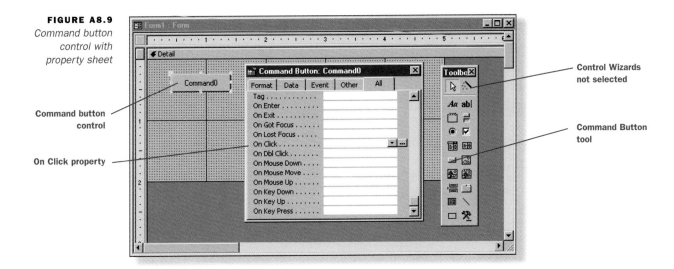

FIGURE A8.9
Command button control with property sheet

Command button control

On Click property

Control Wizards not selected

Command Button tool

Creating a Complex Main/Subform

We covered preparation of a main/subform design in Part One of this book. That discussion featured use of the Access Form Wizard to prepare the form. In this section we will build the order entry form by hand, using a join query as the data source for the form.

Starting with a Join Query

We must join the four main tables used in the order form: Customers, Orders, Order Items, and Products. You read about this design in the "Relational Database Concepts" section of Unit 6. The database design is shown in Figure A6.2. We actually need two queries: one that joins the Orders and Customers tables, and another that joins the Order Items and Products tables. These queries are already created and stored in the Hunter97.mdb database. They are called Customer/Order Join and Order Items/Products Join. The first one will be used for the main form fields, the second query for the subform fields.

Access will *automatically* link the main form and the subform if both contain a field with the same name that is also the primary key of the underlying table. If the two forms are based on queries, as they are here, you must use the subform property sheet to name the link field(s), in this case the OrderNumber field.

 NOTE *If you have created a relationship between the two tables, Access will automatically link the main form and subform. This relationship exists in the Hunter97.mdb database.*

Create the Main Form

The next step is to create the main form. In this case, the main form contains the order information including customer number, order number, order date, and all the name and address information from the Customers table. These fields have been dragged to the query. Remember to leave room for the subform in the lower portion of the screen; we'll add it shortly. Save this form.

Create the Subform

Next, create the subform that contains the individual items with this order. This form will have no header or footer, and should have just a single line in the Detail section. In the subform's property sheet select Datasheet as the default view. Save this form with a different name than the main form.

Add the Subform to the Main Form

The final design step is to drag the subform from the Database window to the lower portion of the main form's Design view. Access will create a subform control to hold the subform. We will have to link the two forms' Order Number fields through the Link Child Fields and Link Master Fields properties in the subform's property sheet. We'll demonstrate this in the following activity.

GUIDED ACTIVITY

8.3   Creating an Order Main/Subform

In this Guided Activity you will prepare an order main form with a subform, beginning with a blank form.

1. Close all windows and return to the Hunter97.mdb Database window.

2. As described earlier, our form will use two queries that have been saved in the Hunter97.mdb database. Switch to Form mode, and click the New button to create the main form. Select the Customer/Order Join query as the data source for this form and select Design View. Click OK to open a blank form.

3. Choose the Form Header/Footer command from the View menu to create a Form Header and Form Footer. Increase the size of the Detail section of the form to about 4 inches.

4. In the Form Header section create a label box for the form title. In this box type Hunter River Order Form and press **Enter**. With the box still selected, choose Bold and make the font size 14 points. If the box does not expand automatically to fit the font size, increase the size of the Form Header section to accommodate this label box.

5. In the Detail section drag the OrderNumber and OrderDate fields from the field list. Although placement is not critical, refer to Figure A8.10 after step 20 for suggested locations.

6. Repeat step 5 with the CustomerNumber field, just beneath the OrderNumber field.

7. Add the FirstName field to the form. Change its attached label to read Sold To:. Place LastName to the right of the FirstName field, and then delete its label. Drag the LastName control over near the FirstName field.

8. Add all of the address fields to the form, placing them directly beneath the name controls. Delete all of the attached labels. Resize the fields to fit their contents.

9. Also add the EmployeeID, TaxableSale, and MethodOfPayment fields to the form.

10. Next, we are ready to save the main form. Use the name Hunter River Main Order Form. Don't close the main form—we will want to add the sub-form to it later.

11. Click in the Database window (or press **F11**) to bring it to the foreground. With the Forms tab selected, click the New button to create the subform. Access will open another Form window while leaving the previous Form window open.

12. Choose the Order Items/Products Join query as the data source for the subform. Choose Design View for the new form, and then click OK to open a blank form.

13. Drag the following fields to the Detail section of the subform, all on the same line: ProductNumber, OrderQuantity, Description, and UnitCost. Delete each attached label. You will want to resize the fields to fit their contents.

14. We need to add a calculated field to the subform. Click the Text Box button in the Toolbox. Then position the pointer to the end of the line and click the left mouse button. Make the attached label of this field Extended Cost.

15. Type the expression =[UnitCost]*[OrderQuantity] inside the new text box and press **Enter**. Don't forget the equal sign. While this control is still selected, change its Decimal Places property from Auto to 2. Its Name property should be Extended Cost. The Format property should be Currency.

16. Click in the dark gray area outside the light gray area of this form. Access will display the form's property sheet. Change the Default View property to Datasheet View.

17. Save the subform as Hunter Order Subform and close its Form window.

18. Click in the main form window (or use the Window command from the menu bar) to make it active. Press **F11** to show the Database window. Drag the subform you just saved from the Database window to the lower portion of the main form and release the left mouse button. Access will create a subform control. Drag its lower border down a little to enlarge the subform. Drag the Form Footer border up to delete most of the space for the footer.

19. With the subform selected, type OrderNumber into both the Link Child Fields and Link Master Fields properties in the subform's property sheet. That will cause Access to display only records in the subform area that match the order number displayed in the main form.

20. Click the Form View button to see what your form looks like. Figure A8.10 shows the subform in place in the main form for the first order. You can examine additional orders by clicking on the bottom record-navigation buttons. If one order has a large number of items, the inner record-navigation buttons can be used to scroll through the items.

21. Save the finished main form design using the same name.

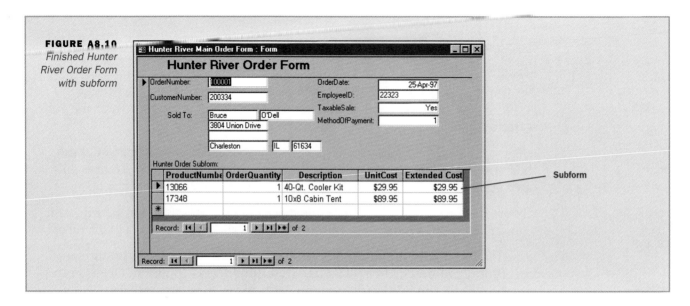

FIGURE A8.10
*Finished Hunter
River Order Form
with subform*

Calculating Subtotals

In our last activity we did not place the Total field on the form. We can sum the Extended Cost calculated field and place it in a control on the form. To do this, add a Form Footer to the subform and place a calculated control in the footer that sums the Extended Cost field. Because the Default View property for the subform is Datasheet View, you will not see any controls that were placed in the subform's header or footer. Create a calculated control on the main form and have it refer to the total field in the subform's footer. The next activity will illustrate this process.

GUIDED ACTIVITY

8.4 Adding a Subtotal Control to the Main/Subform

In this Guided Activity we will take the Hunter River Order Form created in the previous activity and add a control that calculates the total amount of the order items.

1. Close any open windows and return to the Hunter97.mdb Database window. In Form mode, select the Hunter Order Subform. Click the Design button.

2. Choose the Page Header/Footer command from the View menu. Although Access will create a Form Header and Form Footer, they will not display in Form view because we have selected Datasheet View in the property sheet for the subform.

3. Select the Text Box button in the Toolbox. In the Form Footer section, add a text box control beneath the Extended Cost control found in the Detail section.

4. Select the attached label of this control, and then change its caption to `Order Subtotal:` and press **Enter**. You may have to resize the box or choose Format | Size | To Fit to display all of the text.

5. Select the text box control in the Form Footer section. In its property sheet enter `Order Subtotal` for the Name property. In the Control Source property, enter `=Sum([UnitCost]*[OrderQuantity])` and press **Enter**.

You cannot sum the Extended Cost calculated field directly in this expression.

6. Save the subform and close its window.

7. Open the Hunter River Main Order Form in Design view.

8. Select the Text Box button in the Toolbox. Place a text box control beneath the MethodOfPayment control, around the 1.25,4-inch coordinates.

9. Select the attached label, and change its Caption property to `Order Subtotal:`.

10. Select the text box that you just added and enter the following expression in its Control Source property: `=[Hunter Order Subform].Form![Order Subtotal]` and press **Enter**. The equal sign signifies that this is a calculated field; the [Hunter Order Subform]. is the name of the subform control that contains the values used in the calculation; the Form! phrase allows access to the subform's controls and properties; and [Order Subtotal] is the name of the control that contains the value we want.

It might be easier to use the Expression Builder window to create this expression. Click the button with three dots to the right of the Control Source property box.

11. Select Currency for the Format property of this control.

12. Click the Form View button on the toolbar to see the results, shown in Figure A8.11. Save the form and close the Form window.

If Access displays #Error or some other error message in the subtotal control in Form view, double-check that you have entered the proper Control Source expression in step 10. Further, make sure that you changed the Name property of the subtotal control in the Hunter Order Subform in step 5 above.

FIGURE A8.11
Hunter River Main Order Form with subtotal control

Hunter River Main Order Form : Form

Hunter River Order Form

OrderNumber:	100001		OrderDate:	25-Apr-97
CustomerNumber:	200334		EmployeeID:	22323
			TaxableSale:	Yes
Sold To:	Bruce	O'Dell	MethodOfPayment:	1
	3804 Union Drive			
	Charleston	IL 61634	Order Subtotal:	$119.90

Hunter Order Subform:

ProductNumbe	OrderQuantity	Description	UnitCost	Extended Cost
▶ 13066	1	40-Qt. Cooler Kit	$29.95	$29.95
17348	1	10x8 Cabin Tent	$89.95	$89.95
*				

Record: |◄ ◄ | 1 | ► ►| ►* of 2

← **Subtotal control**

Record: |◄ ◄ | 1 | ► ►| ►* of 4

Using the Main/Subform

Although this form is not yet as complete as it might be, we can demonstrate how it can be used to view existing orders or add new orders to the Hunter97 database. To improve the form, you might replace the CustomerNumber text box with a combo box control so that you can search through the customer records for a name. The OrderNumber must be filled in for new orders—you could make this a counter field and have Access fill it in for you. You could replace the Taxable text box control with check boxes for Taxable and Nontaxable. You could add a vertical scroll bar for the subform, removing the navigation buttons area. You could add a command button to close the order form or move on to the next record.

VIEWING EXISTING CUSTOMER ORDERS

To use the form, open the main form from the Hunter97.mdb Database window. Access will display the first record in the Orders table and any matching items from the Order Items table. You can use the main form's navigation area to move through the orders one at a time or go directly to the last order. You can see up to three order items in the subform area; to see additional items, use the subform's record navigation area.

ADDING A NEW CUSTOMER ORDER

To add a new order, open the main form from the Hunter97.mdb Database window. Move to the last record in the main form and click the Next Record button. Access will display a blank record. Place a number in the OrderNumber box and press the **Tab** key. You will move to the CustomerNumber box. Enter a valid customer number and press **Enter**; Access will fill in that customer's information in the rest of the boxes. Then fill in the OrderDate, EmployeeID, TaxableSale, and MethodOfPayment fields. Press **Tab** to move to the subform. Fill in the ProductNumber for the first order item and press **Tab**. Access will automatically fill in the Description and UnitCost fields. Enter an order quantity, and Access will calculate the Extended Cost and Order Subtotal fields. You can add more order items for the current order, or add another order, or close the form. You will add a new customer order as an exercise.

SUMMARY This unit has demonstrated how to create custom forms, beginning with the paper design stage. You can start with an existing form and make modifications in Design view, or begin with a blank form and create the form from scratch. You learned how to build a list box control and an option group control using the Control Wizards.

The Formatting toolbar commands for font, font size, style, and text alignment were covered. You learned how to modify the tab order for a form. Command button controls cause a macro to execute when the user clicks them.

Finally, the unit showed how to create a complex main form with subform. The main form and subform are linked on common values using the Link Child Fields and Link Master Fields properties. You learned how to create a subtotal of fields in the subform, which is displayed in the main form.

Exercises

Use the Hunter River database contained within the Hunter97.mdb file on the Student Data Disk for these exercises.

EXERCISE

8.1

Hunter River Employee Form Design

1. Design a custom form on paper to enter a new employee into the Hunter River database. Use the design of the Employees table to guide your thinking.

2. Use a layout and whatever controls make it easiest to perform this operation. Remember to place similar fields together.

3. What additional fields should be added to the design of this table?

EXERCISE

8.2

Custom Employee Form

1. Using your design from Exercise 8.1, create a custom Access form.

2. Print the Form view for your form.

3. If possible, also print a copy of the Design view of your form. To do this, have the Form Design view on your screen, and then press the **PrtSc** key. Windows will place a copy of the screen in the Clipboard. Open a word processor such as Windows WordPad or your own Windows word processor, and then paste the contents of the Clipboard into a new document. Printing that document may be time-consuming, depending on the speed of your printer and the print resolution you have selected.

NOTE   *The **Alt+PrtSc** command will capture only the active window to the Clipboard, instead of the entire screen.*

4. Save the form as Exercise 8-2.

8.3

Vendors and Products Form Design

1. Design a custom form for Hunter River vendors and products.

2. Your form should include vendor information at the top of the screen and a list of products from that vendor in the lower portion as a subform.

8.4

Custom Vendors and Products Form

1. Using your design from Exercise 8.3, create a custom Access main form and subform for Vendors and Products. Be sure to link the forms together.

2. Print the Design view and Form view for your forms.

3. Save the two forms as Exercise 8-4 Main Form and Exercise 8-4 Subform.

8.5

Modified Vendors and Products Form

1. Modify the form from Exercise 8.4 to include inventory value (unit cost multiplied by quantity on hand) in the subform.

2. Be sure to create a subtotal for all products for a particular vendor.

3. Print a copy of Form view for one vendor's products.

4. Save the form as Exercise 8-5 Main Form.

8.6

Equipment Table

1. Create a new table called Equipment that contains the computers, cash registers, fixtures, display cabinets, storage bins, and other equipment used by Hunter River to display and account for merchandise and customer sales.

2. Develop fields that would be appropriate to calculate age and annual depreciation. One of the fields is a depreciation type for each piece; its codes are

represented by the numeric values 1–5, which stand for the depreciation type. Labels for those types are MACRS, ACRS, Section 168(f)(1), CLADR, and pre-ACRS.

3. Print a copy of the design of this table, using the screen capture to Clipboard procedure discussed in Exercise 8.2.

EXERCISE

8.7 Custom Equipment Form

1. Create a form to enter and view information about the Equipment table. It should contain an option group for the depreciation type field.

2. Create at least one record for the Equipment table, entering it from your custom form.

3. Print a copy of the Form view and Design view for your form.

4. Save the form as Exercise 8-7.

EXERCISE

8.8 Using the Hunter River Order Form

1. Use the Hunter River Main Order Form and subform you created in Guided Activities 8.3 and 8.4 to add a new customer order to the database. The order number is 110003 and the customer number is 281111. Use the current date for the order. The employee making the sale was number 26331. The order consists of a single item, number 20238. The order quantity is 1.

2. Print a copy of the form containing this data in Form view.

Physicians' Medical Clinic: Building a Custom Patient Information Form

PMC management has asked you to prepare a form that shows the patient's permanent information in the top portion of the form. In the bottom part add a subform that shows that patient's visits to the clinic, including the name of the procedure and the cost of that procedure. Remember that each visit should be on a separate line of the subform, in Datasheet view. Print a copy of the form for one patient.

Mr. Greenlee wants you to modify the form for this step so that only the 1997 visits are included in the subform. You will probably create a query for this condition; change the subform's data source to reflect the query instead of the Visits table. Display the total charges for that patient's 1997 visits. Be sure that the subform control is large enough to display all of the charges for that patient's visits. Print a copy of the form for one patient.

UNIT 9

Customizing a Report

This unit covers preparation of customized Access reports. It builds on the discussion of controls found in Unit 7 and on the report introduction in the first part of this book. You will learn how to modify an existing report design, as well as how to format text and controls in reports. Advanced report features are covered, including group reports and linked subreports.

Learning Objectives

At the completion of this unit you should be able to

1. change the design of an existing report,

2. change section size and section properties,

3. use label, text box, line, rectangle, and page break controls,

4. add a calculated field control to a report,

5. create a group report with multiple groups of records,

6. create a report with a linked subreport,

7. build a report cover page in the Report Header section,

8. create custom mailing labels.

Case Study

Although Hunter River has been able to use the standard reports available from the Report Wizard, management wants to prepare custom reports including multiple-level inventory group reports and customer invoices. They would like you to explore using Access to prepare report covers.

Designing the Custom Report

We touched on the design of reports in the first part of this book. With the Report Wizard you can prepare a columnar report, a tabular report, a chart, a group report, or mailing labels. You can let the Report Wizard create the report and then make modifications as necessary. You may have a situation in which you must build the entire report yourself from scratch, such as matching a specific format or working with a large number of fields. You can design a custom report for nearly any situation; the Report Wizard is more limited in formatting and field placement.

Steps in Creating a Custom Report

Although reports allow output only of data values, the steps in creating a custom report are very similar to those for creating a custom form. The emphasis is on creating a design that makes it easy for users to work with the information.

UNDERSTAND THE PURPOSE OF THE REPORT

The first and most important step is to understand the purpose of the report and the kinds of information that it is to provide. What fields are to be included? Must you provide detailed data or summaries? What is the proper sequence for records in the report? How frequently will the report be printed? Talk to the users of the report to learn more about the answers to these questions. And be prepared to make changes to the design after users react to prototype reports.

CREATE THE DESIGN ON PAPER

Sketch rough ideas on paper, before you sit down at the computer. Although some people can create excellent reports directly on the screen, we recommend that you develop ideas first on paper. This step provides feedback on how to display and fit the formatted data fields on the report. Consider using different font sizes in this step to emphasize certain parts of the report. Although it is fairly easy to move controls around the report design, your preliminary design on paper should enable you to initially place fields in their approximate locations.

BUILD THE REPORT DESIGN

You can start with a Report Wizard design and make changes or create a new design by starting with a blank report. We will show Guided Activities for both methods. In either case, Access will place controls in the report design in a manner similar to forms. Of course, some of the controls used in forms are not appropriate for reports. Access reports use five main sections; group reports add group header and footer sections as well. For a complete review on report sections, refer to Unit 5. Our first activity will show how to modify an existing report design. Later activities will start with a blank report.

TEST THE DESIGN

This important step involves taking the report to users and asking for their feedback. Expect them to "take it for a test drive" as they print reports with realistic data. This step usually results in valuable feedback about changes that should be made. Expect users to tell you things that they neglected to mention earlier in the process. Experience shows that once a user can do hands-on work with the real object, good progress is made toward the development of the best design for that object.

MODIFY THE DESIGN

After receiving feedback from users, rebuild the report with corrections and enhancements. Retest the design with users to be certain that the revised report meets their needs.

Changing the Design of an Existing Report

We saw how to make minor changes to a Report Wizard report design in the first part of this book. In that instance we removed a calculated subtotal of a number field that was not meaningful for the group report in which it appeared. The Report Design window is nearly identical to the Form Design window. You can add, move, and resize report controls just as you do form controls. The Report Design View toolbars are shown in Figure A9.1.

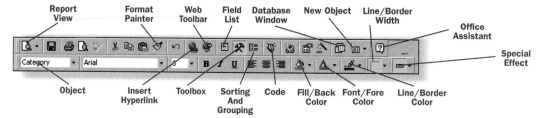

FIGURE A9.1
Report Design View toolbars

The most common type of Access Report Wizard is the group report in which fields are displayed across the page with similar records grouped together. Unless otherwise specified with the Caption property, the field names are used for column headings. Column widths match the field sizes, with one Detail section row per record. Access will try to fit wide reports in landscape orientation. If there are too many fields to fit on a standard page, the extra fields are printed on another sheet of paper. You may need to make changes to column widths, rearrange fields, use two or more Detail section rows to hold the fields, or add dates and other system functions to the report. You might want to add another level of grouping to the report, or place a graph in the report. Graphs are covered in Unit 10 of this book.

Selecting Controls

The basic procedure to change the report is to first select the control(s) you want to change, and then apply the change. To select a single control, click anywhere within that control's box. To select several controls, hold down the **Shift** key and select the controls by clicking within them. To select a group of adjacent controls, place the pointer outside that group; while holding down the left mouse button, drag the pointer to create a rectangle that goes through a portion of the controls in the group.

Resizing and Moving Controls

TIP

Sometimes it is simpler to delete a line and add it again than to make changes to an existing line.

As covered in previous units, you can change the size of a control by dragging one of its seven sizing handles to the desired location and then releasing the mouse button. Use the Undo button on the toolbar to reverse the effects of the last change made. The upper left corner of each control box contains its move handle. Drag this handle to move the control. Many controls have an attached label. If you position the pointer between the text box and its label, the pointer will change to a hand with outstretched fingers. Dragging the control in this configuration will move both control and label. If the hand has an outstretched index finger, you will move only one control, not both.

Remember that lines and rectangles are also controls. They can be selected and manipulated in the usual way.

Text Formatting

Access reports offer the same text formatting features that we discussed in the previous two units. You can select a font and size for one or more text controls. You can choose bold and italic styles for all or a portion of the text in a control. You can select the underline attribute from the control's property sheet but not from a toolbar button. The alignment for the text in a control can be left, right, or centered. You can also choose General alignment in which numbers and dates are right-aligned and text fields are left-aligned.

Working with Report Sections

As discussed previously, reports contain five or more report sections, each with a specific purpose. The Report Header section provides a way to place a title page at the beginning of the report. It appears only one time per report. The Page Header appears at the top of each page (except the first page if there is a Report Header) and can contain a page title, column headings, page number, system date, and other controls. The Detail section displays the field values for each record in the report. The Page Footer section can contain descriptive information or system fields like date and page number. The Report Footer section appears at the end of the report and contains report summary fields and totals. The Report Footer appears before the Page Footer on the last page of the report. Group header and group footer sections are used for introductory and summary fields for groups of records. You could put the value of the group field in the group header section; place subtotals or record counts in the group footer section.

ADDING OR REMOVING HEADER AND FOOTER SECTIONS

Use the View menu to add or remove headers and footers. There are separate commands for Report Header/Footer and Page Header/Footer. Access will place a check mark next to the command if that particular header/footer pair is active. To remove the header/footer pair, choose the command and the check mark will disappear. By default, a blank report design will contain a Page Header and Page Footer, but not a Report Header and Report Footer.

CHANGING THE SECTION SIZE

You can change the height or width of a section by dragging its borders with the mouse. If there is any extra space above or below the controls in the Detail section, that space will appear between records on the report. The default height for a control is ⅙ inch. You can reduce the Detail section height to that size and have records appear with normal spacing between lines.

 NOTE   *If you choose a larger font size, you may need to adjust the height of the Detail section.*

CHANGING SECTION PROPERTIES

You can view and change section properties in reports and forms. Click anywhere within the section to select that section, and then display the property sheet by clicking the Properties button on the toolbar or by giving the View | Properties command. You can also examine the property sheet for the report by double-clicking in the gray area in the Report window (not in a section) and displaying properties. As with forms, some report properties can be changed only in the property sheet, while others, such as size and color, can also be changed directly in the Design window. The rightmost five buttons on the Formatting toolbar will let you adjust the color and special effects of some controls. You can search Help for more details about setting report properties.

GUIDED ACTIVITY

9.1   Modifying a Report Design

In this Guided Activity you will make changes to a report designed by the Report Wizard to improve the layout. Some of the explanations may seem cryptic—refer to the figures to understand the effect of the changes you are making.

1. Load Windows and start Access as usual. Open the Hunter97.mdb Database window.

2. Switch to Report mode. Select the Product Report By Vendor report and click the Design button. Figure A9.2 shows a portion of this design.

3. Select the Vendor label control in the Page Header section. Drag the right sizing handle so that the label extends to about the 1-inch mark on the horizontal ruler.

4. Next, select the StockNumber label control in the Page Header section. Drag its left sizing handle over to the left to the 1 inch mark. Reduce its width slightly.

5. Repeat steps 3 and 4 with the Category and UnitCost label controls. Widen Category and shrink UnitCost.

FIGURE A9.2
*Report Wizard
group report
design*

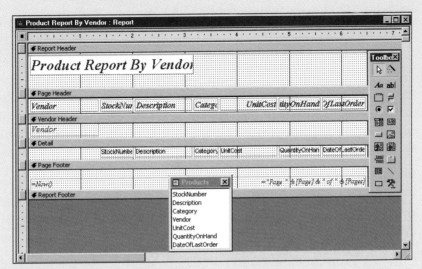

6. We want to move some Detail section group of controls over to the left about 0.5 inch. Place the pointer to the left of the StockNumber field, hold down the left mouse button, and drag a rectangle that includes a portion of the Stock-Number and Description controls in the Detail section. This selects all the controls within the rectangle.

7. With these controls selected, drag the group so that the leftmost control appears at the 1-inch mark. Click once outside the group to deselect these controls. Make sure the controls are aligned with the top of the Detail section border.

8. Now widen the Description text box control in the Detail section by dragging its right sizing handle over to about the 3-inch mark.

9. We need to improve the column headings used in this report. In particular, the DateOfLastOrder and QuantityOnHand labels are much wider than the fields they represent. Drag the lower border of the Page Header section down to about the 0.75-inch mark to make room for changes.

10. Select the line beneath the column headings in the Page Header section. Drag this line down just below the 0.5-inch mark. You are making room for two-row column headings as shown in Figure A9.3 after step 16.

NOTE *Figure A9.3 summarizes the changes you will be making in the remainder of this activity. You can click the Print Preview button after each step to see how your report will look.*

11. Next we will modify the StockNumber label, making it a two-line label with Stock on top and Number on the bottom. Move the pointer just before the "N" in Number and slowly click two times. Then press **Ctrl Enter**; this will instruct Access to insert a line feed and put Number on a separate line. Press **Enter** to complete the change and resize the label control.

12. Move the Description text box in the Detail section to the left, next to the Stock Number control. Drag the right side of the Description text box control out to about 3 inches. Move the Description label in the Page Header section to align with the left edge of the Description text box.

13. Repeat step 11 with the UnitCost label so that it appears on two lines. Right-justify this label. Reduce the size of the UnitCost text box so that its left side is at about the 4-inch mark. Align the UnitCost label and text box on their right sides.

14. Repeat step 11 with the QuantityOnHand label, making it a two-line column heading with spaces between the words.

15. Repeat step 11 with the DateOfLastOrder label, and then split the label into two lines.

16. Click the Print Preview button on the toolbar to view the revised report. Figure A9.3 shows a portion of this output. Save the revised report and close the active window.

FIGURE A9.3
Print Preview for modified group report

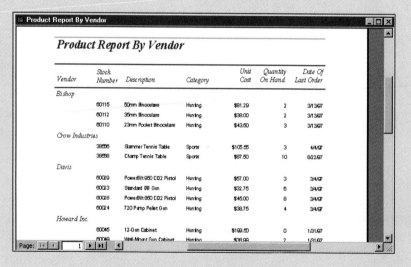

Creating a Custom Report

The 16 steps in the previous activity to modify a Report Wizard design were not hard to perform, but were somewhat tedious. In this section you will create a custom report from scratch, starting with the blank screen and placing controls in the report design precisely where needed. You can design labels that accurately reflect their purpose rather than modify existing labels.

We will focus on four main controls for most reports: label boxes, text boxes, lines, and rectangles. Yes/No form controls such as check boxes and option boxes are not appropriate for most Access reports. In later sections we will show how to add subreport and page break controls.

GUIDED ACTIVITY

9.2   Creating a Simple Custom Report

In this Guided Activity you will create a relatively simple custom report without the Report Wizard.

1. Close any open windows and return to the Hunter97.mdb Database window.

2. Make sure you are in Report mode, and then click the New button. Select the Products table as data source, and then select Design View. Click OK to see a blank Report Design window with three sections on your desktop.

3. In the Page Header section, drag the lower border down to make this section about 1 inch tall.

4. Select Toolbox from the View menu if the Toolbox is not already present, and click the Label button in the Toolbox. In the upper left corner open a label box about 2 inches long. In the label box type Product Catalog and press **Enter**. Use the Font Size box to enter 16 points for this label; note there is no preset choice for 16 points. You may have to resize the box or select Size | To Fit from the Format menu.

5. Click the Text Box button in the Toolbox, and then add a text box control at the 3-inch mark in the Page Header section. Click once on its attached label, and then press the **Del** key to delete the label. In the text box type the expression =Now() and press **Enter**.

6. Next we will add three labels to the lower portion of the Page Header section. Click once on the Label button in the Toolbox, and then create a small label control at the left portion of the section. In the box type Stock and press **Ctrl+Enter**. Then type Number and press **Enter**. With this label still selected, click once on the Bold button on the toolbar to make the label bold. See Figure A9.4 after step 11 for placement of these labels.

7. Create a label for Description and another label for Unit Cost in the Page Header section. Make these labels bold also. Align labels as necessary. You may need to adjust the height of the Description label to make it align.

 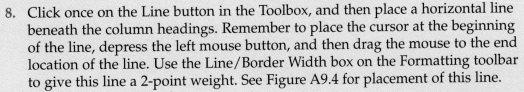

Use the Format | Align | Bottom command to align a group of labels by their bottom edges.

8. Click once on the Line button in the Toolbox, and then place a horizontal line beneath the column headings. Remember to place the cursor at the beginning of the line, depress the left mouse button, and then drag the mouse to the end location of the line. Use the Line/Border Width box on the Formatting toolbar to give this line a 2-point weight. See Figure A9.4 for placement of this line.

9. Next, we will place data values in the Detail section of the report. Drag the StockNumber, Description, and UnitCost fields from the field list box and place them beneath their respective column heading labels. You will have to delete the attached labels for each field.

NOTE *It is easier to place these fields in the middle of the section, click on the attached label to select and delete it, and then drag the text box control to the proper location in the Detail section.*

10. Drag the lower border of the Detail section up so that there is no white space below the text box controls.

11. Make the following changes to the size of the Detail section controls: shorten the StockNumber box, lengthen the Description box, and shorten the UnitCost box. Figure A9.4 shows the proper location and size of the fields for this and the next step.

FIGURE A9.4
Report Design view

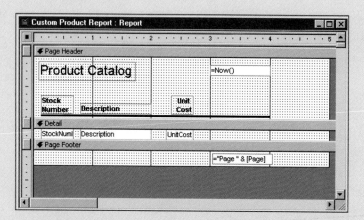

12. Finally, in the Page Footer section place a text box to contain the page number. Delete the attached label box. In the text box type `="Page "&Page` and press **Enter**. This expression will place the word `Page` in the report, and then concatenate the report page number to it. Notice that there is a single space inside the quotation marks so that the page number is separated from the word *Page* by one space.

13. Save the report under the name `Custom Product Report`.

14. To view the results of this report, click once on the Print Preview button on the toolbar. A Zoom view (fit to window) of the report is shown in Figure A9.5. Notice the placement of the page number in the bottom middle of the report.

FIGURE A9.5
Print preview for custom report

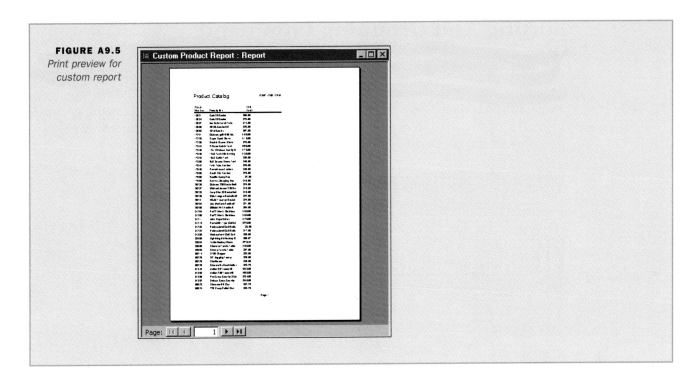

Other Custom Report Options

Most of the customizing techniques we developed in working with forms also work with Access reports. We will first highlight those tools that worked with forms, and then introduce new choices.

Format Menu Choices

As with Access forms, you can select page and report headers as well as footers from the Format menu. In fact, other Format menu choices such as Snap To Grid, Size To Grid, Size To Fit, and Align also exist. These commands affect the size and position of controls in the report design. Refer to Units 7 and 8 for more details on these choices.

Page Break Control

Access ordinarily will print the Page Header section at the top of each page, and then print as many Detail section lines as will fit on the page, reserving space at the bottom for the Page Footer section. Some reports have a great deal of information in the Detail section, and you may prefer that each record's Detail section appear on a separate printed page. Place a page break control at the point in the Detail section where you want the printed page to break. This is typically at the bottom of the section, below all the controls in a section. The symbol for a page break control in a section is a group of six dots near the vertical ruler. Access will still print the Page Footer section at the bottom of a page, even with a page break control in the Detail section. You can also produce a page break with the Sorting And Grouping dialog box, discussed next.

Sorting And Grouping Command

The Sorting And Grouping command from the View menu allows you to specify the sort order for records that appear in the report as well as to determine whether the report will group similar records together. This command produces the Sorting And Grouping dialog box shown in Figure A9.6 with Vendor selected as the group field. The upper portion of the box is used for sorting instructions; the lower part describes group properties for each sort expression.

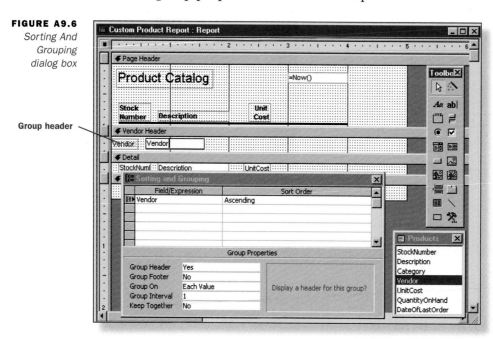

FIGURE A9.6
Sorting And Grouping dialog box

Group header

The first column in this box provides the field or expression for sorting the records in the report. The second column is used to declare an ascending or descending sort based on the first column field or expression. The top Field/Expression row will be the primary key for the sort; later rows represent secondary sort keys. You may have up to 10 sort and group fields or expressions.

For example, if you wanted to sort by Vendor and group by that field, click once on the Field/Expression row in the Sorting And Grouping dialog box. Choose the Vendor field, and use the default Ascending sort order. Go to the Group Properties portion of the box and set the Group Header property to Yes. Access will immediately create a group header section in your report design. You can then drag the group field from the field list, placing it in the group header as shown in the figure. We will demonstrate this in the next activity.

The other group properties are used to create a group footer section and to specify whether the grouping is to be done on the entire value (default) or on a certain number of prefix characters. For instance, if part numbers contained a prefix that denoted a certain product class, you could group on just that prefix or use the entire part number. The Keep Together property is used to keep parts of a group— the header, detail records, and footer— together on the same page. The default value is to print the header whether the rest of the group can fit on the same page.

If you base the report on a query that contains sorted fields or groups, Access will automatically place these instructions in the Sorting And Grouping dialog box. Likewise, if you modify a group report created by the Report Wizard, sorting and grouping instructions will already be placed in the dialog box. You can make changes as needed for your report design.

GUIDED ACTIVITY

9.3   Creating a Simple Group Report

In this Guided Activity you will modify the previous report design to display product records in groups.

1. Select the Custom Product Report you created in Guided Activity 9.2. If you have not already completed this activity, do so at this time. Open this report in Design view.

2. If it is not already present, display the Sorting And Grouping dialog box by clicking the Sorting And Grouping button on the toolbar or by giving the View I Sorting And Grouping command. Drag the dialog box over to the side of the desktop so that it does not interfere with the report design.

3. In the first row of the upper grid of this box, select the Vendor field and press **Enter**. Access will make this the first sort field and fill in Ascending in the second column of the grid.

4. Set the Group Header property for this row to Yes. Access will add a new section to the report, called Vendor Header.

5. Drag the Vendor field from the field list box to the Vendor Header section, placing it at the 0.5-inch mark. See Figure A9.6.

6. Click the Print Preview button to view the report. Figure A9.7 shows the results of this group report. Save the report design changes and close the Report window.

FIGURE A9.7
Print preview for custom group report

Custom Product Report : Report

Product Catalog   8/24/97 9:13:42 AM

Stock Number	Description	Unit Cost
Vendor.	Bishop	
60115	50mm Binoculars	$81.29
60112	35mm Binoculars	$38.00
60110	23mm Pocket Binocular	$43.50
Vendor.	Crow Industries	
38566	Slammer Tennis Table	$105.55
38568	Champ Tennis Table	$87.50
Vendor.	Davis	
60029	PowerBilt 950 CO2 Pist	$57.00
60023	Standard BB Gun	$32.75
60028	PowerBilt 850 CO2 Pist	$45.00
60024	720 Pump Pellet Gun	$38.75
Vendor.	Howard Inc.	
60045	12-Gun Cabinet	$199.50
60049	Wall-Mount Gun Cabin	$38.99
60046	8-Gun Cabinet	$92.45

Page: 1

OTHER GROUPING FEATURES

Access is able to group records in several ways. We have already shown how you can group by a text field's value or a portion of the field. You can also group based on time intervals or on number or currency ranges, and you can even group a fixed number of records together based on the counter value.

The Group On property is used to determine how the values are to be grouped. Access will display different choices for this property for each field type. The Group Interval property works in conjunction with the Group On property as explained below.

- For text fields, the Group On choices are Each Value (match whole value) and Prefix Characters (match first *n* characters as specified in the Group Interval property).

- For autonumber, number, and currency fields, the Group On choices are Each Value (match the value) and Interval (match values, starting with zero, whose range is specified in the Group Interval property). For example, if you chose Interval for the Group On property, and then specified 10 for the Group Interval property, Access would group records containing number values 0–9, 10–19, 20–29, and so on. For tables containing an autonumber field, the Interval property can be used to group a specified number of records.

- For date/time group fields, choices for the Group On property are Each Value (match precise date or time), Year, Qtr, Month, Week, Day, Hour, and Minute. Records whose Year, Qtr, or Month, and so forth, match will be grouped together. The Group Interval property is used to determine how many units of the indicated time interval will be grouped together; the default value is 1.

PRINTING A GROUP ON A NEW PAGE

You can tell Access to print each new group on a different page by selecting the group header section and then displaying the property sheet for that section. Change the Force New Page property from None to Before Section.

MULTIPLE-LEVEL GROUP REPORTS

A multiple-level group report breaks records into groups and subgroups, using more than one group field. The following activity will show how to create a multiple-level group report that displays Hunter River products broken down by Category and by Vendor within each category.

GUIDED ACTIVITY

9.4 Creating a Multiple-Level Group Report

In this Guided Activity you will create a custom report with multiple group levels.

1. Close any open windows and return to the Hunter97.mdb Database window.

2. Click the New button to create a new report. Select the Products table as the data source, and then select Design View. Click OK to open a blank report in Design view.

3. For this report we will use the product category as the primary group field and the vendor as the secondary group field. In the Page Header section place a Label control that contains the report title, Inventory Group Report. Make the text in this label 18 points. Refer to Figure A9.8 for help in sizing and placing controls.

4. Drag the lower border of the Page Header section down to make room for column headings in your report.

5. Create label boxes and enter the following column headings. Use the default font size but make these headings bold. Leave enough room so that the longer product descriptions can be displayed. Remember that you can always move controls later if they are too close together.

 NOTE *To align groups of controls, select them by* **Shift***-clicking each control, and then click the right mouse button. In the resulting context menu, you will see the Align command.*

```
Stock                               Inventory
Number              Description      Value
```

6. Place a 1-point horizontal line beneath the column headings in the Page Header section.

7. If it is not already present, display the Sorting And Grouping dialog box by clicking its button on the toolbar or by giving the View | Sorting And Grouping command. Drag the dialog box out of the way so that it does not interfere with the report design.

8. In the first row of the upper grid of this dialog box, select the Category field and press **Enter**. Access will make this the first sort field and fill in Ascending in the second column of the upper grid.

9. Set the Group Header property for this row to Yes. Access will add a new section to the report design called Category Header. Also set the Group Footer property for this row to Yes. Access will add a group footer for the Category field.

10. Repeat steps 8 and 9 for the Vendor field. Access will add group sections to the report called Vendor Header and Vendor Footer.

11. Drag the StockNumber field to the Detail section of the report. Remove its attached label. Repeat for the Description field. Enlarge the Description field so that its contents will fit. Adjust the position to fall beneath the column headings.

12. Click the Text Box button in the Toolbox, and then add a text box control beneath the Inventory Value heading. Remove its attached label. Within the box, type the expression =[UnitCost]*[QuantityOnHand] and press **Enter**.

13. In the property sheet for this calculated control, choose the Currency format. Change the Control Name property to Extended. Also select the Right-aligned text style and position the control so that it aligns with its column heading.

14. Drag the Category field from the field list box and place it in the Category Header section. Click the Bold button for both the label and the text box. Move the two controls closer together. Drag the lower border of this section up so that there is no extra blank space below the controls.

15. Repeat the previous step with the Vendor field, placing it in the Vendor Header section. Indent the label slightly to the right. Drag the lower border of this section up to remove extra space.

16. Click the Text Box button in the Toolbox, and then place a text box control in the Category Footer section, beneath the Extended field of the Detail section. In this control give the expression =Sum([UnitCost]*[QuantityOnHand]) and press **Enter**. Use the Currency format and make this control bold. Change its attached label to read Category Subtotal: and adjust spacing so that the controls align. Make the label control bold also.

17. Repeat the previous step, placing another subtotal in the Vendor Footer section. Change its attached label to read Vendor Subtotal: and adjust spacing so that the controls align.

FIGURE A9.8
Final design for multiple group report

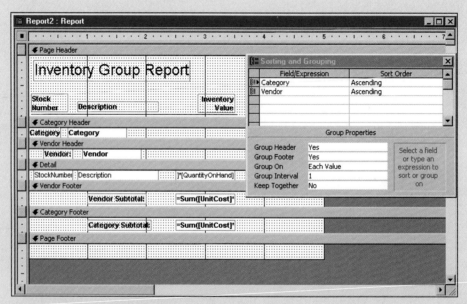

18. Click the Print Preview button to view the finished report. Figure A9.9 shows the print preview. Save this report as Inventory Group Report and close the Report window.

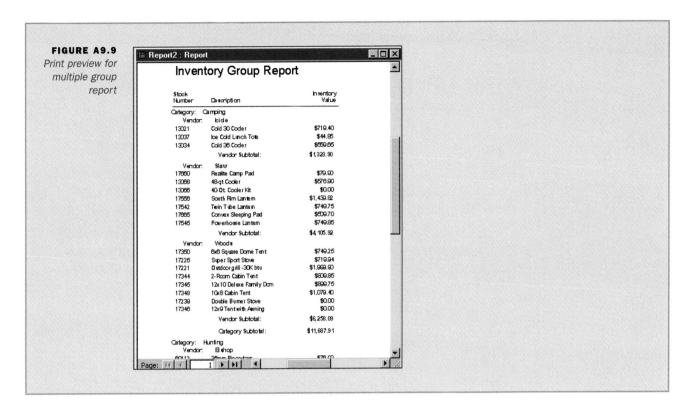

FIGURE A9.9

Print preview for multiple group report

Creating a Report with Linked Subreport

There are instances when it is appropriate to link two or more tables together in a main report with subreport format. This link is accomplished by matching field values. We explored the Hunter River Order Form in the previous unit. We will design a similar report to print order invoices in this section.

The steps to create a custom report with linked subreport are similar to those for main/subforms. First, design both reports on paper. Create the main report, and then the subreport. Then insert the subreport into the main report. You can accomplish this by dragging the subreport from the Database window and placing it in the appropriate report section. Then link the reports by setting the Link Child Fields and Link Master Fields properties as we did with the main/subform. We will illustrate this process with the invoice report created in the following activity.

You can also insert an unlinked subreport into a main report. This has the effect of placing several short reports together on one or more sheets of paper. Although these reports are not specifically linked by common field values, they contain related information. An example of an unlinked subreport would be a departmental report that appears with an employee report.

9.5 Creating a Report with Linked Subreport

In this Guided Activity you will create an invoice report that shows the customer order and order items, similar to the order form from the previous unit.

1. Close any open windows and return to the Hunter97.mdb Database window.

2. Switch to Report mode and click the New button to create the main report. We will use the Customer/Order Join query as the data source for this report. Select Design View and click the OK button to open a blank report.

3. We will create a main invoice report for the order and customer information. Create a label in the center of the Page Header section. In that label place the line Hunter River Sporting Goods. Add a second label control beneath it that contains Wabash Plaza. Add a third label beneath the second that contains Tremain, IN 46263.

4. You will have to pull down the lower border of the Page Header section to make all of these controls fit. Use the pointer to move the controls to center the labels. Make each one appear in bold by selecting it and clicking the Bold button on the toolbar.

5. Add a fourth label control beneath the third that contains CUSTOMER INVOICE. Make this label appear in a 14-point font. Add a horizontal line control beneath the Customer Invoice control. See Figure A9.10 for location of these labels.

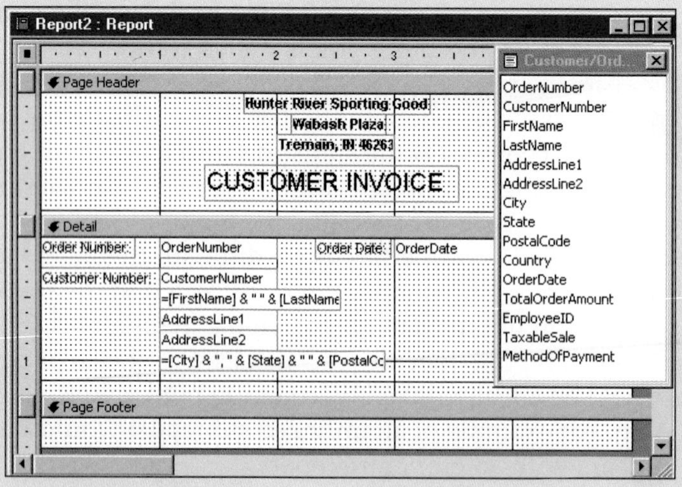

FIGURE A9.10
Main Invoice Report design

6. If the field list box is not already displayed, click the Field List button on the toolbar (or use the View | Field List command). Drag the OrderNumber field from the field list box to the left side of the Detail section. Drag the OrderDate field from the field list to the right portion of the Detail section. Adjust the position so that the label is close to the attached field. Add a space between the words in the two label controls.

7. Drag the CustomerNumber field from the field list box to the Detail section below Order Number. Add a space between the words in its attached label. Beneath the customer number create a text box control for the customer's name. In the box type =[FirstName]&" "&[LastName] and press **Enter**. Delete the unbound control's attached label.

8. If necessary, pull down the lower border of the Detail section to make room for additional fields. Create additional text box controls beneath the customer name box for the AddressLine1 and AddressLine2 fields. Delete the attached labels for these text boxes.

9. Create an additional unbound text box control beneath the AddressLine2 control. In this text box key in the expression

   =[City]&", "&[State]&" "&[PostalCode]

   and press **Enter**. This will create a single concatenated field for the city, state, and zip code. Delete the attached label box. Place a line control beneath the City/State/PostalCode line to separate the invoice header information from the items on the order. Figure A9.12 shows the main report design.

10. Click the Print Preview button to view your main report. Save this report as Main Invoice Report and close its window.

11. With Report mode selected, click the New button in the Hunter Database window. When prompted, select the Order Items/Products Join query as the data source for this subreport. Select Design View, and then click OK to open a blank Report window.

12. We will create a subreport that lists the order items that go with the order information in the main report. Drag the OrderQuantity field from the field list to the Detail section. Delete its attached label and move it to the upper left portion of the section.

13. Repeat step 12 for the Description and UnitCost fields. Delete their attached labels and move them into place. The Description field should be lengthened so that longer descriptions can appear. Access will truncate any description that does not fit.

14. We need to add a calculated control for extended cost. Click the Text Box button in the Toolbox, and then place the control to the right of the UnitCost control. Delete its attached label. In the box, type =[OrderQuantity]*[UnitCost] and press **Enter**.

15. If the property sheet is not already displayed, use the View | Properties command or click the Properties button on the toolbar. With the calculated control still selected, change the Format property to Currency. Change the control's Name property to Extended Cost.

16. Decrease the length of the Detail section so that only these fields are shown. Figure A9.11 shows the subreport design. Save this report as Invoice Subreport and close its window.

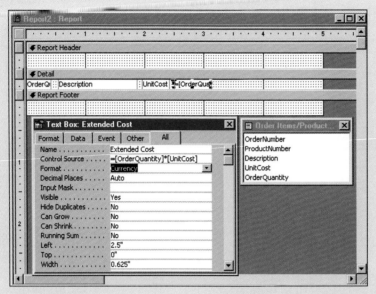

17. Open the Main Invoice Report in Design view. Drag the lower border of the Detail section down to about the 2.5-inch mark.

18. Press **F11** or click the Database Window button on the toolbar to display the Database window. Drag the Invoice Subreport to the 0,1.5-inch position of the Detail section of the Main Invoice Report. Change its attached label to read `Order Items:` and press **Enter**.

19. Select the subreport control and examine its property sheet. In the Link Master Fields property enter `OrderNumber`. Do the same thing for the Link Child Fields property. This will ensure that only the order items matching the order number will appear on the invoice.

20. Click the Page Break button in the Toolbox. Place a page break control just beneath the subreport control in the Detail section. This will cause Access to place each new invoice report on a separate page.

21. Click the Print Preview button to view the results of your invoice report. The preview is shown in Figure A9.12. Save the report again and close the Report window.

FIGURE A9.12
Finished main/subreport

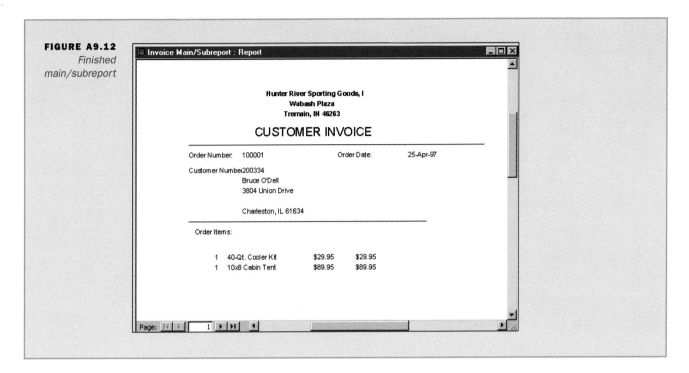

We will save creation of a subtotal control for an exercise at the end of this unit.

Other Custom Report Features

Access provides numerous options for custom reports that make them look better or convey information more clearly. Some of these features are described below.

Creating a Report Header

Certain reports would be more effective if you created a report cover. Printed just one time per report, the Report Header section serves this purpose. The Page Header and Page Footer should not appear on this cover page; you can change the Page Header property on the report's property sheet from All Pages to Not With Rpt Hdr to prevent this from happening.

Suppose you wanted to create a report cover with a large rectangle that sets off the text inside. You might use different fonts and font sizes to highlight certain phrases. Italic and bold styles also help to highlight portions of the text. You might include a date and give credit to the authors of the report. The following activity illustrates this procedure.

9.6 Creating a Report Header

In this Guided Activity you will create a Report Header section that prints a cover for a report.

1. Close any open windows and return to the Hunter97.mdb Database window.

2. Select the Inventory Group Report that was created in Guided Activity 9.4, and then click the Design button.

3. Choose the Report Header/Footer command from the View menu. Access will add sections for Report Header and Report Footer.

4. We will not need the Report Footer section, so drag its lower border up until the section has no height.

5. Drag the lower border of the Report Header section down to about 7 inches on the vertical ruler. If you drag below the current window, Access will scroll the window and display the lower portion of the Report Design screen.

6. Click the Rectangle tool in the Toolbox. Starting with the upper left corner of this control at the 0.5,0.5-inch mark, drag the lower right corner down to the 6,4.5-inch mark and release the left mouse button. Access will scroll the screen downward if you drag the pointer against the lower window section.

7. Next, click the Label tool in the Toolbox. Create a 2-inch long label control near the upper left corner of the Report Header section, inside the rectangle. In this box type `Hunter River Sporting Goods, Inc.` Change it to 12-points and click the Italic button on the toolbar. Access will expand the control box to hold the label. Expect it to take two or three lines inside the box.

8. In the center of the rectangle place a second label. In this box type `Inventory Report by Category and Vendor.` The text in this box should be 18 points and bold. Select the Times New Roman font from the Font box on the toolbar. Resize and move the box manually to fit the text.

9. Below and to the right of the larger box add a text box. Delete its attached label. Inside the text box type `=Now()` and press **Enter**. Access will place the current date and time in this box.

10. Double-click in the gray area of the Report Header section to reveal the property sheet. Under the Force New Page property select After Section. This will cause the Detail section to appear on a new page.

11. Finally, click the Print Preview button to view your report cover as shown in Figure A9.13. Scroll to the next report page to view the regular report. Save the changes made to this report and close the Report window.

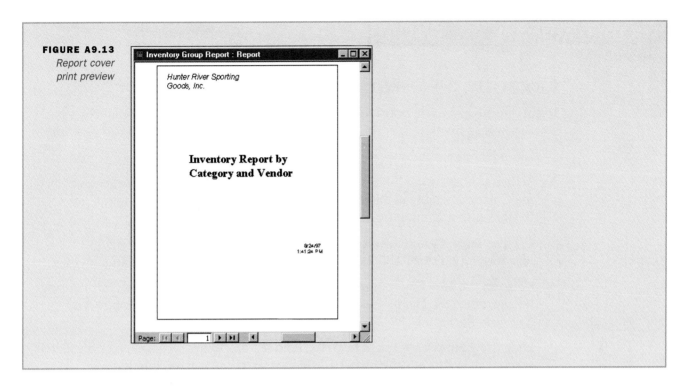

Adding OLE Object Controls to Reports

You can place bound and unbound OLE objects in reports. Unbound objects are frequently used as logos on cover pages or perhaps in a corner of a report page. Bound objects such as employee or product photographs can be added to a report as well. Access supports use of Microsoft Graph to create graphs for reports. We will not cover these types of controls in this unit. Unit 10 covers use of pictures and images in Access reports and forms, along with how to create graphs in reports and forms.

Creating Multicolumn Reports

We learned how to create a multicolumn mailing labels report with the Report Wizard in the first part of this book. In this section we will show how to create a custom mailing labels design, starting with a blank report in Design view.

For a mailing labels report, remove the Page Header and Page Footer sections. This type of report uses just a Detail section. If you wish, you can add a report cover in a Report Header section. However, if you print the report on gummed labels the cover page may not print properly. We frequently use the mailing labels format on regular paper.

The Detail section will contain a control for each line of the label. Drag the section borders in so that the section size is equal to the size of one label. Choose the Print Preview button, and then click the Setup button on the toolbar of the Print Preview window. Adjust the Print Setup dialog box settings to reflect the number of printed labels per row and per page.

9.7 Creating a Custom Mailing Labels Report

In this Guided Activity you will create a three-across custom mailing labels report, starting with a blank report design. The labels are 1 inch high by 2.5 inches wide.

1. Close all open windows and return to the Hunter97.mdb Database window.

2. Switch to Report mode and click the New button to create a new report. Select the Customers table as the data source, and then select Design View. Click OK to start with a blank report.

3. Use the View menu to remove any headers and footers: neither Page Header/Footer nor Report Header/Footer should be checked in this menu.

4. Click on the Text Box tool in the Toolbox. Create a text box control in the upper left corner of the Detail section. Remove its attached label. In this box, key `=[FirstName]&" "&[LastName]` and press **Enter**.

5. Drag the AddressLine1 field from the field list box to the second line of the Detail section. Delete its attached label. Position it so that it touches the first box.

6. Repeat step 5 for the AddressLine2 field.

7. Create another text box for the fourth line of the Detail section. Delete its attached label. In this box type

   `=[City]&", "&[State]&" "&[PostalCode]`

   and press **Enter**.

8. Adjust the size of the fields so that none is wider than 2.5 inches, the width of the label.

9. Drag the right border of the Detail section so that it is 2.5 inches wide. Adjust the height of the Detail section to 1 inch, matching the size of the labels. See Figure A9.14.

10. Click the Print Preview button on the toolbar, and then use the File | Page Setup command. You will see the Page Setup dialog box. Click the Columns tab to view the Grid Settings choices. The most important item to change is the Number of Columns box. For three-across labels, change that value from 1 to 3.

11. Select the Page tab and change to landscape orientation so that all three 2.5-inch columns can print on one sheet.

12. Select the Margins tab of the Page Setup dialog box. Change the top and bottom margins from 1 inch to 0.5 inch to make room for the labels. See Figure A9.15, which shows not only the Page Setup dialog box but also the effects of the changes in the Print Preview screen.

13. Save this report as `Customer Labels 3` and close the Report window.

FIGURE A9.14
Custom mailing label report design

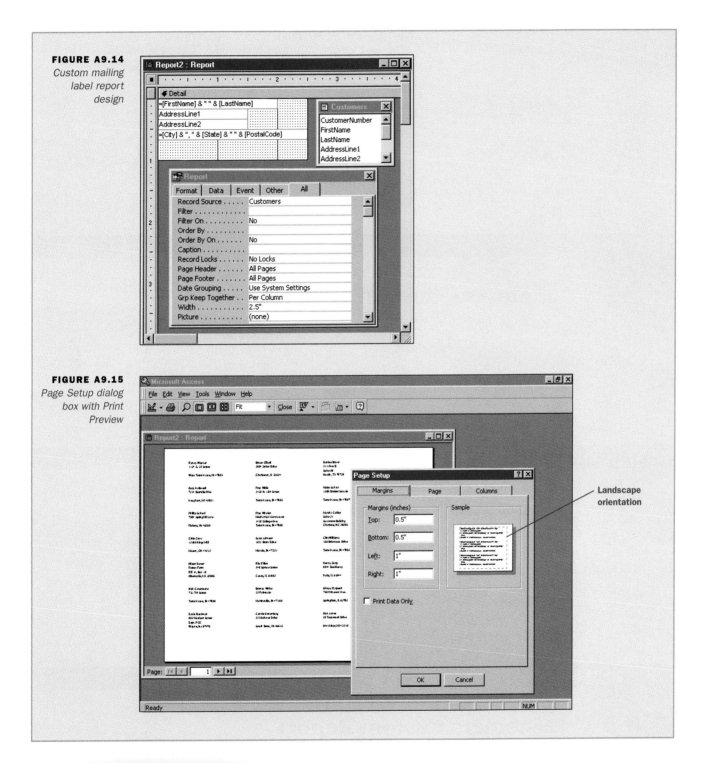

FIGURE A9.15
Page Setup dialog box with Print Preview

Landscape orientation

This unit demonstrates how to create custom reports in Access. It illustrates the use of report sections and shows how to modify an existing Report Wizard design. The unit includes a section on using labels, text boxes, lines, rectangles, and page break controls in custom reports. You learned how to add a calculated field control to a report and to create a multiple-level group report with the Sorting And Grouping dialog box. The unit contains instructions for creating a report with a linked subreport. It concludes with Guided Activities on report covers and custom mailing labels.

Exercises

Use the Hunter River database contained within the Hunter97.mdb file on the Student Data Disk for these exercises.

EXERCISE

9.1

Employees Custom Tabular Report

1. Use the Employees table to prepare a custom tabular report. Include all of the fields in the report, but do not present groups or totals. Use a suitable title for your report.

2. Print the report and save the report design as Exercise 9-1.

EXERCISE

9.2

Employees Custom Group Report

1. Using the Employees table, create a custom group report showing employee salaries by department.

2. Within each department, sort alphabetically by employee last name.

3. Print the report and save its design as Exercise 9-2.

EXERCISE

9.3

Customers Custom Report

1. Create a custom group report for the Customers table, using all of the fields.

2. Your report should contain two detail lines in a format that makes it easy to read.

3. Leave one blank row between customer names in this report.

4. Print the report and save the report design as Exercise 9-3.

EXERCISE

9.4 Products Custom Mailing Labels

1. Prepare a mailing labels custom report for the Products table. In this exercise you will create a product sales tag.

2. On the first line place the StockNumber field.

3. On the second line put the Description field.

4. On the third line place the Vendor field.

5. On the fourth line place the UnitCost field, displayed in Currency format and shown in bold. Change the size of the UnitCost to 10 points.

6. Arrange the report so that you can print five labels across on a single sheet of paper.

7. Print the report and save the design as Exercise 9-4.

EXERCISE

9.5 Customers Report Cover

1. Modify the report for Exercise 9-3 so that it has a cover page. The cover page should include the current date, a suitable report title, and your name. The title should appear in a 36-point bold font; your name should be in a 24-point font.

2. Enclose all of this information in a rectangle and center the fields vertically on the page.

3. Print a copy of the cover page and save the report as Exercise 9-5.

EXERCISE

9.6 Customer Invoice with Subtotal

1. Modify the invoice report of Guided Activity 9.5 so that it has a subtotal for the Extended field. You might refer to the similar work done in the order form created in Unit 8.

2. Print a copy of the report and save the design as Exercise 9-6.

9.7   Inventory Group Report

1. Modify the Inventory Group Report from Guided Activity 9.4 so that each Category begins on a new page.

2. Print a copy of the report, and save it as Exercise 9-7.

9.8   Report Cover

1. Prepare a report cover for the Inventory Group Report created in Guided Activity 9.4.

2. Print a copy of only the first page of the report, and save the report as Exercise 9-8.

Physicians' Medical Clinic: Building a Custom Report

Physician's Medical Clinic must submit a patient visit report to the regional review board. The hospital has asked you to create a main report, create a subreport, and then prepare a report showing patient visits to PMC. Using the PMC97.mdb database, prepare a custom report that shows the patient's permanent information in the top part of the report. In the lower part of the report list the patient visits to the clinic, including the name of the procedure and the cost of that procedure. Each patient should begin a new page of your report. Patients should appear in *alphabetical* order. The report should include the total charges for the visits shown for each patient. Your report should include a report summary section to include the total charges for *all patients listed in the report.*

APPLICATION

UNIT 10

Using Pictures, Images, and Graphs in Access

This unit explains how to use OLE objects such as pictures and graphic images in Access forms and reports. You will learn how to add a scanned photograph file to a table as a data field. The unit also covers creating a logo with the Windows 95 Paint accessory. You will learn how to create graphs with Microsoft Graph, an OLE utility program packaged with Access 97. The unit covers basic graphing terminology, including the types of graphs that can be prepared with Access. You will learn how to add a graph to a form or report using the Chart Wizard, as well as using the Graph menus directly.

Learning Objectives

At the completion of this unit you should be able to

1. define and use OLE objects in Access databases,

2. capture scanned photographs and place them in an Access database,

3. add an image such as a logo to a form,

4. create a simple logo using Windows 95 Paint,

5. embed a bitmap picture file in an OLE field in an Access table,

6. add a photograph to a form,

7. create a simple chart using the Chart Wizard,

8. add a chart to a form or report,

9. modify graph settings, using the Microsoft Graph utility program.

Case Study

Hunter River wants to explore the use of images in the company database. They want to start with employee photographs before considering adding product photographs. They would also like to include charts and graphs in some of the reports.

OLE Objects in Access Databases

You learned about the OLE object data type in an earlier unit. OLE objects refer to a class of Windows objects that can be linked and embedded in other objects. OLE objects include graphs, sounds, pictures, spreadsheets, or other objects that are OLE-compliant—that is, compatible with the OLE programming specifications that Microsoft created for both Windows and Access. Many Windows applications are OLE-compliant, and most software developers plan to offer this capability in future versions of their programs. The source application program that creates the OLE object is also known as the OLE server.

Linked Versus Embedded Objects

An OLE object can be linked or embedded. An embedded object is stored in the database like other data values. If you double-click the OLE object in a form or report, Access will start the application program that created the OLE object and will display the object for you in that application's window. Any changes made in the object are saved in the database itself when you exit from the application and return to Access. Embedding is the most common way to use OLE objects in Access.

A linked object is similar to an embedded object, but the object itself is saved in a separate file, not saved in the database. A link is created between Access and that file. If you double-click the OLE object in Access, the application that created the object will load. Any changes you make to the object must be saved in a separate file created by the source application. Not all OLE-compliant applications support linking.

In linked objects, changes made to the OLE object are automatically passed on to Access without intervention by the database user. The next time you open a form or report that contains an OLE object, you will see the updated version of the OLE object.

Types of OLE Objects

Logos, images (photographs and drawings), and graphs are the most common types of OLE objects used in Access databases. Logos are used with forms and reports to identify the organization and provide a more attractive look for the form or report. Look at stationery, business cards, and advertisements for samples of corporate or institutional symbols.

The ability to embed digitized photographs or drawings in the database is an extremely important advantage of Access. You can view an image field directly in the form or report, just like a text or number field. No longer do you have to maintain a separate manual filing system for such images. It is relatively easy to use an optical scanner to convert the picture into a digital computer file. We will discuss this procedure later in this unit. There is a disadvantage in using images, however—the file sizes can be quite large, requiring additional hard drive storage space. Fortunately, the cost of hard drives has been falling in recent years.

Microsoft includes an OLE-compliant graphing package in Access. Microsoft Graph is able to prepare sophisticated charts, using data from Access databases and other sources. The charts can be embedded in Access forms and reports. Use of the Graph application is explained later in this unit.

It is possible to include objects such as spreadsheets and graphs from spreadsheet applications as OLE objects in Access forms and reports. You may find uses for other OLE objects like sounds and video, particularly with the growing popularity of multimedia applications. Multimedia refers to the capability to use sound, still video, and animated video images in a personal computer, typically with a CD-ROM (compact disc, read-only memory) drive. For instance, you might have a database about musical compositions. It is possible to embed in or link to the database, for example, images of the composer plus audio samples of the composition. You can also have voice samples in a database.

The Windows Registry

Windows 95 includes an internal database called the registry that maps certain file extensions to a particular source application program. Thus, when you double-click a file name with a particular extension, Windows knows what program to start and opens that file within the application. For example, the BMP extension refers to the bitmap files used in the Windows Paint accessory. Paint is frequently used to insert objects into Access databases. The DOC extension refers to Microsoft Word documents, and MDB refers to Microsoft Access databases. Files with WAV extensions are recorded sounds. There are numerous entries in the registry database. As you add a new OLE-compliant application program to your computer, Windows should update the registry database with information about that OLE server.

When you create an OLE object within Access, Windows will consult the registry and display a list of the types of OLE objects available on your computer. Then, when you select an object type, Access will know which OLE server to associate with that OLE field. We will demonstrate this process in the next section.

Adding a Logo to a Form

This section will demonstrate how to add a color logo to a form. Most Windows users have color monitors but monochrome printers. Color graphics obviously look best when viewed on a color monitor. When you use a monochrome printer to print a form or report containing a color image, some clarity is lost as the printer substitutes shading patterns for colors.

The procedure for adding a logo file to a form is simple. First you must create the basic form with all of the normal controls, leaving space for the logo. We typically place the logo in an image control in the Page Header section so that it appears at the top of the screen. Access will display the types of objects available on your computer. Select the file containing the logo image. Access will embed that object in the frame. To view the object within the form, click the Form View button on the toolbar.

GUIDED ACTIVITY

10.1   Adding a Color Logo to a Form

In this Guided Activity you will place a logo that was created with Windows Paint into an Access form.

1. Start Windows and load Access. Open the Hunter97.mdb Database window.

2. Switch to Form mode and select the Hunter Products form. Click Design.

3. Click the Select Objects pointer in the Toolbox, and then pull down the border of the Form Header section to make room for the logo. The logo is about 1 inch high by 2 inches wide.

4. Click the Image button in the Toolbox. (It is the sixth button down in the right column.)

5. Use the pointer to create a control box in the middle right portion of the Form Header section. The box should be 1 inch high by 2.25 inches wide.

6. Access will display the Insert Picture dialog box and ask you to select the graphic file name. In the File text box enter the path and file name for the file. The Hunter logo is stored in the Hunt2.bmp file from the Student Data Disk.

7. Click OK and Access will embed the logo in the form. If your box is not quite large enough to hold the logo, the Format | Size | To Fit command will enlarge the box to fit the logo. The form design is shown in Figure A10.1.

FIGURE A10.1

Form with the logo in an image control

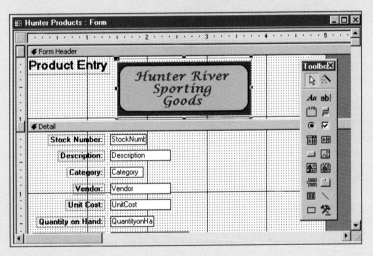

8. To view the form with the logo, click the Form View button on the toolbar, or give the View | Form View command. If you don't have a color monitor, the logo has a light gray background with a dark gray border. *Hunter River* is in dark blue, and *Sporting Goods* is in hunter green.

9. Use the File | Save As command to save this form as Hunter Products Form. Close the Form window and return to the Hunter Database window.

Creating a Logo File with Paint

Most logos are created by artists and can be scanned into a computer file. The logo in the previous activity was created by a nonartistic person (the author!) in Windows Paint. The technique is not difficult, although it does require some knowledge of the Paint accessory program. If you are not familiar with this product, refer to Windows online Help for help. The following activity will guide you through it one time.

GUIDED ACTIVITY

10.2   Creating a Logo with Paint

In this Guided Activity you will learn how to create a simple logo file, using the Windows Paint accessory program. This activity is not necessary for using Access or completing any other guided activities.

1. Make sure Windows is loaded. Click the Start button in the taskbar and slide the mouse pointer up to Programs.

2. Start the Paint accessory located in the Accessories program group. The Paint application window is shown in Figure A10.2. The tool buttons are at the left edge of the screen and the color grid is at the bottom portion.

FIGURE A10.2
Windows Paint application

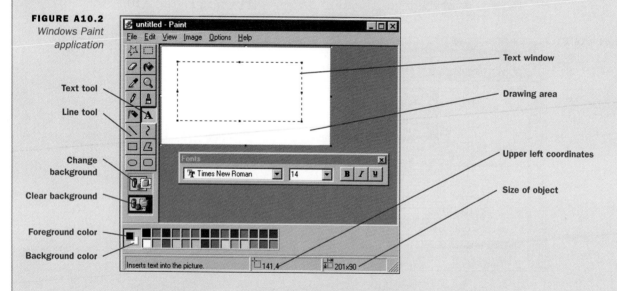

3. Click the Text tool button in the Paint Toolbox, the fifth button in the right column. It shows a capital *A*.

4. Position the pointer in the drawing area and drag the area for your text to appear. The coordinates for the upper left corner and the size appear in the status area of the Paint window. The Fonts toolbar will also open at the top of your screen. On the Fonts toolbar, select the Times New Roman font in the first combo box. Select Bold and Italic, and then choose 14 points for the font size.

5. Click once on the royal blue button in the lower portion of the Paint window to select this color for your text. Click once in the text box in the drawing area. Then type `Indiana State` and press **Enter**. On the next line press **Spacebar** two times, and then type `University`. (You may use the name of your own school, if you wish.)

6. Click once on the Line tool button in the Toolbox. A line-weight box will appear beneath the Toolbox. Click on the middle line weight.

7. Click the Rounded Rectangle tool button in the Toolbox, the bottom button in the right column. Select the middle Rectangle button that appears beneath the Toolbox, signifying you want a solid box with a border.

8. Next, left-click the black button in the Paint color grid, and right-click the light gray button in the Paint color grid. The latter produces the gray background color.

9. Move the crosshairs pointer to a position in the upper left corner of the drawing area. While holding down the left button, drag the mouse to the right and create a rounded rectangle that is a little larger than the text you're going to place in it. Be careful not to touch the text with your rounded rectangle. When you have created the correct size, release the left button. Paint will create a solid gray rounded rectangle with a black border.

10. Click once on the rectangular selection tool at the top of the right column of the Toolbox. Locate the pointer above and to the left of the text, and then hold down the left mouse button and drag the mouse to include all of the text in the box. If you make a mistake, repeat the dragging.

11. Move the pointer into the dotted-line box around the text, and then hold down the left button and drag the dotted-line box on top of the gray rounded rectangle. Maneuver it until the text is centered over the gray rounded rectangle, and then release the button. The text will remain in the scissors box. You can move the dotted-line box until you are satisfied with its position.

12. Before saving the logo, drag the lower right corner of the drawing area up tight around the logo. You may have to move the logo itself closer to the upper left corner of the drawing window. You want to have the smallest possible excess drawing area around the logo when you place it in an Access form or report.

13. To save your logo, choose the Save command from the File menu. When prompted, type in the name ISULOGO or another suitable name for your school. Paint will add the BMP extension and save the logo file on your disk drive. See Figure A10.3. You can use this logo in an Access form or report. Close the Paint window.

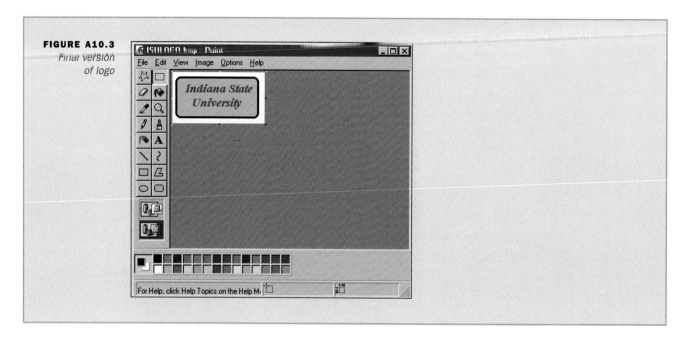

FIGURE A10.3
Final version of logo

The Paint program has limited drawing capabilities. Other Windows drawing programs like CorelDraw offer more sophisticated features and extensive clip-art collections of predrawn artwork that can be incorporated into logos and other graphic designs.

Embedding Bound OLE Objects in Access

The logos from the previous section are unbound image objects—that is, they are not associated with record values. We placed them in the Form Header section of the form. This section will explore use of bound objects that are embedded into the Access database as OLE object fields. In particular, we will demonstrate how to place color photographs into the Employees table of the Hunter97.mdb database. Then you can place them in bound object frames in the Detail section of Access forms and reports.

Taking the Photographs

When taking photographs of individuals, your subjects should be well-lit with bright colors. If possible, use a flash mounted on the camera. We recommend that you set the camera in a position to take head and shoulder portraits. By using a tripod you can be sure that each photograph is consistent in content. You can use two different types of cameras, explained next.

DIGITAL CAMERA

Medium cost ($300–$600) digital cameras can be used to take photographs electronically, skipping several stages in the process. That is, the camera scans the image as it takes the picture and stores the image in a computer file inside the camera. Most digital cameras come with a cable to connect to a computer's serial port; some newer ones have a small disk or card that can be inserted into the computer, speeding up image transfers. Although digital camera images are relatively low resolution, they save the cost of film and processing and provide the image immediately. Look for improvements in resolution, better storage technology, and lower cost soon.

NORMAL FILM CAMERA

Most people will use a normal film camera to take the photographs. Use color film for best viewing results with color monitors. The prints can be the normal size provided by your film processor. We recommend that you take some trial prints first to be sure of your camera settings and the camera location. If you do this test, have the subject hold a small card with the camera settings so that the settings can be identified. After the prints are made, you must scan the image to produce a computer file, explained next.

Scanning the Photographs

Although we will not illustrate the scanning process in a Guided Activity, it is useful to discuss how you might accomplish this important process. A scanner is an optical device that shines a bright light on the document and converts its image into a digital file for storage in the computer. Typically, a scanner attaches to a special interface card installed in your computer. It comes with software to capture the document and manipulate the image electronically before the image is saved. Many scanners come with a version of Adobe Photoshop software.

TYPES OF SCANNERS

There are three basic types of scanners: hand-held, single-sheet-fed, and flatbed scanners. Hand-held scanners require that the user carefully roll the scanner over the image. Rubber wheels underneath the scanner provide a means of keeping the scanner straight as it is drawn across the object, and they also measure the speed at which the scanner is moving. Hand-held scanners are less expensive than other types, but can produce good results for small objects. There are more problems associated with larger documents. With a hand-held scanner you must make several passes and "knit" the images together with the scanning software, a problematic operation for most people.

Single-sheet-fed scanners will pass a photograph or single-sheet image through the scanning window, much as a fax machine scans a document. You cannot pass thick objects or books through a single-sheet-fed scanner.

Flatbed scanners look like copy machines. You place the object to be scanned underneath the cover and command the scanner to begin. The scanner will illuminate the object and adjust the size automatically to match the object's size. The flatbed scanner is able to scan a document as large as its bed permits, usually in one pass. The flatbed scanner is much faster than most hand-held scanners and is designed for large scanning volumes.

SCANNER SETTINGS

You have some choices to make when scanning the photographs. The image size and number of colors affect the physical size of the scanned image file. Remember that these files can become quite large. Keep the image size small, perhaps 2 × 2 or 2 × 3 inches. Most scanner software can produce images with 16 or 256 colors. Although images with 256 colors are more pleasant to look at, their files take up far more space than those of images with 16 colors. This is particularly important for Access OLE object fields for which there is an image for every record in a table. You can view 16-color scanned images quite well, even when your Windows video driver is installed for 256 colors. We suggest that you stay with 16-color scanned images to save space.

SCAN FILES

Your scanner will create digital files containing the scanned image. You may have some control over the type of file created. Because you must use an OLE server application to embed the images in Access, use a file type that is compatible with your OLE server. Windows Paint is able to read both BMP (bitmap) and PCX (PC Paint) format files, two popular scanner file types.

The scanned photographs in the Northwind.mdb sample database packaged with Access are approximately 2 × 3 inches; they use 16 colors and occupy about 22KB each if saved as a Paint bitmap file. The image files included on the data disk for this book are slightly smaller (2 × 2 inches) and take up about 12KB per image.

Embedding the Image in an Access Table

We assume that the images will be stored in OLE object fields within an Access table. You must first define the table and its fields within Access. Select that table and switch to Datasheet view. Then select the record and OLE object field to contain the image. Choose the Object command from the Insert menu. As with image objects, Access will ask you to specify the path and file name for the OLE image to be embedded in that record. Don't forget to use the file extension, usually BMP or PCX with Paint files. Access will save the image in the database itself; you no longer need to store the image as a separate file.

 By default Access will embed *the current object in the database. The Link button in the Insert Object dialog box lets you create a* link *to the object so that if it subsequently changes, the changes will be captured in the database. Use embedding whenever possible to simplify the database.*

You must repeat this process for each record in the table, inserting the OLE object with the Insert | Object command. After you return to Access from Paint, Access will place the name of the OLE server in the table, in this case Bitmap Image, indicating that the value for that field is available in Paint. If you have another graphics program installed in your computer, its name might appear instead of Bitmap Image.

Viewing the OLE Images in Datasheet View

To view the OLE object in Datasheet view, select a record and double-click the OLE field. Access will start the OLE server application that created the OLE image. In our example this would be Paint. We will show how to add the OLE field to a form or report in a later Guided Activity. The following activity will show how to add a picture to an Access table.

GUIDED ACTIVITY

10.3   Adding a Picture to a Table

In this Guided Activity you will create a small table and insert photographs into that table. The photographs are stored as Paint bitmap files on the data disk.

1. Close any open windows and return to the Hunter97.mdb Database window in Access.

2. Change to Table mode, click New, and select Design View. Click OK to create a new table design.

3. The first field in the table is called EmployeeNumber and is AutoNumber type. With this field selected, click the Primary Key button on the toolbar to make this the primary key for your table.

4. The second field is called EmployeePhoto and is of the OLE Object type.

5. Use the File | Save command to save this table under the name OLE Example. Click the Table View button on the toolbar.

6. Position the pointer on the EmployeePhoto field of the first record. Then select Object from the Insert menu.

7. Click the Create From File button.

8. In the File text box, enter the file name E1.PCX and click OK. This file contains the scanned image of the photograph. Make sure that the path is set to the same folder that holds your data files. Use the Browse button to search for the files.

9. Repeat steps 6–8 for the second record. The photograph file for this record is called E2.PCX.

10. To view the photograph, double-click the EmployeePhoto field in either record. Paint will start and display the photograph.

11. When you are finished viewing the image, choose the Exit And Return To OLE Example command from the File menu in Paint.

12. Close the Datasheet window. Your changes are automatically saved in the OLE Example table. You will continue this activity as an exercise at the end of this unit.

Adding a Photograph to a Form

One important advantage of using a graphical user interface such as Windows is the ability to display photographs in forms and reports. Once you have embedded the photographs in an Access table, those fields can be placed in a form or report just as any Access field can. In fact, you can even use the Form Wizard to create the form. Because the OLE field has been embedded in the table, Access uses the OLE server to display the object.

Whether you use the Form Wizard to build the form or create it manually from a blank form, you will place a bound object control in the Detail section. Remember that a bound object is linked to a particular record in the underlying table or query. Each time you move the record pointer, Access will display the correct photograph in a control box in that form. As with other graphic objects, the time to display the photograph is directly related to the speed of your computer and video subsystem.

GUIDED ACTIVITY

10.4   Adding a Photograph to a Form with Form Wizards

In this Guided Activity you will use the Form Wizard to create a form with photographs and then make some changes to the design manually.

1. Close any open windows and return to the Hunter97.mdb Database window.

2. Switch to Form mode and click the New button.

3. Select the Employee Photos table, and then select Form Wizard. Click OK to create the new form.

4. Select the EmployeeID field, and then click the > button to place it in the form.

5. Repeat step 4 with the FirstName, MiddleInitial, LastName, Department, and Photograph fields. They will appear in the form in this tab order. Click Next to go on.

6. Select the default form style, Columnar, and click Next.

7. In the next dialog box, choose the Standard form style and click Next.

8. Finally, use the title Employee Information for this form. Click Finish to open the form with data in it. Notice that the default size for the Photograph field is larger than the image.

9. Click the Design View button on the toolbar. Notice that the photograph control box is nearly 2 inches long. Click once to select this box. Using the pointer, drag the lower right sizing handle to the left so that the box is approximately 1.5 by 1.5 inches.

10. Click the Form View button on the toolbar to see the photograph in its new aspect ratio. Figure A10.4 shows the finished form in Form view.

FIGURE A10.4
Form Wizard form with resized photo control

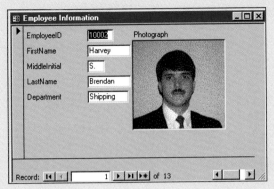

11. Use the File | Save command to save the form as `Employee Information`. Use the Record navigation buttons to examine the remainder of the records in your form. When you are finished, close the active window.

Graph Basics

You are already familiar with graphs. We see graphs in the newspaper and on television almost every day. They are a powerful way of visually displaying trends and patterns in numeric data. We use graphs to help interpret the datasheet that contains the actual data values.

Basic Graphing Terminology

The numeric values or data points for a graph are found in a datasheet. You can use data values from an Access table or even import data from an external application such as Excel or Lotus 1-2-3. We'll talk more about this option later in the unit.

Graphs display values from one or more data series in a chart. A data series is a set of data values from one row or column of the datasheet, such as Annual Sales or Annual Expenses.

The data values are plotted on the chart as a symbol called a data marker. The data marker is a bar, a shape, or a symbol. In cases where there are multiple data series in the same chart, Access will use different colors, shading patterns, or shapes to distinguish each series.

The legend is contained in a box that identifies the colors, patterns, or symbols used with each data series in the chart. The legend gives the name of each data series.

Most Access graphs plot data in a rectangular grid with horizontal and vertical axis lines. The *y*-axis is known as the value axis; data points are plotted on the *y*-axis for most chart types. The *x*-axis is known as the category axis; the data categories are printed as labels on the *x*-axis. 3-D charts use the *z*-axis for the value axis; the *y*-axis represents data series names, and the *x*-axis represents category names. Only the pie chart does not use the rectangular grid system. Each axis has tick marks that represent a scale or category on that axis.

You may also place labels on the graph to describe parts of the chart. Called chart text, these labels may be attached to an item of the graph (such as an axis or data marker) or may stay unattached. Attached text automatically moves with an item when it is repositioned. Unattached text can be positioned anywhere on the chart. Tick mark labels are examples of attached text. You can create a chart title to explain the overall contents of the chart. Axis labels describe the axis. Data labels describe individual data points and may be the value of the data point or some other description.

Types of Charts in Microsoft Graph

Access provides 16 chart types for displaying data. The choice depends on the data itself and on what message you are trying to convey with the data. We will look at the main chart types and discuss when you might choose each one. After choosing a chart type, you can customize your graph by choosing from a wide range of options.

AREA CHART

The area chart shows values over time. It emphasizes the magnitude of the values by displaying them in different shaded regions or areas. If you display multiple data series, the data values are "stacked" one on top of another.

BAR CHART

A common chart is the bar chart. Access uses horizontal bars to represent the magnitude of values in different categories. Bar charts are used to compare individual items with other items rather than to the whole. Access 97 introduces special cone, cylinder, and pyramid varieties of the bar chart in which the bar is replaced by another shape.

COLUMN CHART

Similar to a bar chart, a column chart uses vertical bars to represent the magnitude of values over time or in different categories. Column charts compare individual items with each other rather than to the whole. Access 97 introduces special cone, cylinder, and pyramid varieties of the column chart in which the column is replaced by another shape.

LINE CHART

A line chart uses a line to connect data values over time. It shows trends or patterns in the data values. Although similar to an area chart, a line chart emphasizes the rate of change rather than the magnitude of the change.

PIE CHART

A pie chart is a circular chart whose pieces are proportional to the magnitude of the data values plotted in it. The pie chart illustrates how a whole is broken into components. A pie chart always contains just a single data series. You can emphasize a single element of the pie by exploding it—slicing it and pulling it out slightly—from the rest of the pie.

XY (SCATTER) CHART

The XY chart is the traditional graph in which each point's coordinates are plotted against the *x*-axis and *y*-axis, often looking somewhat scattered. For instance, you might plot Advertising Expenses (*x*-coordinate) against the Sales (*y*-coordinate) to see the effects of advertising on sales. For XY charts you must have two data values for each point that is to be plotted. The bubble chart is a variety of the XY scatter chart in which the plotting symbols are represented by bubbles. The size of the bubble is proportional to the value of a third variable.

3-D CHARTS

The 3-D chart shows a three-dimensional view of a regular chart. There are 3-D versions for area, bar, bubble, column, cone, cylinder, line, pyramid, and pie charts. With some chart types, the 3-D version makes it easier to see movement in the data series. However, you cannot display another data series along a third dimension with a 3-D chart; Access simply adds depth to an existing two-dimensional chart.

Graph Options

The menus in Microsoft Graph offer extensive customization for most of the chart types. You can add gridlines to the chart to help the viewer compare the scale tick marks with plotted points. Data series in bar and column charts can appear side by side or can be stacked on top of each other. Bars can be distinct or can overlap. You can remove the normal space between the categories. For line and XY charts you can select lines, markers, or both for plotted points. You can display line chart data in high/low, high/low/close, or open/high/low/close formats, particularly useful for analyzing stock market price data. You can display the *y*-axis as a logarithmic scale for data series with high variability. You can see graph samples within the Chart | Chart Type menu option of Graph. We'll cover Graph later in this unit.

Methods of Creating Access Graphs

There are four ways to create a graph in Access. The simplest way is to use the Chart Wizard. The procedure is straightforward, but you may not end up with quite what you wanted. Although you can make changes to the graph's design, it is usually simpler to start over again and build a new graph with the Chart Wizard.

The second way to begin is with a blank form or report, selecting the Graph button from the Toolbox. After placing this control in the form or report, you then answer questions presented by the Chart Wizard. This method enables you to add a graph to an existing form or report, and it has the advantage of simplicity, because the Chart Wizard does all the work.

The third way is to call the Microsoft Graph program from within Access and build a graph from scratch. This method is not used as often as the previous two, but can be used to modify the graph design of an existing graph. In the latter case, double-clicking on the graph will start the Graph application. We will cover this in a later section of this unit.

There is a fourth way to place a graph object in Access. You can link to an OLE graph created outside Access, for example, in Excel or Lotus 1-2-3 or in a separate graphing program like CorelDraw or Windows Paint.

Using the Chart Wizard

The easiest way to add a graph to a form or report is to use the Access Chart Wizard. You don't create a separate graph object. Rather, create a new form or report with the wizard, and select Graph as the subtype. Access will then display the appropriate screens and ask you a series of questions about the content of the graph. After answering the questions, you can view the finished graph. If the graph is not quite correct, you can make changes to the graph settings manually or create a new graph with the Chart Wizard.

We will assume you are creating a form with an embedded graph. The steps are the same with a report. Switch to Form mode and click New. The next step is to choose the data source for the graph. You may choose a table or query from the list displayed by Access. Then pick the Chart Wizard and click OK.

Next, select the fields to graph and those for labels, as shown in Figure A10.5. Remember that only numeric fields can be graphed; you must include at least one number field to go on to the next step.

FIGURE A10.5

Field selection list for Chart Wizard

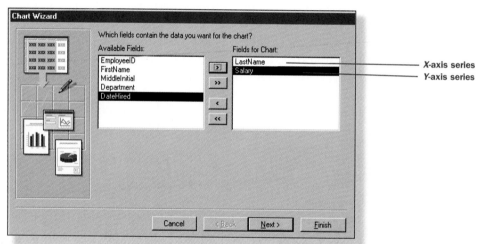

You will next see a screen with images of some chart types. Click the desired chart type, and then go on to the next screen. See Figure A10.6 for the Chart Wizard chart types. Provide a title for the graph, and then click Finish to view the graph. Access will quickly generate the necessary graph settings and create the graph for you. If you are satisfied with the graph, use the File | Save command and give the form a name. If you are not satisfied with the graph design, switch to Design view. Access will display the graph image for you in Design view. If you double-click the graph, the Microsoft Graph OLE application will start and you can make changes as needed. Conversely, you can delete the graph and restart with a new form.

FIGURE A10.6
*Chart Wizard
chart types*

Column Chart
button

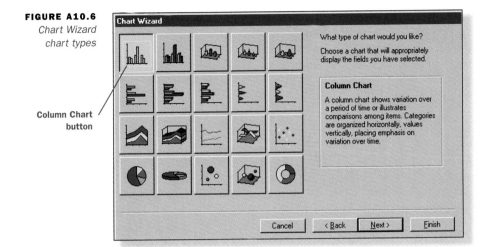

GUIDED ACTIVITY

10.5 Adding a Graph with the Chart Wizard

In this Guided Activity you will build a form with a graph created by the Chart Wizard.

1. Start Windows and load Access. Open the Hunter97.mdb Database window.

2. Switch to Form mode and click the New button.

3. At the next dialog box select the Employees table as the data source and select Chart Wizard.

4. Click OK to begin the Chart Wizard.

5. The Chart Wizard will display a field list and ask you to select fields to be graphed and to appear as legend labels. Select the LastName field and click the > button. Select the Salary field and click the > button. See Figure A10.5 previously shown. Click Next to go to the next step.

6. You will see icons representing the types of charts available in the Chart Wizard. Select the Column Chart button as highlighted in Figure A10.6. This is the chart type with vertical bars, shown at the left in the first row of charts. Click Next to go to the next screen.

7. Next, the Chart Wizard will display the layout for the chart, with LastName on the x-axis and SumOfSalary on the y-axis. Double-click the SumOfSalary box, select None from the Summarize options, and then click OK. The Chart Wizard will place Salary on the y-axis. Click Next to go on.

8. When prompted for the Graph Title, enter Employee Salary Graph and click the Finish button to see the graph, shown in Figure A10.7. The Salary field is plotted as a vertical bar or column. The x-axis contains the last name of the employee receiving that salary.

FIGURE A10.7
Finished Employee Salary graph

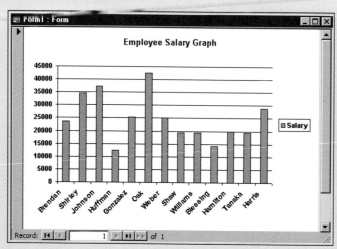

NOTE   *We resized the graph to fully display the names. The Chart Wizard may not do a good job of formatting the graph with regard to size, scale formats, and so forth. We will show you how to make the customizing changes within Microsoft Graph to produce a finished graph.*

9. Save the graph with the File | Save command. Use the same name as the title, `Employee Salary Graph`. Close the open window.

Adding a Graph Control to a Report

You can add a graph control to a form or report in the same manner as other Access controls. First open a new form or report, selecting the data source table or query, and choosing Design View. Add any other controls as necessary, and then click the Graph button in the Toolbox, or use the Insert | Chart command. Use the mouse to open a graph control box in the form or report.

At this point the Chart Wizard takes over, asking similar questions about the graph. Because you have placed the graph in an existing form or report, Access will ask if you want to link the graph to the other data in the form or report. If you reply affirmatively, you will have an opportunity to specify the link fields, similar to the subform and subreport controls we covered in the first part of this book. The following example will show how to place a graph in a custom report, along with the data that the graph represents.

GUIDED ACTIVITY

10.6   Adding a Graph Control to a Custom Report

In this Guided Activity we will start by opening a simple custom report, and then add a graph control to the report design.

1. Close any open windows and return to the Hunter97.mdb Database window.

2. Switch to Report mode and select the 1996 Employee Salary Report. Click the Design button.

3. Use the mouse to pull down the lower border of the Page Footer section to contain the graph. The lower border should be at around 4 inches on the vertical ruler.

4. Click the Chart option in the Insert menu. Drag the mouse to create a graph control that fills the entire Page Footer section, starting at the 0,0-inch coordinates.

5. After a few seconds, Access will display the opening Chart Wizard screen. In the top portion is a list box that asks for the data source for the graph. Specify the Employees table and click Next.

6. Select the Salary field and click on the > button to add that to the chart. Repeat the process for the LastName field, and then click Next.

7. Click the Bar Chart icon in the Chart Wizard screen (the first item in the second row), and then click Next to go to the next screen.

8. The Chart Wizard will display the layout of the graph with fields located on the chart. Double-click the SumOfSalary field, select None from the Summarize options, and then click Next. See Figure A10.8.

FIGURE A10.8
Chart Wizard layout screen

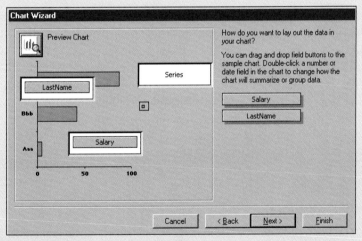

9. In the next screen select the No Field choice in the Report Fields and Chart Fields boxes. We will not link this graph to the report records because we are using all of the records in the graph. Click Next again.

10. In the next screen enter 1996 Salaries as the graph title. Click the Finish button to return to the report design.

11. Click the Print Preview button on the toolbar to see the report and the graph.

12. Use the File I Save As command to save the report as Employee Salary Report with Graph. Close the report.

Printing a Graph

You can print the form or report containing the graph as usual, either by issuing the File | Print command or by using the Print Preview button on the toolbar. You may need to experiment with the settings in the Print dialog box to bring out the features of your charts. Remember that most printers can only approximate the full-color shades of your charts when printing in black-and-white gradations.

Importing External Data into Graph

Microsoft Graph was designed as a separate, general-purpose Windows graphing application. As a result, it is possible to use data from sources other than Access. You can bring data or a chart directly from a Microsoft Excel spreadsheet or use the File | Import command to use data from other sources. As mentioned previously, you can also type data directly into the datasheet. We will not illustrate this feature here, but you can check online Help for more information. Unit 13 covers importing and exporting data.

Modifying Microsoft Graph Settings

When you created a form or report graph with the Chart Wizard, Access called up Microsoft Graph in the background to create the settings. To make changes in the graph settings you must use Graph itself. Because Graph is an OLE application, you can double-click the graph control in Form or Report Design view to open the Graph application window on your desktop. Then you can view the current graph settings and make changes as needed. Figure A10.9 shows the Microsoft Graph window for the Employee Salary graph we built in the first activity of this unit.

FIGURE A10.9
Graph window with Employee Salary graph

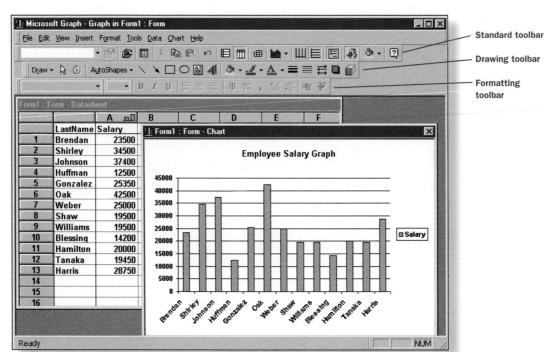

Graph Datasheet Window

In the upper portion of the window is the graph datasheet, used by Graph to hold the data values to be plotted. In this case it contains the two columns, LastName and Salary, that we chose in the Chart Wizard. The rows of the graph datasheet represent sample values drawn from records in the Employees table.

There are three selectable toolbars in the Graph window of Figure A10.9. The top one is the Standard toolbar used for making changes to graph and chart settings. Next, the Drawing toolbar is used for drawing lines, arrows, and text. Your Drawing toolbar may appear at the bottom of the screen. The bottom Formatting toolbar is for formatting data values and various parts of chart text. Each toolbar can be selected or deselected with the View | Toolbars command.

You can use the values in the datasheet for the graph, or can type in new ones. It is also possible to import values from other applications using the File menu, discussed earlier in this unit.

You can move around the Datasheet window with the mouse or the arrow keys. The scroll bars let you see cells that are not shown. You can resize the Datasheet window as needed to view more of the datasheet. The datasheet in Figure A10.9 has been resized to show all the datasheet, so scroll bars are not needed.

You may want to select a portion of the datasheet for your graph. You can drag the cursor over the desired cells or use the buttons on the toolbars. To select all the cells in a row or column, click the row or column selector button at the left or top of the row or column. In most cases you will choose all cells from the datasheet for your graph. If you don't want to use all the data, it is better to use an Access query to limit the records that are to appear in the graph. The Data menu lets you specify whether the data to be plotted is in rows or columns of the datasheet. You can also include or exclude portions of the datasheet from this menu.

FORMATTING THE CELLS

Graph will use the field format from the Access table or query as the default for that field in the datasheet. You can reformat selected cells in the datasheet with the Format | Number command or use the Formatting toolbar buttons. Cell format affects both the way the values are presented in the chart and the way the scale tick marks appear. You can add dollar signs, insert commas and percent signs, select the number of decimal places, show negative numbers in parentheses, or display numbers in another color. You can create custom formats for numeric and date/time values. Use Graph's online Help to view Format menu choices.

Use the Format | Column Width command to change the column width in the datasheet, or drag the column divider as you would in a spreadsheet. Remember that Access may require wider columns for large numbers in particular formats. Use the Format | Font command or toolbar buttons to choose the font for text in the datasheet and in the graph. You can select the font, style (bold, italic, underline), and font size with this menu.

Graph Chart Window

In the lower portion of the Graph window shown in Figure A10.9 is the chart resulting from the current graph settings. In this instance the salaries are displayed

TIP

Use the right mouse button when the chart is selected. Access will display a context-sensitive menu for most of the frequently used graph settings.

in a column chart with the employee names shown on the *x*-axis below the chart. The Chart window has been resized and moved to better display both windows.

THE CHART MENU

You can select a new chart type from the Chart menu. There are 14 standard chart types available and 20 custom types. You can also add your own user-defined chart types. Each chart type has multiple subtypes that are depicted graphically in the Chart Type dialog box when you select a particular chart type. The large button at the lower right corner of the Chart Type dialog box lets you display your chart in that flavor.

The 3-D column version of the Employee Salary chart is shown in Figure A10.10. Notice that the Salary values in the datasheet were formatted to Currency format with 0 decimal places; the graph automatically picked up this format. You can further customize charts with the Chart Options menu described next. Changing to a new chart type will cancel any changes made previously, so select the desired chart type *first*, and then make more modifications with the Insert menu.

FIGURE A10.10

The 3-D column version of the Employee Salary graph

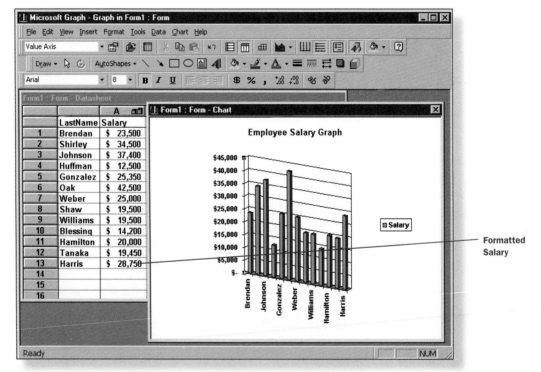

THE CHART OPTIONS DIALOG BOX

In addition to the Chart menu choices for chart type, you can modify chart settings with the Chart Options dialog box found in the Chart menu. The Titles tab lets you modify the chart title and titles attached to the axes of the chart. The Axes tab controls the display of the *x*-axis, *y*-axis, and *z*-axis in a chart. (All three axes appear in Figure A10.10.) The Gridlines tab lets you determine whether horizontal or vertical gridlines appear in the chart; you can select major and/or minor gridlines to appear. Both Figure A10.9 and Figure A10.10 display horizontal gridlines. The Legend tab lets you control the placement of or remove the legend box from the chart. You can use the pointer to move the legend box to another location on the chart. The Data Labels tab is used for placing a data label next to the plotted value of each point. (There are no data labels in Figure A10.10.) You can add a small data table with values beneath the graph with the Data Table tab. Many of the Chart Options choices are also available on the Standard toolbar or by double-clicking the particular graph component.

Making and Saving Changes in Graph

Microsoft Graph can be called only from a Windows application that is configured to use its objects. Because Graph is an OLE application, any graph created by it is embedded in the Access database and *not* saved as a separate file. You can make an unlimited number of graph setting changes while working in Graph. Graph will immediately display the new chart. Many users will begin with a Chart Wizard chart, and then make embellishments within Graph.

When you have finished work on the graph, use the Exit & Return command from the File menu to return to Access with the updated graph. Note that changes made to data values in the Graph datasheet are not transferred back to the Access datasheet.

Changes in Underlying Data Values

As with other Access embedded objects, any changes made to the data values in Access will be reflected in the graph the next time it is opened. For instance, if we make a salary change in the Employees table, that change will be reflected in the column chart in the Employee Salary report.

GUIDED ACTIVITY

10.7 Modifying Graph Settings

In this Guided Activity you will use Microsoft Graph to make changes to a graph created with the Chart Wizard.

1. Close any open windows and return to the Hunter97.mdb Database window.

2. Switch to Form mode and select the Monthly Product Sales form. Click the Design button.

3. While in Design view for this form, double-click the graph to start Microsoft Graph. After a few seconds, you will see the Microsoft Graph window as shown in Figure A10.11. If the Drawing and Formatting toolbars don't appear, use the View | Toolbars command to turn them on.

4. Notice that the sales amounts in the datasheet and the tick mark labels in the chart are not formatted. Click the cell in the datasheet above the Net Sales cell to select that column. Issue the Format | Number command and choose Currency; select 0 decimal places. Click OK.

FIGURE A10.11

Graph window for Monthly Product Sales form

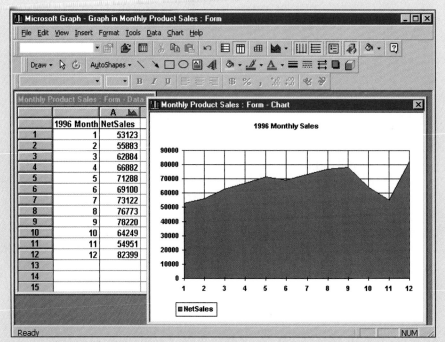

5. Graph will immediately format the datasheet and change the tick mark labels in the chart. Next we will modify the chart's title. Click the Chart window to make it active, and then issue the Chart | Chart Options command.

6. Select the Titles tab, then click once in the Category (X) Axis box. Type `Month` and click OK. Graph will place the word Month in the *x*-axis title block.

7. Click once on the chart title, 1996 Monthly Sales. Then give the Format | Font command. From the Size box choose 14 points, and then click OK. Graph will increase the size of the title. Press **Esc** to remove the handles in the title box.

8. Choose the 3-D version from the Chart | Chart Type menu: select the first sample in the second row and click OK. Graph will redraw the chart with a three-dimensional effect.

9. Click the Arrow button on the Drawing toolbar to place an arrow in the chart. The cursor will appear as crosshairs. Move the mouse pointer to a point above the chart, and then hold down the left mouse button and drag it to the December (Month 12) sales amount. Graph will draw an arrow pointing toward the December sales peak.

10. Next, we'll add an annotation to the arrow. Without issuing any other commands, key the phrase `Holiday Sales`. Graph will open a text box in the center of the chart and place the text in this text box. Press **Esc** to close the window.

11. Use the pointer to drag this text box to the end of the arrow. Release the left mouse button, and then press **Esc** to remove the handles from the text. Your finished chart should look like Figure A10.12.

FIGURE A10.12
Modified graph

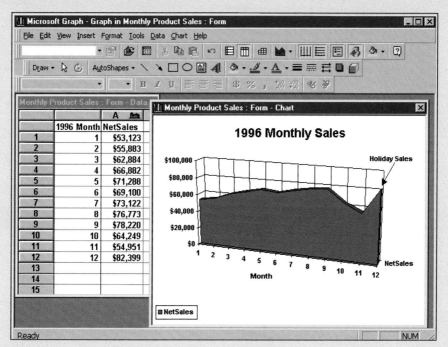

FIGURE A10.12
Modified graph

12. Choose Exit & Return from the File menu. When you return to Access, you should see the modified graph embedded in the sales form. Close the active Form window, saving changes to the form.

NOTE *If you do not want to keep the changes made in Microsoft Graph, simply don't save the form when you close its window in Access. Or use File | Save As/Export to save it under a different name.*

SUMMARY

This unit has demonstrated how Access handles images as database objects. You can add a logo or a digitized photograph to a form or report in an Unbound Object control. For images that are associated with specific records, you can insert images directly into a table with the Insert | Image command. For those who are artistically inclined, Windows Paint can be used to create a logo image. Other graphics programs can be used for more sophisticated images. The Chart Wizard makes it easy to add a chart or graph to a form or report. Microsoft Graph is the OLE server that actually creates charts and graphs within Access. By double-clicking the chart in Design view, you can start Graph and make changes to the design of the chart. When you exit Microsoft Graph, the changes are made to the graph.

Exercises

Use the Hunter River database contained within the Hunter97.mdb file on the Student Data Disk for these exercises.

EXERCISE

10.1

Hunter River Logo

1. Use Windows Paint to create a logo file for the parent corporation, Hunter River Sporting Goods, Inc. You may choose the font and any colors used.

2. Print a copy of your logo using the Paint File | Print command.

3. Save the logo using the name Huntlogo.bmp.

EXERCISE

10.2

Hunter River Custom Form

1. Create a custom form for Hunter River customers.

2. Place the logo from the first exercise in the Form Header section.

3. Print a copy of your form, and save it as Exercise 10-2.

EXERCISE

10.3

Employee Photos

1. Continue the work begun in Guided Activity 10.3, adding the next three employee photographs to the OLE Example table.

2. Use the bitmap files called E3.pcx, E4.pcx, and E5.pcx contained on the Student Data Disk.

3. Print a copy of the datasheet that shows "Bitmap Image" in records 3–5.

EXERCISE

10.4

Employee Entry Form

1. Create a form, using the OLE Example table from Exercise 10.3.

2. Display the EmployeeNumber and EmployeePhoto fields in the Detail section.

3. Print a copy of the form for record 4.

4. Save the form as Exercise 10-4.

10.5

Employee Service Chart

1. Use the Chart Wizard to prepare a graph showing the length of service of each Hunter River employee.

2. You will first have to create a query with a calculated field whose calculation is =Date()-[DateHired]. You can also use the Access DateDiff( ) function to find the difference between two dates.

3. Use a column chart.

4. Save a copy of the form as Exercise 10-5, and print the chart.

10.6

Plan I Employees Chart

1. Prepare a form with a 3-D chart that shows the salary and bonus for the table called Plan I Employees.

2. Your chart should display both salary and bonus as individual data series in three-dimensional form, rather than adding them together.

3. Use appropriate chart text.

4. Save the form as Exercise 10-6, and print a copy of the form.

10.7

Expense Pie Chart

1. Prepare a custom report containing the basic data and a pie chart for the following expense data collected by Joleen Branch, the summer accounting intern at Hunter River.

Expense Category	1997 Amount
Salaries	$303,219
Operating Costs	$106,410
Cost of Goods	$445,200
Overhead	$45,331
Taxes	$104,882

2. The graph control should go in the Page Footer section of the report.

3. Show the percentage (of the total) for each piece of the pie chart,

4. Save the report as Exercise 10-7 and print a copy of the report.

EXERCISE

10.8   Vendor Products Graph

1. Create a form with a bar chart that shows the *count* of the number of products from each vendor.

2. The title of the chart should be 1997 Vendor Products.

3. Use a 3-D effect for the chart.

4. Save the chart as Exercise 10-8 and print a copy of the form.

Physicians' Medical Clinic: Using Graphics in a Form

As a member of the new Total Quality Management program, you have been asked to add patient photographs to the PMC97.mdb database. You arranged to have photographs taken and then scanned them into PCX files, using a flatbed scanner. Modify the Patients table to hold photographs as OLE object fields. If you cannot create your own photographs, you may use the files named E1.pcx...E13.pcx from the Student Data Disk as your patient image files.

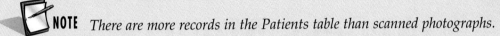

NOTE *There are more records in the Patients table than scanned photographs.*

Prepare a new form or modify an existing form (and save it under a different name) that will display patient information along with a small photograph of each patient. Surround the photograph with a clear (transparent) rectangular box. What other graphic objects would be appropriate for use in the PMC97 database? Break your list into bound objects and unbound objects. Prioritize each list, and prepare an estimate of the expected number of objects per patient.

APPLICATION

UNIT 11

Introduction to Access Macros

This advanced unit introduces Access macros, in effect miniature program statements you create that save time by automating certain keystrokes and mouse commands. The unit describes how to create a macro, including how to set macro arguments. Several macro examples are given. The unit includes a section on debugging (finding and correcting mistakes in) Access macros. This unit also shows how macros can be used to expedite operations on forms and reports. Macros are attached to command buttons and form properties to automate certain activities. More macro actions are illustrated in the activities. Several macro examples are given, including the creation of an Access macro that executes automatically when the database is opened.

Learning Objectives

At the completion of this unit you should be able to

1. create and run a simple macro,

2. create a macro group,

3. use conditions in a macro,

4. run a macro in single-step mode,

5. use the Action Failed dialog box to debug macro errors,

6. discuss what events can occur when you use a form,

7. list the advantages of attaching macros to properties of forms and controls,

8. describe the steps in creating and using switchboard forms,

9. create a macro that opens a form and positions its window at the correct location,

Case Study

To make it simpler for Hunter clerks, management wants to explore automating Access database functions. They want you to create command buttons for automatically opening forms and printing reports. The purchasing agent wants to know if it is possible to create a form that would automatically keep the Products and Vendors forms synchronized.

10. attach a macro to a command button on a form,

11. attach a macro to a property of a form or a control,

12. create an alphabetical lookup macro,

13. print a form or report with a macro,

14. create an auto-execute macro for a database.

Macro Basics

A macro is a list of actions or tasks that you want Access to perform that have been saved with a name. Access will execute the actions in the order they appear on your list. You can create macros that cause actions to be executed only if certain conditions are true. Once a macro has been created and saved, you can reuse it repeatedly. There is a Macros tab in the Database window, just to the right of the Reports tab. You can select a macro from the macro list and then choose the Run, Design, or New buttons from the tab. After describing the advantages of macros, we'll demonstrate how to create a macro.

Advantages of Macros

Macros are efficient—the list of actions, however long, is automatically executed when you run the macro. You don't have to rekey the commands or reissue the mouse commands. In fact, a macro will execute the list of actions much faster than you can do by hand. Needless to say, macros are 100 percent accurate. The same commands are executed each time, regardless of the user's experience with Access.

You can place a command button into a form that causes a macro to execute when the button is clicked. That macro can perform some actions, run a query, invoke other macros, print a report, or open another form. The user can choose whether to run the macro from the form.

You can do error checking with a macro, employing more sophisticated rules than are possible with the Validation Rule property of the form or a validation rule attached to a single field in a table. This ensures that the data entered into the form is accurate. You can also use a macro to do special lookups, setting the value of other fields based on the values entered into fields on the form. For instance, if a customer order comes in to Hunter River from another state, you could use a macro to choose the sales tax rate that is appropriate for that state.

Macros help you automate certain repetitive tasks that are done every time a certain event occurs, such as when you close a form or the workday comes to an end. You attach the macro to form properties, as discussed later.

You can also use a macro to find and filter records in a form. You can attach that macro to a command button so that the user can run the macro at will. You can also transfer data into (import) and out of (export) Access automatically with a macro.

The Macro Window

To switch to Macro mode from the main Database window, click the Macros tab or issue the View | Macros command. The Macros icon looks like a scroll on which you could list actions. You will see the list of macros saved in the current database. If there are no macros shown on the Macros tab, the Run and Design buttons will be dimmed. Only the New button can be used at this time.

After switching to Macro mode, click the New button to create a new macro or click the Design button to modify an existing macro. Access will display the Macro window shown in Figure A11.1. The first column contains the list of actions in your macro. The second column is used for comments about the macro's actions. The lower section of the Macro window will display the arguments for each action. Arguments are similar to properties—they contain additional instructions for carrying out an action. The lower section will be empty if you have not selected any actions for the macro. You can press **F6** to move between the top and bottom sections of the Macro window.

FIGURE A11.1
Macro window
Design view

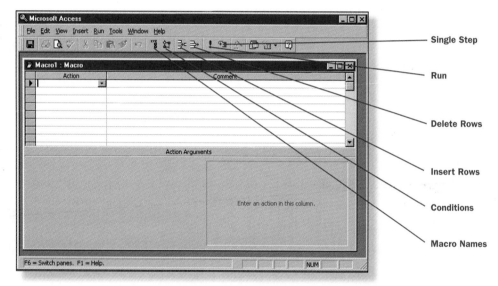

The Macro toolbar accompanying the Macro window is shown at the top part of Figure A11.1. You can choose options from this Macro toolbar that open additional columns in the Macro window. The Macro Names button lets you assign names to individual macro actions in a macro group. The Conditions button lets you create conditions that determine when a particular group of actions are to be executed. The Run button (exclamation point) will run the macro in the Macro window. The Single Step button will cause the macro to run a single line at a time and is used for debugging purposes. We'll discuss the Macro toolbar in more detail later.

Designing a Macro

As with other database procedures, it is helpful to first think through what you want the macro to accomplish. If you go straight to the Macro window and start creating your macro, it is easy to overlook some steps and end up with a macro that is more difficult to change. Make a list, on paper, of the desired actions. Leave some blank lines so that you can fill in tasks that you forgot initially. Talk through your steps with a colleague, even speak them out loud if you're alone. Make changes as necessary to fit the situation you are modeling. We will present more about macro design when we get to creating custom applications in Access.

Creating a New Macro

After you click the New button on the Macros tab in the Database window, Access will open an empty Macro window. You can add actions to the new macro in at least two ways: you can select from the action list in the Macro window, or drag objects from the Database window to a macro action cell. We'll discuss the first method here.

It is customary to put a blank action in the first cell of the macro and use its comment line to describe the purpose of the macro. Access will ignore the line if there is no action there. You can also use blank actions later in your macro to describe groups of actions that are related.

CHOOSING AN ACTION

The pointer is located in the first cell in the action list of Figure A11.1. If you click the arrow, the drop-down list of almost 50 actions is displayed. Nearly all the commands that you can choose from the menu bar are included in this list, although they may have slightly different names in the Macro window. For example, the second entry in the action list is ApplyFilter. This action will apply an Access filter in the same way as the Apply Filter | Sort command from the Records menu in the Form window. The Actions Reference online Help screen is shown in Figure A11.2 with the complete list of macro actions, grouped by task. Click any action for detailed help and examples.

FIGURE A11.2
Online Help screen for macro actions

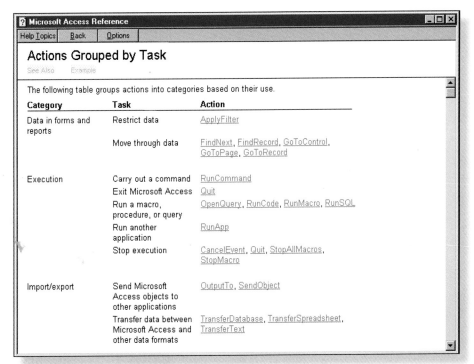

Microsoft Access Reference

Help Topics   Back   Options

Actions Grouped by Task

See Also   Example

The following table groups actions into categories based on their use.

Category	Task	Action
Data in forms and reports	Restrict data	ApplyFilter
	Move through data	FindNext, FindRecord, GoToControl, GoToPage, GoToRecord
Execution	Carry out a command	RunCommand
	Exit Microsoft Access	Quit
	Run a macro, procedure, or query	OpenQuery, RunCode, RunMacro, RunSQL
	Run another application	RunApp
	Stop execution	CancelEvent, Quit, StopAllMacros, StopMacro
Import/export	Send Microsoft Access objects to other applications	OutputTo, SendObject
	Transfer data between Microsoft Access and other data formats	TransferDatabase, TransferSpreadsheet, TransferText

SETTING THE ACTION ARGUMENTS

Once you have selected an action for a particular cell, Access displays its arguments in the lower pane of the Macro window. You can make entries in the lower pane to further specify the action. For instance, if you select ApplyFilter as the action, Access shows two action arguments, Filter Name and Where Condition. You must specify the name of the filter in the first argument; it is optional to use the Where Condition argument. If you need help on a particular argument, click once on its line and look at the lower right portion of the bottom pane for a brief explanation. If you need more assistance, press the **F1** key to invoke the standard Access help system for that argument.

You can select argument values from drop-down lists that Access presents, or you can type them directly in the lower pane. You can also drag database objects to the argument area where appropriate. When you have filled in the arguments for the first action line, move to the second line and repeat the process of selecting an action and setting its arguments.

If you want to open a form or report, it is easy to drag it from the Database window to the action portion of the Macro window. First rearrange the windows so that both are visible (you can move them manually or use the Tile command from the Window menu). Then switch the Database window to Form mode and drag the form to the Macro window. Access will insert an OpenForm action and automatically fill in the arguments with the name of the form you dragged. If you selected a report, Access will insert an OpenReport action in Print Preview. If you drag another macro from the Database window, Access will insert a RunMacro action into the current Macro window.

Modifying Your Macro

Developing a macro is somewhat different from other Access activities. In fact, it is more like writing a computer program in which you make small changes and try to run the macro. When it doesn't run, you analyze the problem, make changes accordingly, and try to run it again. This iterative process is normal and should not be a cause of worry. It is rare that your macro will run properly the first time! This section describes how to make changes to the macro in the Macro window. A section on troubleshooting macros appears later in this unit.

DELETING, MOVING, AND INSERTING ROWS

If you need to make changes to the macro, Access will let you delete an action or move it to another location. In either case, click the row selector button at the left of the action row. To delete that row permanently, press **Del**. To move the action to another row, drag it to the desired location and release the left mouse button. To insert a new action row, click the row selector just below where you want the new row, and then use the Insert | Row command or click the Insert Rows button.

COPYING ROWS

You can use the Windows Clipboard to copy a single cell, a row, a set of rows, or the entire macro. First you must highlight the text to be copied. In the case of a single row, click the row selector button at the left of the Macro window. If you want to select more than one row, hold down the **Shift** key and click other rows; Access will highlight all the rows you have selected. In the case of a cell, drag the mouse pointer over the text to be copied. Then choose the Copy command from the Edit menu (or use the **Ctrl+C** shortcut command).

Then move the pointer to the macro location where the row(s) are to be copied and click once. Use the Paste command from the Edit menu (or use the **Ctrl+V** short-cut command). Access will insert the contents of the Clipboard in the new location. If you want to copy the Clipboard material into a different macro, open the other macro in the Macro window, and then use the Edit | Paste command as before.

TIP

You can also use the File|Save As/Export command to send the selected macro directly to the other database, without using the Clipboard. Select the macro in the Database window, and then issue the command. Follow the directions that follow. Exporting is covered in Unit 13.

COPYING THE ENTIRE MACRO

You might want to use a particular macro with more than one database. As with other Access database objects, you can copy or move an entire macro from the Database window. Switch to Macro mode, and then highlight the macro you wish to copy. Use the Edit | Copy command (or give the **Ctrl+C** shortcut) to copy the macro to the Clipboard. Then open a different database. Click its Macros tab and use the Edit | Paste command to insert the macro from the Clipboard.

Saving the Macro

As with other database objects, use the Save or Save As command from the File menu to save the macro in the database. Remember that the Macro window must be the active window in order for you to see the File | Save command in the menu bar. When choosing a name, *use action terms* to represent the function of the macro. You must save the macro before you can run it. In fact, if you try to run the macro without saving it, Access will offer to save it for you.

Running the Macro

The method for running the macro depends on *where* you are in Access. If you are already in the Macro window and want to test the current macro, click the Run button on the toolbar or use the Run | Run command. If you are in the Database window, click the Macros tab and then select the macro; click the Run button to execute it. If you are in another Access window such as Form, Report, or Query, choose the Macro command from the Tools menu. The macro can run automatically as the result of an event in a form or report or be attached to a command button in a form. You may want to run the macro in single-step mode for debugging purposes, discussed later in this unit.

GUIDED ACTIVITY

11.1 Creating a Simple Macro

In this Guided Activity you will create and run a simple macro that opens the Customers form.

1. Start Windows 95 and load Access. Open the Hunter97.mdb database.

2. Click the Macros tab and click the New button. After a few seconds Access will display the Macro window.

3. Click the Comment box of the first action line in the top pane. Type `Sample Macro that opens the Customers form.` and press **Enter**. Access will move the pointer to the second action line.

4. Click the down arrow in the Action column in the second line and scroll down until you see OpenForm. Select this action for the first task.

5. Click once on the Form Name argument. Either type in `Customers` or choose it from the drop-down list of forms.

6. In the Comment box for this action, type `Open Customers form`, and press **Enter**. Figure A11.3 shows the macro at this point.

FIGURE A11.3
Sample OpenForm macro

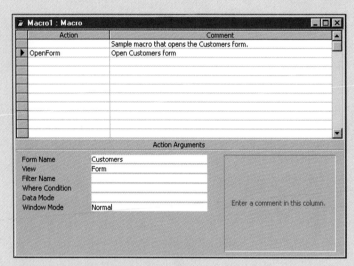

7. Before you can run the macro you must save it. Give the File|Save command and specify `Open Customer Form` as its name.

8. Finally, click the Run button on the toolbar. Access will immediately open the Customers form in Form view and display it on the desktop. Notice that the Macro window remains open in the background.

9. You can scroll through the Customers form as usual. Then close the form by clicking the close button or using its File|Close command. You return to the Macro window. We will make a more elaborate macro in the next section. Close the open Macro window.

Macro Groups

Some macros can be organized as a macro group, a set of related macros that appear together in the same Macro window. When you save the macro group in the database, it appears under the name of the macro group, not the individual macro names within the group. A macro group is useful when you have a group of similar macros for a single form, such as macros attached to command buttons in a menu form. In this example each command button could cause a different form to open or a report to print. These macros would be very similar and can be conveniently combined in a macro group.

Creating a Macro Group

First you must create a new macro. Then click the Macro Names button on the toolbar (or use the View | Macro Names command from the menu bar). Access will open the Macro Name column in the Macro window, to the left of the Action column. Next, insert the actions for the first macro as you normally would, setting the arguments and filling in comments as necessary. When you have entered all the actions for the first macro, type its name in the Macro Name column in the *first* action row. Access will execute the actions in that row and below until it reaches a blank action or a new macro name. You may begin the macro with a blank action and use its comment as a description of the macro.

Go on to insert the actions for the second macro in the group, filling in the Macro Name column with the name of the second macro. Continue this process until all of the actions for each macro in the group have been created and labeled with the correct names. Then use the File | Save command to save the macro group under a single name.

Using a Macro from a Macro Group

Whenever you want to refer to a particular macro within a macro group, use `macrogroupname.macroname` instead. Thus, to refer to the macro named Open Customer Form within the Main Switchboard macro, use the name `Main Switchboard.Open Customer Form`. Otherwise, macros in a macro group are used the same way as an individual macro saved under its own name.

GUIDED ACTIVITY

11.2 Creating a Macro Group

In this Guided Activity you will create a simple macro group that illustrates how the individual macros work. This is not intended to be an example of a complex macro.

1. Close any open windows and return to the Hunter97.mdb Database window.

2. Switch to Macro mode and click the New button to open the Macro window.

3. Click the Macro Names button on the toolbar, or choose the Macro Names command from the View menu. Access will display the Macro Name column in the Macro window.

4. Leave the first action blank, but click once in its Comment cell. Enter the comment `This is a sample macro group.`

5. In the Macro Name column of the second line, type `First`. In the Comment column for that line enter `This is the first macro in the macro group.`

6. In the third line, click once in the Action cell. Click the down arrow and select MsgBox from the list of actions. This action will display a Windows message box with your own message text and title bar. You can choose whether to have the computer beep, and you can set the relative importance of the information with the Type argument. The next step shows how to fill in those arguments.

7. Press **F6** to move to the lower pane of the Macro window. Fill in the following values for the arguments. You can choose the Beep and Type from the drop-down list if desired.

Message	`This is the First macro executing`
Beep	`Yes`
Type	`Information`
Title	`Your Custom Message Here`

8. Press **F6** to return to the top pane. Type this into the Comment cell for the same action line: `Display the custom message box with the first message.`

9. Skip one action line and click the fifth line in the Macro Name cell. Type `Second` and press **Enter**.

10. In the Action cell, type `MsgBox` or select it from the drop-down list.

11. Press **F6** to move to the lower pane. Fill in the following values for the arguments. You can choose the Beep and Type from the pull-down list if desired.

Message	`This is an example of a much longer message that is wider than the width of the box. You can use Shift+F2 to open a Zoom box if desired. Access will automatically widen the message box in order to display as much of your message as possible.`
Beep	`No`
Type	`Warning!`
Title	`Title Space is Relatively Short`

12. Press **F6** to return to the top pane. Type this into the Comment cell of this action line: `Display the custom message box with the second message.`

13. Figure A11.4 shows the Macro window for this activity. Use the File | Save command to save this macro group with the name `Sample Macro Group`.

14. Because this macro group contains individually named macros, use the Tools | Run Macro command to run the macro rather than the Run button on the toolbar. When prompted for the name in the Run Macro dialog box, type `Sample Macro Group.First` and press **Enter**. You should see the message box shown in Figure A11.5. The "i" symbol indicates that this is an information message type. Select OK.

 NOTE *To save time, instead of typing the full name in the Run Macro dialog box, click the down arrow at the right of the box and select the proper macro. Click OK to run the macro.*

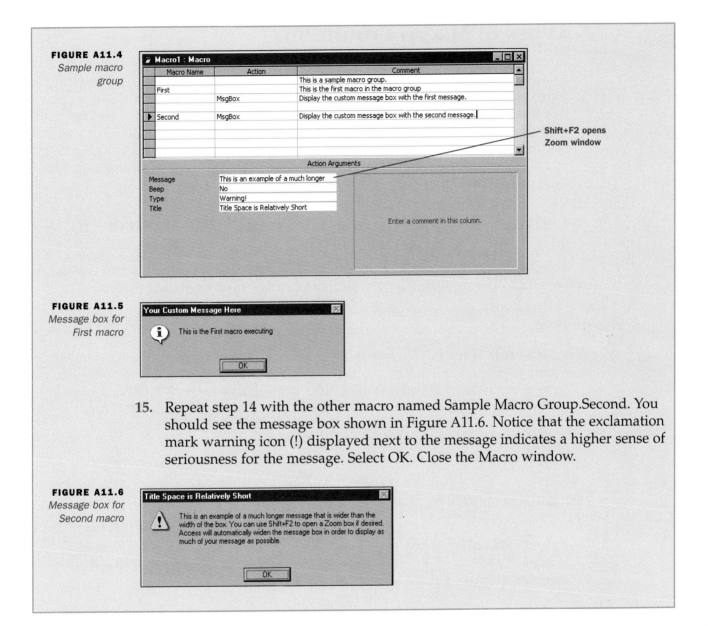

FIGURE A11.4
Sample macro group

FIGURE A11.5
Message box for First macro

15. Repeat step 14 with the other macro named Sample Macro Group.Second. You should see the message box shown in Figure A11.6. Notice that the exclamation mark warning icon (!) displayed next to the message indicates a higher sense of seriousness for the message. Select OK. Close the Macro window.

FIGURE A11.6
Message box for Second macro

Conditional Macros

Access provides a means of testing conditions in macros using conditions, expressions that can be evaluated as True or False. The conditional expression goes in the Condition column. If the condition on a particular action line is True, Access will execute that action. If the condition is False, Access will not execute that action. If the next line's Condition contains an ellipsis (...), Access will apply the same condition as the previous line. In other words, you can conditionally execute a sequence of actions by placing the condition in the first line of the sequence and then writing the ellipsis in each line thereafter that you want to have executed if that first condition is true.

Types of Macro Conditions

In general, you would associate conditional execution of a macro step with control values in the Access object selected. For instance, if the user left blank a particular form control that must be answered, you can have a macro display a message box that instructs the user to make an entry. You can display a message box for one kind of entry and another message box for different entries. You might have a sales tax form that is called up only if the customer is taxable. You can check the number of detail lines used in a form and perform some new-screen actions if that number exceeds a certain count.

Using Control Names in Condition Expressions

Access condition expressions were introduced in Unit 3 of this textbook. Sample expressions with explanations are included in this section. Remember that Access uses the following syntax to refer to control names from forms and reports:

Forms!formname!controlname
Reports!reportname!controlname

As usual, if any of your names has a space in it, you must enclose the name in square brackets. For a macro to make use of a control from a form or report, that form or report must already be open. The macro can open the form itself, or can test whether it is already open with a macro condition and open it if it is not.

Condition	Explanation
Forms!Customers!State="IN"	If the value in the State field in the Customers form is equal to IN….
[Date of Last Order]< "1/1/98"	If the Date of Last Order control value on the form from which the macro was run was prior to January 1, 1998….
Forms!Products!Category= "Camping" AND Forms!Products!Vendor="Icicle"	If the value of the Category control in the Products form is Camping and the Vendor control from the same form is Icicle….
COUNT([LineNumber])> =12	If the total number of entries in the LineNumber field on the form from which the macro was run is at least 12….
[LastName] Is Null	If the LastName field is blank....
IsLoaded("Customers")	If the Customers form is already open on the desktop….

The last condition uses a user-defined function called IsLoaded to determine whether the Customers form is already open in Access. This function was written in Visual Basic for Applications and was included in the Northwind.mdb sample database packaged with Access. It is included in the Hunter97.mdb in the module called UtilityFunctions and can be copied to your own database via the Clipboard.

GUIDED ACTIVITY

11.3   Creating a Conditional Macro

In this Guided Activity you will create a simple conditional macro that tests to see whether a form has already been opened and displays a message accordingly.

1. Close any open windows and return to the Hunter97.mdb Database window. If you are not already in Macro mode, click the Macros tab.

2. Click the New button to create a new macro.

3. Click the Conditions button on the toolbar, or use the View | Conditions command from the menu bar. Access should open a new column to the left of the Action column.

4. Leave the first action empty, but type in its Comment cell: `Sample macro that uses conditions to check for open forms.`

5. In the second row choose OpenForm as the action. The Form Name argument is `Customers`. Leave the defaults for the other arguments. The comment for this action is `Open the Customers form.`

6. Click the Condition cell of the third line and type: `IsLoaded("Customers")`. Press **Enter** to complete the entry. Remember to enclose the form name in quotes and check that you have spelled the name correctly.

7. In the action cell of the third line select MsgBox as the action. The Message argument should be `Customers is open`. Leave the defaults for the other arguments for this action.

8. The comment for the third line is `If the Customers form is open display Open message.`

9. In the fourth line type an ellipsis (…) into the Condition cell, indicating that this action is only to be executed if the previous line's condition is true. The action for this line is Close. The arguments for this action are as follows: Object Type is `Form` and Object Name is `Customers`. The comment for this line is `Close the Customers form.`

10. In the fifth line enter this condition: `Not IsLoaded("Customers")`.

11. In the Action cell choose MsgBox. In this case the Message argument is `Customer is NOT loaded now`. The comment should be `If the Customers form is not open display the Closed message.`

12. Click the row selector button in the third row. Access will highlight the entire row. Choose the Copy command from the Edit menu. This will copy this row to the Clipboard.

13. Click once on the next empty row. Choose the Paste command from the Edit menu. This will copy the contents of the Clipboard into this new row. We need to make some editing changes in this row.

14. Change `Customers` to `Products` in the Condition cell. The easiest way to do this is to drag the mouse pointer across the Customers text, highlighting all of it. Then type `Products` and Access will replace the highlighted text with the new text.

15. Click once on the MsgBox action of this line. Change `Customers` to `Products` in the Message argument in the lower pane and Comment column. The finished Macro window is shown in Figure A11.7. By dragging the column borders, the column widths were adjusted to display the full condition expressions.

FIGURE A11.7
Sample conditional macro

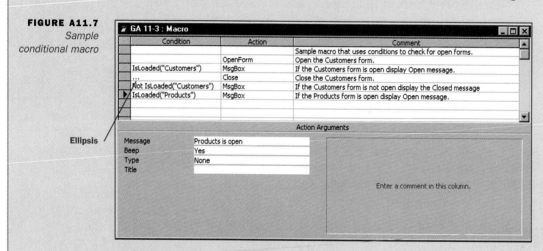

Ellipsis

16. Save your macro with the File I Save command. Use the name `Sample Condition Macro.`

17. To run your macro, click the Run button on the toolbar. Access will open the Customers form and then display the message box confirming that it is open. When you click OK in the message box, Access will close the form. Then you should get another message stating that the Customers form is not open. Click OK and then close the active window.

Debugging the Macro

We use the term debug to describe the process of testing and removing errors ("bugs") from the computer program, in this case a macro. As mentioned earlier in this unit, writing a successful macro (program) is an iterative process. You rarely create a macro that works properly the first few times you run it. In fact, we recommend that new Access programmers build complicated macros in pieces. That is, work on a small portion of it at first until it is correct. Then add more actions in small groups, rather than all at once. Experienced programmers may be able to work with larger groups of actions.

Single-Step Mode

Access provides several built-in debugging tools that help you find errors. Perhaps the most useful of these is single-step mode. In this mode Access will execute your macro just one action at a time. You have a chance to examine the results after each step. You can use the mouse to switch between Access windows on the desktop, picking up clues about what the macro did (or did not) do in the last step. Access will display the next action to be taken in the macro. You can continue in single-step mode or switch to full speed.

To run your macro in single-step mode, click the Single Step button on the toolbar. Or give the Run | Single Step command from the menu bar. In either case, next click the Run button. Access will display the Macro Single Step dialog box shown in Figure A11.8 in the next Guided Activity. The box shows the macro name, condition, action name, and some of the arguments for the next action. You have three button choices: Step, Halt, and Continue. Step will run the action in the dialog box, Halt will stop the macro, and Continue will run the rest of the macro at normal speed. Note that with any method of turning on single-step mode, Access will remain in single-step mode until you switch it back to run mode.

It is possible to insert actions into the macro that cause it to run at full speed for a portion, then switch to single-step mode, and then back to full speed. You can use this method to check parts of the macro that are not working properly, and then to speed past the parts that are working well. The next section will explain how to do this.

You can also switch a macro to single-step mode while it is running by pressing **Ctrl+Break**. This will cause Access to display the Macro Single Step dialog box. You can stop the macro by clicking Halt.

Entering Access Menu Bar Commands in Macros

Nearly all of the Access 97 menu bar commands are available with the RunCommand action, including the Run | Run and Run | Single Step commands. The arguments for this action are listed alphabetically in the Command argument in the lower pane. Simply scroll down to the desired command and click it once.

For example, to switch to single-step mode *inside* the macro, insert a blank row in the macro and choose the RunCommand action. The Command argument would be SingleStep; to go back to full speed, the Command argument would be Run. The macro will run at the indicated speed until you change the speed with another action or change it manually.

If your RunCommand action causes a dialog box to appear, the user can choose a command button from the dialog box. If you want the macro to send something to Access such as choosing a command button in the dialog box, use the SendKeys action in the macro and fill in the Keystrokes argument. For more information on this action, search online Help.

CAUTION   **Experience with Access has shown that some menu bar items do not remain the same between versions of Access. Use RunCommand with caution if you migrate a database application to a new version of Access.**

The Action Failed Dialog Box

Another important debugging tool is the Action Failed dialog box. An error box appears when Access detects an error in your macro. When you click OK, the Action Failed dialog box appears, showing the action and its arguments that caused the error. The only user choice available in this box is Halt, equivalent to stopping the macro. You can study the Action Failed dialog box for clues about why the macro failed to run without error. Remember that a single action may work correctly in one place in the macro and incorrectly in another place, often the result of having the wrong Access object active.

Talking Through the Macro

Our experience in other computer languages shows that you can often find your mistakes simply by talking through the macro steps with someone else. By forcing yourself to explain each line, you often see problems before they are pinpointed. The process of speaking the steps out loud may also help you understand a complicated sequence of actions. Don't hesitate to try this. You may even discover features that were omitted from the macro or implemented clumsily. This is one important reason most programming today is done in teams!

GUIDED ACTIVITY

11.4   Single-Stepping Through a Macro

In this Guided Activity you will use single-step mode to work through the previous macro and explore the Action Failed dialog box.

1. Return to the Hunter97.mdb Database window and select Macro mode.

2. Select the Sample Condition Macro from the previous activity and click the Design button.

3. Click the Single Step button on the toolbar or use the Run I Single Step command from the menu bar.

4. Then click the Run button or use the Run I Run command from the menu bar.

5. Access will run the macro and present the Macro Single Step dialog box. Click Step several times until you see the box shown in Figure A11.8, representing the next action to be executed.

6. Halt the macro, and be sure that the Single Step button is not selected. Click the Run button on the toolbar and wait until you see the first message box that requires a user response.

7. Instead of clicking OK, press **Ctrl+Break** to turn on single-step mode manually. Step through the next action of this macro, then halt the macro.

8. Next we will modify the macro. Click the next open action line and select the RunCommand action. Its Command argument is SingleStep. The comment for this action is Enable single-step mode with RunCommand action.

9. Add one more action line beneath the RunCommand line. Its action is OpenForm and the Form Name argument is Access. Its comment is Open a missing form!

10. Use the File I Save As/Export command to save this macro within the current database under the new name of Single Step Macro.

FIGURE A11.8
*The Macro Single
Step dialog box*

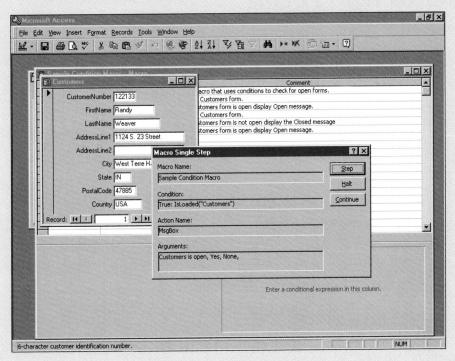

11. Make sure that the Single Step button is not selected and click the Run button. Access will run at full speed until it reaches the RunCommand action, which places it in single-step mode. Click the Step button to execute the last line of the macro.

12. When Access tries to open the nonexistent form named Access, it will display an error message. Click OK, and you will see the Action Failed dialog box of Figure A11.9.

FIGURE A11.9
*The Action Failed
dialog box*

13. After examining the contents of this dialog box, click Halt to end the macro and close the Macro window.

Using Macros with Forms

The most common use for macros is with Access forms. You can use macros in a form menu in which several command buttons are displayed. Clicking the command button runs a macro that opens another form. You can respond to events on forms such as opening the form, moving from one record to another, changing data in a record, deleting a record, and so on. You can synchronize two forms in separate windows by using macros. You can use a macro to set values of controls in forms. You can even print forms with a macro. This section will illustrate many of these macro applications.

Using a Macro to Open a Form

You have learned that the OpenForm action will open an Access form. We want to create a macro that opens a form and, optionally, changes its size and location. We can also attach this macro to a command button so that clicking that button will cause the macro to run.

OPENING A FORM

The OpenForm action causes Access to open the specified form. Its arguments control the Form Name, the View for the form (Form, Design, Print Preview, or Datasheet), and the Filter Name or a Where Condition that restrict the records to appear in the form. You can set arguments for Data Mode (Edit, Add, or Read Only) and Window Mode (Normal, Hidden, Icon, or Dialog). Edit Data Mode permits the user to make changes to existing records. Add Data Mode allows the user to add new records and make changes to existing records. With Read Only Data Mode the user can view the data but cannot make any changes. Hidden Window Mode makes the form invisible when opened on the desktop, and Icon Window Mode opens the form as an icon at the bottom of the screen. Default values for each argument are listed first within each group.

There are two ways to add the OpenForm action to a macro. Earlier in this unit you selected that action from the drop-down list and filled in the arguments as appropriate. You can also drag the form you want to open from the Database window and place it in the macro. Access will automatically add the OpenForm action and place the appropriate values into the arguments. You can make changes to those settings manually if necessary. This method of dragging a database object to the Macro window saves time, especially when you are adding a large number of forms and reports to the macro. It can also reduce errors because you are dragging an existing object instead of typing its name in the argument pane. Of course, if you drag the wrong object it will make the macro incorrect.

MOVING AND SIZING THE FORM

The MoveSize action permits the macro to move and/or resize the active window. You may want to place several forms on the same screen to make room for other Access data objects. MoveSize can be used in Form, Design, and Datasheet views.

MoveSize has four arguments. The Right and Down arguments control the position of the upper left corner of the window, measured in inches from the left and top edges of the window that contains the active window. If you leave these blank, Access uses the window's current settings. The Width and Height arguments specify the dimensions (in inches) of the active box. You can set the default measurement unit to inches or centimeters in the Regional Settings dialog box of the Windows Control Panel.

If you leave the Width and Height arguments blank but change the Right and Down arguments, Access will move the window but leave it in its current size. If you give values for Width and Height but leave the Right and Down arguments blank, Access will resize the window in its current location.

MINIMIZING, MAXIMIZING, AND RESTORING WINDOWS IN A MACRO

The Minimize and Maximize actions will minimize or maximize the active window, similar to clicking those respective buttons in the upper right corner of the window. They have no arguments. The Restore action will restore a maximized or minimized window to its former size. It has no arguments.

GUIDED ACTIVITY

11.5 Creating a Macro to Open a Form

In this Guided Activity you will create a macro that opens a form and changes its size and position.

1. Start Windows and load Access. Open the Hunter97.mdb database.

2. Switch to Macro mode and click the New button to create a new macro.

3. In the first Comment line type `Opens the Customers form and resizes window.`

4. Press **F11** or click the Database button to display the Hunter97.mdb Database window at the side of the Macro window. Adjust the window positions as necessary to view both at the same time. Click the Forms tab in the Database window and locate the Customers form.

5. Drag the Customers form to the Action cell in the second line of the Macro window. Access will create an OpenForm action and assign Customers to the Form Name argument. Use the defaults for all arguments except Data Mode, which should be Read Only. The comment is `Open form.`

6. In the third line choose the MsgBox action. Use the default values for its arguments—we will use the box here to pause the macro until you click its OK button. The comment is `Pause macro.`

7. In the fourth line choose the MoveSize action. In the Right argument enter 3 and for the Down argument enter 1. Leave the Width and Height arguments blank. The comment is `Move form.`

8. Use the File I Save command to save this macro as `Open Customers.`

9. Make sure the Single Step button is not selected. Click the Run button on the toolbar or choose Run from the Run menu. Access will open the form in the normal, upper left corner position on the desktop.

10. Then Access will display the message box. Click OK and watch where the Customers form moves as the MoveSize action is executed. Close the Customers form active window.

11. Next, copy the actions from steps 6 and 7 as the fifth and sixth lines of the macro.

NOTE *You can copy these two actions by using the Windows Clipboard. First select both lines 3 and 4 by dragging their row selector buttons. Click Copy, or click the right mouse button to open the shortcut menu, and choose Copy. Click Paste, or click the fifth line, click the right mouse button, and choose Paste.*

12. The line 6 MoveSize action should leave the Right and Down arguments blank, but use 4 and 2, respectively, for the Width and Height arguments. Its comment line is `Resize form`.

13. Click the Run button (or choose Run from the Run menu) and click Yes to confirm that you want to save the macro before running it. Watch what happens to the form as the macro executes. The final position of the form, along with the macro itself, is shown in Figure A11.10. Note that your desktop may not look just like this one, particularly if you are running Windows at 640 × 480 video resolution. To access the portion of the form that does not appear, you must use the scroll bars in the Form window.

FIGURE A11.10
Macro window and open form after move and resize

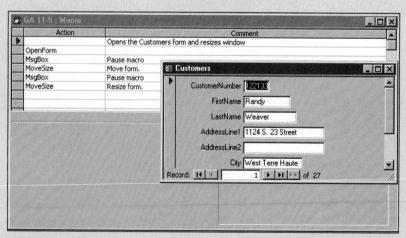

14. Close the Customers form window and the open Macro window.

Using a Command Button to Run a Macro

You can run the macro in the previous activity from the Database window, or directly from the Macro window. But as you create custom applications with macros, it sometimes makes sense to attach a macro to a command button in a form. That way, whenever the button is pushed, the macro attached to it will run. Thus, the user can determine when the macro executes.

To create a command button that opens a form, first create the macro that opens the form and positions it at the desired location. We did this much in the previous Guided Activity. Save this macro. Then open the form that will contain the command button in Design view. Remember, you must add the command button to a *different* form than the one your macro opens. Drag the macro from the Database window to the form in the desired location for the command button. Access will automatically create a command button control and attach the macro to its On Click property. The button will have the name of the macro as its caption. When you open the form in Form view and click the command button, the macro will run and the other form will be opened. The following activity will illustrate this procedure.

GUIDED ACTIVITY

11.6   Creating a Command Button that Opens a Form

In this Guided Activity you will create and save a short macro that opens a form, and then attach it to a command button in another form.

1. Close any open windows and return to the Hunter97.mdb Database window.

2. Switch to Macro mode and click the New button to create a new macro.

3. Position the Database window so that it is next to the Macro window.

4. Click the Forms tab in the Database window and locate the Customers form. Drag it to the first line of the Macro window and release the left mouse button. Access will create an OpenForm action with the Customers form name.

5. Add a MoveSize action. Make the Right argument 3 and the Down argument 1.5 with blank values for the Width and Height arguments.

6. Use the File|Save command to save this macro as Review Customers. Close the Macro window.

7. With the Database window still in Form mode, locate the Review Data form. Click the Design button.

8. Click the Database Window button to display the Database window; adjust its position so that you can see both it and the Form window. Click the Macros tab in the Database window to switch to Macro mode.

9. Locate the Review Customers macro. Drag it to the form, placing it at the 2,.5-inch coordinates in the grid. Release the mouse button and Access will create a command button to which the Review Customers macro is attached.

10. You will have to drag the lower right corner of the control to the 3.5-inch mark on the horizontal ruler so that the control is large enough to display its full caption.

11. Click the Form button on the toolbar. Access will display the new form with the command button. Click the Review Customers command button to run the macro attached to that button. Figure A11.11 shows the Review Data form with the Customers form open in the right portion of the desktop. Close the Customers form and the Review Data form without saving changes to the form.

Form with macro command button and open form

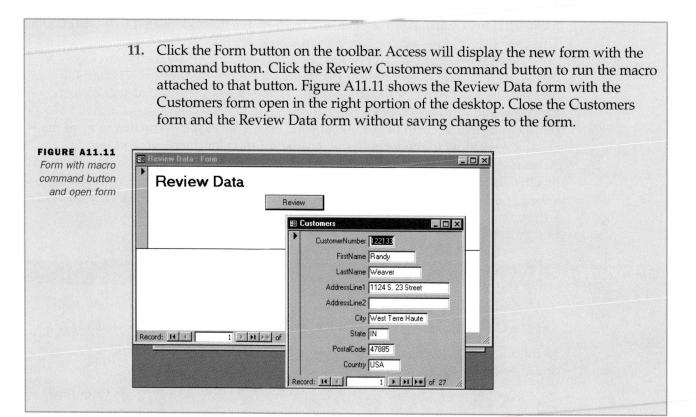

Responding to Events on Forms

Access can react to certain things that occur when you use a form, called events. You can use a macro to respond to these events when they occur. Events include such things as opening the form, moving from one record to another, double-clicking a control on the form, changing data in a record, and so forth. Typically, the event is described by a property of the form or a property of the controls in a form. A complete list of the events and associated properties is contained in the Microsoft Access *Getting Results* manual. You can also search Access online Help for additional help about events and their properties. A subset is described in this section.

FORM EVENTS

These events describe activities that pertain to the entire form. You can attach macros to properties of the form. They apply to both the form and all its controls.

OPENING A FORM The property for this event is called On Open, and it refers to the process when the form is first opened but before the first record is displayed. You could use this event to run a macro that closes another form that is already open or to open a custom dialog box in which the user enters criteria for what records are to be displayed or printed.

MAKING A RECORD THE CURRENT RECORD The property for this event is called On Current. It occurs just before a particular record becomes current, when the form is opened or when the focus moves from one record to another. You could use this property to synchronize records in two forms by calling a macro that matches a control value in the current form with a value in another form. Remember that you can use the GoToRecord macro action to go to a specific record within a form.

CHANGING DATA IN A RECORD   The properties for this event are called Before Update and After Update. Access will save the changes made to a record after you move out of the record. The time just before the update is performed is called Before Update; the time just after the update is made is called After Update. You can use the Before Update property to run a macro that validates the data just entered before it is saved. That macro can cause other actions to occur if the data prove to be invalid, such as displaying a message box or resetting the value of the control before it is saved. After the update is performed, you could use a macro to make changes in another form or table that uses the values just changed. This could be a log entry signifying that a change was made to a record in the table.

DELETING A RECORD   The On Delete property describes the macro that should be run just before the record is actually deleted from the database. You might display a message box asking the user to confirm that the record is to be deleted, or you might use a macro to make an entry in a transaction log that records the deletion action as well as some user identification and the time.

CLOSING A FORM   The On Close property is used to specify what actions are to take place after you have closed the form but before it disappears from the screen. You might make a log entry as to who used the form.

CONTROL EVENTS

These events refer to specific controls. The macro must be attached to properties of an individual control in order for that macro to run. Some control properties are very similar to those used for the form.

SELECTING A CONTROL   The On Enter property refers to the process when you have moved to a control and just before it has the focus. You might use a macro with the property to display instructions for that control. Of course, each control would need different instructions. You could make the instructions optional by supplying a command button to run the macro instead of automatically running it whenever the control is selected.

CHANGING DATA IN A CONTROL   The Before Update and After Update control properties exist for individual controls as well as for the form as a whole. You can do validation for a specific control when these events occur, or do it for the entire record at once with the earlier events.

DOUBLE-CLICKING A CONTROL   The On Dbl Click property can be used to start a macro when you double-click a particular control. You could use this event to open another form that displays additional information.

CLICKING A COMMAND BUTTON   Described in the previous section, the On Click property can be used to run a macro whenever a command button control is clicked on the form. This is appropriate for optional user choices.

TIP

To save time and avoid spelling errors, you can click the down arrow at the end of the property line and Access will display the names of all macros stored in your database. Simply scroll down and select the desired macro.

LEAVING A CONTROL   The On Exit property is used to run a macro when you are leaving a control. You might use this property to run a GoToControl macro that changes the tab order of the form. This property is less frequently used.

ATTACHING A MACRO TO A PROPERTY IN A FORM

First create and save the macro you want to attach to a form property. Then open the form in Design view. Display the property sheet by clicking the Properties button on the toolbar or by using the View | Properties command from the menu bar. Click the form background to select the form. If you are changing the properties of a specific control, click that control to select it. The property sheet for the form or control should be open on the desktop. Click once on the On Click property line and select the name of the macro to attach to that property. If the macro is part of a macro group, type in the name of the macro group first, followed by a period, and then the individual macro name. Figure A11.12 shows the property sheet for a command button control.

FIGURE A11.12
Property sheet for command button control

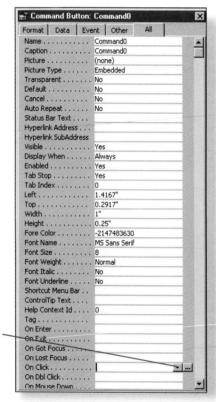

Click here to see the list of macros.

Using a Macro to Synchronize Two Forms

We showed how to synchronize a main form and its subform earlier. When you move to a different record in the main form, Access automatically moves the record pointer in the subform to the matching record. We used common field values in the Link Child Fields and Link Master Fields properties to synchronize the main form and subform within one Form window. You do not need a macro to keep the main form and subform synchronized.

There are advantages in using two *separate* Form windows, rather than a single main/subform design. For instance, you might have two separate forms open on the desktop, one for Products and the other for Vendors. If you move to a new record in the Products form, Access can automatically display the record for that product's supplier in the Vendors form on the screen. By having the forms open in their own windows, you can move or resize the forms independently. Here you would need a macro to keep the forms synchronized and in their desired locations.

You can use a macro to display or hide controls in one form based on values in another form. For example, suppose you have a customer form and are checking the accounts receivable records to see whether that customer is a good credit risk. You might display a previously hidden warning message if that customer has a bad payment history, as well as open another form to show the customer's payment information.

SYNCHRONIZING WITH THE OPENFORM ACTION

You must first decide which form will handle the synchronizing. Typically, this form is the one you will spend more time working with. Call this form the controlling form. Attach a macro to a command button in the controlling form that opens the secondary form and determines which records to display. The macro can use the Where Condition argument in the OpenForm action to make sure that the secondary form displays only records that match a control value in the controlling form.

For instance, suppose you made Products the controlling form. Create a macro that opens the Vendors form. The Where Condition argument in the macro would use an expression like:

```
[VendorName]=Forms!Products![VendorName]
```

In this case the first VendorName field refers to a control in the Vendors form that is being opened, and the second VendorName refers to the value currently in the Products form. When Access runs this macro and opens the Vendors form, it will display only the records that match this condition. If you move the record pointer in the controlling form and click the command button, it will reopen the secondary form and show records that match the new Supplier ID field value.

KEEPING TWO FORMS SYNCHRONIZED

Access provides the On Current property to *keep* two forms synchronized as you move from record to record in the controlling form without having to reopen the secondary form. Create a macro to open the secondary form as before, but attach it to the On Current property of the controlling form, instead of a separate command button. Use the same Where Condition in the macro to ensure that the records match. However, this time add a condition to the OpenForm action line in the macro that causes the OpenForm to execute only if the secondary form is already open. That is, if the secondary form is not already open, the macro does nothing. If it is open, the macro repositions the record pointer to match the record values.

To test whether the secondary form is loaded, use the IsLoaded( ) module that was introduced earlier in this unit. It is contained in the Modules section of the Hunter97.mdb database and can be copied to your own database as needed. It was written by Microsoft and included as part of the Northwind database as an example of a user-defined function. Inside the parentheses of this function, specify the name of the form in quotes. Access will test whether that form is already loaded and will return True if it is open and False if it is not loaded.

GUIDED ACTIVITY

11.7 Using a Macro to Keep Two Forms Synchronized

In this Guided Activity you will create a macro to keep two forms synchronized.

1. Close any open windows and return to the Hunter97.mdb Database window.

2. Switch to Macro mode and click the New button.

3. In the first line's Comment cell, write `Sample macro to keep two forms synchronized.`

4. In the Action cell of the next line enter `OpenForm`. The comment for this line is `Open Vendors form if it is not already open.`

5. The arguments for this action are shown below. Note that the matching fields in the Where Condition don't need to have the same name. In the Vendors table we used VendorName, but in the Products table we used Vendor to refer to the same thing.

Form Name	`Vendors`
View	`Form`
Filter Name	
Where Condition	`[VendorName]=Forms!Products![Vendor]`
Data Mode	`Read Only`
Window Mode	`Normal`

6. Save this macro as `Show Related Vendor`. Close the Macro window.

7. Switch to Form mode. Locate the Products form and click Design.

8. Double-click the form to open the property sheet for the form. (Or use the View | Properties command.)

9. In the On Current property, type `Show Related Vendor` and press **Enter**. This will cause Access to run the macro of that name every time a new record becomes current in the Products form. Save the form. Switch to Form view. The Vendors form will open per the macro instructions.

10. Without closing the Products form, use the mouse to drag the form's title bar over to the right side of the desktop.

11. Select the Vendors form. Move it to the left side of the desktop so that both forms are visible.

12. Click the Products form to make it active. Move the record pointer in this form and watch as Access keeps the Vendors form current with information about the vendor of each product. Figure A11.13 shows the two synchronized forms.

FIGURE A11.13
Forms synchronized via On Current property

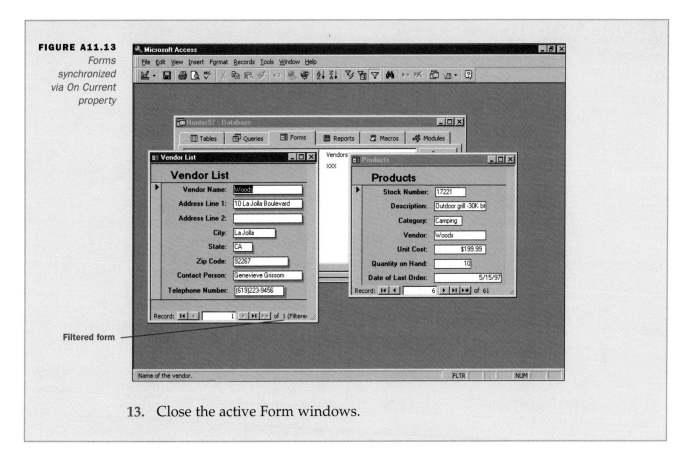

Filtered form

13. Close the active Form windows.

Filtering Records with a Macro

We can use the Where Condition argument of the OpenForm action to limit the form to records that match that condition. For more complex situations that tend to recur, use a filter instead. The Filter Name argument of the OpenForm action can hold the name of a filter that you have saved as a query. The filter can be used to restrict the records that appear in a form, or to sort the records that appear in the form.

You can also use the ApplyFilter action to invoke a filter for a form that is already open. It has just two arguments, Filter Name and Where Condition. You must use one or both of these arguments when you add the ApplyFilter action. If you use both arguments, Access will use the filter first, and then apply the Where Condition to the records that match the filter. The ApplyFilter action can be used with Form, Design, and Datasheet views.

One interesting use of the ApplyFilter action is to create an alphabetical filter using command buttons to represent letters of the alphabet. You can set up a single form to look up records in your database based on the first letter of the relevant field or control. We will demonstrate this in the following activity in which you will build a customer lookup macro that displays only those customers in a specific alphabetical letter range.

11.8   Creating an Alphabetical Lookup Filter

In this Guided Activity you will create an alphabetical lookup macro group that displays customers according to their last name. Each macro in the group will apply a filter for that letter range.

1. Close any open windows and return to the Hunter97.mdb Database window.

2. Switch to Macro mode and click the New button to open a new macro.

3. Click the Macro Names button (or give the View | Macro Names command) to display the Macro Name column of the macro group.

4. In the Comment cell of the first line, enter Alphabetical filter attached to command buttons in Customer Lookup form.

5. The name of the first macro is A-E. Its action is ApplyFilter. The Comment cell should contain Display customers whose last names begin with A-E.

6. Press **F6** to move to the lower pane of the Macro window. The Where Condition for this macro is: [LastName] Like "[ABCDE]*" Thus, any customer whose last name begins with the letters *A* through *E* will meet the condition.

7. Press **F6** to return to the upper pane. Click the row selector button next to the Macro Name column to select the row. We will copy this row for the other macros.

8. With the row selected, choose the Copy command from the Edit menu (or use the **Ctrl+C** shortcut command). Access will copy the macro line to the Clipboard.

9. Move the pointer to the row below the A–E macro and choose Paste from the Edit menu (or use the **Ctrl+V** shortcut command). Access will copy the A–E macro from the Clipboard back into the macro. Change the name of the second macro to F-K, change the comment cell, and change the Where Condition to [LastName] Like "[FGHIJK]*".

10. Repeat step 9 for the remaining three letter groups. Use the following groups: L–P, Q–T, and U–Z. Adjust the Macro Name cell, the Comment cell, and the Where Condition for each macro.

11. When all of the alphabetical letter macros have been created, add one more macro that shows all of the records without applying any filter conditions. Call this macro All, and give its action as ShowAllRecords. This action has no arguments. The comment is Shows all customers. The macro is shown in Figure A11.14.

12. Save the entire macro group under the name Alpha Filter Buttons.

13. Close the Macro window, and then switch to Form mode.

FIGURE A11.14
Finished alphabetical filter macro group

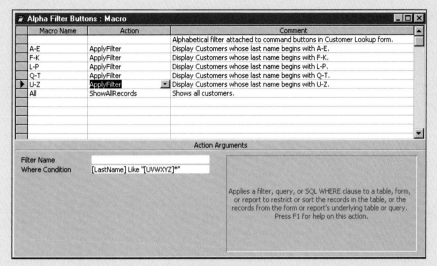

14. Locate the Customer Lookup form and open it in Design view. This form uses a sorted query as its record source. The form already contains the command buttons for the letter groups. You must assign the appropriate macro from the macro group to each button.

15. Click the A–E command button to select it. If the property sheet is not already displayed, click the Properties button on the toolbar or choose the Properties command from the View menu.

16. Click the On Click property, and then click the down arrow at the right edge of the box. Scroll down until you have located the Alpha Filter Buttons.A-E macro. Press **Enter** to assign the Alpha Filter Buttons.A-E macro to that button.

17. Repeat step 16 with the other four letter groups, each time selecting the appropriate macro name at the end of the macro group name.

18. Repeat step 16 for the All button. Its On Click property is Alpha Filter Buttons.All. Figure A11.15 shows the form in Design view.

FIGURE A11.15
Lookup form with command buttons and attached macro

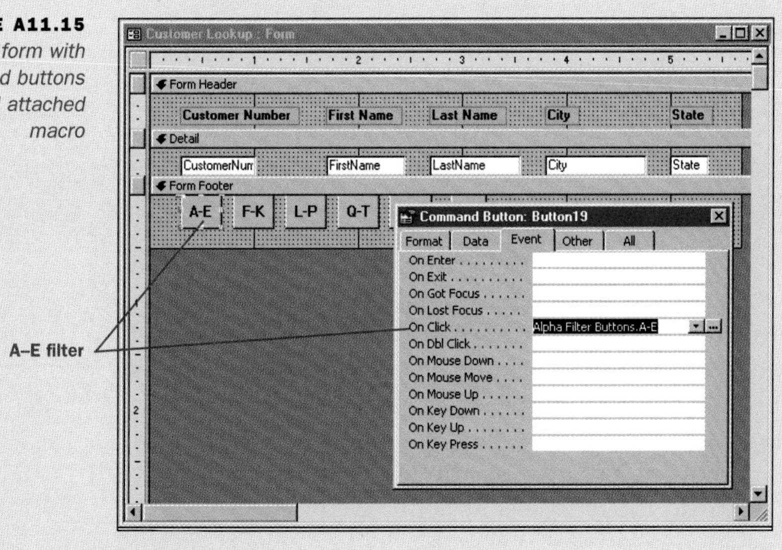

19. Click the Form View button on the toolbar to see the finished form. Figure A11.16 shows the form with the A–E button selected. Notice that only customers whose names start with the letters A–E are displayed on the form. Save the changes to this form and close the active Form window.

FIGURE A11.16
Customer Lookup form with A–E macro filter in use

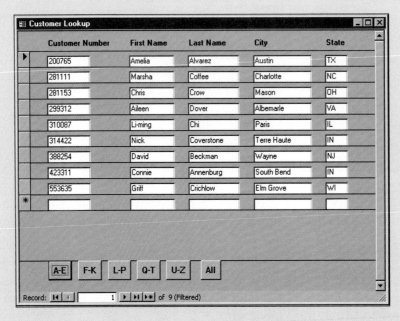

Moving Between Controls in a Macro

You can move automatically between controls and records with your macro. There are three GoTo actions in Access. GoToControl lets you move the focus to another field or control in the current table, query, or form. GoToPage moves you to the specified page in a multipage form and puts the focus in the first control on that page. GoToRecord moves to a specified record or a new record in the current form, table, or query. You can study the arguments for these actions in the online Help system.

You might choose to move to a different control than the tab order specifies because of a certain condition in the form. You might skip irrelevant controls or display only controls that the user is authorized to view. You might want to position the focus in a certain control prior to executing another macro action.

Using a Macro to Find a Record

You can use the FindRecord action to locate the first record after the current record that matches certain criteria. You can search through a table, a form, or a query. There is an argument for each of the seven options in the Access Find In Field dialog box. You specify the value to search for along with the search direction and other criteria. You can specify whether the entire field or the start of the field must match the search text.

To use this action, have your macro move the focus to the control or field that you want to search. Add the FindRecord action to the macro, and then fill in its arguments as shown in Figure A11.17. The Find What argument must be supplied so that the action knows what to look for. You can specify text, a number, or a date in this argument. The other arguments are optional; their default values are shown in the figure.

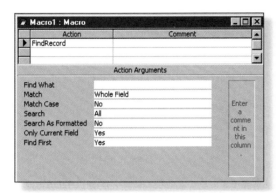

The FindNext action can be used repeatedly to find other occurrences of the data matching the previous FindRecord action. For example, you might use the FindRecord action to find the first instance of a particular customer. The FindNext action can cycle through other instances of the same customer.

Using a Macro to Set Values in a Form

You can reduce errors and make work easier for a user by having your macros set values for controls, fields, and properties. You can set the value of a control equal to the value of a different control on this or another form. You can hide or display a certain control based on conditions in the form. For instance, you might have a warning box if the customer's account balance is over a certain limit or add a message to a report based on a similar condition. You can lock command buttons so that they cannot be selected if certain conditions are true.

SETVALUE ARGUMENTS

The SetValue action is used for setting a value within the macro. This action has two arguments, Item and Expression. Item is the name of the control or property that is to be changed, and Expression contains the new value for that item. If the item refers to a control on the form from which it is called, you can refer to that control by its name alone. If the item refers to a control or property elsewhere, you must give the full name such as Forms!formname!controlname.

CONVERTING A CONTROL TO UPPERCASE CHARACTERS

You can use the SetValue action to convert all the characters in a control or field to uppercase values. This is particularly useful when several people input data values inconsistently. Create a macro with a single SetValue action. Its Item argument should be the name of the control you want to convert to uppercase. The Expression argument should be UCase(fieldname). Attach this macro to the After Update property of that control on the form. Whenever someone changes the value of the control, this macro will run and do the conversion. Suppose the field you want to convert is called TypeOfInsurance. Set the following arguments:

Item	[TypeOfInsurance]
Expression	UCase([TypeOfInsurance])

NOTE *The square brackets are necessary if the field name contains embedded spaces.*

SETTING VALUES FOR NEW RECORDS

You can use a macro to preset values for controls in new records. Suppose you were working with a Vendors form that opens a New Products form to add a new product. The macro can use the SetValue action to set the value of the VendorName field in the New Products form to that in the Vendors form. Not only does this save time, but it ensures that relational integrity is maintained between the related tables.

Requiring an Entry in a Control

You may want to be certain that a field in a form always has a value in it with a Not Null validation rule. You can create a macro that contains the validation rule and attach the macro to the form's Before Update property. Note that you can't attach the macro to an individual control, because that macro will run only if the user makes a change in the form.

Printing Forms with a Macro

We discussed earlier how to use the OpenForm action in a macro to display a form in Print Preview. The user can decide whether to print the form. But you may want the macro to make all of those decisions and insulate the user from needing to know how to use the Print Preview window.

The PrintOut action can also print the active form, report, query, or table. If the desired print object is not active, your macro can use the SelectObject action to make it active; that is equivalent to clicking the object's title bar with the mouse. The PrintOut action contains arguments for all of the options in the Print dialog box except Print to File. You can set the print range, print quality, and number of copies, and can set any collating instructions within the macro arguments.

It is practical to attach a print macro to a button on a form. By clicking that button the user can cause the print macro to run. You can use another pop-up form to let the user make decisions about the various print options, or go with the values already saved in the macro's arguments.

Printing Reports with a Macro

There are two ways to print a report with a macro. The OpenReport action gives more flexibility to the user, including the option to use Print Preview. The Print action introduced in the previous section can also be used to print a report when all of the options have been preassigned. Each is described in this section.

Using the OpenReport Action

The OpenReport action has four arguments, listed below. Use this action when you want to open the report in Print Preview, or when you want to apply a filter or a Where Condition that restricts the number of records that print. This macro uses the current values in the Print dialog box for such things as the print range, print quality, and number of copies. If you want to set these items, use the PrintOut action described below.

Argument	Explanation
Report Name	This is the name of the report within the database to print. It is a required argument.
View	The default is Print, which causes the report to print immediately. You can also select Print Preview, or Design view, in which case the user will see the report design.
Filter Name	This is the name of a query or a filter that has been saved as a query, and will restrict the records that qualify for the report.
Where Condition	This allows you to specify a simple SQL Where clause or Access conditional expression, also limiting which records qualify for the report.

Using the PrintOut Action

The other way to print a report is with the PrintOut action. The PrintOut action will print the currently selected object. This action allows the macro to set values in the Print dialog box such as print range, print quality, number of copies, and collating instructions. The arguments here pertain only to the Print dialog box, not to the name of the report. PrintOut will only send the report to the printer, not let the user enter Print Preview. Use the OpenReport action if you want the user to have the Print Preview option.

There is a way to limit which records qualify for the report and still use the PrintOut action. First use the ApplyFilter action to set a filter, and then invoke the PrintOut action in the macro. As with macros of other applications, there are numerous ways to accomplish the same task.

Using a Print Menu

The Access documentation refers to a switchboard or menu form as a menu of command buttons or switches that enable the user to choose between several alternative courses of action. You might create a main switchboard with two command buttons—one to View Forms and the other to Print Reports. The macros attached to those buttons can cause other switchboard forms to appear. The print switchboard could contain an option group with radio buttons that let the user choose which report should be printed. The following activity demonstrates creation of a print menu macro.

11.9   Creating a Print Menu Macro

In this Guided Activity you will create a macro that displays a menu of report names. Then you will create a switchboard form. Clicking a command button on the form will cause a macro attached to that button to run, printing a report.

1. Close any open windows and return to the Hunter97.mdb Database window.

2. Switch to the Macro mode and click the New button.

3. When the Macro window opens, click the Macro Names button on the toolbar (or use the View | Macro Names command) to display the Macro Name column.

4. On the first line enter this comment: `This is a macro group that will print reports from the Hunter97 database.`

5. On the second line type `Labels` as the macro name. The action is OpenReport. Its Report Name argument is `Customer Mailing Labels`. Leave Print Preview as the view for all reports in this activity.

NOTE   *As you begin to type in the name of the report, Access will fill in the rest of the name for you.*

6. Repeat step 5 with the `Salary` macro name. Its report is `Employee Salary Report`.

7. Repeat step 5 with the `Inventory` macro name. Its report is `Inventory Group Report`.

8. Repeat step 5 with the `Product` macro name. Its report is `Product Report by Vendor`. Figure A11.18 shows the completed macro.

FIGURE A11.18
Report Switchboard Buttons macro group

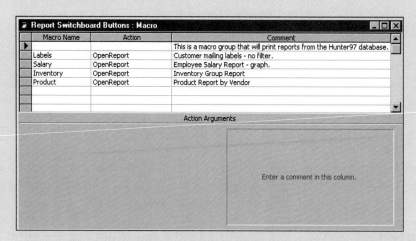

9. Save the macro with the name `Report Switchboard Buttons`. Close the Macro window.

10. Switch to Form mode, click the New button, and then select Design View and click OK to make the Report Switchboard form.

11. Place a large label control in the upper left corner of the form. In the box, type `Report Switchboard` and press **Enter**. Click the Bold and Italic buttons. Adjust the size to 18 points and use the Format | Size | To Fit command to make the box fit the text. Pull the bottom border of the Detail section up to about 1.5 inches.

12. Make sure the Control Wizards button is not selected. Click the Command Button tool on the Toolbox and create a command button control to the right of the form title, near the top of the form. Make it about 1 inch long.

13. Change the name of the control from Command 1 to `Labels`. Click the Bold button on the toolbar. In the On Click property of that control type `Report Switchboard Buttons.Labels`.

14. Repeat steps 12 and 13 for the other three buttons. Their labels should be the same as the macro names (Salary, Inventory, Product). Fill in the On Click property of the three controls with the appropriate macro names (`Report Switchboard Buttons.Salary`, `Report Switchboard Buttons.Inventory`, `Report Switchboard Buttons.Product`). The form is shown in Figure A11.19.

FIGURE A11.19
Report Switchboard form with command buttons

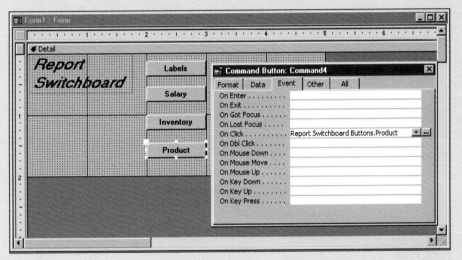

15. Click the Form button to view your form in action. Click the Labels button and watch Access display the Print Preview of the mailing labels report. Try out each of the other reports.

NOTE
If you spell one of the report names incorrectly, Access will display a warning message and the Action Failed dialog box. You will have to go back to the Report Switchboard macro in Design view to make the corrections.

16. Save the form with the name Report Switchboard. Close any open windows. We will modify this form as an exercise in Unit 12.

Creating an Auto-Execute Macro

If you create a menu-driven application with Access macros, you may want to have an auto-execute macro stored in the database that will automatically display an opening menu. This macro is saved as the special name AutoExec. The next time you open the database, Access will run this macro without user intervention. If the macro displays a main switchboard, the user can pick from custom screens without having to know anything about the Access menu system. Each database you use can have one AutoExec macro stored within it.

If you do *not* want the auto-execute macro to run when the database is opened, hold down the **Shift** key when you select the database with the File | Open Database command. In this case you will see the usual Database window.

Command Line Auto-Execute Macro Startup Option

It is possible to create a Windows 95 shortcut that will start Access with different command line options. In the Target box in the shortcut Properties dialog box, specify the folder where Access is stored, and then add the name of the database, followed by any command line options. See Figure A11.20 for the Access shortcut Properties dialog box.

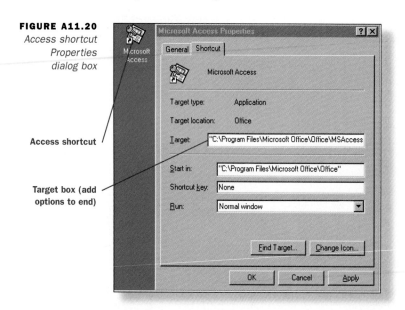

FIGURE A11.20
Access shortcut Properties dialog box

Access shortcut

Target box (add options to end)

You can run a startup macro automatically with the /x command line option. That is, add the name of the database file and /x followed by the macro name to the end of the Target box in the shortcut Properties dialog box. Windows will start Access, automatically load that database, and then execute the macro named. The following command line will start Access, open the Hunter97.mdb database, and automatically execute the Main Switchboard macro found in that database:

```
C:\Program Files\Microsoft Office\Office\MSAccess.exe
Hunter97.mdb /x Main Switchboard
```

You can also type that line in at the Run command of the Start menu. You are not limited to a single shortcut; create a shortcut for each application or special startup condition that your users will encounter. Shortcuts take up very little space on the disk and add to the convenience for users.

Other Access command line startup options are available:

- `/excl` will open the database in exclusive mode (otherwise opened in shared mode)

- `/ro` will open the database in read-only mode (no changes permitted)

- `/compact <target database>` will compact a database

- `/repair` will repair a damaged database

- `/convert <target database>` will convert a database from an earlier version

- `/profile <user profile>` substitutes a different user configuration for Access

- `/user <username>` gives a specific user name

- `/pwd <password>` gives a specific user password

- `/nostartup` will prevent the loading of the Access startup dialog box

GUIDED ACTIVITY

11.10 Creating an AutoExec Macro

In this Guided Activity you will create a simple macro and save it as AutoExec and then load the database and have it automatically execute.

1. Close any open windows and return to the Hunter97.mdb Database window.

2. Switch to Macro mode and click the New button.

3. On the first Comment line type `Runs automatically when you open the database.`

4. In the second line's Action cell use the MsgBox action. This will simulate the opening of a menu switchboard that we'll develop in Unit 12.

5. In the Message argument type `This opens automatically!`

6. Use the File | Save command to save this macro as `AutoExec`.

7. Close the Macro window, and then close the Hunter97.mdb Database window.

8. Open the Hunter97.mdb Database window as usual, and notice how the message box appears without further commands. Click OK to clear the message box.

9. For now, we will rename the AutoExec macro so that it does not open each time we open the Hunter97.mdb database. Switch to Macro mode, and click once on the AutoExec macro.

10. Choose the Rename command from the Edit menu. Give it the new name AutoExec NOT.

11. Close the Hunter97.mdb database and reopen it. Did the macro run automatically?

SUMMARY

This comprehensive unit showed you how to create Access macros that automate keystrokes and provide menus for applications. Macros consist of two parts: actions and arguments. There are nearly 50 actions for such tasks as opening forms and reports, filtering records, displaying messages, and moving forms on the screen. You can attach macros to command buttons or to events associated with forms and controls. When the command button is clicked or the event occurs, Access will automatically execute the macro.

Macros must be saved before they can be run. You can click the Run button on the toolbar or use the Run | Run command to execute the macro. For debugging purposes, switch to Single Step mode before you run the macro. Access will let you step through each macro action in order to pinpoint problems. If the macro fails to execute, Access will display the Action Failed dialog box; study this dialog box to learn what went wrong.

You can add conditions to Access macros by clicking the Conditions button; only actions whose Condition expression is true will be executed. You can group similar macros together with the Macro Names button, saving them in a single macro. Refer to the individual macro with the *macrogroupname.macroname* format. Macro groups are useful for storing macros to be attached to command buttons on the same form.

If you name a macro AutoExec, it will be loaded automatically when the database containing the macro is opened. You can override this feature by holding down the **Shift** key when you open the database. Access command line options can be used to open certain databases or perform certain macros when Access is started. Modify the properties of the Access shortcut to set the appropriate options.

Exercises

Use the Hunter River database contained within the Hunter97.mdb file on the Student Data Disk for these exercises.

EXERCISE

11.1 Open Employees Form

1. Create a simple macro that opens the Employees form, displays a message box that states a message that the Employees form is open, and then closes the form.

2. Be sure to print a copy of the macro.

3. Save it under the name `Open Employees`.

EXERCISE

11.2 Modified Employee Form Macro

1. Modify the macro from Exercise 11.1 so that it tests whether the Employees form is already open before opening the form.

2. Print a message that is appropriate if the form is already open.

3. When you test your macro, be sure to test it both with the Employees form open and not open prior to executing the macro.

4. Save this macro as `Open Employees2`.

5. Print a copy of your macro.

EXERCISE

11.3 Inventory Group Report Macro I

1. Create a macro that opens the Inventory Group Report in Print Preview.

2. Your macro should display a message box that explains the options available to the user in Print Preview. Don't worry about trying to actually print the report. *(Hint: Don't use the Print action for this macro.)*

3. Save this macro under the name `Preview Inventory Group Report`.

4. Print a copy of your macro.

EXERCISE

11.4

Simple Macro Group

1. Create a simple macro group in which the First macro contains a MsgBox action that gives the name of that macro.

2. Use the Edit | Copy command to copy that macro to the Clipboard, and then paste it into the macro group at a lower position. Change the macro name to Second and modify the message box and comment accordingly.

3. Repeat the process with the Third macro.

4. Print a copy of your macro before running it with the Tools | Macro command.

5. Save the macro group with a name of your choice.

EXERCISE

11.5

Open and Move Form Macro

1. Create a macro that opens the Employees form in Datasheet view and in read-only data mode.

2. Your macro should move the Employees form to the right side of the desktop.

3. Your macro should also open the Managers form in Form view and place it on the left side of the desktop.

4. Save the macro as Exercise 11-5.

EXERCISE

11.6

Alphabetical Filter Macro

1. Modify the alphabetical filter form and related macro group to use more command buttons.

2. Your new form should have no command button with more than three letters.

3. Print a copy of your macro.

EXERCISE

11.7

Validation Macro I

1. Open the table called Test Values, which has two fields. The first field is called ID and is counter type. The second field is called TextField and is text type.

2. Create a new form to receive data for this table.

3. Create a validation macro that replaces whatever you type in the TextField control with the uppercase equivalent.

4. Attach the macro to the appropriate property of the form.

5. Use the form and try typing in different combinations of lowercase and uppercase values. See what your macro does to those field values.

6. Print a copy of your macro.

EXERCISE

11.8

Validation Macro II

1. Create a macro that opens the Products form and limits records to the Camping category.

2. Print a copy of your macro.

3. Save your macro as Exercise 11-8.

EXERCISE

11.9

Validation Macro III

1. Modify the macro from Exercise 11.8 to allow the user to specify which product category will be displayed.

2. Save the macro as Exercise 11-9.

3. Print a copy of your macro.

EXERCISE

11.10

Inventory Group Report Macro II

1. Create a macro that will open the Inventory Group Report in Print Preview.

2. Your macro should display only those products that have a positive inventory balance.

3. Save your macro as Exercise 11-10.

4. Print a copy of your macro.

APPLICATION

Physicians' Medical Clinic: Using a Macro to Automate Steps

One of the analysts in the PMC Data Processing department wants to know how Access macros can be used to automate some steps for the clinic. You have agreed to create a few sample macros.

1. Create an alphabetical filter form that displays patients by their last names. Show several fields from the Patients table.

2. Create a macro that opens a form at a certain location on the desktop and displays all patients for a particular insurer. Your macro should allow the user to specify which insurer is used.

3. List four more macro opportunities that would be appropriate for the PMC97.mdb database and that would demonstrate some of the power of Access macros.

UNIT 12

Building an Application with Access

This unit illustrates how to create a complete application using Microsoft Access. An application is a coordinated set of database objects—tables, forms, macros, queries, reports, modules—that enable a user to maintain the data for an organization's database. The unit begins with a discussion of the systems analysis and design process and then continues with a discussion about designing an Access application. The Northwind Traders application from Microsoft is examined. The unit includes the development of a working application for the Hunter River Sporting Goods store. The unit concludes with a discussion of advanced application techniques that are illustrated in two other applications packaged with Access.

Learning Objectives

At the completion of this unit you should be able to

1. describe the purpose of systems analysis and design,

2. list the steps in designing an Access application,

3. use some advanced techniques used in Access applications,

4. run an existing Access application,

5. create a menu switchboard form,

6. add Paint pictures to a switchboard form,

7. create macros that cause actions to occur when command buttons are clicked,

8. start an application automatically when the database is loaded.

Case Study

To simplify use of the Hunter River database, you have been asked to prepare a menu-driven database application. The application should have a main menu that describes the various options for the user, including viewing forms, printing reports, and so forth. The menu should have command buttons to activate each option, with submenus for specific forms and reports. You should use Access macros to accomplish the tasks in the system.

Designing an Application with Access

An Access application is a coordinated set of database objects—tables, forms, macros, queries, reports, modules—that enable a user to maintain the data for a particular set of tasks, whether they be business forecasting, accounts receivable, inventory control, or hospital administration. The Access application is a customized information system for the organization. Instead of using the regular Access menus, the application presents a set of custom menus designed specifically to accomplish the data management tasks. Thus, individual users of the application do not need to know very much about Microsoft Access to operate your application.

The overall process of developing any information system begins with systems analysis and design, described next.

Information Systems Analysis and Design

The process of investigating an organization and evaluating its information needs is called systems analysis. The systems analyst will spend a great deal of time interviewing users, examining existing documents, and evaluating current procedures. Careful attention is paid to the flow of data and information through the organization. It is not possible to develop a usable information system without having arrived at a thorough understanding of the needs of the organization. The end result of the systems analysis is a set of general recommendations for what ought to be done to provide the necessary information.

The next phase, in which detailed specifications are generated, is called systems design. In this phase the analyst designs tables, forms, reports, and procedures that will solve the information problems. Users are given an opportunity to react to prototype forms and reports. These prototypes are working models that provide a realistic preview of how the system will perform. The design phase is usually performed in several iterations. That is, the analyst prepares some forms and reports, and then modifies them in accordance with user feedback. The process is repeated until all the users—whatever their competence—are satisfied that the system is providing the proper kinds of information.

It has been our experience that users rarely "tell" the entire story to analysts the first time around. Some users don't have the time to get fully involved with the project until the last minute. Other users may not have a realistic view of *what* information they need. Frequently, a user tells the analyst one thing and then changes directions once the user has a chance to work with a prototype form or report. Perhaps it is just a normal part of human nature to solve problems in layers. Whatever the case, it is vital to allow ample time for systems design and modification. Needless to say, Access can accommodate the needs of a range of users, providing an effective tool for rapid development of sophisticated and visually attractive database objects. And those objects can be modified just as quickly to meet changing requirements.

Components of an Application

An application consists of the database objects we have been developing throughout this book. In fact, the Database window lists *all* of the objects associated with an application. But the glue that holds them together is a series of menu forms called switchboards that present choices for users. When the user presses a button on a switchboard form, a macro executes and brings another switchboard form, report, or query into play.

TYPICAL MAIN SWITCHBOARD

Although the specific tasks for each application are different, most follow a similar pattern. Many main switchboards present a menu with these choices:

- View Forms
- Print Reports
- Perform Summary
- Database Window
- Exit from Microsoft Access

The View Forms selection lets the user view data, make changes, and add new data to tables in the database using Access forms. The second choice provides a means of printing reports. Both of these options would have secondary menus to let the user select a particular form or report to work with. The Perform Summary option allows the user to cause something to happen after the data are entered, such as closing out the month's accounts and posting them to the journal. The Database Window choice lets the user work directly with the Access Database window. The third and fourth selections might not be present in all applications. The last button is used to terminate the application, close Access, and return to Windows.

OTHER SWITCHBOARDS

The first two choices in the previous menu hint that there will be further choices for what forms or reports are viewed. In fact, macros attached to the command buttons in the main switchboard can open other switchboard forms that let the user choose from available database objects like forms and reports. You might imagine an upside-down tree or pyramid shape in which the top of the pyramid is the main switchboard. As you go down the pyramid it gets wider, reflecting the fact that more lower-level forms become available. We will demonstrate this principle later in this unit.

Steps in Developing an Application

The first step in developing an Access application is to do the systems analysis and decide what information the organization needs. Database design follows, with the development of tables and fields for the database. For a review of database design see Units 1 and 6.

COMPLETE THE DESIGN OF TABLES AND FIELDS

It is very important to complete the design of tables and fields, including properties, before going on to create forms and reports. If you establish properties for the fields in

Table Design view, Access will copy those properties into forms that you create. However, any changes made to table and field properties *after* a form is created will not be copied to the form's properties. Particularly important are the Format, Caption, Default, Validation Rule, and Validation Text properties. Also important is the field's Description property, which becomes the StatusBarText property for a form control containing that field. Unit 2 contains a review of table design.

DEVELOP FORMS AND REPORTS

Once the tables have been defined, it is appropriate to develop the forms and reports that the organization needs. Typically, these are developed with the cooperation of the users so that changes can quickly be made where necessary. Access provides a flexible environment to modify objects and add new objects without affecting existing objects. But if you change a table, you may have to modify each form and report that uses the modified table. Microsoft may correct this deficiency in a future release of Access. Units 4, 5, 7, 8, and 9 contain a review of form and report design.

NOTE *If you add or change a validation rule for a field in a table, Access will offer to check all the existing data in the table. However, a modified property is not automatically copied into the same-named property in the form.*

DEVELOP MENUS ON PAPER

At the same time, the analyst can begin developing a set of menus on paper in outline format. Remember that good menus don't offer the user too many choices on one screen. A rule of thumb suggests that no more than four to six menu choices should be given in one menu. If you have more choices than that, consider combining menu items or splitting the menu into two or more lower-level menus.

Your menus should use descriptive labels with action words on the command buttons so that the user understands clearly what that command button does. For instance, View Forms and Print Reports leave little to the imagination. Although the Database Window label is somewhat confusing, your switchboard form can provide an explanatory message for the user.

BUILD SWITCHBOARD FORMS

Once the menu structure is established, you can build the switchboard forms that display the menus. Most analysts will build the forms one at a time, not trying to tie them all together at once. In fact, you can build the form with its command buttons but not attach the macros until a later time.

CREATE MACROS THAT CAUSE ACTION TO OCCUR

Once the forms are well into development, it is time to create the macros that cause action. See Unit 11 for a discussion of Access macros. Many applications will have an AutoExec macro to open the Main Switchboard form when the database is opened. You will have macros that are attached to the On Click property of the command buttons in the switchboard.

In a change from previous versions of the Northwind database, Microsoft has used event procedures, written in Visual Basic for Applications, to activate such actions as clicking a command button. Although the event procedures use Visual Basic statements instead of macros, for purposes of this textbook little is lost by using macros. Therefore we will use macros in nearly all situations for event processing.

NOTE One situation where Visual Basic is preferred occurs when you are distributing your application with the run-time version of Access. Visual Basic can be used to trap errors and handle them "gracefully"; when a macro encounters an error, it could terminate abruptly, displaying the Action Failed dialog box and stopping the entire application. For more information about Visual Basic, see Access online Help or refer to the Building Applications *manual available for Access 97.*

TIE MACROS TO SWITCHBOARD BUTTONS

After testing the macros and forms separately to be sure that they are correct, it is time to put them together with the switchboards. The Northwind Traders database (Northwind.mdb) packaged with Access provides a useful example of an Access application. We will use this application to demonstrate how to prepare a custom application in the next section.

The Northwind Traders Application

Northwind Traders is a small import/export business specializing in gourmet foods from around the world. The database is documented in the Microsoft Access *Getting Results* manual. The Tools | Relationships diagram is reproduced in Figure A12.1. This query shows the eight main tables in the Northwind database and the relational links between tables.

FIGURE A12.1
Northwind database design Relationships diagram

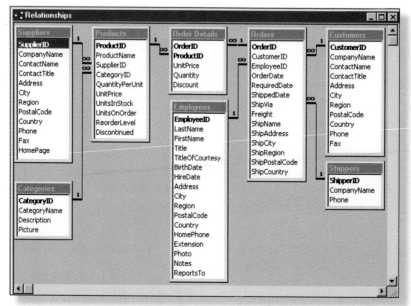

NOTE If your computer does not have the Northwind.mdb sample database available, check with your instructor or lab assistant.

You will note several similarities between the Hunter River database and the Northwind Traders database. Both databases have tables for customers, employees, products, suppliers, orders, and order details. Northwind adds tables for product categories and shippers. This database comes with a large number of orders (more than 800) and otherwise is about the same size as the Hunter River database.

When designing this application, Microsoft chose to subdivide larger forms with tab controls. Thus more space can be given to controls in each tab of the form. In previous versions, forms were larger or used smaller controls spaced more closely.

MAIN SWITCHBOARD

The Northwind main menu is a form called Main Switchboard, shown in Figure A12.2. It features several large command buttons that lead to other forms for viewing forms and printing reports. The lighthouse at the left is a bitmap picture; it reproduces better in color on the screen than in this textbook. The stylistic Northwind Traders logo at the bottom is part of the bitmap image.

Access 97 offers the Tools | Startup command that lets the developer specify an opening form and other options for the application. The Startup dialog box is shown in Figure A12.3. The opening Display Form for the Northwind application is the Startup form, which gives instructions for using the database to learn Access. In a normal application, you would use the name of the Main Switchboard form here. You can also restrict users from accessing the Database window, menus, and various toolbars. Use the Application Title box to give the title bar name for your application; the Application Icon box is used for the small icon that appears in the title bar. If these two boxes are left blank, the Microsoft Access icon and name appear in the title bar.

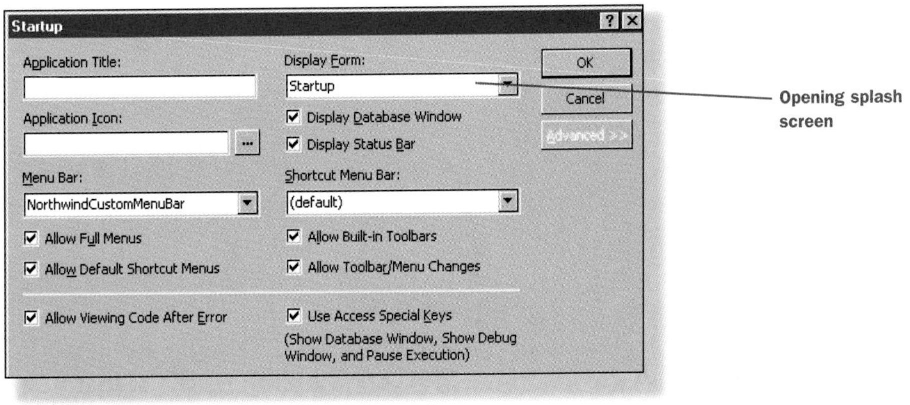

FIGURE A12.2
Main Switchboard form

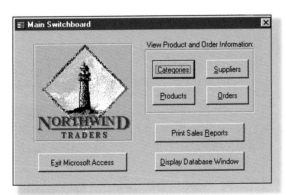

FIGURE A12.3
Startup dialog box including Advanced options

Opening splash screen

OTHER FORMS

The Categories form is shown in Figure A12.4. It displays information about product categories stored in the Northwind database. The database designer chose to leave you in this menu until you specifically choose to return to the Main Switchboard by clicking the close button. The Products and Suppliers forms are essentially similar to the Categories form.

FIGURE A12.4
Northwind Categories form with subform

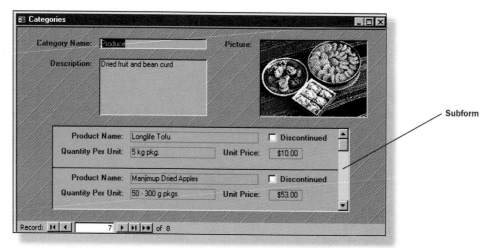

The Orders form is more comprehensive, combining elements of main and subform controls along with a command button to print the order. Figure A12.5 displays the Orders form. This form was also displayed in Unit 3 as an example form with many different types of controls.

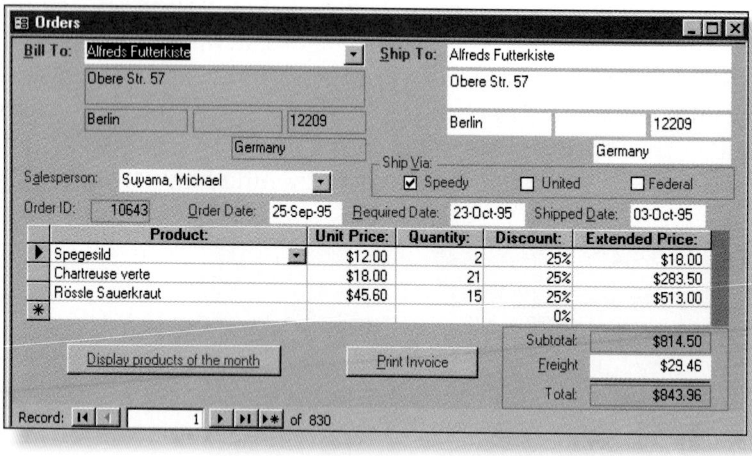

FIGURE A12.5
Northwind Orders form

The Sales Reports form is shown in Figure A12.6. It lists three types of reports with option buttons for each report type. The label control in the left center part of the form gives an explanation for the user. The Sales by Category report features a list box in the lower portion of the dialog box where the user can choose a particular category. After selecting the type of report, the user can click one of the two command buttons at the right to choose Print Preview or Print to the printer. Notice that this form has an option to return to the main menu; click Cancel and control automatically passes back to the Main Switchboard. You would have to

FIGURE A12.6
Northwind Sales Reports form

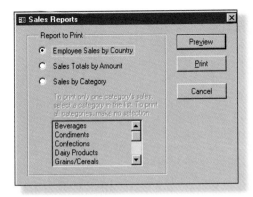

select Print Reports again from the Main Switchboard to return to this menu.

The last choice in the Main Switchboard form, Display Database Window, will close the Main Switchboard and display the Northwind Database window. To return to the Main Switchboard, switch to Form mode and open the Main Switchboard form.

Although the various switchboards, forms, and Print Preview window are depicted individually in the last four figures, the Northwind database designer chose to open the dialog boxes on top of the Main Switchboard window. Thus, you would see the other boxes and sense the hierarchy of menus as the application operates. From the macro discussion in Unit 11 you know that it is possible to hide a box, using the Window Mode argument of the OpenForm action.

TIP

We recommend that while developing an application you not actually exit from Access with this choice. Rather, have this choice close the Main Switchboard form and return to the Database window. Only when the application is fully tested should this choice actually close Access. That way you save time by not constantly restarting Access during the testing period.

OPERATING THE NORTHWIND TRADERS APPLICATION

There are three ways to start an application. As discussed in a previous unit, you can create a macro called AutoExec and save it in the database. When you open the database, that macro will run automatically unless you hold down **Shift** while opening it. The AutoExec macro would open the Main Switchboard form and allow the user to make further choices in that form.

As described earlier in this unit, you can use the Tools|Startup command to declare a form to automatically display when the application opens. Specify the Main Switchboard as the Display Form. You can bypass the startup form by holding down the **Shift** key when you open the database.

Because the Northwind database is used to demonstrate all facets of Microsoft Access, it is not set up to run automatically. To run the application the user must open the Northwind database, and then manually switch the Database window to Form mode. The user next locates the Main Switchboard form and clicks the Open button to open the form.

The user sees the main Northwind Traders menu shown in Figure A12.2. Selecting any of the six command buttons on the right side of the form will cause something to happen. The left button will close the database and exit from Access.

The following activity will let you try out the Northwind Traders application. In it we will also describe some of the underlying Access objects that make the application work.

12.1   Using the Northwind Traders Application

In this Guided Activity you will load the Northwind database and work through the menus and forms of the Northwind Traders application. See your instructor or lab assistant if the Northwind.mdb database is not available in your computer.

1. Start Windows 95 and load Access as usual.

2. Open the Northwind database. It is customarily installed in the Samples folder. If the opening startup screen appears, click OK.

3. Switch to Form mode. Select the Main Switchboard form and click Open. Access will display the main menu previously shown in Figure A12.2.

4. Click the Categories button in the Main Switchboard. Access will display the Products form shown in Figure A12.4. Click the Record navigation buttons at the bottom of the form to scroll through the eight product categories now in the database. When finished, click the close button in the Categories title bar.

5. Click the Orders command button in the Main Switchboard. Access will open the Orders form and display the first record as shown in Figure A12.5. You can use the Record navigation buttons in the lower portion of the form to scroll through the various orders booked by Northwind. The subform middle of the main form contains the products that belong to each order.

6. When finished with the Orders form, close its window by clicking the close button. You will return to the Forms Switchboard.

NOTE *Better form design might suggest that you have a larger command button to close this form and return to the Main Switchboard. We will create such a command button in the Hunter River application later in this unit.*

7. Now select the Print Sales Reports button in the Main Switchboard. You should see the Sales Reports form previously shown in Figure A12.6.

8. Let's take a look at the design of the Sales Reports form. Click the Design View button on the toolbar (or give the View | Form Design command from the menu bar). To enlarge the display, click the maximize button in the upper right corner of the Sales Reports Form window. Display the property sheet for the form. Your desktop should look like Figure A12.7. You may have to drag some of the boxes around to reveal parts of the design.

NOTE *Notice that the caption of the form in Figure A12.6 (based on the Caption property) is different than the actual name in the title bar in Figure A12.7.*

9. Click the Preview command button in the form. Scroll down in the property sheet to display the On Click property. Notice that [Event Procedure] appears on that line. This indicates that a Visual Basic program is used to control what happens when someone clicks this button.

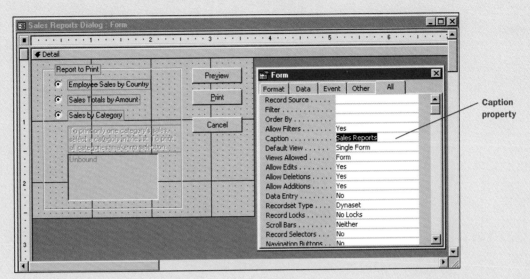

10. Click once on the On Click property line to select it. Click the ... button at the far right of the On Click property line to open the module window for this procedure, shown in Figure A12.8. The operational line is `PrintReports acPreview`. This Visual Basic statement instructs Access to use another user subroutine called PrintReports to do the actual printing. The acPreview term is used as an argument for that subroutine, indicating the Print Preview function is to be used instead of regular Print. Click the close button to close the module window.

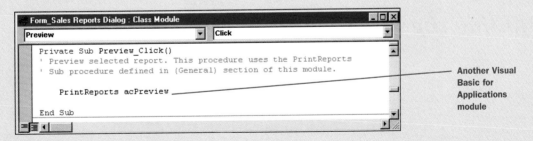

11. Now select Form view for this form. Click the Sales by Category option button, and then select Confections from the list box. When ready, click the Preview button. After a few moments to process the more than 800 order records, Access will display the Print Preview window shown in Figure A12.9. (Your window should not be maximized.) The window is shown maximized to display more of it. Not only does the report group data so that only the Confections are shown, but an Access graph is also prepared and displayed in the same window.

12. When you have finished viewing this preview, click the close button. Access will close the Preview window and return to the Main Switchboard form.

FIGURE A12.9
Northwind Sales by Category report for Confections

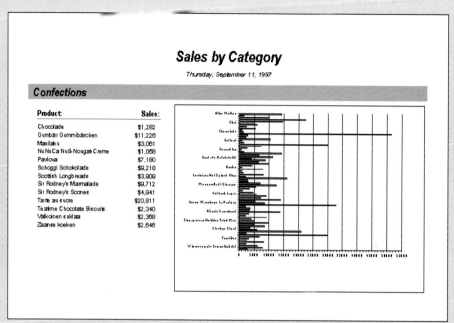

13. From this form click the Display Database Window button. The Main Switchboard form will close and you will effectively leave the application. If you had clicked the Exit Microsoft Access button, Access would have closed the Northwind database and terminated.

Building the Hunter River Application

The remainder of this unit will deal with creation of an application for the Hunter River Sporting Goods store. First we will deal with the systems analysis and design process, and then look at menus. Because we have dealt with this organization throughout the textbook, many parts of the application have already been created.

Analyzing the Hunter River System

Recall that Hunter River is a medium-sized retail sporting goods store selling a wide variety of products in several product categories. From the discussion of relational database concepts in Unit 6 we developed the database design shown in the Relationships window of Figure A12.10. The main tables are shown in this diagram, along with principal relational links between tables.

We have already developed forms and reports for most of the tables in this database. Now we need to provide forms for viewing customers, products, vendors, employees, and orders. We need reports for many of the same tables, plus a few other reports that deal with customers, employees, accounting data, and sales over time. Our application will parallel the Northwind Traders application in some respects.

FIGURE A12.10
*Relationships
window for
Hunter database*

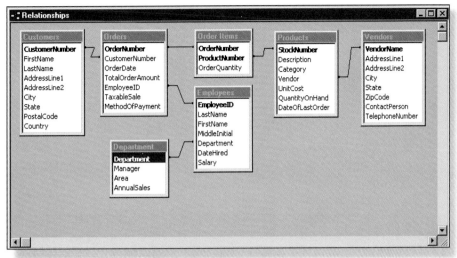

Developing Menus

We will have a Main Switchboard form to start the Hunter River application. It will have choices for:

- View Forms
- Print Reports
- Show Summary Sales
- Quit Application

These choices will be represented by a macro group with individual macros for each button.

VIEW FORMS MENU

The View Forms menu should present menu items for Customers, Employees, Products, Vendors, Department, and Orders. We also need a button to return to the Main Switchboard menu. The forms called by the command buttons should allow users to view and make changes to data as well as to add new data. All forms already exist within the Hunter97.mdb database.

PRINT REPORTS MENU

The Print Reports menu should have choices for Customer Labels, Salary, Inventory, and Product reports. All reports already exist within the Hunter97.mdb database.

The sequence of our development of the application is shown below. We will do the first four items in Guided Activities, with the last three items left as exercises at the end of the unit.

- Create the Main Switchboard form, including command buttons.
- Create the Main Switchboard Buttons macro group with individual macros for each command button. Attach these macros to the Main Switchboard buttons.

- Create the Forms Switchboard form, including its command buttons.

- Create the Forms Switchboard Buttons macro group with individual macros for each command button. Attach these macros to the Forms Switchboard buttons.

- Create the Reports Switchboard form, including its command buttons.

- Create the Reports Switchboard Buttons macro group with individual macros for each command button. Attach these macros to the Reports Switchboard buttons.

- Create the dialog box and form to show summary sales for a specified period of time.

GUIDED ACTIVITY

12.2 Building the Main Switchboard Form

In this Guided Activity you will create the Main Switchboard form with a textured background, the Hunter logo, and the four command buttons.

1. Close any open windows, and then close the Northwind Database window with the File | Close command, if it is not already closed.

2. Open the Hunter97.mdb database and click the Forms tab.

3. Click the New button to create a new form. In the New Form dialog box click Design View, then click the OK button.

4. Using the mouse, drag the form borders so that the form is approximately 4 inches wide and 2.75 inches tall. If necessary, move the Toolbox and property box to the side.

 5. Click the Unbound Object Frame tool in the Toolbox. Use the mouse to create an unbound object frame control that covers the entire surface of the form. If you need help with controls, refer to Units 7 and 8.

6. After you have created the unbound object frame control, Access will display the Insert Object dialog box and prompt you for a file. Select Paintbrush Picture and click the Create From File button. Use the file named Texture.bmp that is found on the Student Data Disk.

7. Access will place this background picture on the form. Adjust the size of the form to fit the picture.

 8. Click the Rectangle tool in the Toolbox, the tenth box down in the left column. Use the mouse to create a large rectangle control in the center of the form, leaving about one-half inch on each side and one-quarter inch on top and bottom.

9. With the rectangle control still selected, click the Special Effect drop-down arrow (last on the right) on the Formatting toolbar. From the drop-down menu, select the Sunken button for a 3-D effect.

 NOTE *Use the Access ToolTips to explore the purpose of each of the buttons in the Special Effect menu.*

10. Click the Fill/Back Color drop-down arrow on the Formatting toolbar. Click the medium green shade, fifth from the left in the second row. Your form should look like Figure A12.11.

FIGURE A12.11
Main Switchboard background controls

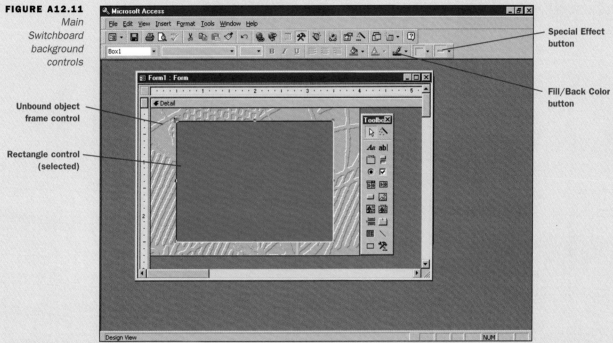

Unbound object frame control

Rectangle control (selected)

Special Effect button

Fill/Back Color button

 NOTE *Your computer's Windows color settings might not match those used in this textbook. In that case use your own discretion to select a pleasing color.*

11. Click the Image tool in the Toolbox, the sixth button in the right column. Use the mouse to create a control in the upper portion of the inset box in the form. This control should be nearly as wide as the box and about an inch tall. Refer to Figure A12.12 for precise placement. When prompted in the Insert Picture dialog box, select the file called Hunt2.bmp on the Student Data Disk. Access will place the Hunter River logo in the control. Adjust the size of the control to fit the logo.

12. Click the Command Button tool in the Toolbox, the sixth button in the left column. Make sure the Control Wizards button is not selected. Create a command button underneath the logo, nearly as wide. Remember to leave room to place four buttons in the space available.

13. Repeat step 12 with three more command buttons. Use the mouse to move and resize the controls in the form as necessary. It takes some practice to get the buttons to be the same size. See Figure A12.12 for placement and size of these controls.

 NOTE *To make four buttons exactly the same size, place one button in the form, then copy it to the Clipboard. Paste it three more times in the proper places for the other buttons.*

14. Now we need to place the labels in the command buttons. Click the first button to select it, and then use the mouse to highlight the Command3 text. In its

FIGURE A12.12
Main
Switchboard
form with
command button
controls

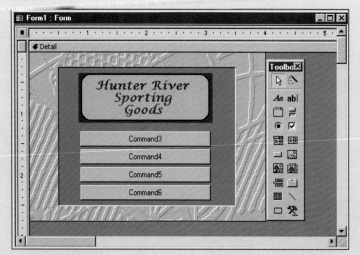

place, type View Forms and press **Enter**. With the control still selected, click the Bold button on the toolbar.

15. Repeat with the other three buttons. The labels are Print Reports, Show Summary Sales, Quit Application. Alternatively, you could fill the labels in the Caption property of each control. Turn on Bold for each label.

16. Click in the gray area outside the form to select the form. In the form's property sheet change the Navigation Buttons property to No. (Menus do not need navigation buttons.)

17. Use the File|Save As/Export command. The name should be Main Switchboard.

NOTE *If this object already exists in your database, you may replace it with the current copy.*

18. Click the Form button to change to Form view. Your Main Switchboard should look like Figure A12.13. We resized the Form window to enclose just the Main Switchboard form. Close the form. In the next activity we will build some of the macros in the Hunter River application.

FIGURE A12.13
Finished Main
Switchboard form

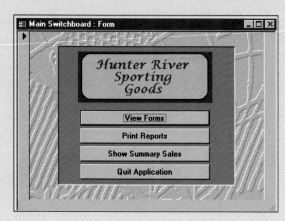

12.3 Creating the Main Switchboard Buttons Macro Group

In this Guided Activity you will create the macros that operate the menu buttons in the Main Switchboard form.

1. Close any open windows and return to the Hunter97.mdb Database window. In Macro mode click the New button to create a new macro.

2. With the Macro window open, click the Macro Names button on the toolbar to display the Macro Name column. You could also use View | Macro Names from the menu bar.

3. In the first line fill in this Comment: `Attached to the buttons on the Main Switchboard form.`

4. On the second line fill in the name `View Forms` in the first column. In the Action column select the OpenForm action. The Form Name argument is `Forms Switchboard`. The Comment is `Open the Forms switchboard form to open the forms in your application.`

5. Repeat the previous step for the second button. The Macro Name is `Print Reports`. The action is OpenForm, and the Form Name argument is `Reports Switchboard`. The Comment is `Open the Reports Switchboard to select and print a report.`

6. Repeat step 4 for the third button. The Macro Name is `Show Summary`. The action is OpenForm, and the Form Name argument is `Show Summary Sales`. The Comment is `Open the Show Summary Sales dialog box.`

7. For the fourth button use the Macro Name `Close Application`. The Action is Close. The Object Type argument is `Form` and the Object Name argument is `Main Switchboard`. The Comment is `Close the Main Switchboard form and return to the Database window.`

8. Save the macro under the name `Main Switchboard Buttons`. The macro is shown in Figure A12.14.

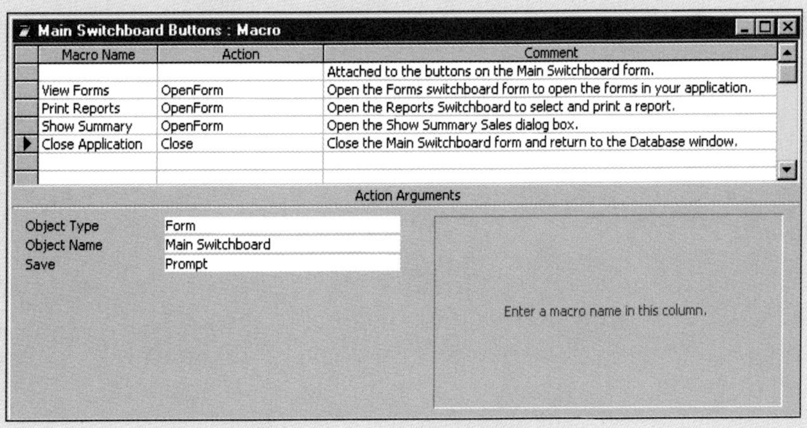

FIGURE A12.14
Main Switchboard Buttons macro group

9. Close the Macro window.

10. Finally, we need to attach these macros to the command buttons in the Main Switchboard form. In the Hunter97.mdb Database window, switch to Form mode. Select the Main Switchboard form and open the form in Design view.

11. Double-click the View Forms command button to display its property sheet. In the On Click property, enter `Main Switchboard Buttons.View Forms` and press **Enter**. This notation means to run the View Forms macro within the Main Switchboard Buttons macro group.

 NOTE *Click the down arrow at the end of the On Click property line to display a list of all the macros currently residing in the database. Scroll down to the desired one, making it easier to enter the name of the macro.*

12. Repeat the previous step with the other buttons, as shown below:

Button	On Click Property
Print Reports	Main Switchboard Buttons.Print Reports
Show Summary Sales	Main Switchboard Buttons.Show Summary
Quit Application	Main Switchboard Buttons.Close Application

13. Use the File | Save command to save the modified form. Close the Form window.

In the next activity we show how to create the Forms Switchboard form.

GUIDED ACTIVITY

12.4 Creating the Forms Switchboard Form

In this Guided Activity you will create the Forms Switchboard menu. If you need help with the details of this form, refer to Guided Activity 12.2 where similar procedures were done.

1. Close any open windows and return to the Hunter97.mdb Database window.

2. Switch to Form mode and click the New button.

3. In the New Form dialog box select Design View and click the OK button.

4. Adjust the size of the form by dragging the borders so that it is 2 inches tall by 4 inches wide.

5. Place an unbound object frame control inside the form that occupies that entire form. Click the Create From File button. Specify the Texture.bmp bitmap image for the background, just as we did in the Main Switchboard, and click OK.

6. Place a large rectangle control in the left portion of the form, starting at the 0.25,0.25-inch coordinates and stretching to the 2.5,1.7-inch coordinates. Click the Back Color Transparent and Sunken special effect buttons on the

Formatting toolbar for this control. You will see the texture pattern shown through this control.

NOTE *If you have trouble selecting the proper control, select the texture object, and then press the* **Tab** *key to cycle through all of the controls in the form.*

7. Place another rectangle control to the right of the first, centered in the remaining space within the form. This rectangle should also be transparent and sunken, both set on the Formatting toolbar. Figure A12.15 shows the form so far.

FIGURE A12.15
Preliminary design of Forms Switchboard

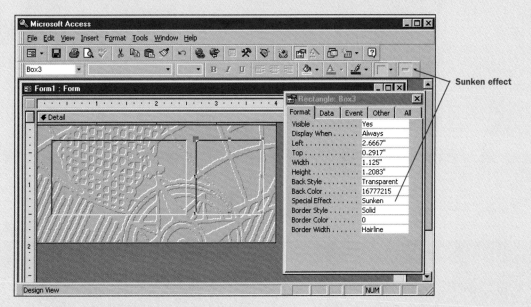

8. Place six 1-inch wide command buttons in the left rectangle and one larger button in the right rectangle. You may need to resize the buttons slightly to hold the caption. It is also possible to reduce the font size slightly to make the caption fit. The command buttons in this activity use the 10-point font size and are bold.

9. Click outside the form in the gray area to select the form property sheet. Set the Scroll Bars property to Neither. Set the Navigation Buttons property to No. Figure A12.16 shows the way this form should appear after the command buttons and labels are added.

10. Save the form as Forms Switchboard and close the Form window.

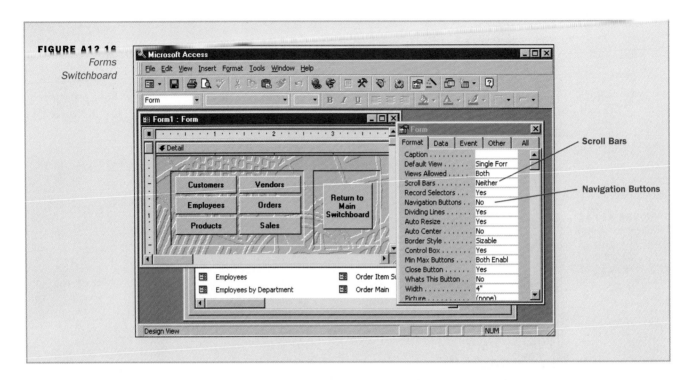

FIGURE A12.16
Forms Switchboard

Scroll Bars

Navigation Buttons

In the next activity we will create the macro group that will be attached to command buttons in the Forms Switchboard form.

GUIDED ACTIVITY

12.5 Creating the Forms Switchboard Buttons Macro Group

In this Guided Activity you will create the macros that operate the menu buttons in the Forms Switchboard form. If you need help with details, refer to Guided Activity 12.3 where similar procedures were done.

1. Close any open windows and return to the Hunter97.mdb Database window. Switch to Macro mode and click the New button.

2. When the Macro window opens, click the Macro Names button on the toolbar.

3. In the Comment cell of the first line enter `Attached to buttons on the Forms Switchboard form`.

4. In the Macro Name cell of the second line enter `Customers`. The Action is OpenForm. Press **F6** to move to the lower pane. The Form Name argument is `Customers`. Press **F6** to move to the upper pane. The Comment is `Open the Customers form`.

5. Repeat step 4 with the following information for the remaining five command buttons. (*Hint:* Copy the first macro and make changes.)

Button	Action	Form Name	Comment
Employees	OpenForm	Employees	Open the Employees form.
Products	OpenForm	Products	Open the Products form.
Vendors	OpenForm	Vendors	Open the Vendors form.
Orders	OpenForm	Orders	Open the Orders form.
Sales	OpenForm	Sales	Open the Sales form.

6. The last macro in this group is named Exit. Its Action is OpenForm, and the Form Name argument is Main Switchboard. If the Main Switchboard is already open, Access will switch to that window without closing the Forms Switchboard window. The comment for this action is Return to the Main Switchboard form. The final macro group is shown in Figure A12.17.

FIGURE A12.17
Forms Switchboard Buttons macro group

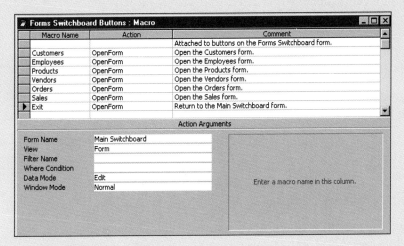

7. Save this macro as Forms Switchboard Buttons and close the Macro window.

8. Switch to Form mode in the Hunter97.mdb Database window. Locate the Forms Switchboard form and click the Design button.

9. Double-click the Customers command button to display its property sheet. In the On Click property enter Forms Switchboard Buttons.Customers and press **Enter**. To save time, you can click the down arrow on that property line and select the macro name from the list box.

10. Repeat the procedure from step 9 for the remaining six command buttons:

Button	On Click Property
Employees	Forms Switchboard Buttons.Employees
Products	Forms Switchboard Buttons.Products
Vendors	Forms Switchboard Buttons.Vendors
Orders	Forms Switchboard Buttons.Orders
Sales	Forms Switchboard Buttons.Sales
Return to	Forms Switchboard Buttons.Exit

11. Save the form and close the Form window.

In the next activity we show how the Hunter River application works.

GUIDED ACTIVITY

12.6 Running the Hunter River Application

In this Guided Activity you will work with the partially complete Hunter River application.

1. Close any open windows and return to the Hunter97.mdb Database window. Switch to Form mode.

2. Select the Main Switchboard form and click Open. Access will open the Main Switchboard menu we created in a previous activity.

3. Click the View Forms button to open the Forms Switchboard.

4. At the Forms Switchboard click the Customers button. Access will display the first record of the Customers form.

5. Close the Customers form by clicking the close button. You should return to the Forms Switchboard menu, which is still open on the desktop.

6. Try out the other menu choices in the Forms Switchboard. When you are satis-fied that all are working, click the Return to Main Switchboard button in the Forms Switchboard.

 NOTE *You will create a Sales Summary form as an exercise.*

7. Click the Print Reports button in the Main Switchboard. What does Access do in this case? You will complete the application as an exercise.

8. Quit the application by clicking the Quit Application button in the Main Switchboard. Close the Forms Switchboard.

Other Application Techniques

This section will discuss some techniques that make your applications easier to use. It also presents the two sample teaching applications that come with Access.

Placing a Picture on a Command Button

Access can display words or a picture on a command button. The Caption property is used for a label, and the Picture property is used for the bitmap image. We rec-ommend that a label be added to the form itself, near the button, to define the pur-pose of the button. You can also use the ToolTips property of the command button control to define its purpose. The following activity demonstrates how to place a picture in a command button.

GUIDED ACTIVITY

12.7   Creating a Command Button with a Picture

In this Guided Activity you will create a form with a command button that contains a bitmap image instead of words. You could use this technique in any switchboard form.

1. Switch to Form mode and open a new form in Design view.

2. Add a command button in the upper left corner of the form. It should be about one-half inch square, but the size is not critical. You will resize the button to fit its picture.

3. Double-click the command button to display the property sheet if it is not already visible.

4. Click the Picture property once to select it, and then click the Builder button (...) at the right end of that line. You'll see the Picture Builder dialog box.

5. Scroll down until you reach the Exit line and click once to select it. You will see the sample command button with that picture in Figure A12.18. Click OK to add this picture to the command button.

FIGURE A12.18
*Picture Builder
dialog box for
command button*

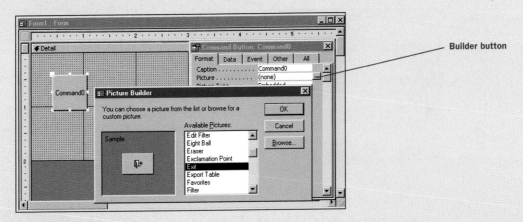

6. Finally, add a label control just beneath the command button with the following text: Close Window. Access will *not* let you have both a caption and a picture for a command button, but you can add a descriptive label adjacent to the button.

FIGURE A12.19
*Command
button with
bitmap picture*

7. Figure A12.19 shows the finished form with this command button. It would look better if you turned off the scroll bars and navigation area. Of course, to make it work you would have to create a macro with the Close action and then insert its name in the On Click property of the command button on the form. Close the form without saving it.

Creating an Opening Splash Screen

If you would like to display a bitmap image before your Main Switchboard menu appears, create and save a bitmap image with the same name as the database in the same folder. The bitmap file must have the .bmp extension. Next create a shortcut for your application's .mdb file. Double-click the shortcut to start the application. Access will display the bitmap splash screen for a few seconds and then load your database and execute any startup procedures or AutoExec macros in your database.

Creating Custom Menus

Access has a Menu Builder available though the Menu Bar property of a form. Click the Builder button (...) at the end of the Menu Bar property line and the Menu Builder dialog box will appear. You can start with the existing Access menus and make changes or begin with the Empty Menu Bar selection and build up a custom menu. Select a template, and then follow the instructions to create the menu choices.

Shortcuts to Command Buttons

Access lets you use a single letter to activate a command button. In the Caption property of the command button control, simply place an ampersand (&) before the

FIGURE A12.20
Command button captions with shortcut letters

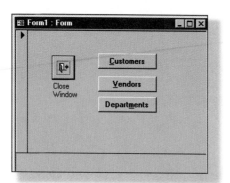

letter you want to act as a shortcut to that command button. For example, if you used the caption &Customers, Access will display the caption on the button as <u>C</u>ustomers. Likewise, &Vendors would display as <u>V</u>endors and Depart&ments would display as Depart<u>m</u>ents. To select one of these command buttons, either click the button with the mouse or press the underlined letter. As with Windows menus, make sure you do not have duplicate shortcut letters in the same form. See Figure A12.20.

Sample Teaching Applications Packaged with Microsoft Access

Although we will not illustrate these techniques in this textbook, along with Northwind two other sample applications packaged with Access provide innovative ideas for applications. The Orders application is a sophisticated order entry and invoice printing system for the Northwind Traders company. The Solution application offers structured assistance to those who want to build their own applications; highlight a component in this Access application and a special help system will show how to create that component. Contact your instructor or lab monitor if these databases are not installed on your computer.

THE ORDERS APPLICATION

When you open the Orders.mdb database, an AutoExec macro automatically opens the Orders form and hides the Database window. This application displays a custom user interface in the main menu, shown in Figure A12.21. Access also displays a custom help system called Show Me that contains references to various parts of the Orders application. You can select an item and learn how that portion of the application was built. Microsoft invites you to copy any part of this application into your own database.

FIGURE A12.21

Orders application showing custom menu bar and toolbar

Product details

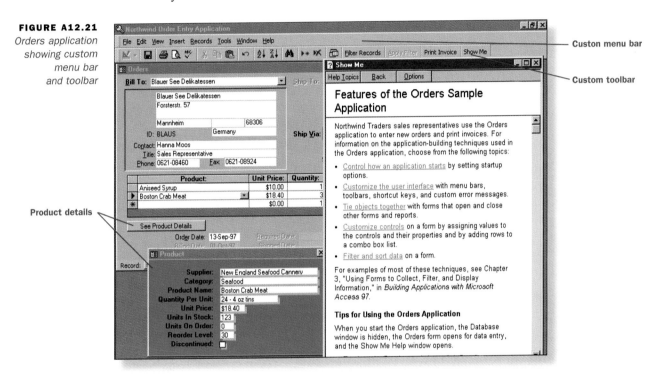

THE SOLUTIONS APPLICATION

The Solutions.mdb database was designed to teach you how to create very sophisticated applications. It organizes the help tips by categories in a form called Solutions. Figure A12.22 shows the Solutions form, which contains examples for the "Create advanced reports" category. The Solutions database's Show Me help system gives step-by-step instructions for reproducing the example forms, reports, and interface elements commonly found in Access applications. Figure A12.23 shows a portion of the Show Me help for the first report example from the previous figure.

This database makes extensive use of Visual Basic for Applications modules; those techniques are beyond the scope of this textbook. You can learn more about modules by reading the *Building Applications with Access 97* manual and by studying the Show Me help screens.

FIGURE A12.22
Solutions database
with Show Me
examples of
application
components

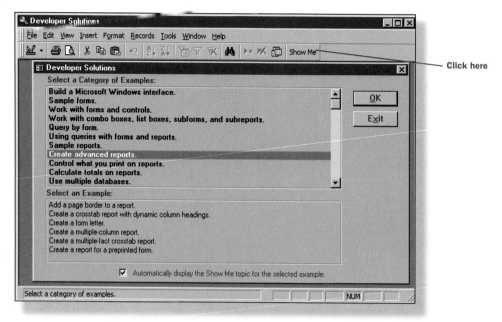

Click here

FIGURE A12.23
Show Me help
for creating a
form letter with a
page border

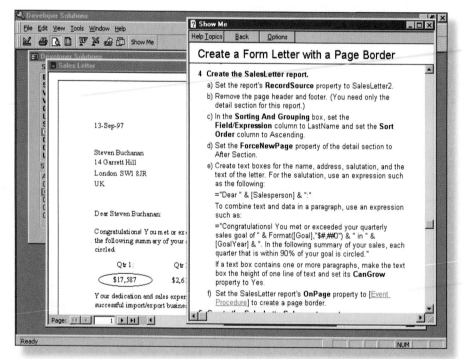

The Microsoft Access Developer's Toolkit

The Microsoft Access Developer's Toolkit enables the professional developer to create and distribute custom applications for clients. The Developer's Toolkit contains a run-time version of Access that enables the client to run the Access application without having to purchase a separate copy of Access. The Developer's Toolkit comes with a Windows 95 Help compiler that enables the developer to create a custom help system for your application. Additional custom controls are packaged with the Developer's Toolkit to augment your application. The Developer's Toolkit also contains the *Microsoft Access 97 Language Reference* manual, a printed version of the online language reference help.

To use the Developer's Toolkit to create an application for distribution, you must have a full version of Access. First create the application under Access as usual, testing it fully. When ready to create the portable version of your application, install and start the Developer's Toolkit. It will load and then ask a series of questions about your application. The Setup Wizard will create a set of disk images on your hard drive that can be copied onto floppy disks, complete with an installation program on disk 1. When the end user runs the installation program, it will create the application on the user's hard drive and install the run-time version of Access. The custom application will appear with its own icon on the Windows 95 Start menu.

Applications running in the run-time mode do not offer all Access features. For instance, you cannot view objects in Design view nor make changes to the design of database objects. The user will not see the Database, Macro, or Module windows for your application. Some menu options are unavailable. That means that your application's switchboards and other objects must offer *all* the functionality required to complete its tasks.

 NOTE *You can also start the regular Access program in run-time mode by using the /runtime command-line option.*

SUMMARY

It is relatively simple to create custom applications in Access. Switchboard forms contain command buttons with menu choices. Attach a macro to the On Click property of the command button to cause some action when the user clicks the button. Microsoft packaged three applications with Access 97 to give you ideas about custom applications. If you name a macro AutoExec, it will execute automatically when you open the database unless you hold down the **Shift** key while you do so. The Tools | Startup menu gives several other startup choices. Access also supports command-line startup options.

Exercises

Use the Hunter River database contained within the Hunter97.mdb database file on the Student Data Disk for these exercises.

EXERCISE

12.1

Reports Switchboard Form

1. Create the Reports Switchboard form for the Hunter River application.

2. The switchboard should allow for five reports (Customer Labels, Customers, Employee Salary, Inventory, and Product Report By Vendor) and have a Return to Main Switchboard button.

3. You should add other features such as texture and background rectangles, similar to the Forms Switchboard developed in this unit.

4. Print a copy of the Reports Switchboard form in Form view.

EXERCISE

12.2

Reports Switchboard Buttons Macro Group

1. Create the Reports Switchboard Buttons macro group, with individual macros for the buttons in the Reports Switchboard form.

2. Attach these macros to the buttons in the Reports Switchboard form.

3. Print a copy of the design of your macro group.

4. Print a copy of the finished Reports Switchboard form in Design view.

EXERCISE

12.3

AutoExec Macro

1. Create an AutoExec macro that opens the initial Main Switchboard form.

2. Remember that you can defeat an AutoExec macro by holding down the **Shift** key when you open the database containing that macro.

3. Print a copy of the design of your AutoExec macro.

EXERCISE

12.4

Show Summary Sales Dialog Box

1. Create a Show Summary Sales dialog box that can be used to show total sales for a particular period of time. Refer to the Northwind Traders database for an example of this form.

2. Remember that the user must input data for a period that contains some orders, based upon the Orders table in the Hunter97.mdb database.

3. Print a copy of the dialog box's design.

EXERCISE

12.5 Command Button Pictures

1. Create a form with three command buttons: Open, Save, and Exit.

2. Place a picture on each button. Use appropriate pictures from the Builder.

3. Print a copy of the form, and save it as Exercise 12-5.

EXERCISE

12.6 Custom Command Buttons

1. Create a form with three command buttons: Open, Save, and Exit.

2. Create captions for the buttons as follows: <u>O</u>pen, <u>S</u>ave, E<u>x</u>it. Make sure that you provide for the underlined letters.

3. Print a copy of the form, and save it as Exercise 12-6.

Physicians' Medical Clinic: Building an Application with Access

At this time the clinic is primarily concerned with handling patient records and billing, so you have been asked by Dr. Greenway to focus on developing a design for this portion of the system. Your assignment has been structured in the parts below.

1. Design the menus that PMC could use for this patient records system. Consider the forms and reports that would be appropriate for this system.

2. Create Access switchboard forms for the main menu, Forms menu, and Print menu. Build macros that will handle moving between the switchboards and the appropriate forms and reports.

3. Create simple forms and reports that reflect the information displayed in the forms and reports switchboards. Make sure that your system actually produces the desired output.

UNIT 13

Connecting Access and Other Data Files

In this unit you will learn how Access can exchange data with other compatible applications such as other Access databases, text files, popular spreadsheet programs, other databases, and network SQL server software. The Link Tables command lets you open data table files from other applications without first translating them to the Access file format. You will learn how to use the Import and Export commands to read and write files from other applications. The unit concludes with a macro that can be used to transfer data automatically.

Learning Objectives

At the completion of this unit you should be able to

1. list data types that are compatible with Microsoft Access,

2. describe the differences between linking, importing, and exporting data files,

3. use the Windows Clipboard to copy objects between databases,

4. link an external data file to Access,

5. import a data file into Access,

6. export an Access table to another data file,

7. copy files between different Access databases,

8. use a macro to transfer data between Access and other packages.

Case Study

Occasionally Hunter River needs to exchange data with other organizations that do not use Microsoft Access. You have been retained to show management how to import and link data from other databases, and to export data.

Compatible Data Types

Access provides data translators for many popular data types. The data translators are able to convert the data from one format to another without much intervention on the part of the user. Each new version of Access has new or improved data translators. Microsoft has promised to make more translators available in the future, particularly for use with mainframe or minicomputer databases. Table A13.1 shows the compatible data types.

 NOTE *Not all the data translators are installed automatically with Access 97. Use the Setup program to install missing translators, or see the Office 97 ValuPack on the CD-ROM.*

TABLE A13.1
Compatible data types

TYPE	PROGRAMS
Database	Microsoft Access 1.x, 2, 7/95, 97 (MDB)
	dBASE III, IV, IV+, 5 (DBF)
	Microsoft FoxPro 2.x, 3.x (DBF, DBC)
	Paradox 3.x, 4.x, 5.x (DB)*
	ODBC (SQL Server, Oracle)
Spreadsheet	Microsoft Excel 3, 4, 5, 7/95, 97 (XLS)
	Lotus 1-2-3 (WK1, WK3)*
Text Files	Fixed-Width, Delimited (TXT)
	Rich Text Format (RTF)
Internet	Hypertext Markup Language (HTM, HTML)
	Microsoft Internet Information Server (IDC, HTX)
	Microsoft Active Server Pages (ASP)

*Available only in Office 97 ValuPack on the CD-ROM.

Linking External Files

Access is able to read and write certain external data files directly. The File | Get External Data | Link Tables command lets you open a table file in its native format from another database application (or Excel spreadsheet or text file) and treat it as if it were an Access object. You can open a datasheet containing the data file and then use it in a query, form, or report. Any changes you make to field values in the file are automatically made in the file itself, unlike the File | Get External Data | Import procedure, in which changes are made only to the internal Access table, not the external file.

Although you cannot change a linked file's structure, you can assign values to its properties after it is linked. You can add descriptions to the fields, particularly if the field names were not very descriptive. You can change the Format, Decimal

Places, Default Value, Validation Rule, and Validation Text properties for each field in the linked file.

Linking the File

To link a table stored as an external file on your PC or a network, switch to Table mode in the Database window. Issue the File | Get External Data | Link Tables command and select the type of file you wish to link from the Link dialog box. There are eight external file types available in Access 97, and more will probably be available in the future. After you specify the type of file to link, Access will display in the Link dialog box a list of files including the designated file name extension in the default drive and folder. Then select the desired file and click Link.

Access will create a link to the external data file and then allow you to specify any index files that are to be loaded. Specify the index files by name, and then click the Close button. Index files allow much faster access to the table's contents. Although Access is able to build its own indexes to database files, any changes made to the linked table while in Access would not be updated in the index files unless they are also linked at this time. Access cannot build indexes for linked tables. Finally, if you do not wish to link any additional files at this time, close the Link dialog box.

Using a Linked File

Access lists linked tables on the Tables tab of the Database window with a special symbol, an arrow pointing to an abbreviation of the file type. The arrow signifies that this is a linked table, available to but not a part of the current database. You can use the table as long as the file remains linked. Access will automatically create the link whenever the database containing the linked table is opened. In fact, the link remains active until you highlight the linked table and press **Del**. If you delete the linked table, only the link is erased. The data in the table remain unaffected. You can later establish a link again if one is desired.

If another user makes a change to the linked file, that change is automatically made available to Access. Of course, if you opened the external file in exclusive mode, nobody else will be able to view the file as long as you have open the database that contains the link.

GUIDED ACTIVITY

13.1   Linking an External Data File to Access

In this Guided Activity you will link to an external data file found on the Student Data Disk and use it in Access.

1. Start Windows 95 and load Access. Open the Hunter97.mdb database.

2. Choose the Get External Data command from the File menu, and then select Link Tables.

3. In the Link dialog box select dBASE IV (*.dbf) in the Files Of Type box. Access will display all files in the current folder with the .dbf file name extension.

4. Highlight the Prospect.dbf file and click Link. When Access displays a list of index files, click the Cancel button.

5. Access will create the link to the external database file and display a message for you if the Link is successful. Click OK, and then click Close to close the Link dialog box.

6. You should see the Prospect table listed among those in the Hunter Database window. Access uses a special table symbol (with an arrow) in front of the linked file to signify that it is a linked table rather than an internal table.

NOTE *If there were another table called Prospect already in this database, Access would have named the linked table as Prospect1.*

7. Double-click the Prospect table in the Database window and Access will open that table in Datasheet view, shown in Figure A13.1. Then close the open window.

FIGURE A13.1
Datasheet view of linked Prospect table

Linked table

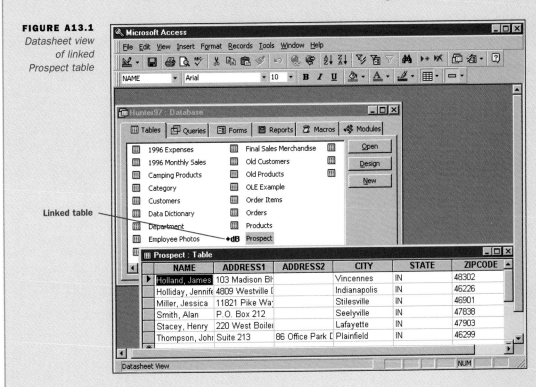

Importing Other Files into Access

As mentioned earlier, you can import data from an external file directly into a table in an Access database. The process begins by opening the Access database into which you want to import the data. Choose the Get External Data | Import command from the File menu. Access will display the Import dialog box, asking you to select the type of data file to import. You can also enter the drive, folder, and file name of the external data file directly.

After you specify the data source, Access will show all files that match your specification. After selecting the file, click the Import button. Next you may see an

TIP

If the spreadsheet import operation takes an unusually long time, it may be because many errors are occurring. To cancel the import operation, issue the Ctrl+Break command.

Import Options dialog box that is specific to the kind of file import being done. The following sections describe the import options when importing spreadsheet, database, and text files.

Importing a Lotus or Excel Spreadsheet

For spreadsheets, you will see the Import Spreadsheet Wizard dialog box shown in Figure A13.2. You can select a range of cells to import or bring in the entire spreadsheet. If the first row of the worksheet's data range contains the field names, click the option button to indicate that the field names are available. Otherwise, when you create a new table Access will number the fields and you should give proper names to the fields after the import is complete.

GUIDED ACTIVITY

13.2   Importing a Spreadsheet File

In this Guided Activity you will import an Excel spreadsheet file into Access, creating a new table. The file is found on the Student Data Disk.

1. Close any open windows and return to the Hunter97.mdb Database window. Click the Tables tab.

2. Choose the Get External Data | Import command from the File menu. Access will display the Import dialog box with the various data source types. Select the Microsoft Excel (*.xls) file type.

3. Select the drive and folder that contains the Excel XLS file, and then select the proper file, in this case Stocks.xls. When you are finished, click the Import button to translate the Excel file into the Access data format.

4. Access will display the Import Spreadsheet Wizard dialog box, along with the first sheet in your spreadsheet, shown in Figure A13.2. Click Next to go on.

FIGURE A13.2
Import Spreadsheet Wizard dialog box

Field names

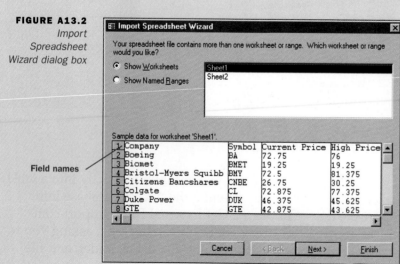

5. In the next Wizard window, click the option button next to First Row Contains Column Headings. Access will reconfigure the datasheet shown in the window so that the data begins on row 1, with field names as column headings. Click Next to go on.

6. Click Next in the next dialog box to signify that you want to store the data in a new table in the Hunter97.mdb database.

7. The next wizard dialog box lets you specify field options for each column in the spreadsheet. You can choose to not import a column, select the field type, and build an index for each field. We'll accept the default here, so click Next to go on.

8. The next wizard dialog box allows you to create a primary key for your table. You can have Access add a primary key (AutoNumber field), select one field from the table itself, or have no primary key. Click Next to have Access create a primary key field.

9. In the last wizard dialog box, enter the name of the table that Access will use. In this case, enter `Stock Portfolio` and click Finish.

 NOTE *If your copy of Hunter97.mdb already contains this name, go ahead and replace it with this copy.*

10. Access should display an information box stating that it has successfully imported the Stocks.xls file. Access will automatically open a new table to hold the data. If another table of the same name already exists within the current database, Access will ask if you want to replace the existing table with the newer one. To see what Access brought into the Hunter database, click OK to close the message box.

11. Return to the Database window. Scroll down until you see a table named Stock Portfolio in the list. Click the Open button to see the contents of this table.

12. Adjust the column widths of the datasheet by dragging the border between the columns so that you can see the entire contents of each field. Figure A13.3 shows the Datasheet view for this table.

13. Close the open Datasheet window. Click OK to accept changes in the table layout.

FIGURE A13.3
Datasheet view for imported spreadsheet table

Stock Portfolio : Table

ID	Company	Symbol	Current Price	High Price	Low Price	Number Shares
1	Boeing	BA	72.75	76	44.375	100
2	Biomet	BMET	19.25	19.25	11.5	100
3	Bristol-Myers S	BMY	72.5	81.375	57.125	100
4	Citizens Bancsh	CNBE	26.75	30.25	26	380
5	Colgate	CL	72.875	77.375	58	100
6	Duke Power	DUK	46.375	45.625	37.375	100
7	GTE	GTE	42.875	43.625	30	200
8	Hewlett-Packard	HWP	82.75	96.625	45.875	200
9	Eli Lilly	LLY	99.75	102.875	60.875	66
10	Southwest Airlin	LUV	25	29.875	15.5	100
11	Novell	NOVL	16.75	23.25	13.75	100
12	Telecommunica	TCOMA	18.1875	20	12.5	100
13	Wal-Mart	WMT	24.125	27.625	20.5	100
(umber)						

Record: 1 of 13

Importing a dBASE or Paradox Database Table

The database program data sources will usually translate completely without displaying any further dialog boxes. Access is able to read the table definition information and create a new table automatically. You are not given the option of appending the external data to an existing Access table. To do this, first import the file into a new table, and then copy records from the new Access table into the Windows Clipboard. Copy those records from the Clipboard into the existing Access table.

Importing Data from Another Access Database

The first choice for the file type data source in the Import dialog box is Microsoft Access. You will be asked to specify the name of the other Access database. Then you will see the Import Objects dialog box, in which you can specify what type of database object you want to import. You can select from Tables, Queries, Forms, Reports, Macros, and Modules by clicking the appropriate tab. Access will display all objects of the selected type, similar to the Database window. You have the option of importing the definition alone or the definition and the data. Importing the definition alone means that you bring in the design of a table but none of the data in that table. The definition-and-data option appears only for tables. For other types, only the structure is imported. Other options are shown in the lower part of the dialog box. Importing from another Access database is left as an exercise.

Importing Text Files

Data in text files can appear in fixed-width columns or as delimited data. Access will import data from either kind of text file. Fixed-width text files allocate the same number of positions for a particular field in each record; you could draw a vertical line between fields. Delimited files separate fields with a punctuation character, usually a comma, and surround text fields with a delimiter, usually the quote character. The next two sections will describe importing from text files.

FIXED-WIDTH TEXT FILES

A fixed-width text file uses specific starting and ending points for each field; the same field in different records uses the same number of characters. Two fixed-width records from the stock table might look like:

```
5 BOISE CASCAD NYSE    37.375   47.5    23         2000
6 BOEING       NYSE    72.75    76      54.625      500
```

Notice that there are no delimiters or separators with this data format. You must provide the starting position and width for each field in the file for importing and exporting. We will illustrate this dialog box in a later Guided Activity where we export fixed-width text records.

When importing a text file, you will see the opening Import Text Wizard screen. In the lower portion is sample data from the text file, similar to what appeared with the Import Spreadsheet Wizard. The wizard will examine the data and determine whether it is in delimited format or fixed-width column format. Other choices in later Import Text Wizard screens include:

- Set the location of field breaks by clicking between fields

- Store data in an existing table, or place it in a new table

- Provide information about each field, including name and data type; create an index on that field; or skip that field in the import operation

- Define the primary key (let Access add the field, or use an existing field, or have no primary key)

- Assign the Access table name for the imported text file

DELIMITED TEXT FILES

In the default specification for delimited files, text is delimited with the double quote character (") and fields are separated with the comma. That means that the text field values are enclosed in double quotes, with a comma between each two fields. The following line shows what a delimited record from a stock price table would look like:

```
6,"BOEING","NYSE",72.75,44.375,76.625,500
```

The two text fields are enclosed (delimited) with quotes, and all fields are separated by commas. The number fields at the end represent high price per share, low price per share, purchase price per share, and number of shares. With delimited text files, fields take only as many characters as needed; long fields use more space while short fields take less space.

The following activity shows how to use the Import Text Wizard to import a delimited text file and append it to the end of an existing table. The Import Text Wizard choices for delimited text files are slightly different than for fixed-width text files.

GUIDED ACTIVITY

13.3 Importing a Delimited Text File

In this Guided Activity you will import into Access a delimited text file and append it to an existing Access table.

1. Close any open windows and return to the Hunter97.mdb Database window.

2. Select the Get External Data | Import command from the File menu.

3. In the Import dialog box choose Text Files (*.txt, *.csv, *.tab, *.asc).

4. In the Select File dialog box highlight the file called Camp29.txt. This file contains new camping products to be added to the database. Click the Import button to start the Import Text Wizard.

5. Access will display the opening Import Text Wizard box, shown in Figure A13.4. Notice that all the text fields (including field names in the first row) are

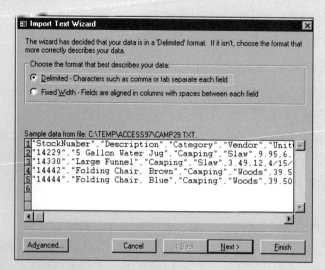

enclosed in quotes and fields are separated with commas. Click the Delimited option button in this dialog box, and then click Next to go on.

6. In the next wizard dialog box, click the First Row Contains Field Names option button. Access has already recognized that the comma is the delimiter that separates fields and the text qualifier is the double quote character. Click Next to go on.

7. In the next wizard dialog box, click the option button in front of In An Existing Table, instructing Access to add the data to the end of the table. Select the Camping Products table, and then click Finish.

 To save time when importing records from the same text file, you can save the import specifications. See the section following this Guided Activity.

8. Access will perform the import, adding the new camping products to the end of the Camping Products table. Click OK in the import results box, and then open the Camping Products table.

9. The Camping Products table is shown in Figure A13.5. The last four records with stock numbers beginning with 14 are the new ones brought in from the delimited text file. Close the active Table window to return to the Database window.

FIGURE A13.5
*Camping Products
table with four
imported records*

	StockNumber	Description	Category	Vendor	UnitCost	QuantityOnHar	DateOfLastOrder
▶	13021	Cold 30 Cooler	Camping	Icicle	$59.95	12	5/4/97
	13034	Cold 36 Cooler	Camping	Icicle	$129.95	7	5/4/97
	13037	Ice Cold Lunch	Camping	Icicle	$14.95	3	5/4/97
	13066	40-Qt. Cooler K	Camping	Slaw	$29.95	0	4/15/97
	14229	5 Gallon Water	Camping	Slaw	$9.95	6	6/29/95
	14330	Large Funnel	Camping	Slaw	$3.49	12	4/15/95
	14442	Folding Chair, E	Camping	Woods	$39.50	8	4/3/95
	14444	Folding Chair, E	Camping	Woods	$39.50	0	12/20/94
*							

Camping Products : Table

Record: 14 ◀ 1 ▶ ▶I ▶* of 8

SAVING TEXT IMPORT SPECIFICATIONS

If you frequently import data from the same text file, you can save time by saving the import specifications in the database. Create the specifications as usual, through step 7 of the previous Guided Activity. At the last step in the Import Text Wizard, click the Advanced button. Access will display your settings in the Import Specification dialog box shown in Figure A13.6. Make any changes, and then save the specifications.

FIGURE A13.6
*Import
Specification
dialog box*

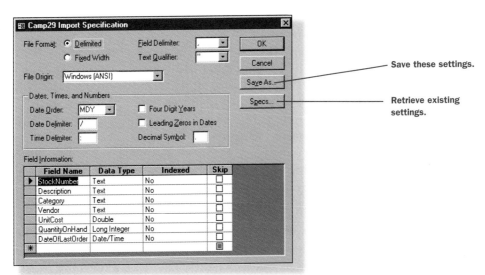

Camp29 Import Specification

File Format: ⊙ Delimited   Field Delimiter: ,   OK
           ○ Fixed Width   Text Qualifier: "   Cancel

File Origin: Windows (ANSI)   Save As... — Save these settings.
                               Specs...   — Retrieve existing settings.

Dates, Times, and Numbers
Date Order: MDY   ☐ Four Digit Years
Date Delimiter: /   ☐ Leading Zeros in Dates
Time Delimiter: :   Decimal Symbol:

Field Information:

	Field Name	Data Type	Indexed	Skip
▶	StockNumber	Text	No	☐
	Description	Text	No	☐
	Category	Text	No	☐
	Vendor	Text	No	☐
	UnitCost	Double	No	☐
	QuantityOnHand	Long Integer	No	☐
	DateOfLastOrder	Date/Time	No	☐
*				

When you import text that follows these specifications later, you can skip the steps in specifying how the data is formatted in the text file. Simply begin the Import Text Wizard, and then click the Advanced button. At the Import Specification dialog box, click the Specs button, and then choose the previously created import specification and click OK. Access will use your settings for subsequent import operations.

HANDLING IMPORT ERRORS

If Access detects any errors in the import process, it creates a special table called Import Errors that contains the description of each error. Check the Database window in Table mode for this table. When an error is found in the import process,

Access does not actually import the data. Correct the error and repeat the File | Get External Data | Import command.

Exporting Data Files from Access

Just as we are able to import data directly into Access from external data files, so can we use Access to create external data files from Access tables. The procedure is similar to the Import process. First select the desired table in the Database window. Choose the Save As | Export command from the File menu, and then choose between saving the table to an external file or database, or saving it within the current database under a new name.

If you select external file Access will display a Save Table dialog box. Select an external file type from the list of available types. As with importing, the Access .mdb file is the default type. Access will prompt you for the name of the file to save it in, using the default file extension of the destination package. All of the records from that table will be exported to the indicated file. We will illustrate two different export methods in this section.

Exporting Data to a Spreadsheet File

You can export data from Access to the common spreadsheet file formats Lotus 1-2-3 and Microsoft Excel. The procedure is simple: select the table to export, choose the File | Save As | Export command, and then select the type of file in the Save As dialog box. Then give the file name for the export, and click Export. The entire table is saved in the appropriate file format, one field per column and one row per record. Access automatically places the field names in the first row of the spreadsheet file. Text fields are converted to spreadsheet labels. Numeric and yes/no fields are converted to spreadsheet values. For the latter, Yes is saved as a 1 (or True) and No as a 0 (or False.) Where possible, field format properties are converted to corresponding cell formats. Date fields are converted to dates in the spreadsheet file and given a date format. When you examine the spreadsheet file, widen the spreadsheet columns to view the full data field.

CAUTION

If you are exporting to an application outside of Windows 95 or NT, use a file name that follows the older MS-DOS 8.3-character file name restriction (8 characters for the name followed by a period and 3-character file name extension). However, if you do use a long file name, Windows 95 will also prepare a unique shortened name such as Finals~1.xls.

GUIDED ACTIVITY

13.4 Exporting Data to a Spreadsheet

In this Guided Activity you will export a table to a Microsoft Excel spreadsheet file.

1. Close any open windows and return to the Hunter97.mdb Database window.

2. Click the Tables tab to switch to Table mode; select the Final Sales Merchandise table.

3. Give the File | Save As | Export command. In the Save As dialog box, select To An External File Or Database and click OK.

4. In the Save Table dialog box, choose the Microsoft Excel 97 (*.xls) file type in the Save As Type box.

5. In the Save Table dialog box, select the folder and file name for your spreadsheet file. In this case, Access will fill in Final Sales Merchandise.xls. Click Export to send the Access table to this file.

6. If you have Microsoft Excel or another spreadsheet program that can read an .xls file, retrieve the exported file and view its contents. Figure A13.7 shows the spreadsheet displayed in Microsoft Excel version 97.

FIGURE A13.7
Final Sales Merchandise Excel spreadsheet

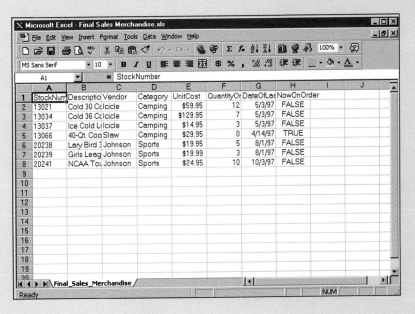

Exporting Data to a Fixed-Width Text File

Unlike the method used to export the entire table to a spreadsheet file, with fixed-width text files you must create and use an import/export specification. This describes the fields that are to be included in the text file, the field type, the starting location, and the number of characters to use for each field. This specification can be saved with an appropriate name and reused later for import or export jobs. If you try to export without an import/export setup in place, Access will stop the process and display a warning message box.

13.5 Exporting Data to a Fixed-Width Text File

In this Guided Activity you will create an export specification and then export data from the Vendors table to a fixed-width text file.

1. Close any open windows and return to the Hunter97.mdb Database window.

2. Switch to Table mode. Select the Vendors table but do not open the table at this time.

3. Choose the Save As | Export command from the File menu. In the Save As dialog box, select To An External File Or Database and click OK.

4. In the Save Table dialog box, select Text Files in the Save As Type box. Accept the default name of Vendors.txt and click Export to start the Export Text Wizard.

5. Click the Fixed Width option in the opening Export Text Wizard dialog box. Access will redisplay the sample field display as fixed-width fields. Click Next to go on.

6. In the next Export Text Wizard dialog box, you are given a chance to change column widths by dragging field boundaries. Make the following fields narrower: VendorName, AddressLine2, ContactPerson. See Figure A13.8. Click Next to go on.

FIGURE A13.8
Export Text Wizard dialog box for changing field widths

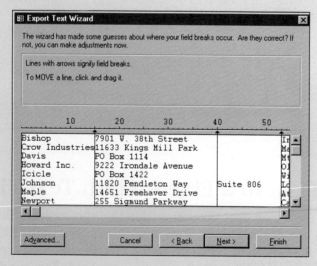

7. In the final Export Text Wizard dialog box, click the Advanced button to open the Vendors Export Specification dialog box shown in Figure A13.9. Each export field has an entry in the table for name, starting position, and width (in number of characters). Click Cancel to close this Advanced options box.

8. Click the Save As button to save this specification. Use the default name Vendors Export Specification for this specification. You can reuse this specification for export in the future. Click OK to return to the Export Text Wizard.

FIGURE A13.9

Vendors Export Specification dialog box

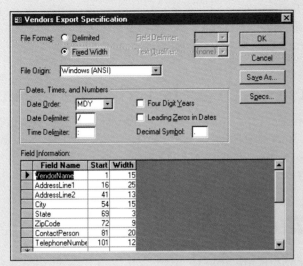

9. Click Finish in the Export Text Wizard dialog box. Access will notify you when the text file has been exported. Click OK to close the message box. Figure A13.10 shows the Vendors.txt file in the Windows 95 Notepad window. Notice that some of the fields have been truncated on their right sides according to the export specification you prepared. If the Notepad window is open, close it.

FIGURE A13.10

Fixed-width text file displayed in Notepad

Exporting Other Data Objects to an Access Database

You can export any Access database object to other Access databases. The process is similar to the table export procedure demonstrated in the previous two Guided Activities. First select the database object to export, and then use the Save As | Export command from the File menu. Select To An External File Or Database in the Save As dialog box. In the Save dialog box, select the appropriate Access database and click the Export button. Access will then ask you to confirm the name of the object in the new database. Click OK to complete the export. We will leave this as an exercise.

NOTE *If you need to export an Access 97 table to an earlier version of Access, first export to an intermediate file format that can be read by both Access versions. For example, export a table from Access 97 to the dBASE IV format, then import that table into Access 2.0 or Access 95. Most table properties and all data will be maintained.*

Exporting Access Objects to HTML Documents

We have already covered saving Access tables, forms, and reports as HTML documents in earlier units. Access 97 has a new File | Save As HTML command for this purpose, or you may use the File | Save As | Export command and choose HTML document as the file type. See Units 2 through 5 for several examples.

Using the Windows Clipboard to Exchange Files

Many Windows applications are able to swap data via the Windows Clipboard. The procedure is simple: highlight text to be copied in the sending Windows application, and then use the Edit | Copy command from that package. Whatever was selected is copied from that application into the Clipboard. Then switch to the receiving Windows application and use the Edit | Paste command to transfer the data from the Clipboard.

For instance, you can highlight records in an Excel or Lotus 1-2-3 spreadsheet under Windows and then go through the Clipboard to copy those records into an Access table. The copy can be as new records, or you can replace existing records with the contents of the Clipboard. Some Windows applications cannot create data values that are compatible with Access tables—try the Clipboard method with a small sample.

Using a Macro to Transfer Data

You can use a macro to automate and make virtually foolproof the process of transferring data from one data file to another. Although macros were covered in an earlier unit, it is appropriate to cover the specific transfer actions here, now that you are familiar with linking, importing, and exporting in Access.

Transfer Macro Actions

Access offers three macro actions for transferring data between itself and external applications and files. You can specify transfers for databases, spreadsheets, and text files. These actions produce the same results that you could produce with the File | Get External Data | Import, File | Save As/Export, and File | Get External Data | Link Tables commands from the menu bar.

The TransferDatabase action is used to import, export, or link data between the currently open Access database and a compatible external database file. There is an extensive set of arguments for this action, including settings for type of transfer, type of database including path where the database file is located, object type (if you are transferring from another Access database), name of source file, and object name in the destination database. You can transfer just the structure of an object or the structure and its embedded data values.

The TransferSpreadsheet action is used to import or export data between the currently open Access database and a compatible external spreadsheet file. Like the previous action, there are arguments for type of transfer, type of spreadsheet (Lotus or Excel), Access table name, spreadsheet file name (with full path), specifying whether the first row contains field names, and spreadsheet range to import. If you are appending spreadsheet rows to an existing Access table, you must have a compatible structure in terms of the type and sequence of data fields.

The TransferText action is used to import or export data between the currently open Access database and a delimited or fixed-width text file. Arguments include type of transfer (import delimited, import fixed-width, export delimited, export fixed-width, export Word for Windows merge, link delimited, and link fixed-width), text options specification name, Access table name, text file name, and whether the first row contains field names. The same data compatibility rules apply to spreadsheet and text files, particularly if you are appending data to an existing Access table.

A Data Transfer Macro

If you have not already studied macros in Unit 11, you should do so at this time. The data transfer macro should use the general macro structure of other macros in this book. You can link the data transfer macro either to a command button or to a property of a form. The transfer itself is straightforward, once the proper instructions are placed into the transfer action arguments.

The following simple macro will export Employee data to a dBASE IV file. All of the arguments are set as constants within the macro itself, but you can use a form to receive special instructions from the user when the macro runs, placing those instructions in the arguments of the macro. To place the contents of a form control in an argument, use the format =Form!formname!controlname. Fill in the appropriate names for the form and the control in the expression.

GUIDED ACTIVITY

13.6 Using a Macro to Transfer Data

In this Guided Activity you will create a simple macro to automatically export data from an Access table to a dBASE IV database file.

1. Close any open windows and return to the Hunter97.mdb Database window.

2. Switch to Macro mode and click the New button to open the Macro window.

3. Leave the first line's Action cell empty and enter the following comment in the first Comment cell: Sample data transfer macro.

4. In the second line's Action cell, choose the TransferDatabase action. The arguments for this action and the comment are shown in Figure A13.11. Enter each argument in the lower pane of the Macro window. You may need to specify a different location for Database Name if your computer does not have a folder

called C:\My Documents\. This argument specifies where the dBASE file will be created; if the path does not already exist, Access will display an error message and halt the macro.

FIGURE A13.11
Macro TransferDatabase action arguments

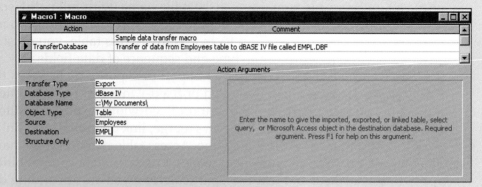

5. Use the File | Save command to save the macro under the name Transfer Employee Data.

6. Run the macro by clicking the Run button on the toolbar (or use the Macro | Run command from the menu bar).

7. Access will create the dBASE IV database file named Empl.dbf in the C:\My Documents\ folder. If the file already exists, Access will replace it with the current contents of the Employees table without warning you.

8. Close the active Macro window to return to the Database window.

SUMMARY

Access is able to exchange files with other Windows applications, including databases, spreadsheets, and text files. It can import data into Access so that it becomes a part of the database. Access can link tables to other database applications so that changes made in that external database also are evident to Access. Access can export data in other formats, including those already mentioned and HTML file formats. Access also contains macro actions to transfer data between Access and other file types.

Exercises

Use the Hunter River database contained within the Hunter97.mdb file and the Physician's Medical Clinic database contained within the PMC97.mdb file on the Student Data Disk for these exercises.

EXERCISE

13.1

Importing a Lotus Spreadsheet

1. Import the spreadsheet file called Adbudget.wk1 from the data disk to the Hunter97.mdb database. You may need to install support for this type of import operation from the Office 97 ValuPack on the CD-ROM.

2. Create a new table.

3. Use the named range called ITEMS from the spreadsheet. The first row of this range contains the field names.

4. Print a copy of the contents of the imported table within Access.

EXERCISE

13.2

Export Query to Text File

1. Export the query called Alphabetical Customers to a delimited text file called Alpha.txt.

2. Print a copy of the text file.

EXERCISE

13.3

Link to Paradox Database

1. Link the Paradox 3.5 table called Teams from the data disk.

2. Its password is *team165*. The password is case-sensitive.

3. This table gives a partial list of the teams in several of the sports leagues that are administered by Hunter River.

4. Print a copy of the contents of the table, and then delete its link from the Database window.

EXERCISE

13.4

Data Transfer Macro

1. Modify the sample macro shown in Guided Activity 13.4 so that it is launched with a command button on a form.

2. The form should have a control in which the user enters the names of the table and the external data file.

3. Your macro should use those values in the arguments of the TransferDatabase action.

EXERCISE

13.5

Import Access Table

1. Import the table called Visits from the PMC97.mdb database into the Hunter97.mdb database.

2. Print the datasheet for this table from the Hunter97.mdb database.

EXERCISE

13.6

Export Macro to Access Database

1. Export the macro called Filter Buttons from the Hunter97.mdb database to the First.mdb database.

2. Use the same name in the new database.

3. Will the new macro run correctly in the First.mdb database? Explain what is needed to make it work correctly.

APPLICATION

Physician's Medical Clinic: Importing and Linking

PMC is exchanging a patient list with one of the local HMO organizations. After some discussion, you have learned that the HMO can accept data as delimited text files or as dBASE IV files. Prepare a patient list for all fields in both formats, and print a copy of the delimited text file.

INDEX